The Rise of the Laity in Evangelical Protestantism

Why have the ordinary people in the church largely been written out of political and ecclesiastical history? Whatever happened to Luther's Reformation doctrine of the priesthood of all Christian believers? To what extent has evangelicalism fulfilled its promise as an inspirational and liberating power in the lives of the many it has influenced?

The rise to prominence of an active laity is one of the most remarkable yet least-discussed aspects of the modern church. Despite the insistence of post-Reformation Protestantism on the possibility of direct interior access to God for every person, such has been the preoccupation with clerical leadership that only one or two episodes of lay participation are widely known. *The Rise of the Laity in Evangelical Protestantism* is the first comprehensive investigation of the part played by non-ordained men and women in the life of the church, including the development of Christian critiques of the clergy. Exploring a phenomenon stretching from Britain and Germany to the Americas and beyond, it considers the successes and failures of evangelicalism, as an anti-establishmentarian and at times profoundly individualistic movement, in enabling the traditionally powerless laity to become enterprising, vocal and influential in the religious arena and in areas affecting politics and culture.

Fifteen original research-based essays cover themes that include early controversy over lay preaching, the lay component of German Pietism, the religious leadership roles of women in America and Britain, the staffing and direction of overseas Christian missions, and implications for the future shape of evangelical Christianity arising from developments within the Southern Baptist and Charismatic movements. Asking whether we have finally arrived at a church of the laity, *The Rise of the Laity in Evangelical Protestantism* offers an unrivalled examination of how evangelicalism has influenced the silent lay majority from the Reformation to the present day, and how representatives of that majority have in turn changed the face of the church and of their own communities.

Deryck W. Lovegrove, a Fellow of the Royal Historical Society, has written extensively on themes including religious dissent, itinerant preaching, the church and war, and the development of English and Scottish evangelicalism. He has recently retired from teaching at the University of St Andrews and is the author of *Established Church, Sectarian People: Itinerancy and the Transformation of English Dissent, 1780–1830* (CUP, 1988).

The Rise of the Laity in Evangelical Protestantism

Edited by Deryck W. Lovegrove

London and New York

First published 2002
by Routledge
11 New Fetter Lane, London EC4P 4EE

Simultaneously published in the USA and Canada
by Routledge
29 West 35th Street, New York, NY 10001

Routledge is an imprint of the Taylor & Francis Group

Typeset in Times by M Rules
Printed and bound in Great Britain by
Antony Rowe, Chippenham, Wiltshire

British Library Cataloguing in Publication Data
A catalogue record for this book is available from the British
Library

Library of Congress Cataloging in Publication Data
A catalog record has been requested

ISBN 0–415–27192–4 (hbk)
ISBN 0–415–27193–2 (pbk)

To the countless unrecorded followers of Jesus Christ who have faithfully exercised the royal priesthood

Contents

Contributors

Clyde Binfield is Professor Associate in History, University of Sheffield

Neil T.R. Dickson is Assistant Principal Teacher of English, Kilmarnock Academy, Kilmarnock, Scotland

Crawford Gribben is Research Fellow, Centre for Irish-Scottish Studies, Trinity College Dublin

Bruce Hindmarsh is James M. Houston Associate Professor of Spiritual Theology, Regent College, Vancouver

Helen M. Jones is a committee reporter in the Department of the Official Report, House of Commons, London

Timothy Larsen is Professor of Church History, Tyndale Seminary, Toronto

Deryck W. Lovegrove recently retired as Lecturer in Ecclesiastical History, University of St Andrews

Mark A. Noll is Professor of History, Wheaton College, Wheaton, Illinois

Hans Otte is Head of Archives for the Lutheran Church of Hanover

Mark Smith is Lecturer in the Modern History of Christianity, King's College London

Carl R. Trueman is Associate Professor of Church History and Historical Theology, Westminster Theological Seminary, Philadelphia

Andrew F. Walls was Founding Director of the Centre for the Study of Christianity in the Non-Western World, University of Edinburgh, and is currently Curator of the Centre's Collection of Documents

Marilyn J. Westerkamp is Professor of History, Merrill College, University of California Santa Cruz

David F. Wright is Professor of Patristic and Reformed Christianity, University of Edinburgh

Malcolm B. Yarnell, III is Dean of the Faculty and Vice President of Academic Affairs, Midwestern Baptist Theological Seminary, Kansas City, Missouri

Editorial note

This book has its origins in gratitude felt for the idealism, teaching and example received in earlier decades from ordinary Christians, both men and women. Most of them are destined to remain unknown figures, their very existence preserved for posterity only in the form of names on membership lists. Yet they are part of one of the greatest, if least examined, aspects of modern church history – the vast and increasingly important company of active lay Christians who together give tangible expression to the concept of the church as being the body of Christ.

More immediately this volume of essays arose out of an international conference of historians held at the University of St Andrews in July 1999 to examine the reappearance of the doctrine of the general priesthood of believers at the Reformation, and its connection with the increasing prominence of the Christian laity in the post-Reformation church. The papers delivered at St Andrews considered the extent to which these developments constituted a process of emancipation and explored connections between the rise of lay involvement and the spread of Protestant evangelicalism.

In planning and editing both conference and book I have incurred many debts of gratitude, not least among them those to academic friends and colleagues. In this connection I would like to thank Professor Stewart Brown of the University of Edinburgh for his early encouragement and Professor Mark Noll of Wheaton College, Illinois for his unfailing patience, wisdom and support throughout the various stages of organization. I would also like to express my thanks to all those who helped to explore the subject by giving papers at the conference. The combined expertise of so many scholars working in related fields enables large subjects such as this to be tackled, which otherwise would remain beyond the scope of any single individual. It is my hope that the resulting volume will stand as a permanent tribute to their work and effort.

Particular mention must be made of the generous financial help received from the British Academy for the support of the St Andrews conference. Special thanks are also due to the following bodies and persons for their courtesy in granting permission to publish extracts from manuscript and other material in their possession: the Archives of the Evangelical-Lutheran State Church of Hanover in respect of the Ephoralarchiv Clausthal-Zellerfeld quoted in Chapter 4; the Director and Librarian of the John Rylands University Library, Manchester in respect of the Early Methodist Volume of correspondence quoted in Chapter 5; Messrs Taylor & Francis in respect of material in Chapter 7 originally published in M.J. Westerkamp, *Women and Religion in Early America, 1600–1850*; representatives of the Massey and Pye-Smith families in connection with family papers quoted in Chapter 12; and Dr J.S.T. Garfitt, Chairman of the Council of the Oxford Pastorate in respect of the Minutes of the Pastorate Council quoted in Chapter 13.

To my friend and long-time colleague Dr James Alexander go my thanks for his translation expertise. Similarly, for his help in dealing with the problems of modern on-line computer technology I must not forget my friend and pastor, the Revd Ben Pieterse. The task of editing a multi-author book is never simple, but I would like to pay tribute to the patience of those friends and colleagues who have contributed to this volume. They have responded with constant cheerfulness, good humour and grace to my many queries, and are collectively responsible for any merit this book may have. Its faults by now are mine alone, and for them I take full responsibility. Finally, I would like to thank my beloved and longsuffering wife, Barbara, who thought I had retired but alas has had to endure a significant delay in the urgently needed restoration of our eighteenth-century house.

Deryck Lovegrove
Kilry, Glenisla
September 2001

Chapter 1

Introduction

Deryck W. Lovegrove

> The pope or bishop anoints, shaves heads, ordains, consecrates, and pre-
> scribes garb different from that of the laity, but he can never make a man
> into a Christian or into a spiritual man by so doing. He might well make a
> man into a hypocrite or a humbug and blockhead, but never a Christian or
> a spiritual man. As far as that goes, we are all consecrated priests through
> baptism, as St. Peter says in I Peter 2, 'You are a royal priesthood and a
> priestly realm.' . . . whoever comes out of the water of baptism can boast
> that he is already consecrated priest, bishop, and pope . . .[1]

With these words from the first of his three great Reformation tracts of 1520,
Luther, with characteristic forthrightness, undid the neglect of centuries and
restored to the centre of Christian thought the biblical doctrine of the priesthood of all believers. In our own secular and sceptical age, almost 500 years
after Luther's fundamental questioning of the nature of the church, the doctrine is again being reconsidered and accorded a new prominence in Christian
thought. Yet the present context seems to encourage a certain distortion of its
original meaning. In an increasingly individualist society, which demands
professional expertise and specialization but displays deep-seated distrust
and dislike of professions and their monopolies, the concept of the general
priesthood often appears to be construed as a vehicle for asserting the rights
of the individual believer against the pretensions and restrictions of the
ordained ministry. Nor have modern attempts to widen the range of those
involved in ministry removed the sense of two conflicting groups. Despite the
apparent blurring of the lay–clerical boundary achieved by the growth in
part-time vocations, the concept of non-stipendiary ministry has been dismissed by at least one commentator as a device for closing the church's mind
to the general priesthood and for creating the impression that a vocation to
the ordained ministry is superior to any other.[2]

At the beginning of the new millennium, when church membership figures
in many of the traditional denominations are falling steadily and the number
of ministerial vocations appears to be in decline, increasing attention is being

given to the potential of lay Christians. In a recent radio interview an Anglican bishop suggested that the days of the traditional episcopate were numbered and that, although leaders would always be needed, the emphasis in future would be upon the church's membership. In similar vein, the May 2000 General Assembly of the Church of Scotland began with a report from its Panel on Doctrine which recognized the ministerial role of each church member.[3] In much of this contemporary focus it is difficult to avoid the impression of an organization being driven by external considerations. Given the publicity accorded to the failings of the ordained clergy, there is the feeling that in falling back upon the laity the church, to some extent, is returning to the concept of the general priesthood as a last resort when traditional patterns of ministry have been found wanting.

Yet, if there are these negative undertones, there are important positive aspects to the new lay emphasis. In many respects it reflects the progress made by popular education and the scope offered in modern societies for the development of the individual. The traditional gulf between a learned clerical elite and the untutored masses has ceased to exist. Higher education has become available to a sizeable section of the populace only within the last three or four decades, but already the new situation has produced within organized Christianity a generation of worshippers which is no longer content to be merely the passive recipient of professional ministry. In the secular climate of the late twentieth and early twenty-first centuries the church finds itself knowing more clearly than for most of its history the precise extent of its membership and in a practical sense almost every denomination, whether retaining a parish structure or not, has been forced to adopt a gathered form of organization in which an active understanding of membership and its attendant responsibilities is assumed. In this situation, given the hostile or, at best, neutral attitude of modern society, it can be argued that for the church to make any future progress, exclusive reliance upon a professional ministry is no longer possible. The resource implications of operating in a broadly unsympathetic environment are that the church is being compelled to return to its roots and reconsider its very essence.

Any idea that the New Testament provides a simple or even single understanding of the organized church is quickly rejected once a careful study is made of the text. Even within the pages of the canonical books there is evidence of a struggle between the freedom of the Spirit and the demands of order and regularity. The former is represented most plainly by the writings of the apostle Paul, for whom authority based upon structure is always subordinate to that which issues from the Spirit's endowment.[4] According to his model the church is essentially a non-hierarchical body whose members share in the ministry of the gospel and are differentiated from one another by function rather than status. By the time the reader reaches the Pastoral Epistles status differentiation has become more evident and is based upon a regular structure of leadership involving bishops, elders and deacons. A similar if less differentiated structure is found in the First Epistle of Peter, but there the emphasis on office explicitly retains the concept of an active membership. The Petrine description of the general body of believers as 'a royal priesthood' constitutes the formal basis of the doctrine with which this book is concerned.

Before considering the long neglect of the general priesthood, it is important to clarify the principal ideas that lie behind its New Testament formulation. As with so many Christian ideas its origins lie in the religious identity and cultus of ancient Israel. The Israelites, in keeping with their self-identity as the chosen people, construed their unique revelation as involving both the ongoing worship of God and the mediation of the divine will to the nations at large. Although a priestly class developed, through which religious life was channelled and expressed, the people as a whole, at least in principle, assumed this religious calling.[5] Following the death and resurrection of Jesus, early Christian thought transposed the idea of collective priesthood from the people of the Old Covenant to those who constituted the new Israel, the members of the Christian church. In place of the imperfect representation of Israel by the office of high priest went the perfect and endless representation of the new people of God by the risen and ascended Christ acting as eternal high priest. In the new context, priesthood as a description of the Christian people, or *laos*, was given a collective meaning. The people of Christ are a royal priesthood. Because of their position *en Christo* they are given to participate in the sole priesthood of the ascended Lord, though they are never individually priests. While the general priesthood as a concept is intrinsically opposed to clerical pretensions it is not antiministerial. But, by the same token, priesthood cannot simply be construed in terms of the ordained ministry. The ministry functions in New Testament thinking wholly within, rather than apart from, the general priesthood shared by all Christian believers. As the exercise of the gift of preaching constitutes part of the worship offered to God by the general priesthood, so also do the other gifts distributed by the Holy Spirit throughout the whole body of believers. Historically, it was the undue exaltation of the preaching gift (including the administration of the sacraments and discipline) and the neglect of the rest that led to the disappearance of the doctrine.[6] As a concept general priesthood allows no room for pride and differentiation of status. Christians can only be true to their collective priestly calling when they emulate the high priestly example of Christ in his willingness to embrace a life of suffering, obedience and service.[7]

Yet, in spite of the respect evident in the apostolic period for the collective spiritual authority of the church, the abiding presuppositions concerning the importance of ecclesiastical office were also forged in antiquity. They should not be regarded as a later, medieval development.[8] As early as the time of Clement of Rome and Ignatius of Antioch, at the turn of the second century, proper organization and order within the church had become all-important, with the institution itself becoming to all intents and purposes a legal entity. All that remained essentially was for Cyprian in the middle years of the third century to formalize the separation between the threefold clergy and the laity, and to emphasize the exclusive authority of the former, especially with regard to the Christian sacraments and ordinances. By then the lay believer's freedom for action had shrunk to little more than the private sphere of personal devotion.[9]

With the conspicuous exception of the monastic movement, and especially the appearance of the mendicant friars in the early years of the thirteenth century, the high Middle Ages saw clerical theory elevated to such a degree that any concept of a wider priesthood was virtually obscured. Even the Franciscans were compelled to turn away from their lay roots in spite of their founder's innovative realization of the wider priesthood in 1221 in the founding of the lay brotherhood known as the Tertiaries. As the *New Catholic Encyclopedia*, under the entry for 'Laity in the Middle Ages', observes:

> Unfortunately, the subsequent institutionalization of the Franciscans was a sign that the Church was not prepared to pay a sufficiently high price to retain the allegiance of the masses, i.e., a religious order with a predominantly lay character. After 1242 no lay brother could be appointed to offices in the order.[10]

The first signs of a more questioning spirit towards the prevailing scholastic mood of professional exclusivity came with the insistence of Marsiglio of Padua in his *Defensor Pacis* of 1324 that the power of the priesthood wrongly extended to matters of discipline, a realm which properly belonged to the whole church. Spirituality was not the exclusive possession of the clergy, nor did their hierarchy of authority rest on any substantive scriptural basis.[11] Some 50 years after Marsiglio, John Wyclif went even further, rejecting the traditional feudal understanding of relationships within the church and arguing instead that all Christians owed direct allegiance to God by virtue of his grace. In terms of their spiritual 'tenure' all were equal, whether pope or layman, prince or peasant.[12] Over the following century, his followers, the 'Poor Preachers', put this principle to the test by taking to themselves the right to propagate the teachings of the Bible read in the vernacular and publicly to attack those aspects of the late medieval priesthood which appeared to contradict scripture.

There was, in the situation which Luther and his fellow reformers inherited, a sharp dichotomy in Christian thinking about the priesthood. Both as a group and as individuals the clergy aroused contempt and hatred in the popular mind. Yet at the same time there was enormous respect for the priestly office and for what the priest alone could do. In that context Luther's affirmation of the priesthood of all believers, when delivered into the wrong hands – for example those of Carlstadt or the German peasants – was capable of producing a situation that their author never intended. No more in Luther's mind than in Paul's was the essential spiritual equality and active role of believers (their membership of the royal priesthood) an intrinsically antiministerial concept. Nevertheless, not least because of its unacceptable social implications, the doctrine ran into the sand during the later stages of the Reformation.

To many observers the new presbyters within the reformed churches of western Europe looked little different from the old priests in terms of their relationship to the laity. The surviving 1587 version of the English 'Book of Discipline', which was not printed until 1644, makes it clear that active involvement in the church was regarded as wholly a clerical matter, with the ruling elders and deacons, no less than the other officers, considered to be ministers.[13] Within ecclesiastical leadership hierarchy had given way to parity, but the emergent Calvinism was demonstrating atavistic tendencies. Among the many strands of continuity with the past that characterized the Reformation era, the persistence of clericalism, or what Professor Ward with regard to a later period has termed 'punditry', was arguably the most prominent and significant. Not until the Enlightenment brought a new focus upon the development of the individual through education, encouraged the growth of religious pluralism and toleration, and challenged the monopoly of state churches, were the full implications of the general priesthood of believers able to emerge.

It could be argued that its realization as a doctrine depended on a changed conception of the church: that just as its demise had accompanied the successful penetration by Christianity of sections of early Greek and Roman society, so its rediscovery followed the move away from territoriality towards the position where the church was seen once more as a 'pure' body in which all members had the potential for exercising a priestly role. Even within denominations such as the Church of England, which maintained a strong state connection, the secular character of society and the growing appreciation of the church's missionary task led to calls, such as that made by the London barrister Horace Mann in 1853, for 'aggressive Christian agency' encompassing lay as well as clerical teachers of religion: advocacy, in other words, of an active priestly role for lay Christians.[14] Alongside this change in the understanding of the church went a new view as to what constituted faith: a recovery, for the main part in the eighteenth century within Protestant circles, of the immediate sense of the forgiveness of the individual by Christ, rather than a process mediated by the sacraments of the institutional church through its clergy.

The 'rise' of the laity, or the rediscovery of their significance, owed much to a gradual loss of confidence by the professional priesthood under assault from secular quarters, but it would be a mistake to underestimate the staying power of old attitudes or the strength of conservatism within the churches. In many respects the recovery of the doctrine of the general priesthood will be seen in the pages of this volume to be hesitant and often more hypothetical than real.

Within mainstream historiography the subject has languished in almost total oblivion. The first significant modern treatment of the doctrine by Roman Catholic theologians came in November 1964 during the Second Vatican Council with the publication of the *Dogmatic Constitution on the Church*. This stated that the faithful

> are by baptism made one body with Christ and are constituted the People of God; they are in their own way made sharers in the priestly, prophetical and kingly functions of Christ; and they carry out for their own part the mission of the whole Christian people, in the Church and in the world.[15]

Within Protestant circles there have been many references to the doctrine, especially in the context of Luther studies, but few extended treatments from an historical perspective. Perhaps unsurprisingly, two of the most significant contributions have come from scholars with a Methodist background. In the early 1960s Cyril Eastwood published two volumes in which he traced the doctrine from its origins in biblical thought up to the present day, making extensive use of primary sources.[16] His study gives considerable space to the developing theology of priesthood, with its specific application to a clerical caste, and to the correspondingly diminishing scope for an active laity, but pays little attention to wider social and organizational factors. More recently, Professor Ward's essay 'Pastoral office and the general priesthood in the Great Awakening' has examined the post-Reformation fortunes of the idea during the seventeenth and eighteenth centuries.[17] Among the important points discussed in this work is the continuing tendency of organized Christianity, even in its most popular forms, to lapse into a professional mentality – an approach which neglects many of the ministerial gifts and vocations with which the church is endowed.

In spite of the scarcity of historical discussion concerning the developing role of the laity in the modern church, individual aspects of lay ministry, especially within the context of the developing evangelical movement, have attracted considerable attention. The contribution to Methodism by non-ordained class leaders and preachers of both sexes has been examined by scholars such as Deborah Valenze, David Hempton and, most recently, Marilyn Westerkamp,[18] but other aspects have also featured in modern studies. The importance of lay leadership in the eighteenth-century Scottish Highlands has been considered by John MacInnes and Steve Bruce, the place of lay piety in the American middle colonies by Marilyn Westerkamp and the extensive but almost unknown activities of Dissenting itinerants in the English countryside by the editor of this present volume.[19] In addition to these works, broadly focused upon evangelical practice, a useful examination of the wider lay constituency of the Church of England prior to the onset of revival has been provided by W.M. Jacob.[20] In summary, there has been no shortage of detailed specialist studies, especially in recent years. What is lacking is a work that looks at the contribution and role of the religiously committed laity over a wide historical canvas.

The purpose of the present volume, therefore, is to examine the complexity of the doctrine of the general priesthood against the changing fortunes of post-Reformation Protestantism. Though the concept of an active laity is not confined to one section of the western church, whether Protestant or Catholic, its recovery in modern times appears to be connected intimately with the rise of pan-Protestant evangelicalism with its strong emphasis on personal faith and conversion. This is the underlying hypothesis that the book as a whole sets out to examine. If scholars have neglected to study this development it is in part due to the fact that it is the modern history of the Christian rank and file. Moreover, as some of the later essays in the book suggest, the doctrine appears to be leading the church into organizationally uncharted waters where the outcome for traditional leadership structures is not easy to predict.

The divisions chosen for the book are broadly chronological. Part I traces the somewhat elusive connection between Luther's theoretical restatement of the doctrine and its realization in the wave of popular evangelical activity at the beginning of the eighteenth century. The Reformation concept of lay priesthood, as a fusion of progressive and traditional elements, asserted the spiritual equality of baptized Christians and the irrelevance of rank to faith, yet at the same time demanded continuing respect for ecclesiastical as well as social leadership. This ambiguity was still evident among the puritan descendants of the reformers and, in the English context, shifted decisively towards the full democratic potential of the doctrine only when puritanism had lost its association with the religious establishment.[21] At the popular level the potential for change showed itself from the period of the English Commonwealth onwards as a rash of Independent congregations produced a vibrant and literate lay religious culture whose paradigms were based upon experience rather than formal scholastic theology. In particular this important transition revealed itself in the vogue for writing personal accounts of conversion. These, though to some extent stylized and produced under clerical supervision, marked the emergence of the lay believer from a position of absolute dependence upon the professional ministry.[22] In Germany the full flood of evangelical revival, seen in the Pietist movement within Lutheranism, brought lay Christians from the humblest origins face to face with clerical pretension at its most outspoken. As a mass movement Pietism was deeply influential on lay religious practice. In certain territories its adherents were branded as heretics, chiliasts and exponents of inner light and the resulting proscription caused a drift towards more tolerant areas. Yet, in spite of this enforced migration, the wider effect of the rise of Pietist schools and social institutions was the development in many territories of a fruitful interaction between the Protestant clergy and the laity.[23]

From the issues surrounding the re-establishment of the doctrine, attention shifts in Part II to the coincidence between its eighteenth-century flowering and the Age of Enlightenment. To what extent was this a necessary relationship, with the two movements intimately connected? How far did the coincidence depend upon accidental factors and even demonstrate contradictions? The individualism expressed in the work and writings of the early Methodist preachers, class leaders and Sunday school teachers may have been consonant with Enlightenment values, as recent scholars suggest, but it seems unlikely that there was any significant intellectual debt. The new vein of evangelical self-awareness had less to do with contemporary secular individualism than with the corporate identity of the emerging community of faith.[24]

Within that community the worth of the individual, the contemporary spirit of toleration and, in some cases, the wider availability of education, combined to begin the process of liberation for one section of the laity in particular – women. Two of the chapters discuss the contribution made by strikingly dissimilar sections of the female Christian constituency: at one extreme the handful of white British aristocratic patronesses of eighteenth-century evangelical religion;[25] at the other the much larger body of American women that became publicly active during the Great Awakenings.[26] The latter, running counter to contemporary norms, included a number of uneducated black women. To the casual observer British female aristocrats such as the Countess of Huntingdon appeared to represent no threat to established social or religious conventions. Their respect for rank appeared absolute, their deference to the clergy and traditions of the established churches secure, and their observance of the limits of female activity unexceptionable. In reality, their religious employment of the home, their own recognized domain, and their use of personal wealth to fund networks of proprietary chapels staffed by clergymen whose evangelical sentiments they admired, gave them a disproportionate influence. By contrast with the complaisance they inspired, the rising religious profile of American women challenged the cultural expectations of emergent republican society. In the new social order women were expected to play a subordinate role. Yet female religious leaders continued to appear and the manifest vocations of the increasing numbers of women who functioned as preachers and exhorters, both within traditional denominations and black organizations such as the African Methodist Episcopal Church, demonstrated that the supernatural force which inspired the evangelical movement, the operation of the Holy Spirit, would never coexist comfortably with established structures of authority, be they white, male or clerical.

As the doctrine of lay priesthood began to find tangible expression through the vehicle of religious revival, so points of tension developed and these are examined in Part III. Settled clergy, especially those within religious establishments, resented unauthorized and apparently unsupervised forays into traditional areas of ministerial responsibility by poorly educated laypeople.

When these irregular activities coincided with periods of social and political crisis, pressure to take action became irresistible. In the ensuing debates not only were the alleged deficiencies of the lay agents thoroughly rehearsed and returned with spirit, but the discussion turned at a deeper level towards a reassessment of the entire lay–clerical relationship which had characterized the ancien régime. Some of the bitterest moments of controversy occurred during the late 1790s and in these it is difficult to escape the conclusion that the new assertion of lay power within the church had become more than a little anticlerical.[27] Given the tendency for this lay activity to be associated either with membership of non-established denominations, or with reforming movements such as Pietism or Methodism, running counter to the mainstream within the territorial churches and showing a strong tendency towards the formation of small groups for more serious Christians, it is tempting to draw conclusions that link the empowerment of the laity with a fundamental shift in ecclesiastical polity. The examples offered by America up to the mid-nineteenth century suggest that while no simple connection can be drawn between the spread of evangelicalism and the extension of lay opportunity, their parallel development owed much to the growth of three new aspects of church organization: itinerancy, voluntary association and disestablishment.[28] Even within the voluntary churches, however, old habits died hard. Methodism in particular witnessed the reassertion of clerical dominance following the death of its founder, as Conference, Wesley's effective successor, restricted its membership to the body of travelling preachers. In response to this blatant attempt to exclude laymen from the central decision-making process, the small but democratic Methodist New Connexion was formed in 1797 with opposition to clericalism as its primary objective. Its affirmation of the general priesthood appears from the beginning to have had as much to do with the spread of secular liberalism as with the assertion of biblical doctrine, and it maintained its principled position only until the clerical hegemony within the Methodist mainstream had succumbed to the mounting democratic pressures of late Victorian society.[29]

Part IV looks beyond these tensions to one of the dominant features of the new age – the burgeoning missionary movement. In the sphere of overseas missions the unprecedented growth experienced in the nineteenth century might have been expected to create new opportunities for a restive laity. The personnel requirements of the various Protestant denominations, in what became their greatest phase of numerical and geographical expansion, manifestly outstripped the resources of the professional ministry, making it necessary from the outset for the new voluntary societies to augment their ranks with lay recruits. The modern missionary movement might have presented the greatest opportunity up till then for the reassertion of lay priesthood unimpeded by clerical restrictions or professional jealousy. The question, therefore, is whether the popular image of the lay missionary operating in the South Sea islands or in darkest Africa suggests that, in the area of overseas missions, the laity eclipsed the clergy in significance. The facts suggest otherwise – that not until lay professionalism and the demand for female personnel altered the character of the work towards the end of the nineteenth century did clerical status cease to be the missionary norm and domination of the movement by the ordained ministry begin to falter.[30]

The entrance of the lay professional may have come relatively late in the development of Protestant missions but when it did it offered an outlet for female expertise as well as providing a more general emancipation. At the time domestic society still largely adhered to traditional, male patterns of recruitment. The valedictories held at the turn of the twentieth century for the young professionals engaged as staff for the growing number of missionary hospitals and schools highlighted the curious position in which these specialist missionaries found themselves, caught as they were between the traditional passivity of the laity and the professional ministry of the church. In practice, the specialized nature of their work and its remoteness from the home base allowed them, as the quintessential products of congregational polity, to resolve the implicit tension between these two conservative forces.[31]

If late Victorian professionalism widened the scope of the Nonconformist laity, the same cannot be said for undergraduate religion at Oxford and Cambridge. There the prevailing spirit of student agnosticism appeared to observers to be compounded by clerical indifference. The third essay on missions examines the way in which this mood of complacency and drift was reversed between 1893 and the Second World War by the creation of an Evangelical Pastorate within the University of Oxford. By the early 1940s the work of the Pastorate had revolutionized the religious atmosphere of the university, demonstrating evangelical Christianity as a positive and constructive force, capable of attracting considerable numbers of the rising generation of lay leaders and of influencing them towards an active understanding of the faith.[32]

The final section of the book, Part V, considers the apparent antithesis of clerical domination – the emergence of a church with no formally differentiated leadership, in which the royal priesthood of the faithful is once again an important doctrine. As early as the seventeenth century the appearance of the Quakers marked the first formal rejection of the lay–clerical distinction within the modern church, but it was not until the development of Brethrenism in the late 1820s that a movement arose that would carry the principle to the heart of evangelical Protestantism. Out of the tensions and jealousies between evangelical and non-evangelical clergy within the Church of Ireland over the employment of lay preachers sprang a movement in which the members saw themselves as belonging to a corporate priesthood enjoying perfect spiritual equality. At its most radical, reality coincided with theory as members of Brethren assemblies broke bread together and spoke for their mutual edification as the Spirit gave them utterance. Yet the movement's innate conservatism made it wary of democracy and led to a reliance upon strong leadership. In other ways also it generated its own spiritual elite, demonstrating that, in the very attempt to recreate a biblical model of the active Christian community and to avoid human constructs, there were significant pitfalls to avoid.[33]

Among the Southern Baptists of America a different kind of obstacle to the general priesthood emerged in the form of extreme individualism. Whereas seventeenth-century separatist writers, such as John Smyth, had emphasized a corporate, Pauline understanding of the church as an integrated body of believers and had maintained a conventional regard for ministerial leadership with respect to preaching and the ordinances, influential Baptist thinking at the turn of the twentieth century adopted a post-Enlightenment individualism, which insisted upon the ability of the human soul to deal directly with God. The outcome of this approach was the creation of a body composed of atomistic believers possessing an attenuated Christology, an impoverished understanding of church and ministry and an undue regard for the autonomy of the human will.[34]

The appearance since the 1960s of what has become known as the Charismatic Movement may seem to mark both the full emancipation of the laity and the disappearance, or at least the imminent demise, of the classical model of the hierarchical church. Some of the principal ingredients of charismatic experience unquestionably centre upon the laity, but closer examination suggests that the movement as a whole does not admit of such simple analysis. Though the focus may have moved away from traditional forms of hierarchical leadership, the tendency among house churches to create quasi-episcopal figures shows that the image of a lay movement under the sole direction of the Spirit needs, at the very least, to be qualified. Nevertheless, the new approach has widened participation in worship and ministry and brought charismatic concerns and practices to mainstream congregations. Ultimately, the test of authenticity is, as Irenaeus insisted in the second century, that the church is recognized and defined by the presence within it of the Spirit of God.[35]

Viewed against the overall development of ecclesiastical polity the position of the laity has undoubtedly changed since the Reformation. Yet, even if so strong a term as 'emancipation' can be applied, the extent to which that development can be interpreted as a return to the primitive simplicity and directness of early Christianity is open to question. Not only is it debatable whether the changes that have occurred are as extensive or as simple as they might seem, but also whether they have been driven by Christian principle or by external forces. Given the process of continuous adaptation envisaged by some within the present day Charismatic Movement, it seems unlikely that either the rise or the full emancipation of the laity can ever be treated simply as a reversion to type, however compelling the biblical model may be. Rather, it is more helpful to regard it as a further stage in what has become the continuous evolution of the institutional church.

Notes

1 M. Luther, 'To the Christian nobility of the German nation concerning the reform of the Christian estate', in *Luther's Works*, ed. J. Pelikan and H.T. Lehmann, 55 vols, St Louis: Concordia; Philadelphia: Fortress Press, 1955–86, vol. 44, pp. 127, 129.

2 W.R. Ward, 'Pastoral office and the general priesthood in the Great Awakening', *Studies in Church History* 26, 1989, 326.

3 *Reports to the General Assembly 2000*, Edinburgh: Church of Scotland, 2000, pp. 13/8–14, §§ 3.3–3.4.

4 H. von Campenhausen, *Ecclesiastical Authority and Spiritual Power in the Church of the First Three Centuries*, trans. J.A. Baker, London: Black, 1969, p. 69.

5 Exodus 19.3–6 *(N.I.V.)*: 'Then Moses went up to God, and the Lord called to him from the mountain and said, "This is what you are to say to the house of Jacob and what you are to tell the people of Israel: '. . . Now if you obey me fully and keep my covenant, then out of all nations you will be my treasured possession. Although the whole earth is mine, you will be for me a kingdom of priests and a holy nation.'"'

6 Notwithstanding the direct but theoretical relationship between the collective priesthood of Israel and the general priesthood of the Christian community, Colin Bulley has recently suggested that the creation of the special, ordained Christian priesthood (and, therefore, the eclipse of the general priesthood) arose in part from the church's desire to relate the practical example of Old Testament worship and literature to its own life. See C. Bulley, *The Priesthood of Some Believers: developments from the general to the special priesthood in the Christian literature of the first three centuries*, Carlisle: Paternoster, 2000.

7 The definition of general priesthood in this paragraph owes much to the discussion of the doctrine to be found in C. Eastwood, *The Priesthood of All Believers: an examination of the doctrine from the Reformation to the present day*, London: Epworth, 1960.

8 Campenhausen, pp. 293–4.

9 Ibid. pp. 299–300.

10 *New Catholic Encyclopedia*, 15 vols, New York: McGraw-Hill, 1967, vol. 8, p. 333.

11 C. Eastwood, *The Royal Priesthood of the Faithful: an investigation of the doctrine from biblical times to the Reformation*, London: Epworth, 1963, pp. 165–6.

12 Ibid. p. 173.

13 P. Collinson, *The Elizabethan Puritan Movement*, 2nd edn, London: Methuen, 1982, p. 299.

14 While Mann's report advocates lay agency as part of a collective response by the various denominations to the problem of urban irreligion, its author clearly envisages an expansion of existing Anglican efforts as part of that process. *British Parliamentary Papers, 1851 Census Great Britain, Report and Tables on Religious Worship England and Wales, Population 10*, Shannon: Irish University Press, 1970, pp. clxi–clxvii.

15 C.J. Barry (ed.) *Readings in Church History, Vol. 3, The modern era 1789 to the present*, Paramus, NJ: Newman Press, 1965, p. 538. The original can be found in Vatican II, 'Lumen gentium', ch. 4, § 31, 21 November 1964.

16 See above, notes 7 and 11.

17 See above, note 2.

18 D.M. Valenze, *Prophetic Sons and Daughters: female preaching and popular religion in industrial England*, Princeton, NJ: Princeton University Press, 1985; D. Hempton, *The Religion of the People: Methodism and popular religion*

c.1750–1900, London: Routledge, 1996; M.J. Westerkamp, *Women and Religion in Early America, 1600–1850: the puritan and evangelical traditions*, London: Routledge, 1999.

19 J. MacInnes, *The Evangelical Movement in the Highlands of Scotland: 1688 to 1800*, Aberdeen: Aberdeen University Press, 1951, ch. 6; S. Bruce, 'Social change and collective behaviour: the revival in eighteenth-century Ross-shire', *British Journal of Sociology* 34, 1983, 554–72; M.J. Westerkamp, *Triumph of the Laity: Scots-Irish piety and the Great Awakening, 1625–1760*, New York: Oxford University Press, 1988; D.W. Lovegrove, *Established Church, Sectarian People: itinerancy and the transformation of English Dissent, 1780–1830*, Cambridge: Cambridge University Press, 1988.

20 W.M. Jacob, *Lay People and Religion in the Early Eighteenth Century*, Cambridge: Cambridge University Press, 1996.

21 Ch. 2, C.R. Trueman, 'Reformers, puritans and evangelicals: the lay connection'.

22 Ch. 3, C. Gribben, 'Lay conversion and Calvinist doctrine during the English Commonwealth'.

23 Ch. 4, H. Otte, 'The Pietist laity in Germany, 1675–1750: knowledge, gender, leadership'.

24 Ch. 5, B. Hindmarsh, 'Reshaping individualism: the private Christian, eighteenth-century religion and the Enlightenment'.

25 Ch. 6, H.M. Jones, 'A spiritual aristocracy: female patrons of religion in eighteenth-century Britain'.

26 Ch. 7, M.J. Westerkamp, 'Taming the Spirit: female leadership roles in the American Awakenings, 1730–1830'.

27 Ch. 8, D.W. Lovegrove, 'Lay leadership, establishment crisis and the disdain of the clergy'.

28 Ch. 9, M.A. Noll, 'National churches, gathered churches, and varieties of lay evangelicalism, 1735–1859'.

29 Ch. 10, T. Larsen, 'Methodist New Connexionism: lay emancipation as a denominational raison d'être'.

30 Ch. 11, A.F. Walls, 'The missionary movement: a lay fiefdom?'

31 Ch. 12, C. Binfield, 'Industry, professionalism and mission: the placing of an emancipated laywoman, Dr Ruth Massey 1873–1963'.

32 Ch. 13, M. Smith, 'A foundation of influence: the Oxford Pastorate and elite recruitment in early twentieth-century Anglican evangelicalism'.

33 Ch. 14, N.T.R. Dickson, '"The church itself is God's clergy": the principles and practices of the Brethren'.

34 Ch. 15, M.B. Yarnell, III 'Changing Baptist concepts of royal priesthood: John Smyth and Edgar Young Mullins'.

35 Ch. 16, D.F. Wright, 'The Charismatic Movement: the laicizing of Christianity?'

Part I

The priesthood of all believers

From principle to practice

Chapter 2

Reformers, puritans and evangelicals

The lay connection

Carl R. Trueman

Introduction

It is a truism that the immediate theological and cultural roots of modern evangelicalism lie in the world of the Enlightenment and beyond. In America the democratization of Christianity witnessed by the rise of field meetings, the different kinds of revivalism associated with figures such as Jonathan Edwards and Charles Finney, and the importance of the Scofield Reference Bible, is a well-documented phenomenon.[1] In Britain the impact of the Wesley brothers and George Whitefield in the eighteenth century, the Welsh revivals of the nineteenth and early twentieth centuries, and the rise to prominence of various parachurch organizations, such as the Inter-Varsity Fellowship (now the Universities and Colleges Christian Fellowship), the Evangelical Alliance, and the British Evangelical Council, have all helped to shape British evangelicalism at its deepest level.[2] Nevertheless, to study evangelicalism simply in terms of the developments which have taken place since the early eighteenth century is inadequate. To attempt an explanation of the movement purely in terms of monoglot Anglo-American sources and categories, which take no account of important trajectories stemming from the broader European traditions of Protestant theology of the sixteenth and seventeenth centuries, is surely as short-sighted a move as the old-fashioned attempts to explain the Reformation as a complete intellectual and cultural break with the Middle Ages. At the very least, the conflicts between Remonstrants and Counter-Remonstrants in Holland, the appearance of Socinianism as a challenge to orthodoxy, the rise of German Pietism, the impact of the Moravian movement and, above all, the Reformation, must be taken into account if a full-orbed understanding of modern evangelicalism is to be achieved.

Such an undertaking is too vast for a chapter like this to begin to tackle, for each of the above topics deserves at least a monograph to itself. What is intended is a brief outline of how the Reformation, at least in the writings of Luther, embodied elements which gave the laity a particular theological importance. Though the rhetoric and emphases surrounding this theme were swiftly modified to suit circumstances, the deep concern for all Christians and for individual religious experience, which remained at the centre of Reformation and post-Reformation thinking, paved the way for the rise during the eighteenth century of what can be recognized as modern evangelicalism.

The importance of Martin Luther

The choice of Martin Luther as a representative reformer requires no justification. It is obvious that much of the Reformation agenda was set by his theology. Equally, it is well known that his distinctive eucharistic views continued to determine the hostile relations that existed between Lutheran and Reformed communions long after his own demise. For later evangelicalism his singular importance lies in the fact that his theology reflected the initial concern of Protestantism with what might be called 'democratizing' or, perhaps better, 'antihierarchical' spirituality or Christian experience. As this chapter will argue, this is not to say that Luther intended to democratize the church but rather to reconceive Christian experience as something essentially non-hierarchical. His basis was a theology whose consequence was to redefine the role of the institutional church. Such a concern runs throughout much of Luther's writings but finds its fullest expression in four specific ideas: individual conversion, the priesthood of all believers, Christian freedom, and Christian calling. As the interest here is with the development and application of these concepts in a post-Reformation setting, each merits a brief exposition.

Individual conversion

The famous account of Luther's conversion, given in the preface to the Wittenberg edition of his collected Latin works in 1545, is riddled with chronological difficulties.[3] These, however, are of little concern compared to the main thrust of the passage, wherein the struggles of the individual Luther with the God hidden in the biblical text are described in graphic detail. The struggle with temptation, the struggle with the law and judgement, the struggle with despair and anger are followed by the liberty of enlightenment, joy and peace. Whatever one's feelings concerning the source of Luther's account – whether it represents an application to himself of the experience described by Paul in Romans 7 and 8, or whether it represents the refraction of Pauline theology through the lens of Augustinian introspection – there is no doubt that conversion profoundly shaped the way he read the Bible and understood the Christian encounter with God. Law and gospel, despair and hope, became the basic theological and existential categories for understanding human experience of the divine. While the immediate antihierarchical potential of this might not be obvious, it was rooted deeply in a theology which saw individual experience of grace and personal assurance of God's favour as essential, in contrast to the typical medieval church-mediation of the former and outright rejection of the latter.

The antihierarchical theological thrust of Luther's understanding and experience of conversion should not be underestimated. By making salvation, and especially assurance of salvation, something which was normative for believers and not mediated by any church hierarchy – a reality that was available directly via the grasping of God's word by faith – Luther effectively undercut the whole elaborate medieval sacramental and penitential system, rendering it unnecessary.[4] By making salvation available to all through God's word and emphasizing personal, unmediated assurance of faith, Luther linked his theology to an experience theoretically open to all and not under the control of the institutional church. This was a profoundly liberating move in terms of the church laity. Furthermore, as directly picked up by Christian writers such as John Bunyan and John Wesley, the Luther-style conversion experience became part of standard evangelical literature, culture and experience.

The priesthood of all believers

Luther formulated his understanding of the universal priesthood of all believers in 1520.[5] This is significant, for at one level the term captures in a nutshell Luther's understanding of grace, justification and salvation. These are not mediated via the institutional church or by the priestly hierarchy of that church, but are the direct privilege of every believer who through faith can have dealings with God in Christ on a personal basis. This is effected through the word of God – in scripture, in preaching and in the sacraments. In each case there is an immediate grasping of God in Christ through the faith of the individual. In each case believers are assured of God's favour not by their standing in the visible church but by the personal possession of what God has done for them in Christ. Within this scheme the role of the church, of the institutional priesthood and of the mass is radically transformed. The church is the servant of Christ proclaiming his word to the world. The institutional priesthood becomes the body which, as much for convenience sake as for anything else, is there to preach the word and point to God's promises. The mass becomes not a sacrifice which makes grace available in and of itself, but an act which, like preaching, underlines and offers God's promise of salvation in Christ. The whole notion of an elite priesthood, which in some way constitutes an intermediate spiritual group between the laity and God, is thus abandoned.[6]

At another level, however, we must beware of placing too much stock in the terminology of the universal priesthood. Luther used the term in 1520 in large part to make a specific polemical point against the overweening theological and soteriological pretensions of the Roman clergy and it was not in itself as theologically significant as the underlying ideas. The year 1520 was in many ways make-or-break for the Lutheran Reformation. After inconclusive meetings with the church authorities at Augsburg and Leipzig and while awaiting the inevitable bull of excommunication, Luther published his three greatest treatises: *To the Christian Nobility of the German Nation*; *The Babylonian Captivity of the Church*; and *On the Freedom of the Christian*. In these works he stated his emerging Reformation theology in a sharply polemical manner and made a last (somewhat unconvincing) attempt to appeal to the Pope. It was in this climate that the language of universal priesthood came to the fore, though this did not in itself represent an underlying change or radical development in theological perspective. It was rather an attempt to give full expression to the content and implications of salvation by grace through faith which had been developing in his mind since approximately 1515, while at the same time making a sharp polemical criticism of the Roman church's priestly pretensions. In the early 1520s, therefore, the rhetorical power of the term was in many ways as significant as the theological point being made – a point which had in effect been made by Luther on earlier occasions without using this kind of language.[7]

Furthermore, it is important to note that what Luther was emphatically not doing was using the concept of universal priesthood as a means for determining the institutional structure of the church. In the mind of the German reformer, at least, this priesthood was intended as pointing towards an antihierarchical understanding of salvation; it was not intended in the first instance as pointing towards or demanding a democratic or antihierarchical view of church government. It gave the laity a theological significance they did not have previously by tearing down the pretensions of the medieval priesthood but in Luther's mind it afforded no mandate for ending all notions of hierarchy in the visible church, even though it required a rethinking of the functions of that hierarchy.[8]

The freedom of the Christian

The third element in the antihierarchical theology of Luther is his stress on Christian freedom. Again a phrase which comes to the fore in 1520, at the height of Luther's controversy with Rome, the language of freedom must to a large extent be understood as the specific expression of his ongoing theological commitments in the heat of contemporary debate. The theological point being made by Luther is that Christian salvation does not consist in obeying particular rules and instructions but in faith in Jesus Christ. While medieval churchmen may have taught that the individual must attend mass, do good works, obey the church's teaching and attend confession in order to have any chance of salvation, Luther confidently proclaims that salvation is accomplished in Christ and that believers' good works follow as a response to God's prior grace in Christ.[9] The believer is thus free from the obligations imposed by a corrupt church because his salvation is not mediated through human institutions but by Christ. In essence the point is the same as that contained in his writings prior to 1520; what is new is the accent now placed upon individual freedom as a means of theological point-scoring against Roman opponents.

The Christian's calling

The fourth element in this antihierarchical theology is that of calling. Here, Luther attacks the distinction between sacred and secular callings by asserting the God-given and approved validity of all Christian tasks, from that of the humble peasant crofter to the highest government or church official. No longer can the individual in the monastery or the cleric claim to be superior to the ordinary believer; no longer can the world be divided between those with sacred callings and those with secular tasks. In his address *To the Christian Nobility* Luther makes the following statement:

> To call popes, bishops, priests, monks, and nuns, the religious class, but princes, lords, artizans, and farm-workers the secular class, is a specious device invented by certain time-servers; but no-one ought to be frightened by it, and for good reason. For all Christians whatsoever really and truly belong to the religious class, and there is no difference among them except in so far as they do different work.[10]

Again, as with the notions of universal priesthood and freedom, this is yet another application and expression of the theology of grace epitomized in Luther's conversion. What it does is to abolish the divisive hierarchy between the sacred and the secular, and to accord parity to all things in the spiritual realm.

What is significant about Luther's teaching on calling, however, is that it also reflects the limits of the democratizing tendencies of his theology. The idea ties in with his teaching on the two kingdoms and highlights the fact that, while he may have democratized salvation by taking it out of the hands of an institutional church, which in the spiritual kingdom was acting as a high-handed mediator between God and humanity, he was nevertheless not democratizing society or the institutions which formed its constituents. The concept of calling cuts both ways: on the one hand, no one can claim spiritual superiority on the grounds of a sacred calling or position, since all callings are now sacred; on the other hand, everyone's calling is God-given and thus no individual has grounds for attempting to overthrow the given secular order on the basis of the democratization of the spiritual order. The conclusion to be drawn from this is that since the social hierarchy as it now exists is God-given, rejection or rebellion against that hierarchy is effectively rejection and rebellion against God.[11]

This is an extremely important point. Luther's thought is more subtle than many have given it credit for. The two kingdoms idea, with its strict demarcation between the world of social discourse, public righteousness, and daily life and the world of individual salvation, righteousness before God, and spiritual life, effectively serves to demarcate the bounds and the application of the teachings embodied in the notions of universal priesthood and Christian freedom. These are ultimately categories which refer to the spiritual and not the material world. Thus their strict democratizing tendencies, in Luther's mind at least, are restricted to that sphere. What he is doing is to allow for a universal, egalitarian attitude to grace and conversion, while setting up barriers which prevent this Reformation programme being carried across into the secular field.

Failure to spot this subtlety, or fear that others might fail to spot it, lay behind much of the early Catholic opposition to Luther. Indeed, in the context of a discussion of the priesthood of all believers, David Bagchi makes the following observation concerning Luther's early Catholic opponents:

> [T]he controversialists in general were much less antagonistic to Luther's doctrine of the priesthood of all believers than might have been supposed. Their objection, as with some of Luther's other teachings, was prompted largely by the possibility that the rabble might understand it out of ignorance or malice . . . Cochlaeus, Fisher, Bartholomeus Usingen, Eck, Arnoldi Von Chiemsee, Johannes Gropper, and Jodocus Clichtoveus all accepted the universal priesthood, provided that it did not detract from the special priesthood.[12]

The last caveat, referring to the fact that Luther's Catholic opponents still held to an elite priesthood above and beyond that of all believers, should not obscure the point that Luther's use of this terminology in itself does not appear to have overly concerned orthodox Catholics. Indeed, Bagchi mentions only one Catholic who wrote against the idea and that from a perspective eerily reminiscent of John Wyclif![13] What was at issue was the way in which the language of universal priesthood could be abused by more radical and less subtly learned elements for anarchic and disruptive ends.

In fact, as regards the universal priesthood, what are found in Luther are two related but formally separable phenomena. On the one hand, the theology of grace, justification and conversion places the individual and Christ firmly at the centre with no hierarchical mediation whatsoever. From this flow various consequences: the need for comprehensible preaching of the word, for the vernacular mass and for accurate and clear translations of the scriptures into the vulgar tongue. They are accompanied by an emphasis upon the individual wrestling with God. All point towards lay participation in church life and represent an empowerment of the laity, since they hand laypeople direct responsibility for their own salvation.

On the other hand, there is Luther's rhetorical language concerning universal priesthood, Christian freedom from the law and the spiritual equality of all earthly callings, both spiritual and non-spiritual. In context this rhetoric is simply a particularly pointed way of expressing the theological underpinnings of his Reformation programme. To the untrained ear, however, in the context of early sixteenth-century Saxony and beyond, it had a socially revolutionary sound which made it attractive to various nascent nationalist and radical groupings. To the oppressed peasants, labouring under intolerable conditions, and to the German knights, resentful of German taxes paying for Italian excess, the rhetoric of Luther was a rallying call for revolution and rebellion.

This is an important point, since it helps to explain both the dramatic success of the initial Lutheran reform programme in Germany and, more significantly for the theme of this volume, the disappearance of the rhetorical emphasis on universal priesthood and freedom in later Protestantism. Talk of Christian freedom and universal priesthood struck a clear chord with the crescendo of nationalism, anticlericalism and peasant unrest which afflicted the German territories in the early sixteenth century. Luther's rhetoric was seized upon by various groups. It provided them with a vocabulary for articulating and justifying their various protests and a means of turning their social grievances, the stock-in-trade of alehouse conversation for the past 150 years, into a religious crusade.[14] As such, they divorced the language from the theology and turned Luther's Reformation into a social and political revolution. The disasters of the so-called Peasants' War and of Münster served to demonstrate both to Luther and others the dangerous ways in which the rhetoric of freedom and priesthood could be used. Accordingly, once the polemical heat of 1520 had passed, such language became less common.

It is important to remember, therefore, that the language of freedom and priesthood was in part a polemical ploy, intimately related to the political and theological climate of 1520. The loss of the specific language of freedom and priesthood does not necessarily indicate a shift in theological belief. It may instead point to a change in the polemical context, where it was as important not to concede ground to libertines and radicals through ambiguous terminology as to criticize the practice of prelacy within the Roman hierarchy.

Given Luther's emphasis on calling and upon the two kingdoms, it would be wrong to categorize his theology as either providing an ideological basis for a complete emancipation of the laity or as representing a radical individualism. It was neither. The emphasis upon calling in the social and political sphere had its corollary in the theological realm. Luther's emphasis upon individual conversion, assurance and faith was not an attempt to set the individual in general opposition to all forms of corporate authority but rather a specific response to the particular problem of how men and women could stand as righteous before a holy God. In doing so he called into question the institutional church's pretensions, both political and theological. Yet, as his later opposition to the fanatics demonstrates, he had no intention of putting the Bible into the hands of the laity simply for each believer to do with it as they would. His emphasis upon the fundamental perspicuity of scripture did not deny a role in the church for theological professionals nor did it insist that each person was as competent to discern the meaning of scripture as everyone else.[15] Thus, the need for proper theological education was maintained by Luther and his followers and the respect for church tradition, particularly patristic theology, remained within the Reformation programme despite adherence to the notion of scripture alone.[16] Both factors reflected the reformer's acknowledgement that scriptural authority could not exist in a vacuum but needed to be set in a critical relationship to the doctrinal and exegetical traditions of the church. One could not simply dispose of the teaching magisterium of the church. It was necessary to replace it with an authoritative concern for responsible biblical exegesis conducted in the corporate setting of academy and church, and related to the traditions of the past. Once that basic reality was acknowledged, theology became in part at least the corporate activity of the educated church leadership and not something in which anyone could indulge. Thus again, universal priesthood and freedom were delimited by the theological constraints which Luther's understanding of the word, as the word given within the Bible, imposed upon it. As in the social sphere, where a God-given hierarchy existed, so in practice in the religious sphere a similar hierarchy continued to exist, albeit within a different soteriological framework.

The Reformation and beyond

Luther's Reformation, then, was a combination of two separate and, to an extent, incompatible ideological emphases. On the one hand, the notions of individual conversion, justification through faith and the authority of a perspicuous scripture, all served, potentially at least, to empower the laity: to place the individual, outside formal, institutional frameworks, in the theological driving seat. On the other hand, the notions of calling and the need to fill the power vacuum left by the disposal of the Roman curia with something which would prevent the proliferation of sectarian lunacy, served radically to delimit and control the power and freedoms of the laity. What will be argued in the rest of this chapter is that evangelical[17] Protestantism, particularly in England, remained relatively faithful to these two aspects: the universal, lay orientation and the educated, more authoritarian, dimension of the Reformation programme well into the seventeenth century. It will be suggested that the decisive change occurred in the aftermath of the Clarendon Code in the 1660s, when the ejection of most puritan clergy from the establishment effectively shifted the balance within the English puritan tradition in favour of a more pietistic theology.

Given the somewhat rhetorical and polemical purpose of Luther's language concerning universal priesthood, it is hard to believe that the infrequency of the term in later Reformed Protestantism is at all significant from a theological perspective. John Calvin makes little of the language and, in connection with I Peter 2.9 makes only a passing reference to the idea, typically focusing his attention instead on the priesthood of Christ.[18] Nevertheless, in Calvin, as in evangelical Protestantism in general, the foundations of the idea are all there: the centrality of assurance, the immediacy of the believer's communion with God in Christ, the unmediated access of the believer to the Father through Christ and the corollaries in church practice (namely, the vernacular scriptures, an emphasis upon the clear preaching of the word and a focus upon the sacraments as acts of promise rather than physical channels binding believers to an institutional hierarchy possessing a monopoly on grace).

What was arguably of more significance to the rise of the laity in Protestantism than the change of language was the development of the theory of the just rebellion against corrupt and idolatrous powers. If any theological shift in the aftermath of the Reformation emphasized the importance of the laity as a group, then the alteration in this aspect of religio-political theory must surely be the one. While the theory itself was essentially a pragmatic response by individuals such as John Knox to the fact that certain countries were never going to become Protestant or even tolerate Protestantism of their own accord, it also marked a fundamental abandonment of the very ideological framework used by Luther to defuse the socially revolutionary implications of the ideas underlying his notion of the universal priesthood and of Christian freedom. Now specific theological concerns were to be allowed a direct and dramatic role, not simply within the heavenly kingdom but also within the earthly kingdom. This meant that individual conversion, church commitments and theological convictions were seen to be of immediate political importance. The theory of the just rebellion was, on one level, the formal ideological acknowledgement of the political power and social importance of such hallmarks of Protestantism as conversion, justification by faith and scripture alone. As such, it further underscored the need to educate the laity about theological matters, not simply for the benefit of their own souls but also for the shape and stability of society as a whole.

Education can, of course, be construed either as a liberating or as a socially controlling phenomenon and so it is worthwhile at this point to look briefly at the development of Protestant theology in terms of its pedagogical context. At the level of the intellectual elite the most significant post-Reformation development was that of Protestant scholasticism.[19] It is important to note at the start of any discussion of this particular phenomenon that the rise of Protestant scholasticism did not in itself represent the development of a theology which was in intent and purpose remote or elitist. It was rather a natural and inevitable development in Protestant theological pedagogy. As Protestant theology became established at the national level it moved from the pulpit into the university. Thus, in the late sixteenth and seventeenth centuries, the phenomenon of Protestant scholasticism developed. Much ink has been spilt in this particular area and most of it, one must add, to little scholarly profit. Talk of scholasticism as incipient Enlightenment rationalism, as a 'hardening' of the kerygmatic theology of the reformers or as an attempt to obscure simple biblical truth is largely misplaced.[20] Scholasticism was simply the pedagogical method which was employed in the university context, built around the question and answer framework of so-called disputed questions, best represented in the *Summa Theologica* of Thomas Aquinas. Using this method and the technical theological language developed by the church during the patristic and medieval periods, the heirs of the reformers elaborated the inner structures of their theology in a complex and detailed way which enabled them to combat various theological enemies and to develop and maintain a normative Protestantism, whether Lutheran or Reformed, which was capable of defining itself over against its rivals.

In addition to the adoption of the scholastic forms of university discourse, Protestantism also absorbed much Renaissance rhetorical practice. Thus, for example, the proofs of God's existence reappeared in Protestantism at this point but not in their medieval form, where the strength of the arguments lay in the underlying metaphysics or logic of the proofs themselves. In Protestant scholasticism the proofs more often drew their strength from the consent of the nations, or from rhetorical tricks of persuasion, than from metaphysical presuppositions and were thus tailored to convincing not metaphysicians but ordinary congregations of God's existence.[21]

Finally, the Protestant emphasis on philology – a basic element of elite theological education in the late sixteenth and seventeenth centuries – should not be seen as another subversion of lay-oriented religion. From its very inception, Protestantism had been the religion of the Book and, with its concerns for the unique authority of scripture as revelation and for the perspicuity of the same, it inevitably had a profound concern for textual and linguistic issues. One has only to think of the importance of Erasmus' Greek text of the New Testament for the initiation of the Lutheran Reformation to see the truth of this. In the 150 years after Luther Protestantism developed an increasing linguistic and textual expertise, culminating in the seventeenth century in the work of such men as Brian Walton, James Ussher, John Lightfoot and Edward Pococke.[22] What must be appreciated, however, is that such scholarship, technical as it was, was not antithetical to the theological emphases which aimed at the laity but arose directly from them: the need for a sound biblical text, for correct exegetical procedures and for a better understanding of the world of the Bible derived directly from a desire to make the scriptures comprehensible and accessible to all, a desire which arose from the antihierarchical theology of the Reformation.

Protestant scholasticism was, methodologically speaking, the inevitable result of moving a discipline into a university setting which was rooted in the culture of medieval and Renaissance pedagogy. It also represented the necessary outcome of aspects which, as previously noted, were implicit in the Reformation project itself: a desire to develop and define correct doctrinal and exegetical norms in order that true theology might be expounded and defended, and that ministers might be equipped with a thorough knowledge of the biblical text, thus enabling them to communicate its message to their congregations. It was, therefore, in some ways the heir to some of the authoritarian aspects of Luther's original breakthrough, in that it placed the keys to knowledge in the hands of church leaders and not fanatics. But in other ways it was tailored towards the doctrinal well-being of the church as a whole, including the laity and, in theory at least, pointed to the notion of church leaders being the theological servants of the laity.

It is necessary to guard against any tendency to equate the rise of a scholastic university Protestantism with a collapse or frustration of the lay focus of the theology of the reformers. A number of factors served to prevent this being the case. First, it is important not to confuse categories. As noted above, scholastic theology was not a different theology to that of the reformers but simply a different form of the same theology. It was Protestant theology expressed in the forms demanded by the pedagogical and polemical requirements of the university setting. It is thus hardly the place to look for the lay dimension, or popular ministerial effectiveness in post-Reformation Protestantism, any more than the modern-day university medical lecture theatre is necessarily the place to judge the effectiveness of general medical practitioners. In England and Holland, at least, leading exponents of Protestant scholasticism maintained a strong interest in the day-to-day work of the church. Thus, William Perkins, whose work entitled *A Golden Chaine* has been credited in some of the more naïve readings of seventeenth-century puritanism with single-handedly scholasticizing English puritan thought, was primarily a preacher whose first calling was as a minister of the gospel and whose terrifying pronunciation of the word 'damn' was still talked about years after his death. In addition, much of his work was concerned with the issue of personal assurance of salvation and this, combined with the rise in puritan casuistry, indicates the profound concern that puritan pastors and theologians maintained for the spiritual well-being and maturity of their various flocks.[23] In Holland, probably the greatest scholastic Protestant thinker of them all, Gisbertus Voetius, not only published a multi-volume work of classic disputed questions, but also produced an influential handbook of instruction on elementary Christian piety – and all of this while conducting regular catechetical classes at an orphanage in Utrecht, classes to which, incidentally, he gave priority over meetings with leading theologians and politicians.[24] It is also possible to mention William Ames, Richard Sibbes, Thomas Goodwin, John Owen and Richard Baxter – probably the five most influential puritan intellects of the seventeenth century, all of them adept at refined theological reflection and yet all of them pastors who ministered to congregations which were not composed of men and women of the same theological acumen as themselves. In the works of all these writers it is possible to trace the impact – sometimes profound – of the scholastic method and the medieval and Renaissance metaphysics of the university culture of their day. Yet they exhibit the same concern for conversion, faith, assurance, day-to-day piety and Christian experience which first marked the reforming work of Luther, Calvin and their colleagues a century earlier.[25]

The reasons for this lay focus are obvious: the same underlying emphases upon individual responsibility, conversion, the need for faith and thus the need to understand the central message of the scriptures remained as constants in orthodox Protestant soteriology. These factors combined in the seventeenth century with the need to educate the flock concerning their own theological identity at a time when subtle variations within Protestant theology carried with them dramatic social and political consequences. Thus, in Holland, Voetius's catechizing of orphans fulfilled the same function in the orphanage as his disputed questions did with students in the university: it secured a particular constituency for the Reformed faith over and against the Remonstrant alternatives. Those alternatives had profound domestic and international political implications, since Arminianism was seen by the Dutch Reformed Church as essentially a pro-French commitment. The same was true, in a different context, of Perkins' preaching in England, which served to point his hearers towards the need for a more thorough reformation of the Church of England and a more vital piety than formal state religion required. As the seventeenth century developed, so the need to influence the laity and to shape the way it thought became steadily more important as the social and political stakes increased.

If Protestant scholasticism represented the natural outcome of pedagogical developments and certain Reformation concerns, it nevertheless constituted at a self-conscious level the activity of an intellectual elite. Of more immediately positive significance for the lay orientation of post-Reformation Protestantism was the continued emphasis upon preaching. As noted earlier, the Reformation concern for preaching arose directly from the view that salvation, accessible to all, was grasped by faith in the word of God as found in scripture, scriptural preaching and the sacraments duly administered in the context of the word. The focus of Protestant theological education remained that of the preaching ministry even within the scholastic training of the seventeenth century.[26] Preaching like scholastic theology had a dual function. On the one hand, it communicated the word of God to the congregation and acted as the immediate means of their salvation and growth as Christians. On the other, it was also a means of educating the congregation concerning sound doctrine, good exegesis and becoming Christian conduct. It thus reflected the dual aspect of the Reformation noted above: the liberation of the individual by the placing of responsibility for salvation firmly in the believer's own hands and the delimitation of this new-found freedom by the establishment of norms of Christian belief and conduct. Hence, puritan works place great emphasis upon the high calling of the preaching ministry. It is not something to which all should aspire but a vocation reserved for those who possess a profound experience of God's grace, a great burden for the lost and, of crucial importance, the theological competence not to make major mistakes in the pulpit or give the impression that preaching is a task for the untrained person.[27]

These concerns are reflected in many ways in the practice of the so-called prophesyings which developed in Elizabethan England. A practice initially started in Zürich, the prophesying was a gathering of ministers and ministerial students, some of whom would take it in turn to expound a particular scripture passage in front of the others.[28] This placed the practice of homiletic interpretation in a communal setting which both allowed ministerial self-regulation to take place before budding preachers were let loose on unsuspecting congregations and defused the potential dangers of excessive individualism by enabling factors such as homiletic tradition and the opinions of other, more learned ministers to operate. Thus, a method of elite ministerial control was applied to a procedure whose end purpose was the education of the laity.

The dangers of unregulated and unlearned preaching were all too obvious in the rise of the mechanic preachers during the English Civil Wars of the 1640s and the simultaneous proliferation of radical sects and enthusiasts.[29] The pressure exerted by these groups, with all the social chaos they were perceived to threaten, was not dissimilar to that placed on the early reformers by Thomas Müntzer, the Peasants' War and the later debacle at Münster. Arguably, the experience of the 1640s led to a hardening of Presbyterian attitudes not only to radical sectarians but even towards those who advocated congregational Independency.[30] The idea of a gathered church of professed believers smacked too much of Anabaptism or a dangerous social dualism to be tolerated. The distinction between the visible order and the invisible order, the priesthood of all believers, was becoming too blurred for comfort.

The last aspect of Protestant practice that merits discussion in the present context is that of catechizing. Like preaching it represents the acknowledgement by the ministerial elite of the need to educate everyone concerning the things of God. While the sermon was one way in which theological reflection was communicated to the congregation, individual and family catechizing represented a second, complementary approach. As with preaching, it was both the result of the lay orientation of the theology of individual salvation and assurance which flowed from the Reformation and a means of controlling and regulating the theological convictions of the laity. In a world where Luther's subtle distinction between the two kingdoms had largely become blurred, as epitomized by the rise of the theory of the just rebellion, regulation of the congregation's theological views had an acutely important political as well as soteriological function. Thus catechizing, as a means of driving home pulpit theology around the family fireside, reflected the importance of the laity in ways different from those normally involved in the ministry of the gospel.

Luther had himself been the author of catechisms and in the developing Reformation, both Lutheran and Reformed, catechisms held a place of honour as basic statements of the essentials of the faith.[31] The most famous puritan examples are the Larger and Shorter Catechisms of the Westminster Assembly. The latter, with its well-known first question and answer, 'What is the chief end of man? Man's chief end is to glorify God and to enjoy him forever', exerted a formative influence on household piety from its inception, an influence which continues to this day in some of the more remote areas of the Scottish Highlands and Islands. Nevertheless, the practice of puritan catechizing was not restricted to the official documents of key assemblies, for many puritans wrote their own. Thus, for example, John Owen, the great Independent, wrote catechisms for use with his own congregation. Indeed, in his introduction to these works he stated that, after preaching the gospel, he considered catechizing to be the single most important task of the pastor as it was that which established individuals in their knowledge of the truth. This was a view held by many puritans including the greatest catechizer of them all, the indefatigable Richard Baxter.[32] For this reason Owen produced two catechisms, one for the young and unlearned so that they might have ready answers for basic theological questions and a second which dealt in closer detail with the person and work of Jesus Christ. They functioned as a progressive course in theology.[33] Their style was typical of the genre: basic questions, straightforward answers and a series of relevant scripture proofs (although the 'proofs' were not so much proof texts as signals to diligent readers concerning where to find exegetical help on the point in question from the various standard biblical commentaries). The thrust was, therefore, both doctrinal and exegetical, with catechisms providing a basic and normative framework within which the laity would be able to understand the Bible for themselves. In the catechism as in the sermon the concerns of the theological elite were clearly visible. That elite wished both to empower the laity by placing the Bible and its contents into the hands of everyone, while at the same time providing a controlling framework for understanding the text which would steer the reader away from error.

To summarize, the post-Reformation period, while losing to a large extent the rhetorical language of the universal priesthood, yet maintained those theological concerns which in a specific polemical context the language was meant to convey. Indeed, the emphasis of the reformers on conversion, faith, assurance and the authority and perspicuity of scripture provides the basic matrix within which the various developments of Protestant thought and practice, from the scholastic disputations and linguistic researches of the university to the catechizing of the unlearned villager, should be understood. The need for everyone to take charge of their own salvation imposed responsibilities on those in positions of authority and profoundly shaped the way in which they went about their daily theological business.

The implications for the history of evangelicalism

What are the implications of all this for the history of evangelicalism? First, some useful observations can be made using David Bebbington's fourfold grid of conversionism, activism, biblicism and crucicentrism as the standard starting point for modern discussions. It is immediately obvious to any student of the sixteenth or seventeenth century that all four characteristics are rooted in the Reformation, even if they undergo certain developments in later periods. Conversionism is paradigmatic for much of Protestantism after Luther, resting as it does upon the notions of sin, faith and assurance which the reformer himself brought to the fore. It is only necessary to look at the lives of, say, John Calvin, Theodore Beza, William Perkins, William Ames, Thomas Goodwin or John Bunyan (the list could be extended) to see how central is the notion of personal conversion to Protestantism in the sixteenth and seventeenth centuries. Indeed, such conversionism is an integral part of the theology these men represented.

Second, the activist dimension is also evident: preaching and catechizing with a deep existential concern for the souls of others, a concern which flowed directly from the conversionism mentioned above, were central to the work of both the reformers and their immediate heirs and not simply an innovation by eighteenth-century divines. The theology underlying the notion of universal priesthood brought with it both privileges and responsibilities, and these responsibilities found their outlet in activism – perhaps not the field-preaching of Whitefield but certainly the visitations and catechetical work of men such as Baxter and Owen.

As for biblicism and crucicentrism, that these are hallmarks of sixteenth- and seventeenth-century Protestantism surely needs no restatement. It can be argued that certain evangelical positions concerning scripture, which are often seen as Enlightenment developments, can be traced back through the history of the church and that a strong stance on justification by faith is also a hallmark of crucicentric evangelicalism. In practice Bebbington's last two categories clearly point us once again to the sixteenth- and seventeenth-century theological roots of eighteenth-century evangelical developments.

As a result of this, it is obvious that writing the history of evangelicalism requires the whole movement to be set to some extent within the context of the sixteenth and seventeenth centuries. The four characteristics of evangelicalism were not new in the eighteenth century but represented the continuous outworking of elements established within evangelical Protestantism at a very early stage in its development. If a case is to be made, therefore, for the distinctive character of eighteenth-century evangelicalism, the focus has to be upon the ways in which these four elements were changed, modified or differently understood, or how they were given an altered significance during this period.

Here, the seventeenth-century historian moves beyond his strict sphere of competence and into the realm of speculation. However, it would seem that one key discontinuity between the puritan theology of the seventeenth century and much of the evangelicalism of the eighteenth is that of the university context. Certainly in the form of English and Dutch puritanism, seventeenth-century Protestantism represented a successful marriage between academic theology and pastoral concern, whereby supremely accomplished learning connected with the life of the everyday believer through the media of sermons, catechisms and the pastorates of men who were well versed in scholastic theology. As such, it held two apparently incompatible strands of Protestant thought and life together: the need for a responsible, learned and theological approach to the biblical text and the belief that every individual, from the greatest to the least, had the responsibility to believe in God for their own salvation. Events in the latter part of the seventeenth century, however, served to rupture this relationship.

In England the Restoration of 1660 and the subsequent imposition of the Clarendon Code effectively terminated puritanism as a movement and excluded not only serving puritan ministers but also subsequent generations of Nonconformists from both the Anglican ministry and, more importantly, from the universities. When nearly 2,000 puritan ministers left the established church in 1662, they took their theological tradition away from its academic roots in a university culture which stemmed from the Middle Ages and had been modified by the Renaissance. Their heirs in English Nonconformity were often men of formidable intellect – the names of Isaac Watts and Philip Doddridge spring immediately to mind – but they were not university men. They were not schooled in the language and thought forms of their puritan forebears and the theology they expounded did not coincide with that of their heritage in some of its most important aspects.[34]

Had the puritans remained within the university system change would still have been inevitable. The impact of Enlightenment philosophies on institutions of higher learning effected a change within the structures of academic life scarcely less far-reaching than the impact of the Aristotelian renaissance of the twelfth and thirteenth centuries. Whether it was Lockean empiricism in England, or Cartesianism in Holland, the result was the implementation of new philosophical paradigms which had a profound effect upon the way university education in general, and theology in particular, was conceived and pursued. Ultimately, the result was that the two sides of theology, the intellectual and the lay, largely went their separate ways, with academic theology becoming further and further removed from the conversionism, activism, biblicism, and crucicentrism which lay at the heart of the Reformation programme.

In conclusion, therefore, two simple points can be made. First, the lay focus found in eighteenth-century evangelicalism is rooted in the Reformation of the sixteenth century and represents simply the latest phase of Protestant lay concern. As such, it must be understood as a development of the Reformation, not as an innovation of the Wesleys, Whitefield or whoever else. Second, if evangelicalism is in some way distinct from the Reformation in terms of its understanding or application of the four evangelical characteristics, then these differences must be understood within the context of wider changes in the intellectual and social culture. Given the evident continuities between evangelicalism and the Reformation, the key question becomes why such differences arose. The answer to this lies not in any internal theological considerations or developments but in the wider context in which the movement developed. Central to the question, almost certainly, were the changes in university culture that took place at the start of the eighteenth century.

Notes

1 See N.O. Hatch, *The Democratization of American Christianity*, New Haven: Yale University Press, 1989; C.E. Hambrick-Stowe, *Charles G Finney and the Spirit of American Evangelicalism*, Grand Rapids: Eerdmans, 1996; B.B. Warfield, *Perfectionism*, Philadelphia: Presbyterian and Reformed, 1958, pp. 3–63; G.M. Marsden, *Fundamentalism and American Culture: the shaping of twentieth-century evangelicalism 1870–1925*, New York: Oxford University Press, 1980.

2 For a good general account of all of these, see D.W. Bebbington, *Evangelicalism in Modern Britain: a history from the 1730s to the 1980s*, London: Unwin Hyman, 1989.

3 The account is frequently cited in selections of Luther's writings or in works about him, e.g. W. Pauck (ed.) *Luther: lectures on Romans*, London: SCM, 1961, pp. xxxvi–xxxvii. On subsequent pages Pauck also discusses some of the problems raised by the account.

4 See, for example, Luther's arguments in the preface to the Epistle to the Romans, the theses for the Heidelberg Disputation, and 'The Freedom of a Christian'. Translated texts can be found in J. Dillenberger (ed.) *Martin Luther*, New York: Anchor, 1961.

5 The definitive account of Luther's development up to, and including, the crucial year 1520 is M. Brecht, *Martin Luther: his road to Reformation, 1483–1521*, trans. J.L. Schaaf, Minneapolis: Fortress Press, 1985.

6 Luther's soteriology is expressed in two of the major treatises of 1520, 'On the Freedom of the Christian' and 'The Babylonian Captivity of the Church'.

7 See especially Dillenberger, *Luther*, pp. 345, 349, 407–8.

8 Thus, preaching and administration of the sacraments are still tasks reserved for a particular group, but this is essentially for the sake of convenience, and on the basis of mutual consent. Ibid. p. 349.

9 Ibid. p. 69.

10 Ibid. p. 407.

11 See Luther's treatise of 1523, 'Secular Authority: to what extent it should be obeyed', Dillenberger, *Luther*, pp. 363–402.

12 D.V.N. Bagchi, *Luther's Earliest Opponents: Catholic controversialists, 1518–1525*, Minneapolis: Fortress Press, 1991, pp. 137–8.

13 The controversialist's name was Wolfgang Wulffer. Bagchi, ibid. p. 138.
14 'The gospel of social unrest: 450 years after the so-called "German Peasants' War" of 1525', in H.A. Oberman, *The Dawn of the Reformation*, Edinburgh: T. & T. Clark, 1992, pp. 155–78.
15 On university life and pedagogy in the Reformation, see H.A. Oberman, *Masters of the Reformation*, Cambridge: Cambridge University Press, 1981.
16 On the importance of patristic studies to the Lutheran Reformation, see P. Fraenkel, *Testimonia Patrum: the function of the patristic argument in the theology of Philip Melanchthon*, Geneva: Droz, 1961.
17 The term 'evangelical' is used here to denote those movements within Protestantism which maintained an emphasis upon conversion and preaching in the years subsequent to the Reformation, as opposed, say in England, to the sacramental tradition represented by the followers of William Laud. This use of the term is not in itself an attempt to prejudge the issue of the relationship between seventeenth-century Reformed orthodoxy and eighteenth-century evangelicalism proper.
18 '[N]ow ye are royal priests, and, indeed, in a more excellent way, because ye are, each of you, consecrated in Christ, that ye may be the associates of his kingdom, and partakers of his priesthood.' J. Calvin, *Commentaries on the Catholic Epistles*, trans. J. Owen, Grand Rapids: Eerdmans, 1948, p. 75.
19 On the whole issue of Protestant scholasticism, see the essays in C.R. Trueman and R.S. Clark, *Protestant Scholasticism: essays in reassessment*, Carlisle: Paternoster, 1999.
20 For examples of such interpretations, see B.G. Armstrong, *Calvinism and the Amyraut Heresy*, Madison: University of Wisconsin Press, 1969; E. Bizer, 'Fruehorthodoxie und Rationalismus', *Theologische Studien* 71, 1963.
21 See, for example, the sermon by Stephen Charnock on the existence of God which integrates the proofs into the classic rhetorical device of *persuasio*. S. Charnock *The Existence and Attributes of God*, 2 vols, Grand Rapids: Baker, 1979, vol. 1, pp. 25–88. On this point in general, see R.A. Muller, *Ad Fontes Argumentorum: the sources of Reformed theology in the 17th century*, Utrecht: Utrechtse Theologische Reeks, 1999, p. 18.
22 On this issue in general, see R.A. Muller, *Post Reformation Reformed Dogmatics II: Holy Scripture, the cognitive ground of theology*, Grand Rapids: Baker, 1993.
23 On Perkins' influence, see F.E. Stoeffler, *The Rise of Evangelical Pietism*, Leiden: Brill, 1965; also P.R. Schaefer, 'The spiritual brotherhood on habits of the heart: Cambridge Protestants and the doctrine of sanctification from William Perkins to Thomas Shepard', unpublished thesis, University of Oxford, 1992.
24 On Voetius, see W.J. van Asselt and E. Dekker (eds) *De Scolastieke Voetius*, Zoetemeer: Boekencentrum, 1995, esp. pp. 1–33. His classic treatment of Christian piety is available in a critical edition by C.A. de Niet, *De praktijk der godzaligheid*, 2 vols, Utrecht: De Banier, 1996.
25 Good guides to puritan theology are still few and far between, but the following are worth consulting, in addition to the works by Schaefer and the collection edited by Trueman and Clark cited above: J.R. Beeke, *Assurance of Faith: Calvin, English puritanism, and the Dutch Second Reformation*, New York: Peter Lang, 1991; G.F. Nuttall, *Richard Baxter*, London: Nelson, 1965; P. Toon, *God's Statesman: the life and work of John Owen*, Exeter: Paternoster, 1971; C.R. Trueman, *The Claims of Truth: John Owen's Trinitarian theology*, Carlisle: Paternoster, 1998.
26 John Owen, probably the most sophisticated of the puritan theologians of the seventeenth century, regarded preaching the word, administering the sacraments and

praying for the congregation as the three most fundamental tasks of the Christian ministry. See his 1689 treatise, 'The True Nature of a Gospel Church', in J. Owen, *The Works of John Owen*, 16 vols, Edinburgh: Banner of Truth, 1968, vol. 16, pp. 74–96.

27 This is why Richard Baxter advised all preachers to say at least one thing in every sermon which no member of the congregation understood, in order to preserve the distinction between the ministry and the laity. M. Sylvester (ed.) *Reliquiae Baxterianae: or, Mr Richard Baxter's narrative of the most memorable passages of his life and times*, London, 1696, I.i, p. 93.

28 On the rise of the prophesyings, see P. Collinson, *The Elizabethan Puritan Movement*, Oxford: Clarendon Press, 1967, esp. pp. 168–76.

29 The classic study of these sects remains that by C. Hill, *The World Turned Upside Down*, London: Pelican, 1975.

30 See the discussion of Baxter's attitude to Independency, in C.R. Trueman, '"A meere Catholick"? Richard Baxter on Christian unity: a chapter in the enlightening of English Reformed orthodoxy', *Westminster Theological Journal* 61, 1999, 53–71.

31 For a good discussion of catechisms, particularly as regards their polemical function, see T.J. Wengert, *Law and Gospel: Philip Melanchthon's debate with John Agricola of Eisleben over poenitentia*, Carlisle: Paternoster, 1997, pp. 47–75.

32 Owen, *Works*, vol. 1, p. 465. For Baxter, see the extended discussion of the usefulness of catechizing in his major work on the pastoral ministry, *The Reformed Pastor*.

33 Ibid. pp. 465–6. The text of the catechisms is found on pp. 467–94.

34 See, for example, Doddridge's complete confusion in the face of his hero Richard Baxter's more sophisticated theological work. G.F. Nuttall, *Richard Baxter and Philip Doddridge: a study in tradition*, London: Oxford University Press, 1951, pp. 17–18. For my own comments on the way in which subsequent generations appropriated Baxter, see Trueman and Clark, *Protestant Scholasticism*, pp. 185–6.

Chapter 3

Lay conversion and Calvinist doctrine during the English Commonwealth

Crawford Gribben

The relationship between the pulpit and the pew is surely one of the most potent, important and problematic relationships in practical Christian theology. Since the apostle Paul, Christian preachers have insisted upon their authority and doctrinal knowledge before congregations, which in turn have often insisted on their own independence and the priority of lay experience. The faith of the laity exists in flux. It has rarely been the faith of the theologian.

In general, this tension has been neglected by historians of Christian belief. Ideologies, in many estimations, exist en bloc: Lutherans are assumed to have believed what Luther believed; Calvinists to have followed Calvin's ideas. This type of church history, like the old accounts of national history, has been characterized by a top-down approach. Yet, as David Hall has noted, 'ordinary men and women' in the seventeenth century 'enjoyed a certain measure of cultural and religious independence, the bedrock of which was their ability to read the vernacular Bible'.[1] Reconstructed as a conflict of monolithic movements, the academic discipline we know as church history often has little room for such individual deviation, which marks real theological evolution.

The tendency to prioritize imagined monolithic mass movements has been disrupted recently, however, as historians and theologians have begun to reassess the extent to which seventeenth-century puritans – generally Calvinists – differed from the theological perspective established by Calvin.[2] Crucially, they argue, Calvinists abandoned Calvin's belief that assurance was of the essence of saving faith. Although this debate has done much to improve the contextualization of both Calvin and his puritan successors, it has been crippled by an overemphasis upon theology as it was carried out as a scholastic discipline. Scholars such as R.T. Kendall have focused the debate upon academic treatises and pastoral sermons, rather than the popular reception of the ideas those narratives contained. Despite the immediacy provided by its record of spiritual experience, the literature of lay puritanism has less often been considered. This chapter, then, is an attempt to highlight the records of spiritual experience left by lay puritans in the early 1650s, and to suggest ways in which a recovery of scholarly interest in these records might lead to a more rounded understanding of 'Calvin and the Calvinists'. The wealth of puritan literature that exists allows unparalleled access to lay conversion and Calvinist doctrine as they interacted during the English Commonwealth.

Puritan conversion narratives

Puritanism was an intensely literary culture.[3] As the leaders of a movement born with the vernacular scriptures, the puritan preachers encouraged their congregations to keep written records of their conversion and to read those accounts which others had prepared.[4] Richard Baxter recommended Christian biographies because

> the true History of exemplary Lives, is a pleasant and profitable recreation to young persons; and may secretly work them to a liking of Godliness and value of good men, which is the beginning of saving Grace: O how much better work is it, than Cards, Dice, Revels, Stage-Plays, Romances or idle Chat.[5]

Owen Watkins has recorded the result of this emphasis:

> men and women with no special literary skill developed an ability to analyse and communicate their religious experience; the Puritan culture provided a body of theory, a technique, and a language with which to do so – and there were many dedicated pupils.[6]

This linking of writing to salvation, which Watkins highlights, no doubt helped encourage the dramatic rise in literacy rates among seventeenth-century puritans.

During the first half of the seventeenth century most of the spiritual biographies published were the work of clergy. These preachers used the printed page to validate their call to ministry and their subsequent Christian life. Such books sold well as lay puritans compared their own experiences with those of the preachers. Market demand demonstrated how generations of puritan preachers had fostered intense spiritual concern.

These preachers had imagined the soul's movement from damnation to salvation as a linear progression along a 'teleology of grace'[7] which the theologians described as the *ordo salutis*: predestination, to calling, to justification, to glorification.[8] It was a 'golden chain' which stretched from the eternity before creation to the eternity beyond the earth's dissolution. Thomas Manton later described the idea's most popular metaphor. He envisaged

> a golden chain, the chain of salvation, which is carried on from link to link, till the purposes of eternal grace do end in the possession of eternal

glory . . . [and] an iron chain of reprobation, which begins in God's own voluntary preterition, and is carried on in the creature's voluntary apostasy, and endeth in their just damnation.[9]

Existing to comfort the afflicted and to afflict the comforted, books which dealt with such themes proved to be best-sellers. They suggested various methods of determining one's place in the temporal outworking of the eternal decrees. These discussions were calculated to foster self-scrutiny by constantly raising the spectre of false faith and self-deception. In *The Breastplate of Faith and Love*, for example, an evangelistic title which passed through nine editions between 1630 and 1651, John Preston warned of 'ignorant men, that take not Christ in deed, but onely in their owne fancie'.[10] Richard Sibbes similarly warned against the presumption of saving faith, but highlighted too its opposite danger: 'we are thus prone to presume; so when conscience is awaked we are as prone to despair'.[11] It was a sentiment entirely appropriate to Bunyan's *Mapp of Salvation* (1664): in the early stages of spiritual experience despair was an encouraging sign, but assurance was downright dangerous. Summarizing this teaching three centuries later, the historian William Haller voiced the puritan dilemma: 'we live in danger, our greatest danger being that we should feel no danger, and our safety lying in the very dread of feeling safe'.[12]

Richard Baxter was one of many puritans whose spiritual concerns were aroused through exposure to this genre. In his mid-teens he read *Bunny's Resolution*, and through the reading of this book, he claimed, 'it pleased God to awaken my soul'.[13] Richard Sibbes' *Bruised Reed* also encouraged these aspirations towards godliness, but Baxter began to worry that his experience did not correspond to the paradigm of salvation the preachers had established: he 'could not distinctly trace the Workings of the Spirit upon [his] heart in that method which Mr Bolton, Mr Hooker, Mr Rogers, and other Divines describe'.[14] The preachers' writings thus became the benchmarks of the soul.

Baxter's experience was entirely typical. Traditional English Calvinism propelled the sinner out of passivity into intense self-scrutiny. Alister McGrath has noted:

> At the theoretical level predestination might seem to encourage quietism: if one is elected, why bother doing anything active? In fact its effect was quite the reverse: to ensure that one is elected, one must throw oneself wholeheartedly into appropriate action.[15]

This 'appropriate action' did not simply involve the reading of evangelistic books. Election to salvation was evidenced by true faith; true faith was evidenced by holiness of life. Lay puritans were therefore regularly exhorted to maintain 'commonplace books', ledgers in which the saints tallied up their righteousness each day to validate the reality of their claim to new birth. As in the discussion of salvation, the preachers led the way. Thomas Goodwin's diary recorded 'the account of the work of the Holy Spirit on his soul, in converting him to God, and many of his religious exercises and experiences'.[16] Robert Harris 'marked down his evidences for heaven . . . often subscribed in a book which he had for the purpose'.[17] Richard Sibbes also encouraged his readers to 'keep diaries of [God's] mercies and favours every day'.[18] As Goodwin's son claimed in writing his father's biography, 'nothing so clearly and fully unfolds the work of the Holy Spirit, and the exercise of the soul, in conversion, as a person's diary'.[19]

Although this aspect of puritan culture was rigidly defined by the preachers, it was, paradoxically, to facilitate the emergence of a puritan lay movement. The Independent churches rejected territorial identification in an attempt to include within their membership only those who had been truly born again. Suddenly, the literary self-reflection which the older Church of England preachers had encouraged became a catalyst for the 'conversion narratives' which the Independent churches demanded. These conversion narratives were designed to evidence the validity of the faith of the individual applying for membership of the gathered church. It is impossible to exaggerate the significance of this liturgical innovation. For the first time in those churches loyal to the Magisterial Reformation, lay Christians – both male and female puritans – enjoyed their own ecclesiastical voice.

But the old hierarchies did not completely disappear. The conversion narrative was a genre in which preachers continued to lead the way. Early in the 1650s compilations of conversion accounts were published by millenarian ministers such as Henry Walker, Vavasor Powell, Samuel Petto and John Rogers.[20] One recent historian of the American conversion narrative has argued that this type of writing was the product of its times. Social and political turmoil produced 'an equal and opposite reaction: the emergence of a counter-demand and a heartfelt longing for peace and safety, for comfort and, in a word, for assurance'.[21]

While announcing the innovation, however, the publication of these accounts fossilized the genre. Although in every other respect the Independents insisted on their separation from the older Anglican settlement, their conversion accounts echoed the modes and metaphors which the earlier preachers had established. The attractiveness of losing one's humanity – and therefore culpability – was, for example, a common theme. Decades before the 1650s William Perkins had noted the 'enviability' of a dog or toad for a person under conviction of their sin.[22] In 1653 John Rogers' account of his own conversion remembered 'wishing I were a stone, any thing but what I was, for fear of hell and the devils'.[23] Four years later Thomas Brooks imagined an afflicted conscience longing that it 'might be turned into a bird, a beast, a toad, a stone! Oh that we were anything but what we are!'[24] Even in *Grace Abounding* (1666), John Bunyan would remember envying the condition of the dog and toad . . . yea, gladly would I have been in the condition of the dog or horse, for I knew they had no soul to perish under the everlasting weights of hell for sin, as mine was like to do.[25]

Even in the most radical literary genre the Independents possessed, the radical exponents of the Independent way echoed the soteriological language of the ultra-clerical Anglicans and set a pattern which later puritans would follow.[26]

Thus, establishing a pattern for the perception of conversion, the accounts became highly stylized membership applications, and puritan conversion was subsequently reimagined through the paradigms the genre had established.[27] In particular, as we shall see later, it encouraged the expectation of a two-stage conversion in which radical puritanism – to the extent that it ever deviated from Calvin – seemed to return to an insistence upon an assured faith as the basis for church membership.

Summarizing the earlier part of the seventeenth century, literary critic Stephen Greenblatt has argued that 'among the early Protestants we find almost no formal autobiography and remarkably little private, personal testimony'.[28] By the 1650s the literary temper of English-speaking Protestantism had changed dramatically. Newly emancipated in the Independent churches, lay puritans had found their voice – but discovered they had little choice in what to say.

John Rogers

At the forefront of this radical movement within puritanism were the millenarian and open-Baptist Independent congregations with which John Rogers and John Bunyan were involved. Born only a year apart, Rogers and Bunyan occupied very different places among the radical Independents in 1653. Rogers was an experienced pastor with a university education; Bunyan was a tinker undergoing conversion who would not attain church membership for a further three years. Bunyan only owned a couple of books; Rogers by this time had begun his publishing career and had earned himself a substantial reputation among Cromwell's elite. His work entitled *Ohel or Bethshemesh* (1653) was an apology for Independent church government, and included within it a selection of the conversion narratives provided by members of his gathered church in Dublin.

The accounts in Rogers' collection resemble those found elsewhere in the puritan corpus: there is the same sense of linear progress and final 'arrival' at assurance of faith. Thus one member was 'awakened' under the ministry of Ezekiel Culverwell and was 'satisfied' by Samuel Bolton.[29] Another member was 'prepared' by Sidrach Simpson and Walter Cradock, given 'conviction of sin' through John Owen, and 'received great comforts and assurance of Christ' eventually through Rogers himself.[30]

But while there are allusions to the established paradigm of conversion, there are also distinct novelties about Rogers' approach. The descriptions of the despair of the convicted sinner, for example, evidence a radicalization of the typical puritan discourse. The principal theologians of the Independent movement had argued that a state of 'void' should characterize the convicted sinner. This 'void' was 'an emptiness', a recognition that the individual 'has nothing he can point to, or even reflect upon, including his preparedness'.[31] Thus, for example, Jeremiah Burroughs encouraged those who sought salvation to pray,

> Lord, I am nothing, Lord, I deserve nothing, Lord, I can do nothing, I can receive nothing, and can make use of nothing, I am worse than nothing, and if I come to nothing and perish I will be no loss at all.[32]

Later in the century the Presbyterian Thomas Watson would speak of such humility as 'a kind of self-annihilation'.[33] One recent historian has described this as a 'writing to redundancy', a negation of the self.[34] Denying oneself, therefore, meant exactly that – and in some instances denying the self's existence quite as much as the sin.

Consequently, Rogers argued that 'A true and full perswasion of the way of Christ makes thee see an emtinesse.'[35] This effected a challenge to the puritan representation of conversion as prospective saints struggled adequately to depict this sense of emptiness. Their objective was to silence the egotism of autobiography.

Rogers' congregation adopted various means to this end. Some efforts were linguistic. John Spilman described how he 'fell into great trouble':

> [I] thought I was damned, and utterly lost for all this, still wanting faith, and looking upon my own actings and graces . . . then I discovered the most excellent way, which is Christ and nothing but Christ, and then I grew confident, and full of courage and assurance, and loved Christ, in all, and all that was Christ's, and Christ more than all.[36]

Spilman's writing literally enacts his theology. If the subject of his sentence is himself and his object is Christ, the verb silenced by the incantation of the final clauses demonstrates that in speaking of Christ he ceases to speak of himself. He has been evacuated from his account of himself.

At the other end of the teleology of grace, as repentant sinners entered into assurance of salvation, many of Rogers' accounts prioritized the 'inner light' of dreams and visions above the outward, objective evidence of scripture. Before Rogers arrived in Dublin, for example, Elizabeth Chambers had

> a dream one night of her troubles, a vision of him [Rogers] so plainly, that after he was in Dublin, the first Serm[on] he preached, she told her

friends that this was the man that God had declared to her in a vision, should comfort her soul.[37]

John Cooper had a similar experience, finding confirmation of his faith in a dream which involved Rogers along with the governor of Dublin and the bishop of Clogher.[38] Like John Bunyan in *Grace Abounding*, these believers found themselves the passive subjects of the assaults of dreams and biblical texts. One historian has argued that Rogers encouraged such 'heightened emotionality' as evidence of the operations of grace.[39]

This 'heightened emotionality' certainly encouraged a sustained sense of crisis. This tension emerges in Rogers' perception of the cyclical movement the preachers had encouraged. William Perkins, 'the principal architect of the young Puritan movement',[40] had definitively established the linear paradigm of the 'golden chain', but had also famously argued that each new act of sin requires a new act of conversion. Assurance of salvation was something that could be enjoyed, then lost, and then enjoyed once again. Instantaneous conversion had become a series of conversions. This pattern can be observed in the longest of the accounts included by Rogers, in the narrative prepared by Elizabeth Avery.

Avery's narrative demonstrates the influence of those Independent puritans who emphasized the immediate witness of the Holy Spirit. Assurance for them was not simply a rational conclusion drawn from the observation of increasing holiness in everyday life – it was the effect of the Spirit's direct revelation to the soul. Avery structured her narrative around two crisis experiences, emphasizing her trance and conversion, and the 'voices' that she heard telling her that she was truly saved.[41]

Thus John Rogers, while inheriting the pastoral tensions of traditional Church of England Calvinism, was not a slave to its traditions. The lay members of his church were liberated by his teachings about the Holy Spirit and his permission for their vocal involvement in public worship. But this was an emancipation of the laity which radically redefined who they were – no longer a mixed multitude of elect and reprobate, as Presbyterians and Anglicans had claimed, but a union of visible saints, assured of their salvation, called into the priesthood of all believers, and testifying to the ministry of the same Holy Spirit. It was a pattern that continued after the Restoration, even when puritanism had collapsed into Nonconformity and Episcopalianism was again ascendant.

John Bunyan

The experience of John Bunyan in the early 1650s was markedly similar to the conversions that Rogers recorded. Bunyan was also engaged with the deeply millenarian open-Baptist Independents and, like Rogers' hearers, found himself struggling with the theological traditions of experimental Calvinism.

The links between the two men were not merely circumstantial; later in the decade, after the eclipse of the Fifth Monarchist programme, in which both were involved, Bunyan's church was still actively pursuing links with London radicals – including John Rogers.

By the time that Bunyan came to reflect upon his conversion, and to prepare his spiritual biography for publication, he was active in the ministry of the Independent churches in his locality. Blurring the distinctions between 'clergy' and 'laity', Bunyan never quite made it as a puritan divine, and often flaunted his lack of the formal education that his ministerial peers had enjoyed. It seemed more authentic to be like the unlettered fishermen who first followed Jesus. Richard Baxter typified the attitude of many in describing Bunyan as 'an unlearned Antinomian-Anabaptist', while admitting that he was nevertheless 'an honest Godly man' who 'attained the design of Christianity'.[42] As a common man, ministering to common men, Bunyan's work can be thought of as part of the puritan lay tradition.

His spiritual biography *Grace Abounding* (1666) is the most famous puritan conversion narrative and has been described as 'the apogee of [the] tradition'.[43] It is not an entirely typical example, however. *Grace Abounding* does not demonstrate a dependence upon the linear paradigms established by the puritan theologians, so much as highlight a series of cycles such as that seen in Elizabeth Avery. It imitates the earlier form of personal spirituality, the cyclical soteriology popularized by Perkins.

For this reason the literary critic Anne Hawkins has noted 'an absence of spiritual development' in the book.[44] She concludes that Bunyan's narrative is actually a significant deviation from the standard puritan morphology of conversion: 'an outline of the text reveals that this structural oscillation between progress and regress itself constitutes a definite pattern – one that consists of two series of temptations and two conversion narratives'.[45] Unlike the crisis conversions of St Paul or St Augustine, she concludes, 'Bunyan's lysis conversion is by definition diffuse, cumulative, and repetitive – a conversion model that does not readily lend itself to the narrative dimensions and dramatic potential of spiritual autobiography.'[46]

And yet Bunyan seems elsewhere to place himself well within the orthodox Calvinist tradition. His *Mapp of Salvation*, completed two years earlier, was a theological flow chart of the decrees of election and reprobation in which the believer was encouraged to undertake self-examination: 'Look into thy heart, as in a book, and see if thou canst read the same.'[47] This table was based on a similar diagram published in William Perkins' *Golden Chain* (1590), which was in turn based on a similar chart published in two English translations of Beza's *Tabula* in 1575 and 1576.[48] Beza's work was approved by Calvin and one of the English translations was carried out by Calvin's brother-in-law William Whittingham. Calvin's own writings were not definitive for the English puritan movement, for in England by 1602 the works of Perkins, who died that year, were outselling the works of Calvin, Beza and

Bullinger combined.[49] Nevertheless, Bunyan's *Mapp* exists in direct lineal descent from Calvin's work and from the work of his most prolific Reformation apologists.

One must hesitate, then, in accepting Gordon Wakefield's claim that Bunyan was 'a signal example of Lutheran influence on English Protestantism, tempering Calvinism'.[50] The scholastic treatment of conversion, faith and repentance demonstrate that Bunyan's theology was far from alien to the Calvinistic theology of the English puritan movement.

But if the variety of these assessments demonstrates anything, it is that Bunyan's theology was drawn in several directions at once. The tension between what critics describe as his Lutheran and Calvinist impulses was in essence a tension between his understanding of the scriptural teaching of the application of salvation and the interpretation of his own experience.

Like Elizabeth Avery and others in the conversion-narrative tradition, Bunyan's experience evidences two crises – one of conversion and one of assurance. Echoing the claims of Thomas Goodwin, Bunyan had implied that the 'immediate' witness of the Spirit in assuring the believer of his salvation was comparable to 'a new conversion'.[51] But Bunyan's formal considerations of salvation – like the *Mapp* – did not support any such 'second blessing'. Heart and head were torn apart by the influence of the Independents and Bunyan's considered account of his conversion could not escape their legacy. The conversion-narrative mode was transforming abstract theology into living, breathing accounts of Christian experience and, as such accounts were not closed until assurance had been attained, was transporting the concept of puritan conversion back beyond Perkins to Calvin and his initial teaching that assurance was of the essence of saving faith.

Conclusion

In these two instances, as in many others, puritan conversion narratives effected an emancipation of the laity. Laypeople found a voice within the ecclesiastical institutions of the burgeoning Independent movement. Without formal theological qualifications they were encouraged to testify what God had done for their soul and were given the means publicly to negotiate with the received orthodoxies of experimental Calvinism. As a consequence their experiential analysis of saving faith seemed to echo Calvin's earlier definition. But the manner of their involvement was also of immense significance. With the support of significant elements of the theological and political elite, unlettered men and women were provided with institutional indemnity to declare their views publicly before the church.

Nevertheless, this emancipation was tempered by high levels of clerical involvement. Accounts were collected and prefaced by ministers who were anxious at some level at least to validate themselves and their theology before the world. For the most part, conversion accounts were highly controlled, highly stylized productions whose publication, we can be sure, was designed to consolidate the reputation of the congregation's minister.

But their emancipated laypeople were grappling with Spirit and with scripture and were redefining the very basis of ecclesiastical debate. Accounts of lay conversion no longer tallied with academic presentations of Calvinist doctrine. They could negotiate with the scholastics, for the Son had set them free.

Notes

1 D.D. Hall, 'The Literary Practices of Dissent', in K. Herlihy (ed.) *Propagating the Word of Irish Dissent 1650–1800*, Dublin: Four Courts Press, 1998, p. 13.
2 R.T. Kendall, *Calvin and English Calvinism to 1649*, Oxford: Oxford University Press, 1979; P. Helm, *Calvin and the Calvinists,* Edinburgh: Banner of Truth, 1982; R. Muller, *Christ and the Decrees: Christology and predestination in Reformed theology from Calvin to Perkins*, Grand Rapids: Baker, 1988; A. Clifford, *Atonement and Justification: English evangelical theology 1640–1790: an evaluation*, Oxford: Clarendon Press, 1990, also *Calvinus: Authentic Calvinism: a clarification*, Norwich: Charenton Reformed Publishing, 1996; J.R. Beeke, *Assurance of Faith: Calvin, English puritanism, and the Dutch Second Reformation*, New York: Peter Lang, 1991, also *The Quest for Full Assurance: the legacy of Calvin and his successors*, Edinburgh: Banner of Truth, 1999.
3 See N.H. Keeble, *The Literary Culture of Nonconformity in Later Seventeenth-Century England*, Leicester: Leicester University Press, 1987.
4 See C. Gribben, *The Puritan Millennium: literature and theology 1550–1682,* Dublin: Four Courts Press, 2000, pp. 149–71.
5 S. Clarke, *Lives of Sundry Eminent Divines*, London, 1683, sig. A3v, quoted in O.C. Watkins, *The Puritan Experience*, London: Routledge and Kegan Paul, 1972, p. 1.
6 Watkins, *Puritan Experience*, p. 2.
7 T. Webster, 'Writing to redundancy: approaches to spiritual journals in early modern spirituality', *Historical Journal* 39, 1996, 43.
8 The basis of the puritan idea of a 'golden chain' can be traced to Romans 8.30.
9 T. Manton, *The Complete Works of Thomas Manton*, 22 vols, London, 1870–5, vol. 5, p. 202.
10 J. Preston, *The Breastplate of Faith and Love*, London, 1630, p. 15.
11 R. Sibbes, *The Complete Works of Richard Sibbes*, 7 vols, Edinburgh, 1862–4, vol. 3, p. 34.
12 W. Haller, *The Rise of Puritanism: or, the way to the New Jerusalem as set forth in pulpit and press from Thomas Cartwright to John Lilburne and John Milton, 1570–1643*, New York: Columbia University Press, 1957, pp. 156–7.
13 J.M. Lloyd Thomas (ed.) *The Autobiography of Richard Baxter*, London: J.M. Dent & Sons, 1931, p. 7.
14 Ibid. p. 10.
15 A. McGrath, *A Life of John Calvin: a study in the shaping of western culture*, Oxford: Blackwell, 1990, pp. 242–3.
16 J. Reid, *Memoirs of the Westminster Divines*, 2 vols, Paisley, 1811, vol. 1, p. 320.
17 Ibid. vol. 2, p. 19.
18 Sibbes, *Works*, vol. 3, p. 24.
19 Reid, *Memoirs*, vol. 1, p. 320.
20 M.R. Watts, *The Dissenters: from the Reformation to the French Revolution*, Oxford: Clarendon Press, 1978, pp. 174–9.

21 P. Caldwell, *The Puritan Conversion Narrative: the beginnings of American expression*, Cambridge: Cambridge University Press, 1983, p. 21.
22 M. Mullett, *John Bunyan in Context*, Keele: Keele University Press, 1996, p. 65 n. 78.
23 J. Rogers, *Ohel or Bethshemesh. A tabernacle for the sun*, London, 1653, p. 426.
24 T. Brooks, *The Works of Thomas Brooks*, 6 vols, Edinburgh: Banner of Truth, 1980, vol. 1, p. 437.
25 J. Bunyan, *Grace Abounding*, 1666, §104.
26 Note, for example, these entries in the diary of the eighteenth-century American Calvinist David Brainerd: 'I was much dejected, kept much alone, and sometimes envied the birds and beasts in their happiness, because they were not exposed to eternal misery, as I evidently saw I was . . . I had rather be a beast, than a man without God.' *The Works of Jonathan Edwards*, 2 vols, Edinburgh: Banner of Truth, 1974, vol. 2, pp. 317, 325.
27 A. Simpson, *Puritanism in Old and New England*, Chicago: University of Chicago Press, 1955, p. 2.
28 S. Greenblatt, *Renaissance Self-Fashioning: from More to Shakespeare*, Chicago: University of Chicago Press, 1980, p. 85.
29 Rogers, *Ohel*, p. 412.
30 Ibid. inserted pagination, pp. 2–3, following p. 412.
31 Kendall, *Calvin and English Calvinism*, p. 172.
32 J. Burroughs, *The Rare Jewel of Christian Contentment*, 1648, rpt. Edinburgh: Banner of Truth, 1964, p. 89.
33 T. Watson, *A Body of Divinity*, 1692, rpt. Edinburgh: Banner of Truth, 1958, p. 316.
34 Webster, 'Writing to redundancy', *Historical Journal* 39, 1996, 33–56.
35 Rogers, *Ohel*, p. 250.
36 Ibid. inserted pagination, p. 5, following p. 412.
37 Ibid. p. 406.
38 Ibid. p. 390.
39 C.L. Cohen, *God's Caress: the psychology of puritan religious experience*, Oxford: Oxford University Press, 1986, p. 213 n. 47.
40 Beeke, *Quest for Full Assurance*, p. 83.
41 Rogers, *Ohel*, p. 406.
42 N.H. Keeble, *Richard Baxter: puritan man of letters*, Oxford: Clarendon Press, 1982, p. 24.
43 V. Newey, '"With the eyes of my understanding": Bunyan, experience, and acts of interpretation', in N.H. Keeble (ed.) *John Bunyan Conventicle and Parnassus: tercentenary essays*, Oxford: Clarendon Press, 1988, p. 190.
44 A.H. Hawkins, *Archetypes of Conversion: the autobiographies of Augustine, Bunyan, and Merton*, Lewisburg, PA: Bucknell University Press, 1985, p. 88.
45 Ibid. pp. 90–1.
46 Ibid. p. 92.
47 J. Bunyan, *The Works of John Bunyan*, 3 vols, Glasgow, 1860, vol. 3, insert.
48 G. Campbell, 'The sources of Bunyan's "Mapp of Salvation"', *Journal of the Warburg and Courtauld Institutes* 44, 1981, 240; R.L. Greaves, 'John Bunyan and covenant thought in the seventeenth century', *Church History* 36, 1967, 151–69.
49 I. Breward, 'The significance of William Perkins', *Journal of Religious History* 4, 1966, 116.
50 G.S. Wakefield, '"To be a pilgrim": Bunyan and the Christian life', in Keeble, *Conventicle and Parnassus*, p. 112.
51 T. Goodwin, *The Works of Thomas Goodwin*, 12 vols, Edinburgh, 1861–6, vol. 1, p. 251.

Chapter 4

The Pietist laity in Germany, 1675–1750

Knowledge, gender, leadership

Hans Otte

On 9 January 1735 the vicar of Wildemann, a village in the Harz mountains, received a letter conveying good wishes for the New Year. At that time, to receive a letter like this, carefully written by hand, was not uncommon. Members of the upper classes would send each other greetings letters. On the one hand these missives demonstrated the culture of the sender while on the other they paid homage to the recipient. But this particular letter was strange, so the vicar delivered it at once to his regional bishop, the general superintendent of Clausthal, the principal city of that part of the Electorate of Hanover. In the first place the author (and sender) was a miner. The unusual spelling of many words suggests that he was not much used to writing. Nevertheless he wanted to share in this common usage and so he presented his letter. The content of the letter was even stranger than its form. The sender wrote:

> I wish you a lowly heart so that you need not receive honour from men. Thus saith the Lord: My glory will I not give to another, neither my praise to graven images. Cry aloud, spare not, lift up thy voice![1]

This request was followed by a warning: 'If you do not want to follow the steps of Christ and if you are afraid of hissing and reproach, you cannot be his servant. He that taketh not his cross, and followeth after him, is not worthy of him.'[2] The hidden theme of the letter was the spiritual standing of the laity as compared to that of the clergy. For the author of the letter the parsons and theologians of the established church seemed to be false Christians. Only if they repented could they become true Christians in the same way as the laypeople. The criterion for doing so was simple: 'The [lay Christians] serve God in their hearts, for thus saith God, whose name is holy: I dwell with him that is of a contrite and humble spirit.'[3]

The letter appears to stand in the tradition of mystical Bible interpretation established by Jane Laede. Some of her publications had been confiscated during a raid in Clausthal.[4] The official report to the consistory had warned of the existence of a brotherhood formed by miners and craftsmen. With the passage of time it is no longer possible to tell if this information was correct, but there was certainly a group of people in Wildemann that belonged to a radical Pietist movement. Its members were convinced that true Christians possessed two characteristics: a contrite and humble spirit, which was the prior condition for God to dwell in the soul, and a brotherly love to one's neighbour. Parsons seemed to them to lack both characteristics. Therefore the writer of the letter asked his addressee to change his heart and mind. He should alter his manner of life completely in order to find the way of salvation. The miner mentioned two exemplars of true Christianity: St Paul and Martin Luther. For him St Paul was

> a simple craftsman who knew his craft well. There was no need for him to ask the faithful for money in the way the parsons do. Instead he looked after their souls. He called them brethren and did not receive honour from men.[5]

At this point the author mentioned an important criterion of true faith: it was most important to regard oneself as a true brother and to live and work as one who was an equal among equals. Those who were not born again were opposed to this concept.[6] For those who had been reborn there was no need of an established church or of a clergy that lulled those who had not yet experienced rebirth into a false sense of security. All true Christians despised the visible church as did St Paul: 'They did not consider as holy the confessional, the pulpit, the altar, the baptismal font, but they served God in their hearts.'[7] In the meantime, he suggested, things had changed considerably: 'Martin Luther is dead, and popery has crept in again. So the clergy takes money for confession, for baptizing, for burying, and if you do not have money, you have to borrow it.'[8] This harsh comparison illustrates the self-confidence of the writer of the letter, a miner called Heinrich Jacob Frisch. Using language shaped by the Bible, he displayed a great ability to argue for his views. For him differences in education or class distinction had become irrelevant; the lasting differences between men were caused by their inner qualities.

This example gives an impression of one particular type of Pietist comprising lower-class lay individuals who derived their knowledge and self-confidence from the Bible and from banned radical Pietist literature. Radical Pietism emphasized its essential difference from the established church and traditional social order. Through its tuition laypeople became sufficiently self-confident to express their opinions in larger groups and semi-public surroundings. At the same time, such groups frequently came under political and social pressure. This may have been true for the group to which Frisch belonged in Wildemann. We know little about the group apart from a few names, letters and the official reports that have been preserved. Its members were oppressed by Hanoverian officials and were expelled when they refused to attend the regular church services. At every place in the Harz mountains where such Pietist groups were detected governmental, consistorial and mining authorities reacted violently. The officials were irritated not only by the miners' religious obstinacy but even more by their social refractoriness. At that time the miners were struggling to maintain their social privileges. Population increase had led to a surplus of labour and, therefore, the miners found themselves earning less money. They had been told that working methods had to be modernized and that new pumps were to be paid for by reductions in their wages. These strained relations between the authorities and the miners may even explain why the letter of greeting from Frisch to the vicar of Wildemann, with its complaint about the greed of a clergy that lacked true faith, had been written. But the social background cannot explain everything. The writer was certainly more interested in religious than social matters and his letter may simply have been a suitable vehicle through which to make known his convictions. In 1734, the year that had just drawn to an end, the government had renewed its earlier proclamation, warning people that Pietism was a poison for their souls. The proclamation had been aimed at groups of radical Pietists like the one at Wildemann and it is possible, therefore, that Frisch wanted to express his rancour towards its contents when he wrote the greeting letter to his pastor. The consistory, having designed the proclamation, was sure that all heresies fed one another. The catalogue of Pietist heresies included false interpretation of the blessed sacrament, chiliasm, and false doctrine concerning the reconciliation of all souls (*apokatastasis panton*). The consistory also criticized the rejection of the government and clergy, the disregard for divine worship, the belief in an inner light and attendance at conventicles.[9]

This catalogue of heresies was shaped by a comprehensive publication by Samuel Schelwig (1643–1715), a senior clergyman at Dantzig. In his *Synopsis controversiarum sub pietatis praetextu motarum (Synopsis of Controversies Initiated under the Guise of Piety)* he had classified all the pretended errors of Pietism.[10] He wanted to demonstrate that every Pietist error, even the most innocent, belonged to a great chain of Christian error and heresy. Therefore he placed the principles of moderate Pietists such as Philipp Jakob Spener (1635–1705) alongside the extreme opinions of more radical Pietists. Schelwig regarded himself as a true defender of Lutheran orthodoxy. His view of the relationship between the clergy and the laity was clear and simple: 'The church as a whole is made up of teachers and pupils, of whom, as in the previous debate, it was shown from scripture the former govern by divine right, the latter obey, the former lead, the latter are led.'[11] The superiority of the teacher by comparison with the laity, who were regarded as a mere audience, was established by God. If the true nature of the relationship were not respected, anarchy would follow. Luther's view of the priesthood of all believers was explained by Schelwig in a very simple way: every baptized Christian has the same access to salvation but does not have the same rights. Everyone gains access to that salvation through the preaching of the church. Preaching

takes place at the divine service. Divine service can be celebrated only if there is a public order and a clergy, which is established by God's commandment. Thus the difference between the laity and the clergy is not only part of the public order but also of God's economy since the creation of the world.[12] In a similar way Schelwig argued against the private *collegia pietatis* of the Pietists. Due to God's order to preach (Rom. 10.15–17) the public sermon was the only effective form for the advancement of the gospel.[13] Therefore private conventicles with their non-public preaching impeded the basic order of the Christian religion and, at the same time, brought into contempt both public worship and the blessed sacrament. As these conventicles were private by nature, they were open to every form of abuse in the darkness of privacy. Therefore they caused more harm than benefit to pure religion.[14] Schelwig gave a rather rigid and immovable picture of Lutheranism, one that certainly did not represent mainstream Lutheran theology of the period following 1710. The stringent way in which he defended Lutheran ideas may have been doubtful, but he defined the basic tenets of the conservative position with intellectual accuracy and resolution. He erected strong walls in order to prevent laymen from participating actively in the life of the church and made the situation difficult for those who were genuinely interested in religious questions by enhancing the monopoly of the clergy.

In those territories where that form of orthodoxy existed Pietism had to confine its activities to the private sphere. Most of its adherents were people at the edge of society, either soldiers or craftsmen, who could easily make their way to the next town, or – at the other end of the social scale – members of the nobility, who could ignore the conventional norms of behaviour more easily than people of the middle classes. For example, in Hanover the wife of the prime minister Gerlach Adolph von Münchhausen belonged to a pious circle at a time when Pietism was forbidden.[15] The kind of strict orthodoxy represented by Schelwig gradually disappeared during the second third of the eighteenth century, but until that time private devotions that came to the attention of the authorities were normally treated as being illegal.

In virtually every country in central Europe only one church was regarded as established and as having the particular privilege of a public exercise of religion. In northern Germany and Scandinavia the Lutheran churches had become established in that meaning of the term.[16] Alongside the established church, the Reformed and the Roman Catholic branches of religion enjoyed the lesser privilege of a private exercise of religion. But only these three churches were licensed by the state. Therefore no one could leave them and join a dissenting religious group or convert to another form of religion. There was no such legislation as the English Toleration Act of 1689. Consequently, in Germany and northern Europe there was no equivalent to the small, permanent groups of English dissenters. Yet, as always in Germany, there were exceptions. In some of the smaller territories of the Holy Roman Empire the princes favoured radical Pietism. In these territories, between 1700 and 1750, religious societies were often tolerated and printers of heterodox literature were not prosecuted. From 1690 to 1750 a great deal of unorthodox litera-ture, formerly printed in Britain and the Netherlands, was published in some of the small counties of Hesse.[17] Nevertheless, open toleration of this kind was exceptional during the first half of the eighteenth century. Normally adherents of radical Pietist groups were not permitted broader access to the public. Private reading of pious literature and informal contacts with friends through letters and visits were the only avenues for the pursuit of unconven-tional beliefs that were not closed.

The impression gained thus far is that laypeople had little alternative but to fit into the pattern set by the clerical church and to remain silent, or to develop religious activities on the fringe of the church, or even outside it altogether, in the knowledge that they would experience opposition from the clergy. Yet such an interpretation is too simplistic for the relationship between laity and clergy was complex. Even before the Reformation laypeople had held leading positions in the administration of the church. Acting as patrons or as churchwardens they often exercised tight control over the clergy. Above all many orthodox Lutheran clergy were concerned to strengthen and deepen the religious convictions of their parishioners and some called for greater theological instruction of the laity. Gradually, therefore, the relationship between laity and clergy changed. Inevitably laymen who had been theologi-cally educated and whose interest in religious matters had been awakened constituted a challenge for both clergy and church.

This was the starting point for Philipp Jakob Spener who, in the later years of the seventeenth century, became the senior theologian of Protestant Germany. He exemplified the more traditional and ecclesiastical form of Pietism. Spener revived the term 'priesthood of all believers', thus rehabili-tating a central idea from Martin Luther's early ecclesiology, although he preferred the description 'spiritual priesthood' to 'general priesthood'. He presented his programme of reforms to the church at large in 1675 in a small publication called *Pia Desideria, or heartfelt desires for an improvement of the true Evangelical Church pleasing to God, with some Christian proposals to that end*.[18] His goal was the attainment of a lively faith 'so that the spiritual life of Christian people be so miraculously strengthened, that they should become entirely different people'.[19] His starting point was conventional insofar as he called on his fellow clergy 'to spread the Word of God more abundantly among Christians'.[20] To achieve this goal he listed several steps. First, it would be wise to reinstate the kind of synods that existed in apostolic times. By so doing it would be possible not only for the minister but also 'for other people, blessed with special gifts and spiritual knowledge, to have a say and put their godly view about the matters concerned'.[21] Second, the 'spiritual priesthood' should be restored and then duly exercised.[22] This step aimed at improving pastoral care. Because of the false distinction that had grown up between the ordained clergy and the laity, the so-called laypeople could scarcely avoid being lazy. The result of this was a woeful ignorance leading to irreligion. Such neglect of the spiritual priesthood also meant that ministers were able to do whatever they pleased without fear of effective control or even criticism. Yet it was the duty of Christians to edify their neighbours and for the parson to play a part in this. If the clergyman were negligent he should be admonished in a brotherly way. Spener's third proposition was intended to remind his readers that 'for Christian people it [was] not enough to have some knowledge about Christianity, but they should rather put it into practice'.[23] Consequently, he believed that religious controversies should not be approached merely in an intellectual, theoretical fashion. Mere intellect, he argued, was useless if the individual Christian were not able to be convincing by showing true penitence and living a saintly life. Such considerations called for a careful re-evaluation of the importance of dogmatic differences. For radical Pietists this led to a resolute rejection of all differences between denominations. They understood Spener's suggestions as a plea for an interdenominational approach to Christianity.

Spener's programme aimed at invigorating lay Christian activity and it was only after the lapse of a considerable period of time that conservative defenders of Lutheran orthodoxy such as Samuel Schelwig began to attack his proposals. Schelwig and his fellow critics were afraid of competition for attendants between the private meetings for edification and the ordinary public-worship services of the parish. The tendency of the pious to retreat into private worship became a particular bone of contention. Despite their opposition it was remarkable that Spener's programme at first met with unanimous approval, even beyond the borders of the Holy Roman Empire. His suggestions could be interpreted as providing a summary of a conventional Lutheran programme of reform. At first, therefore, there was little objection to his propositions from orthodox Lutherans. He had, after all, maintained that 'the office of a minister was most important for changing the Church for the better'.[24] Parsons were to retain their precedence as far as the reform of the church was concerned. Hence Spener acted as a mediator in the matter of the reform of the church. He accepted representations from anticlerical elements who believed that the clergy constituted the biggest obstacle in the way to salvation, and who favoured instead the activity of laypeople.[25] But he transformed their objections by linking criticism of the church to a wise programme of ecclesiastical reform. He refrained from recommending use of the various means of coercion that the magistrates were prepared to place at his disposal. His irenic attitude was unusual and represented a break with the customary approach to reform within the Lutheran tradition, which had placed the burden of responsibility upon the secular authorities. At the heart of Spener's method lay his conviction that the individual was of key importance, 'since all of our Christianity exists in inward and renewed people, whose soul is the Faith, and its impact the fruits of life'.[26]

In the writing of *Pia Desideria*, with its plea for a reformation of the church, Spener was able to call upon his experiences with the groups that met for private devotion – the so-called *collegia pietatis*. Some who listened to his sermons had asked him urgently to commence religious exercises on Sundays. They wanted to practise their faith by means of private devotion instead of normal Sunday amusements. The prototypes for these religious exercises were the devotional conventicles found within the Dutch Reformed Church. Some members of Spener's congregation had attended one of these conventicles and wanted to introduce the practice to Frankfurt. Thus the *collegia pietatis* were started at the instigation of certain prominent laymen in Spener's congregation. At first the group gathered in his house. In that way the meeting avoided suspicion and allowed him to forestall any potential separation within his flock. The motor of the process was a lawyer named Johann Jakob Schütz (1640–90). Schütz had been educated in Lutheran dogmatics but, as he puts it, only his head had been touched and not his heart. While reading Johann Tauler, he had experienced a religious awakening as he discovered Tauler's way of using a spiritual key in order to understand God's word in the Bible.[27] From that point Schütz wanted to develop his own religious experience and to share it with others of like mind.

This example shows the importance of the laity in the initial growth of Pietism. Pious laymen acquired knowledge about the forms of devotion they wished to practise and began to question the monopoly of the professional theologians in explaining the Bible. When Spener first published his *Pia Desideria* Schütz was preparing a volume of ethical rules for sincere Christians.[28] He had collected sentences and stories from the Bible and had rearranged them in order to illustrate his rules. This interest in ethics shows that Schütz was closely connected with Enlightenment thinkers. Nevertheless, Spener was still very important for Schütz. As a young man he had encountered certain problems with Tauler's theology and had doubts concerning its compatibility with the Lutheran orthodoxy of his upbringing. Spener had pointed him to Lutheran authors and had quoted Luther's own positive judgement about Tauler in such a way that Schütz had become convinced that Lutherans could read Tauler with spiritual profit. In due course, however, Schütz had emancipated himself from Spener's influence. Following his reading of Tauler he experienced an awakening and thereafter Spener became progressively less important to him as a spiritual guide.

The case of Schütz provides an important illustration concerning the dynamics of lay activity. When the interest in spiritual exercises at Frankfurt had increased Spener had opened the *collegia pietatis* to anyone in his congregation. Schütz, however, wanted a group for sincere Christians only. Little by little he withdrew, forming a new conventicle with his friends without Spener's leadership. This group was strongly influenced by Jean Labadie and later by William Penn.[29] Schütz no longer attended the normal Sunday services. Private edification within his group of reborn believers became sufficient for him. Despite this apparent similarity with the miner Frisch he represents a different type of Pietist layman. He had been well educated and was a member of the bourgeoisie in a large town within the Holy Roman Empire. He had travelled widely through western Europe and had many relatives living in various countries. It was comparatively easy for him and his friends to reject the ordinary Sunday services and the eucharist in a large city such as Frankfurt. No sanctions need be expected, but in smaller places it was more difficult for Pietists not to take part in public worship. Nevertheless, there were also lower-class Pietists in Frankfurt besides pious members of the bourgeoisie. Even servants attended Spener's *collegia pietatis*. But their participation was so extraordinary that it was regarded as a peculiarity. The barriers between the social classes remained, although they had lost much of their separating character, but when Schütz withdrew totally from Spener's *collegia pietatis* and formed his own conventicle he referred to the illiterate people who were in the practice of attending. It appears that he believed that he could gain no further edification from Spener's groups.

Schütz's relationship with Spener shows the importance that parsons had as experts within the Pietist movement. They were able to circulate devotional texts. Many of these texts were examples of pious literature written not by orthodox Lutherans but by authors from other denominations representing various theological schools. During the second half of the seventeenth century the publication of heterodox literature grew rapidly. In the promotion and distribution of this literature Spener played a major part. He refused to dissociate himself from pious authors simply because they espoused certain heterodox opinions. He preferred to take advantage of the outstanding piety of their writing. Its spirituality emphasized the practical aspect of belief rather than dogmatic rigidity and its associated dryness. Spener advised his disciples to ignore any heterodox views they encountered in their reading or, even better, to revise their texts, erasing the heterodox parts according to Lutheran orthodoxy.[30] His promotion of devotional and mystical literature encouraged its circulation. In great measure this stemmed from the influence he enjoyed in his positions as senior minister in Frankfurt, royal chaplain in Dresden and dean of St Nicholas in Berlin. While it is not possible to attribute the increase of heterodox literature to the recommendations of a single man, undoubtedly Spener shaped a new approach to such material and one which subsequent Pietist theologians favoured. In this way they enabled laymen to read such literature with a clear conscience.

Spener's starting point was the reform of the church. He never deviated from this central aim, not even in encouraging individuals to strive for a Christian position in politics, at school or at home. His most influential disciple August Hermann Francke (1663–1727) altered the focus, however, and in consequence his relationship to the laity also changed. Francke's most important achievement was the creation of the *Franckesche Stiftungen*, a complex of schools and institutions at Halle. He had commenced his work with an orphanage, but soon added a range of schools adapted to the needs of the different social classes, a large dispensary for medicine, a book store, a printing press and other manufacturing and trading enterprises. He regarded his institutions as the beginnings of an ecumenical reforming movement that would eventually span the whole world. Every part and every area of life ought to be involved. The ideological source of these institutions was the university at Halle and especially its faculty of theology which would prepare future preachers of the gospel. He believed the various institutions constituted a remedy administered by God in order to prevent the spread of general corruption through the different estates.[31] To use his own terminology, Francke felt sure that the new bodies would demonstrate God's footprints in the world. In this respect he was more concerned than Spener to identify the practical effects of the divine presence within society and to that end he drew up a pedagogical method to help people trace its results.

The essential difference between the two Pietist leaders can be seen clearly as one compares their respective attitudes to the revelations made by so-called extraordinary women. Between 1690 and 1700 there was a wave of enthusiastic visions in several towns in central and northern Germany. These revelations were received by women belonging to the lower classes, among them domestic servants and wives of artisans. The revelations consisted of warnings to the clergy and the local authorities that Christ's return was imminent. The prophetesses were escorted by mentors who interpreted their revelations and defended them against critics. Spener was sceptical. He was sure that the revelations were not from God since they were directed against the divine order as it existed in the state, church and family.[32] Francke, on the other hand, was thoroughly convinced that God revealed his glory through miracles of this nature and would continue to do so in even more dramatic ways. In particular, he favoured the far-reaching character of the revelations, with their tendency to comprehend every aspect of God's creation. Even when the events predicted did not occur he persisted in his opinion that God chose to act in mysterious ways and might, as he put it, show his mercy 'just in an hour that you are not aware of'.[33] He had experienced a strong sense of divine providence at his own conversion. Therefore he advised his hearers to be calm as they waited for God to do his work. He was convinced that there were clear steps leading to conversion for which the individual had to be prepared. To train a pupil up to that point was an important part of his pedagogical programme. But Francke's agenda went further. Conversion was only the beginning of progress through the world. Consequently, the individual believer had to await attentively God's further revelations. He had to observe the signs of the time in order to recognize God's footsteps and to follow them.[34] This combination of quietly waiting for and tensely following God's actions was Francke's method of employing both chiliasm and enthusiasm for the benefit of his institutions. The method determined his relationship to laymen. He wanted to help everybody to be converted and then to show them their destiny within God's kingdom.

When Francke developed a wider network of communication his method proved extraordinarily successful. He called upon a wide range of people, especially those with influence. In his programmatic 'Great Essay', sent to Frederick William I of Prussia in 1716, he asked rhetorically: 'Would it not be great, if the secretaries of State who accompany the kings and princes would wake up and care about God's work more than at any time before?'[35] He recognized that private men acting alone could not bring about a radical change in society. Therefore he tried to gain allies among the nobility. He also wanted to win the youth because he believed that in the longer term he would only be successful if young people spread his ideas. On the one hand he trained young theologians in his schools and institutions, while on the other he ran boarding schools and apartments for noblemen and law students. Not long into the programme Francke gave the following account of his success:

> Since the time when this university was opened, some young noblemen and others who had been converted to God have borne fruit out of the good seed God had put into their souls, when they began to manage their estates or obtained a public office.[36]

Francke's programme was particularly successful in Prussia. His access to friends and patrons in the Prussian administration and at the royal court helped him greatly in stimulating the laity. He was granted privileges for his institutions, was able to promote Pietists in the administration of churches and schools and gained support for his commercial projects. Furthermore, he secured support for his missionaries abroad: not in Berlin, since the king of Prussia favoured projects within the borders of his realm, but in London, Copenhagen and – for a short time – St Petersburg.[37] His missionary enterprises were supported not only by prominent laymen but also by some of the leading theologians in their respective countries. They pursued aims characteristic of Pietism within their own churches, such as the preaching of repentance and conversion and the enhancement of inward piety. Nevertheless, Prussia remained the centre of Francke's work in nearly all matters. The majority of Prussian noblemen were not Pietists yet the Pietists among them became the most influential group at the royal court during the reigns of Frederick I and Frederick William I. At the same time it is remarkable that there was no trace of Pietism among the highest nobility. When the wife of Frederick I devoted herself to Pietist aims, and practised religious seclusion with a small number of fellow believers, she was considered as being eccentric if not a little mad.[38]

Apart from Prussia, Pietist members of the nobility were to be found mainly in central Germany. Several small territories in Hesse and Thuringia were ruled by Pietist princes and counts. Most were impoverished and had problems living within the constraints of their small incomes. Pietist values offered a practical alternative to the baroque pomp and superficiality that characterized the greater courts. Embracing Pietism normally signified the commencement of stringent economies both at court and in the administration. However, some princes favoured Pietism within their territories because of its toleration concerning denominational differences. In territories where Lutherans and Calvinists lived side by side, as in Prussia, Pietism appeared to offer the means of improving peace between them. Though it would be a mistake to reduce the interest shown by the princes in Pietism to a simple calculation of benefits, the movement clearly advanced such interests. Yet it must be stated that in most cases the individual Pietist was primarily interested in demonstrating the fruits of faith arising from his own rebirth. The personal, practical interest in piety took precedence over any larger concern for economy or religious toleration. Despite that the individual focus upon the fruits of faith tended to promote a wider interest in social reforms, with Pietist aristocrats, businessmen and officials improving schools and adding windows and stoves to prisons. Between 1700 and 1750, both at governmental and personal level, Pietist leanings often showed themselves in the founding of orphanages.[39]

The participation of aristocrats in the Pietist movement had consequences for prevailing opinions about social class. Within the inner circle, where the word of God was the guiding principle, no such distinctions applied. But outside those gatherings traditional distinctions were respected. The description of the hours of devotion at the court of Christian Ernest, prince of Saxe-Saalfeld, is typical. The religious exercises were open to everybody, but not everybody could take a seat. The members of the court and the aristocrats sat on divans, people of the middle classes were allowed to sit on chairs, but lower-class participants had to stand.[40]

These observations concerning the nobility introduce a third social group that was attracted to Pietism. For those members of the nobility who were on the edge of bankruptcy and who therefore sought salaried posts in the political administration or army, Pietism offered a convincing way of mastering their lives according to Christian principles. As Pietists they were expected to renounce luxury and to live a life that involved labour. They were not allowed to be lazy as there was always the opportunity to devote their energies to the kingdom of God, even if their income was sufficiently high as to render gainful employment unnecessary. In this way Pietism tended to favour attitudes that were typical of the bourgeoisie.

Laymen who were well educated and had experienced spiritual rebirth tended to gain in self-confidence in their relationship with the clergy and that in turn caused conflict, for the clergy saw themselves as holding the leading position in the church. A particularly well-publicized confrontation was set in motion by a group of aristocratic Pietists in Sweden who maintained close links with August Francke. They had been held in captivity by the Russians at Tobolsk. There they had come to know Halle Pietism through the influence of books and preachers. After the death of Charles XII the absolute monarchy in Sweden was abolished. During the epoch of reforms that followed, the group of Pietist noblemen, who by then had returned to Sweden, tried to alter church order in such a way as to break the predominance of the bishops and priests.[41] They argued that all true Christians and committed members of the church should participate in the election of bishops and that laymen should be appointed as assessors in cathedral chapters, since every true Christian had 'the right to decide on religious instructions and the disagreements which rise from these'.[42] In the end the project failed to gain parliamentary approval, but the episode demonstrates clearly the effect that Francke and his circle had in stimulating lay activity within a Lutheran Church that was dominated by the clergy.

This chapter has examined three types of Pietist. All possessed certain common features: they wanted to turn away from a worldly mind; they focused their attention upon the awakening of the individual soul, which they regarded as immortal; and most looked for the fruits of faith. To this process they applied the term 'conversion'. That became one of the keywords of the movement. Most Pietists regarded conversion as the prerequisite of a fruitful clerical ministry, but since laypeople could also experience the same process, they were in principle regarded as functioning on the same level as the clergy. Thus lay Christians were able to judge the doctrine taught by the professional theologians and, moreover, could share in the interpretation of the Bible. Even Luther in some of his earlier writings had stated that lay Christians had the right to do this. Although circumstances had changed considerably by the end of the seventeenth century, with the concept of rebirth beginning to play a major role within Lutheran thought, the Pietists were prominent in promoting lost aspects of Luther's teaching.

The manner and intensity of conversion corresponded to the age and social class affected. The nobility and higher-ranking bourgeoisie were the most easily able to adapt a Pietist understanding of faith to the teaching of the official church, especially in territories where moderate Pietist doctrine such as that of Spener or Francke had been accepted. In territories where the widely imposed ban on conventicles had not been lifted it was difficult for people from the lower classes to reveal that they had been converted, at least if they did not want to break the rules of local society by joining one of the numerous small radical Pietist groups. Therefore many lower-class Pietists preferred to adopt a reclusive approach to faith. They read mystical literature in private and were anxious not to alert church officials. This is the principal reason for the burgeoning of Pietist literature in those territories whose official church policy rejected the new movement. Many laypeople who never thought of changing church policy became interested in edifying and mystical literature. This was the case not only in small Pietist principalities and in countries where Pietist theologians held leading positions within the church, but also in those territories that refused to tolerate Pietism within their borders. During the period under consideration the publication of religious books and especially of literature inspired by Pietism reached its peak in Germany. In 1740 it was estimated that 75 per cent of all publications were books of piety. The Pietists succeeded in reducing the costs of printing to such a degree that even poor people were able to purchase copies of the Bible and religious tracts.[43]

A second keyword of the Pietist movement was 'community'. This was best expressed by the *collegia pietatis*, regarded by many as the most distinctive feature of the movement.[44] The reborn came together in a community in which denominational and class barriers no longer mattered. Many Pietists were deeply convinced that this spiritual equality was correct. On the other hand it would be wrong to overemphasize the idea of community. There were still differences within and between the various Pietist groups. Between 1675 and 1750 a sundering of class barriers remained very unusual, but it was not completely unknown. The barriers within Pietist communities were not so much removed as became obsolete when they proved to be an obstacle to faith. The community of the pious was in principle universal and everybody was expected to join. As a result Pietists became interested in Christian mission extending to all continents and in the spiritual care of Christians who had left their home country to live in overseas colonies. In this way a relationship between British and German Christians came into being that was more intensive than ever before. Pietists began a missionary movement that remained active into the nineteenth and twentieth centuries, long after the founding generations of Pietists had died.

It was typical of most Pietists to be convinced that a true Christian life must be formed by faith. The coherence between faith and life was emphasized and – in consequence – the believer's responsibility for every moment of his life. Therefore, some groups of Pietists rejected laughing, dancing and every form of levity. They often felt a Christian responsibility which went far beyond their small local sphere. For Halle Pietists economic and social activities formed part of their sense of Christian responsibility. At the same time all Pietists laid considerable stress on the subjective element, since conversion and its consequences were seen to shape the personality. Laypeople in particular looked for new ways to express this subjectivity as a natural consequence of their growing awareness of responsibility. As they did they helped to create new forms of literature such as autobiography and spontaneous lyric poetry which eschewed fixed rules. In this way the new emphasis upon the responsibility of believers became a means of emancipating the laity. It helped to ease the rigidity of orthodoxy and Luther's view of the priesthood of all believers was put into practice. In spite of this the professional theologians retained their leadership, the cases of Spener and Francke being two outstanding examples. Even Count Nikolaus Ludwig von Zinzendorf (1700–60) who, as a member of the aristocracy, could easily have ignored clerical assumptions, found himself having to pass a theological examination and to become ordained in order to win acceptance and to hold his group of Moravian followers together.

One important innovation was the broad respect accorded to female religiosity. Using this term is not meant to imply the speculation of some radical Pietists that postulated the presence of the divine wisdom (*sophia*) in the world and the androgynous origins of mankind.[45] Those who followed that kind of speculation were somewhat isolated. Most Pietist groups accepted the active participation of women in talking about religion, while smaller groups even accepted women as leaders. Consequently, Pietism was attractive to women. Contrary to many forms of religious orthodoxy women were not reduced to listening, singing or praying silently. Theological education was no longer a precondition for taking part in religious affairs. Yet the participation of women was limited. Between 1690 and 1700 the limits were tested only by those famous, extraordinary women who experienced revelations. Only a few, radical Pietists accepted these women as bearers of revelations. The majority of Pietists rejected them because they had left their houses and families in order to proclaim God's revelation. Despite that general rejection this was the first time that the idea of a special affinity between women and religion was publicly expressed. In the nineteenth century the idea was developed with the growth of the conviction that women were particularly susceptible to religious belief.

The last important phase of Pietism was that of Count Zinzendorf and the Moravian Brethren, its significance being judged not so much by the number of its adherents as by its impact upon intellectual discussion. In this period the movement developed new traditions and tendencies.[46] It was characterized by the participation of different social classes: it encompassed the noble count, his wife and people drawn from the lower classes. The largest group of followers consisted of craftsmen and farmers. The incorporation of different tendencies seems to have been one of the guiding principles. At first Zinzendorf and his followers were impressed by Halle and its tradition, but later they adopted increasingly radical ideas. In the 1730s they changed their mind again. As a result of studying Luther's works they adopted his Christology and parts of his doctrine of redemption. Even though most of the changes were initiated and encouraged by Zinzendorf, laypeople also took part in the accompanying discussions. The Moravian Brethren as a group were shaped by their communitarian leanings. They were always small in number and not simply during their radical phase when they found themselves banned in most territories. Their quasi-communitarian life neither convinced orthodox theologians nor the general public. Therefore they had little choice but to found a church of their own. In spite of that many eighteenth-century intellectuals were fascinated by the idea of living as a community and together following Christ as redeemer.

This brief consideration of the Moravian community leads naturally to the question of numbers. Pietism never attracted a majority of Germans. At its strongest as a movement some 40 per cent of the Protestants of Germany counted themselves in some respects as Pietists. Yet in spite of its minority status it was a mass movement, the study of which is of considerable importance. It seems, however, that the qualitative aspect of the movement was even more important than its numerical strength. Even in those parts of Europe such as Scandinavia, where numbers remained small, the impulses imparted to Christianity at large were so strong, especially in terms of activating the laity, that the modern history of the church cannot be written without mentioning the significance of Pietism. Through the movement two important features emerged: an interest in reformulating traditional doctrine and in witnessing real improvements in social life. Changes such as these would not have taken place so readily without the engagement of laypeople who were stimulated by the movement's ideals.

Notes

1 Clausthal-Zellerfeld, Ephoralarchiv, Rep. 3 (Zellerfeld) Nr. 170 (Heinrich Jacob Frisch), Glück zum Neuen Jahr, 9 Jan. 1735, contemporary copy by Johann Georg Hieronymi. The author is quoting John 5.41; Is. 42.8; Is. 58.1. Cf. Manfred Jakubowski-Tiessen, 'Religiöse Konflikte und soziale Proteste', *Jahrbuch der Gesellschaft für niedersächsische Kirchengeschichte* 94, 1996, 123–38; Rudolf Ruprecht, *Der Pietismus des 18. Jahrhunderts in den Hannoverschen Stammländern*, Göttingen: Vandenhoeck & Ruprecht, 1919, pp. 14–18, 66–96.

2 Frisch, n. 1, cf. Mt.10.38.

3 Ibid. cf. Is. 57.15.

4 Cf. Jakubowski-Tiessen, 'Religiöse Konflikte', pp. 124–5; cf. F. Ernest Stoeffler, *German Pietism during the Eighteenth Century*, Leiden: Brill, 1973, pp. 208–12.

5 Frisch, n. 1.

6 Cf. Hans-Jürgen Schrader, *Literaturproduktion und Büchermarkt des radikalen Pietismus*, Göttingen: Vandenhoeck & Ruprecht, 1989, p. 57.

7 Frisch, n. 1.

8 Ibid.

9 Cf. 'Renovation und Declaration der Verordnung vom 15 May 1711 die Fanaticos und Separatisten betreffend vom 28 May/8 June 1734', *Chur-Braunschweig-Lüneburgische Landes-Ordnung und Gesetze, . . .*, Göttingen, 1739, pp. 1067–72.

10 Samuel Schelwig, *Synopsis controversiarum sub pietatis praetextu motarum*, 3rd edn, Wittenberg, 1705. Concerning the controversies about Schelwig's book cf. Johann Georg Walch, *Historische und theologische Einleitung in die Religions-Streitigkeiten der Evangelisch-Lutherischen Kirche . . .*, 5 vols, Jena, 1730–9, vol. 2, pp. 26–30.

11 'Tota ecclesia constat ex docentibus et discentibus, quorum, uti in praecedenti controversia, ex Scriptura ostendebatur, illi de jure divino praesunt, hi subsunt, illi ducunt, hi ducuntur.' Schelwig, *Synopsis*, art. XXIX, q. II, p. 333.

12 Schelwig reiterates this argument: 'Ordini autem et decentiae adversatur, si absque praescitu, consensu et censura eorum, qui ad docendum ducendumque vocati sunt, alii id quod docentium doctorumque est, invadant.' 'They act contrary to [divinely established] order and what is fitting if, without the foreknowledge, agreement and judgement of those who have been called to teach and lead, others usurp the role that belongs to teachers and learned men.' Ibid. art. XXIIX, q. III, p. 314.

13 Ibid. art XXXII, qu. IV, pp. 363–6.

14 Ibid. art. XXVII, qu. X, pp. 306–7.

15 Cf. Ruprecht, *Pietismus*, pp. 135–8. For the situation in Hanover, cf. the brief survey in W.R. Ward, *The Protestant Evangelical Awakening*, Cambridge: Cambridge University Press, 1992, pp. 208–20.

16 Cf. N. Hope, *German and Scandinavian Protestantism 1700 to 1918*, Oxford: Oxford University Press, 1999, pp. 60–71.

17 Schrader, *Literaturproduktion*, pp. 108–223; cf. also W.R. Ward, *Protestant Evangelical Awakening*, pp. 10–13; E. McKenzie, *A Catalog of British Devotional and Religious Books in German Translation from the Reformation to 1750*, Berlin: de Gruyter, 1997, passim.

18 First published in 1675 as a homiletic preface to a new edition of Johann Arndt's *Postil;* American translation by T.G. Tappert, Philadelphia: Fortress Press, 1964; cf. also W.R. Ward, 'Pastoral office and the general priesthood in the Great Awakening', in idem, *Faith and Faction*, London: Epworth, 1993, pp. 177–83.

19 Kurt Aland (ed.) *Pia Desideria. Philipp Jakob Spener*, 3rd edn, Berlin: de Gruyter, 1964, p. 57.

20 Ibid. p. 53; cf. Col. 3.16.

21 Ibid. p. 55.

22 Ibid. p. 58. Cf. Martin Schmidt, 'Spener's Pia Desideria', in idem, *Wiedergeburt und neuer Mensch*, Witten: Luther-Verlag, 1969, pp. 144–9.

23 Ibid. p. 60.

24 Ibid. p. 67. Spener continues with proposals for a reform of clerical education.

25 Spener edited a tract of Jean Labadie and some sermons of Johann Vielitz; cf. Johannes Wallmann, *Philipp Jakob Spener und die Anfänge des Pietismus*, 2nd edn, Tübingen: Mohr Siebeck, 1986, pp. 240–9.

26 Spener, *Pia Desideria*, p. 79; cf. ibid. p. 34.

27 Cf. Wallmann, *Spener*, pp. 302–3.

28 Johann Jakob Schütz, *Christliche Lebens-Reguln oder vielmehr Außerlesene Sprüche aus dem N. Testament*, Frankfurt, 1677; cf. Markus Matthias, 'Collegium pietatis und ecclesiola', *Pietismus und Neuzeit* 19, 1993, 58.

29 Cf. Hermann Dechent, *Kirchengeschichte von Frankfurt am Main seit der Reformation*, 2 vols, Leipzig-Frankfurt a M: Kesselringsche Hofbuchhandlung, 1913–21, vol. 2, pp. 79–85.

30 Cf. Philipp Jakob Spener, *Theologische Bedencken und andere brieffliche Antworten*, 4 vols, Halle 1700–2, vol. 4, p. 127.

31 Otto Podczeck (ed.) *August Hermann Francke . . . Großer Aufsatz*, Berlin: Sächsischen Akademie der Wissenschaften zu Leipzig, 1962, S. 88, Die Universitäten sind dazu 'bequem, dem allgemeinen Verderben in allen Ständen am nachdrücklichsten abzuhelfen'; cf. ibid. pp. 76–7; cf. Carl Hinrichs, *Preußentum und Pietismus. Der Pietismus in Brandenburg-Preußen als religiös-soziale Reformbewegung*, Göttingen: Vandenhoeck & Ruprecht, 1971, pp. 1–125.

32 Ulrike Witt, *Bekehrung, Bildung und Biographie. Frauen im Umkreis des Halleschen Pietismus*, Halle: Franckesche Stiftungen; Tübingen: M. Niemeyer Verlag, 1996, p. 60.

33 Cf. Martin Schmidt, 'A.H. Franckes Stellung', in idem, *Wiedergeburt und neuer Mensch*, S. 205.

34 Francke appreciated the term 'God's footprints' as applicable to the work of the Halle Pietists. Anthony William Boehm employed it when he translated one of Francke's advertising tracts, *Pietas Hallensis: or a publick demonstration of the footsteps of a Divine Being yet in the world: in an historical narration of the orphan house, and other charitable institutions at Glauche near Hall in Saxony*, London,

1705; cf. D.L. Brunner, *Halle Pietists in England: Anthony William Boehm and the Society for Promoting Christian Knowledge*, Göttingen: Vandenhoeck & Ruprecht, 1993, pp. 82–7.

35 Francke, *Aufsatz*, p. 59.

36 Ibid. p. 108.

37 Hope, *Protestantism*, pp. 143–6; cf. Martin Brecht, 'August Hermann Francke und der Hallische Pietismus', in idem (ed.) *Der Pietismus vom siebzehnten bis zum frühen achtzehnten Jahrhundert*, Göttingen: Vandenhoeck & Ruprecht, 1993, pp. 514–31; Renate Wilson, 'Heinrich Wilhelm Ludolf, August Hermann Francke und der Eingang nach Rußland', in Johannes Wallmann and Udo Sträter (eds) *Halle und Osteuropa: zur europäischen Ausstrahlung des hallischen Pietismus*, Halle: Franckesche Stiftungen; Tübingen: M. Niemeyer, 1998, pp. 83–108.

38 Cf. Hinrichs, *Preußentum*, p. 92.

39 Cf. Udo Sträter, 'Pietismus und Sozialtätigkeit', *Pietismus und Neuzeit* 8, 1982, 201–30. In England the charity school movement was strongly influenced by the Halle orphanage; cf. Brunner, *Pietists*, pp. 71–82.

40 Hinrichs, *Preußentum*, pp. 189–90.

41 Cf. Hope, *Protestantism*, pp. 159–60; Hilding Pleijel, *Der Schwedische Pietismus in seinen Beziehungen zu Deutschland*, Lund: C.W.K. Gleerup, 1935, pp. 113–18.

42 Pleijel, *Pietismus*, p. 114. These Swedish reformers made reference to the Prussian pattern, since in Prussia laymen were members of cathedral chapters, whereas the office of bishop had been abolished.

43 Cf. Schrader, 'Pietismus', in Walther Killy (ed.) *Literaturlexikon: Autoren und Werke deutscher Sprache*, 15 vols, Gütersloh: Bertelsmann Lexikon, 1988–93, vol. 14, p. 210; idem, *Literaturproduktion*, pp. 253–67.

44 Especially in Württemberg, pious laypeople took part in gatherings of Pietists known as *Stunden*. Württemberg Pietism is not discussed in this essay extensively as it showed no fundamental difference from the models of lay activity offered by Spener and Francke.

45 Cf. Willi Temme, *Krise der Leiblichkeit. Die Sozietät der Mutter Eva (Buttlarsche Rotte) und der radicale Pietismus um 1700*, Göttingen: Vandenhoeck & Ruprecht, 1998, pp. 311–50.

46 Cf. W.R. Ward, 'The renewed unity of the Brethren: ancient church, new sect or interconfessional movement', in idem, *Faith and Faction*, pp. 112–29.

Part II

Lay religious activity during the Enlightenment

Chapter 5

Reshaping individualism

The private Christian, eighteenth-century religion and the Enlightenment

Bruce Hindmarsh

> When I had thus found the goodness of God to my soul, I could not forbear speaking of it to others.
>
> William Hunter, lay Methodist preacher, c. 1779

In David Bebbington's oft-cited book, *Evangelicalism in Modern Britain* (1989), he argues that activism was a distinctive characteristic of evangelicalism and, indeed, set evangelicalism apart from earlier movements such as puritanism. He argues that the source of this activism was a more robust doctrine of assurance and that this new assurance derived in turn from the new Enlightenment concern with first-hand experience.[1] This chapter is concerned in a complementary way to trace the contribution of the Enlightenment to the rise of an articulate and involved laity in eighteenth-century evangelicalism. The focus of the chapter, however, is on the new forms of individualism and private experience that appeared in the eighteenth century rather than epistemology or religious doctrines. Doctrines such as the priesthood of all believers, the Calvinist concept of vocation and the conviction that assurance is of the essence of saving faith contributed significantly to lay activism, but it is also true that larger shifts in the relationship of self to society helped to shape the unique character of evangelicalism.

Although eighteenth-century writers often referred to their century as an 'enlightened age', it was nineteenth-century intellectual historians who coined the term 'the Enlightenment' to describe the systematic practice of a newly critical philosophy in the late seventeenth and early eighteenth centuries deriving in large measure from the ideas of John Locke and Isaac Newton.[2] Of the many characteristics of the Enlightenment the focus here concerns its individualism. Isaac Kramnick writes, 'There is a profoundly radical individualism at the heart of Enlightenment thought. Its rationalism led Enlightenment philosophy to enthrone the individual as the centre and creator of meaning, truth, and even reality.'[3] The intellectual icons of this individualism include René Descartes with his methodological doubt and his assertion that the thinking self is the one thing of which one can be sure, John

Locke with his sensationalist psychology and his description of the mind as a tabula rasa, or as wax to be moulded and fashioned as one pleased, and Adam Smith with his picture of the competitive individual, ever ambitious, ever striving to better his own condition.

So, another way to construe the task is to ask whether there was an ideology of Enlightenment individualism that underlay the popular practices of an involved evangelical laity in the eighteenth century. The lay followers of Wesley and Whitefield, the motivated laity within the Anglican parishes of evangelical ministers such as Henry Venn or John Newton, the lay members of Moravian communities, and the lay members of Dissenting congregations touched by revival – all of these laypeople were typically active not only in public religious observance but also in hearing and speaking of personal religious experience, hymn-singing, exhorting or even preaching, extemporaneous prayer, and also in private religious practices such as devotional reading, prayer, meditation, fasting and diary-keeping. These practices constituted a culture of lay activism which was new to many evangelical converts. John Pawson wrote that before being introduced to Methodism, 'Going constantly to church and sacrament included the whole of religion, as far as I knew.'[4] But Methodism introduced him to a new set of practices and expectations and he was soon anxiously waiting on the means of grace for the salvation of his soul, and then in due course he joined a class meeting, became a class leader, took up the task of lay exhortation and finally responded to the calling to become an itinerant lay preacher under John Wesley. The laywoman Sarah Middleton likewise told Charles Wesley that she used to 'rest in going to church and sacrament but now I do not rest upon them but upon Christ Jesus *my* Lord and *my* God'.[5]

There were, of course, many ways in which the laity of the church could be active other than as evangelicals. In the ongoing debate about the condition of the eighteenth-century Church of England, some historians claim that the laity were involved and articulate before the advent of evangelicalism, albeit in a different way. For example, W.M. Jacob concludes his study, *Lay People and Religion in the Early Eighteenth Century* (1996), by arguing that the laity

> took the initiative in relatively uncomplainingly supporting the clergy, in developing their own spirituality, in maintaining Christian worship and discipline, in philanthropic works, and in building and improving churches. The Church of England in the first half of the eighteenth century was a communal Church to which the greater part of the population actively adhered, and it was a Church in which the laity played a full part.[6]

Thus the vexed ideal of a fully integrated national church and confessional state was achieved to a remarkable degree in the early eighteenth century. But the keynote in Jacob's analysis is the notion of a communal church and a lay activism that he describes as adherence. Evangelical lay activism will look very different from this as it is seen developing in the second half of the century. As the laywoman Mary Thomas wrote in 1742, 'When I went to Church I seldom found any thing there that disturbed me except it was being there too long. But when I came to hear Mr John Wesley I found nothing but discontent in my mind.'[7] Evangelicals were rarely content only to 'adhere'.

Most eighteenth-century converts were, of course, baptized members of the established church. Indeed, the Church of England could claim the nominal allegiance of over 90 per cent of the population of England throughout most of the century. Consequently, most evangelicals described their experience in terms of passing from nominal adherence to earnest faith, rather than in terms of proselyte conversion. As Sarah Middleton looked back on her life before conversion she was scathing: 'We went to church and did all the outward things [but] we were but baptized heathens.'[8] So often the convert used the metaphor of being woken from a deep sleep to describe their experience, so much so that to be 'awakened' was almost a cliché. Margaret Austin summarized her experience in stark terms when she signed off a letter to Charles Wesley: 'Margaret Austin, awakened by the Reverend Mr Whitefield: Convicted by the Reverend Mr John Wesley: Converted by the Reverend Mr Charles.'[9] The other term that converts often used was 'serious' – as when describing someone as a 'serious professor' to indicate that their religion was more than public observance, more than 'going constantly to church and sacrament'.

The new style of evangelical homiletics also provoked this sense that religion had to do in a new way with one's own individual life. In her letter to Charles Wesley, Margaret Austin told how she was a young single mother who had recently been abandoned by her abusive husband and left to care for two children. She heard Whitefield preach in 1740 and found herself in every sermon he preached. When he preached on Zacchaeus, she said, 'I found I was that person.' When he preached on Saul of Tarsus, again she commented, 'I was much affected . . . finding my self to be the very person.' 'For though I went to church as often as I could,' she wrote, 'I never was struck in such a manner as then.'[10] This was a common refrain in lay narratives of conversion and some listeners thought the preacher could actually read their minds. Margaret Austin felt addressed as an individual in a way that had never happened in all her years at church. This aroused in her a strong desire to get into one of the Methodist bands. Once there she heard the testimonies, sang the hymns and in time passed through the crisis of evangelical conversion, writing her own spiritual autobiography in a letter. Her progression from public religious observance to active and articulate lay piety involved the discovery of private religious experience: the almost startling recognition that religion could address her particular concerns and order her interior life.

To what extent, however, can Margaret Austin's change in lay religiosity be explained by the rise of a new individualism in the Enlightenment? It can safely be assumed that she had not read Descartes' *Discourse on Method* or John Locke's *Essay Concerning Human Understanding*. It will be necessary to take the long way around and tell the larger story of the rise of individualism if the significance of Margaret Austin's experience is to be appreciated.

The rise of individualism: the Renaissance

The nineteenth-century cultural historian Jacob Burckhardt established what has been the standard account of the rise of individualism in the Renaissance, sharply contrasting the medieval and modern sense of self-identity:

> In the Middle Ages both sides of human consciousness – that which was turned within as that which was turned without – lay dreaming or half awake beneath a common veil. The veil was woven of faith, illusion, and childish prepossession, through which the world and history were seen clad in strange hues. Man was conscious of himself only as a member of a race, people, party, family, or corporation – only through some general category. In Italy this veil first melted into air; an objective treatment and consideration of the State and of all the things of this world became possible. The subjective side at the same time asserted itself with corresponding emphasis; man became a spiritual individual, and recognized himself as such.[11]

Thus Burckhardt pointed to Italy and even Florence in the fourteenth century as the specific birthplace of individuality. The poet Dante and the sculptor Cellini were examples of this strong sense of self that was so different from thinking of oneself only as a member of a larger group. This kind of individualism was an amalgam of values and practices, not just philosophy. So the evidence adduced includes portraiture, technology such as the Venetian mirror, and so on, as well as explicit claims that man is the measure of all things. For example, Burckhardt picks up on small details such as the disappearance by 1390 of any prevailing fashion of dress for men in Florence, with each man preferring to clothe himself in his own way.

The French literary critic and historian of ideas Georges Gusdorf has likewise contrasted pre-modern consciousness with this new kind of individualism. Pre-modern consciousness was communal:

> The conscious awareness of the singularity of each individual life is the late product of a specific civilization. Throughout most of human history, the individual does not oppose himself to all others; he does not feel himself to exist outside of others, and still less against others, but very much with others in an interdependent existence that asserts its rhythms everywhere in the community . . . Community life unfolds like a great

drama, with its climactic moments originally fixed by the gods being repeated from age to age. Each man thus appears as the possessor of a role, already performed by the ancestors and to be performed again by descendants. The number of roles is limited, and this is expressed by a limited number of names. Newborn children receive the names of the deceased whose roles, in a sense, they perform again, and so the community maintains a continuous self-identity in spite of the constant renewal of individuals who constitute it.[12]

Both Burckhardt and Gusdorf, then, would say that there was something novel about the way in which Margaret Austin wrote a personal narrative of her religious experience. They would both say that this was all but unthinkable before the Renaissance or outside western civilization. The Burckhardtian tradition has, however, been criticized in the last 30 years both for specific historical claims and for its grand narrative of the 'ascent of man'. Peter Burke, for example, raises three problems. Geographically, there are Japanese autobiographies from the eleventh century and Chinese portraiture from the seventeenth century that call into question the uniqueness of self-consciousness as something peculiarly western. Sociologically, the tiny minority of literate, upper-class males, usually Italian, that is drawn upon to tell the standard story of the rise of individualism raises the question of how far this story may be applied to lower orders of society or to women. And, chronologically, there is evidence of individualism in the Middle Ages, especially from the twelfth century onwards, just as there is also evidence of identity shaped by kinship, guild and city in the early modern period.[13]

The Burckhardtian tradition is thus now seen as a kind of Whig interpretation of the rise of individualism. The result of this recent questioning is that the story of the rise of individualism is now a richer and more complex one. It is necessary to pay more attention to context and to be aware that overlapping and multiple identities have thrived in different times and places, and under various conditions. There is not a simple monolithic and diachronic story of the ascent of western man. Heightened individual self-consciousness may have appeared at various times and places where the right conditions have obtained.

Even after all this throat clearing, a stark contrast remains between people like Margaret Austin who pen autobiographies and people for whom this would not occur. It is still necessary to ascertain the conditions that led to Margaret Austin's sense of individuality. She was a layperson of little education or social stature and a woman, and yet she found a voice within eighteenth-century religion and told her unique story. There were many others like her in the mid-eighteenth century, but precious few in pre-modern times.

Martha Claggett

Another woman's experience serves to illustrate in more detail the private and personal narrative identity of countless evangelical laypeople. One of the Wesleys' first converts was a woman named Martha Claggett. On 24 July 1738, exactly two months after John Wesley's Aldersgate experience, she wrote her spiritual autobiography in a letter to his brother Charles.[14]

As a child she was quite often left alone and would spend her time poring over the pages of a tall leather-bound Bible with woodcut illustrations. Her parents, worried she was becoming too introspective, sent her off to school to develop polite manners. She learned to dance and took great pleasure in what she called 'the vanities of the world', and soon her religious seriousness was forgotten. She was dangerously ill for two years as a young teenager and her condition was beyond the help of doctors. She prayed and got better. Soon, however, she forgot about all this, since she was packed off to London once more, as she says, 'to improve her vanity'. At 22 she was married and found herself entirely preoccupied with her new role. Her greatest trouble, though, had to do with childbirth. This is how she put it:

> I had uncommon sufferings in Child bearing which kept me in continual fear. The enemy took advantage of my weakness and when I had conceived of my fifth child [he tempted] me to use some means to disappoint God's providence in bringing it to perfection, and that way free myself from the pain I so much dreaded.

In other words, she was seriously considering how she could devise a secret abortion. She did not go through with it, and in the end it was this child, a daughter, who would introduce her to John Wesley and the Methodists.

That would be later. In the meantime she had more suffering to endure. A brother she loved died in spiritual anguish. Martha Claggett herself spiralled down into depression, her condition compounded by a run of serious fevers. She sank into spiritual despair and toyed with suicide. Remarkably, she had another six children and her pain in childbirth seemed to get worse with each one, not to mention the growing cares of the household. In her own words:

> I knew not what to do, having none to guide me till God sent Mr Whitefield amongst us. He told me of Original Sin and man's fallen estate. This by sorrowful experience I had proved to be true. He talk'd of a new Birth and Change of Nature, which I thot I had understood, but Since find I did not. I was pleas'd with his conversation and was delighted with singing hymns, when I was sure no one heard me.

Yet Martha Claggett found that as she tried to break old habits she became discouraged. On 29 June 1738 John Wesley visited her and spoke of Christ's love for her in particular. They spent most of the afternoon in prayer and singing. But she still was not sure. She felt so unworthy. A few days later it all began to sink in and she felt Christ was smiling on her. She started practising saying, '*My* Lord and *My* God'. She went to bed strangely peaceful. Then, between three and four in the morning she woke up suddenly, 'in such joy as I never felt before, my Heart overflow'd with the love of God, the Spirit bearing witness that I was the Child of God, and I could not keep joining the immortal choir in their hallelujahs'. That is where her manuscript breaks off.

Like Margaret Austin, Martha Claggett emerged from the silent mass of lay Christians down through the ages, all those who like John Pawson and Sarah Middleton thought that religion consisted entirely in going to church and sacrament – she emerged from this silent throng of laypeople with a name, and a voice, and a story. When we hear the voices of laypeople in the eighteenth century it is often in this autobiographical form of personal conversion narrative. The sense of having been specified, individuated, is strong and even surprising.

The evangelical narrative identity

By definition medieval hagiography was not like that. Saints' lives were woven together out of topoi, literary commonplaces or patterns that overwhelmed the personality of the subjects. Richard Fletcher gives an example in his study of early medieval conversion.[15] Bede's *Life of Cuthbert* in the eighth century tells how the saint was brought pig's lard by a pair of ravens and Bede acknowledges that this was 'after the example' of the *Life of Benedict* written a couple of centuries earlier by Gregory the Great. And behind Benedict's story was yet another of the hermits Paul and Anthony who were sustained by bread brought to them by ravens in the desert. And, of course, this closely resembles the account in I Kings 17 of the prophet Elijah who was fed by ravens beside the brook Cherith. What this one example illustrates is the way that the medieval biographer could draw on an inventory of tales, themes and phrases, and apply these to his subject without constraint. Behind this lay a theological conception of the communion of the saints and the essential unity of sanctity across the ages: there was really only one life of a saint.[16] But the effect of all this was in many cases to efface the personality of the saint, not to mention leaving modern historians scratching their heads and wondering how exactly to use this information.

Some cultural historians suppose that the evangelical conversion narrative is really a hangover from this kind of hagiographical writing, a sectarian or fundamentalist backwater in the modern era, a literary remnant of a spirit-drenched universe that does not fit properly in the age of Enlightenment and rational religion.[17] However, the evangelical genre is not primarily biographical but autobiographical and, moreover, it is truly popular, being written by ordinary folk. That in itself should be enough to place evangelical narrative identity squarely in the modern period. Indeed the genre emerges uniquely in the mid-seventeenth century on the cusp of the modern period. It is not Luther and Calvin who write conversion narratives – we have to piece together the details of their spiritual biographies from fragments in their theological writings – but their later descendants.

Conversion narrative as a popular genre emerges in the mid-seventeenth century in the context of what Ernest Stoeffler calls the post-Reformation experiential tradition.[18] Early examples include August Hermann Francke in German Pietism and John Bunyan in the tumultuous context of English puritanism during the Interregnum. Jerald Brauer argues that conversion was central to puritanism in England and New England, and to the revivals of the eighteenth century. In each of these different contexts the basic nature and structure of conversion was surprisingly similar, though the time it took to pass through the stages of conversion was typically shorter in the later period. The key difference was in the role and consequences of conversion. Conversion functioned within English puritanism as part of an ideal to transform the church and nation and complete the Reformation; in early New England, by contrast, conversion was the bedrock on which church and state rested. In the revivals of the eighteenth century there was a decisive shift away from the centrality of the Reformation, the covenantal community or the godly commonwealth, and conversion existed instead almost wholly for its own sake. The focus now was upon the converted individual.[19]

The rise of individualism: the seventeenth century

The genre itself reflects a high level of individuation. This is what might be expected under the conditions of the early modern world as the individual begins to count in all sorts of ways. As already suggested, the origins of individualism are contested and it is dangerous to take a narrow intellectual view of this development. But in many spheres it is apparent that more weight devolves on the individual as time passes from the late Renaissance into the seventeenth and eighteenth centuries. Charles Taylor summarizes some of the factors:

> of the politics of consent, of the family life of the companionate marriage, of the new child-rearing which develops from the eighteenth century, of artistic creation under the demands of originality, of the demarcation and defence of privacy, of markets and contracts, of voluntary associations, of the cultivation and display of sentiment, of the pursuit of scientific knowledge. Each of these has contributed something to the developing set of ideas about the subject and his or her moral predicament . . . they have helped to constitute a common space of understanding in which our current ideas of the self and the good have grown.[20]

Here, then, it is better if we speak of the conditions of modernity than of the Enlightenment per se. The developments that constitute modernity, including mass communication, efficient transportation and increased mobility, religious toleration, capitalism and consumerism, industrialization, demographic change and political reform – all of these are in place in such a way by the eighteenth century, even if in embryo, that ordinary men and women are left having to find their way in the world in a new manner.

Thomas Cooper, for example, was a layman who kept up a respectable life of church attendance and moral rectitude while an apprentice in the country, but then he moved to London and got into a bad crowd and, as he put it, 'spent a deal of my time in horing, drinking, dancing, plays, and such vice as youth is prone to'.[21] Caught up in demographic change, moving from the morally reinforcing structures of a village apprenticeship to life in an anonymous city – all this had been unsettling, and he and an acquaintance confided in each other at a local pub that their consciences were troubled.

There was so much less certainty about life in the modern world for people like Thomas Cooper. Now there were multiple options in more and more spheres. Occupational surnames such as Smith, Thatcher, Baker, Miller and Taylor bear silent witness to an earlier time of more stable identity. Now there were fewer structures around to dictate the individual's identity. Where once there was a small number of well-defined roles that pre-existed the individual and would be passed on to the descendants, with fixed rights of passage, now the future seemed open-ended. Charles Taylor describes the new form of narrativity that went along with this: 'Rather,' he says, 'than seeing life in terms of predefined phases, making a whole whose shape is understood by unchanging tradition, we tell it as a story of growth towards often unprecedented ends.'[22] That is to say, there were now no scripts to follow.

The result was what some literary historians call the autobiographical moment in western culture.[23] Michael Mascuch traces some of these influences and the precocious acculturation of individualism in England, and notes that, 'beginning in the seventeenth century, Britain [sic] produced a widening stream of narrative autobiographical discourse, whose breadth and depth expanded to Mississippian proportions in the course of the eighteenth century'.[24] One of the most basic material conditions we must bear in mind as we trace this development is the rising level of literacy. In 1640 in England the ability to write was limited to 30 per cent of the male and 10 per cent of the female population. By 1714 the figures had risen to 45 per cent of men and 25 per cent of women.[25] Likewise the output of printed books, serial journals, magazines and newspapers rose steadily throughout the eighteenth century, the price of paper fell and there were increasing numbers of cheap popular books.[26] The seventeenth-century puritans produced large leather-bound folios; the eighteenth-century evangelicals published cheap octavo and duodecimo editions that could be slipped in the coat pocket. The technology of reading and writing not only allowed for the rise of autobiographical discourse, it also encouraged the development of interiority and the practice of communing with one's own thoughts in private.

At precisely this moment in the acculturation of individualism in England, the evangelical narrative of conversion can be discovered flourishing among a numerous laity. Commonplaces, biblical tropes and narrative conventions occur in evangelical autobiography but this is not hagiography, at least not usually. The emphasis again and again in stories such as that of Martha Claggett is that people were surprised to find that the gospel was for them personally. Martha Claggett discovered that the gospel was not merely about playing a role in a pre-determined world – through nominal adherence to the established church and participation in communal ritual – but that it had to do with a deeply personal story that could make sense of her fears in childbirth, her guilt for having contemplated abortion, her grief over her dead brother, her depression, her vanity, as well as her dreams and hopes. After John Wesley's own conversion, he wrote with wonder that God had taken away, he writes, '*my* sins, even *mine*, and saved *me* from the law of sin and death', and he put all these personal pronouns in italics in his journal.[27] Charles Wesley's hymn 'And can it be' was written immediately after his conversion in 1738 and is a study in the same joyous bewilderment:

> Died he for me, who caused his pain?
> For me, who him to death pursued?
> Amazing love! How can it be,
> That thou my God, shouldst die for me.

A later stanza celebrates God's mercy, and concludes, 'For, O my God, it found out *me!*'[28] The italics and exclamation mark are the author's and, indeed, many of his exuberant hymns must have challenged the typesetters. This *Christus pro me* insight occurs elsewhere in church history, in the *Confessions* of Augustine for example, or in Luther's 'tower experience', but it becomes a truly popular one only in the early modern period. By then there are many people who feel themselves to be individuals, not just part of a larger category such as family or race.

When we hear the voices of the laity in the eighteenth century, then, it is typically in the form of autobiographical discourse. Clearly, the rise of an articulate laity owed much to the appearance of a new individualism in society. But there were several directions in which this individualism could have gone. Cultural historians, even those who follow Michel Foucault in decrying the modern individualist self as a delusion, or a form of deep anthropological sleep, still typically write about the secular version of individual self-identity as a normative development in the eighteenth century.[29] In Roy Porter's otherwise brilliant study of madness in England, *Mind-Forg'd Manacles* (1990), he persistently refers to 'sectarian' evangelical autobiography as a 'fundamentalist' reaction against the secular forces of the Enlightenment.[30] David Bebbington has argued forcefully that modern evangelicalism with its stress upon experience is, on the contrary, a robust expression of the Lockean Enlightenment.[31] This chapter argues similarly that the evangelical narrative identity, while embedded in the larger biblical narrative of salvation, is also a vector of the Enlightenment. The appearance in the mid-eighteenth century of a popular genre of religious autobiography, a genre which was both oral and literary, is a development as concrete as the Gin Crisis of the 1730s or the rise in the price of corn in the 1740s and 1750s. It will not do simply to dismiss it as marginal to the forward march of the secular, rational self. The story is more complex (and interesting) than that.

James Lackington: the secular self-identity

To gain an appreciation of the secular self-identity which emerges alongside the evangelical conversion narrative, it is instructive to consider the life of an ex-Methodist named James Lackington, particularly since Michael Mascuch regards Lackington's *Memoirs* as an early and seminal example of the modern identity.[32] James Lackington was a 16 year old in London who went along to a Methodist meeting in 1762. His conscience was awakened under the preaching and a month later he found peace with God. He tried to make a living as a journeyman shoemaker but by the time he was 28 he was penniless. He was able to get a small business loan of five pounds from John Wesley and with that he started retailing books. Beginning with a bag of books he bought for a guinea and sold in an obscure passageway, he built an enormously successful bookselling business in London, so that some 17 years later he boasted an income of £5,000 a year. His secret was the invention of the practice known today as remaindering – the buying and selling of unsold books at below the cover price. In 1793 he bought a block of houses in Finsbury Square for a new shop that he called 'The Temple of the Muses'. The main floor was large enough to drive a coach and six horses around, and the shop quickly became one of the sights to see in London.

Two years after Lackington started this business with the loan from Wesley he left the Methodists and abandoned his evangelical faith. Consequently, when he wrote his *Memoirs* in 1791 he wrote not a conversion but an *un*conversion narrative. Mascuch emphasizes that Lackington's story was deliberately structured to direct his own identity without reference to divine providence or piety of any kind. These were not simply the disconnected anecdotes of an old man: his story had a point. The frontispiece of Lackington's autobiography was an engraved portrait of the author with the caption: 'I. Lackington. Who a few years since, began Business with five Pounds; now sells one Hundred Thousand Volumes Annually.' The complete title of the American edition of the book communicates the same message of Lackington as a self-made man: *Memoirs of James Lackington, who from the* *humble station of a journeyman shoemaker, by great industry, amassed a large fortune and now lives in a splendid style in London containing among other curious and facetious anecdotes, a succinct account of . . . the Methodists. Written by himself.*

A part of what made his book so successful was his witty (indeed scurrilous) exposé of the Methodists as one who had been an insider. The cover hinted of kiss-and-tell revelations in the book. For example, he tells a story of the famous Methodist preacher, George Whitefield, out field-preaching. A young woman in the front of the crowd fell backwards, just under the great evangelist, and lay there kicking up her heels. Seeing her in a kind of convulsion some of the crowd moved to help her and the women drew her petticoat and apron down over her feet, but Whitefield cried out, 'Let her alone! Let her alone! A glorious sight! A glorious sight!' meaning of course that it was wonderful to see a soul overwhelmed by spiritual emotion. But the young men construed his meaning somewhat differently and, when the audience could not stop laughing, Whitefield had to dismiss them. According to Lackington, it became a saying among the young men ever after, when reeling home from the pub, 'A glorious sight, A glorious sight!'[33]

Again, Lackington recounts his previous amours and how he was infatuated with one Methodist sister after another, moving easily from spiritual advice to kisses: 'I assure you, my friend, that we were sometimes like the Galatians of old; we began in the *spirit*, and ended in the *flesh*.'[34] None of this did much for the reputation of Methodism, but it certainly established Lackington's own character as a witty, urbane man about town. And that, of course, was what he was trying to do.

Entertaining stories such as these were embedded in the overall story of Lackington's progress from rags to riches by dint of his own enterprise and stoic self-discipline. He took control of his own identity in secular terms which should be fairly familiar to the modern reader. He constructed his own story, owned his own copyright, and acted as his own distributor. He took advantage of the new legal mechanisms of intellectual property rights. He made his life into a successful commodity and he literally traded on his own identity. And he was good at it. There were 13 editions of his *Memoirs* in his lifetime. He successfully persuaded a vast public audience to sanction his self-identity as a successful individual and bookseller.

Lackington is a good specimen, and an early one, of the modern self-understanding which has been so much discussed of late by moral philosophers, literary theorists, cultural historians and social scientists. He understood himself as clearly bounded, unique and neatly integrated. He was the product of his own choices and he could narrate his life in a way that organized the aimless drift of experience into a coherent story, one that pointed authoritatively to a single retrospective meaning. He was the one to declare this meaning and persuade others of it. This form of narrative identity is sometimes called modern or modernist, bourgeois, or individualist.

Reshaping individualism: the evangelical narrative community

Large numbers of laypeople, however, found their voice through a different kind of narrative than this: namely, a religious one. Societal changes could lead to competing versions of what it meant to be a moral agent among other moral agents. What then was distinctive about the evangelical self-identity? What was the difference between James Lackington and Martha Claggett? Clearly, Lackington was deep in Michel Foucault's 'anthropological sleep', quietly and blissfully eliding the contribution that others made to his identity. But what about these other evangelicals? Were they also a little drowsy?

Historians such as Harry Stout have argued that evangelicals were uniquely adapted to the emerging consumer culture in the eighteenth century, and that they effectively hawked the gospel as a commodity in the marketplace and addressed people as religious consumers – all of this in contrast to the traditional monopoly over religion presumed to exist in the church as established by law and custom.[35] On this reading, evangelicals were profoundly individualist. And yet, if we look closely at the stories told by Martha Claggett and others, we find a surprisingly strong countervailing emphasis upon the community of faith, a community that was as much discovered as it was constructed by human agency. If the evangelical laypeople who wrote autobiographies were individualists of a sort, it should be stressed that they were also communitarians of a sort. The evangelical self-identity owed much to the rise of individualism, but differed markedly from the solipsism of the secular, modern version of the self. Theirs was an important alternative version of Enlightenment individualism.

Repeatedly in these narratives, attention is drawn to the small, intimate group meetings – the bands, societies, and class meetings. Within these groups the fellowship was close and men and women could unburden their souls to each other. Thomas Oliver was one who had heard some Methodist preaching at Bristol and he was soon in deep spiritual concern for his soul. He used to stalk the Methodists, secretly following them to their meetings and eavesdropping on them. As they would sing their hymns he would be outside crying. When they came out he would follow them at a distance, still listening, sometimes following them for over two miles. He knew they had something he wanted.[36] Margaret Austin's desire to join the band meetings was likewise intense and when she did she found there the family she never had. Tellingly, she uses kinship language for the woman who nurtured her – 'Sister Robinson'. When such people were converted they felt they were born again, not in isolation, but into a new family of brothers and sisters. John Newton wrote a hymn to dedicate a new meeting place for his religious society and it includes the following stanza:

> Within these walls let holy peace,
> And love, and concord dwell;
> Here give the troubled conscience ease,
> The wounded spirit heal.[37]

It was within precisely this kind of koinonia that ordinary women and men discovered a new way to understand their religious identity.

These groups and the preachers who led them were the guardians of the evangelical narrative identity. It was within these meetings that the newcomer would hear the testimonies and sing the hymns. Here that they would begin to learn the story and ask themself, 'Could my life be like that in any way?' 'How might I enact, receive or experience that sort of autobiography?' The evangelical conversion narrative is a genre, which means that it has certain conventions. Conventions come out of a community or a tradition (which is a community expressed through time), and these are what connect one narrative to another. Again, this does not mean that everyone's story was the same. All Elizabethan sonnets are not the same, even though they might be written in fourteen lines of iambic pentameter with a limited range of rhyme schemes. The puritan Richard Baxter went through some travail over whether he was only socialized as a Christian rather than truly regenerated. At the end of his anxious soul-searching he wrote, 'At last I came to realize that God breaketh not all men's hearts alike.'[38] There was scope for the personal and unique, even within the larger story.

What then was the pattern that structured these narratives? Unlike Lackington's story, the escalator of progress, Martha Claggett's was a narrative of suffering, humiliation, and redemption. The late Northrop Frye argued that the pattern of original prosperity, descent into humiliation and return is the overall structure of the biblical story and of the mini-narratives within it, such as the parable of the prodigal son. He also argued that this pattern has distinctively shaped much of western literature.[39] This is also true for the narrative identity of many Christians. Their personal story is the biblical story in miniature, an episode in the larger story of God, and it has the same shape. The most famous example is that of Augustine. His story of stealing fruit from an orchard nicely echoes the epic fall from paradise in Genesis, while his later conversion in a garden at Cassiciacum equally corresponds to paradise restored, and so on. For Martha Claggett this pattern was true also, as she remembered the relative innocence of a Bible-reading childhood and the hardening of her heart in adolescence at boarding school. Then just as the promise of redemption followed the biblical fall, so also the word of God entered her experience with Whitefield's preaching and began the process of return. Again, even as the climax of salvation history came with the advent of the Messiah and the Pentecostal experience of the Holy Spirit, so also Martha Claggett and other converts bore witness to a joyous sense of sins forgiven and of new life. Finally, the biblical prophecy of a future new heaven and earth had its counterpart in the hopeful curve of these conversion narratives, projecting the hope of growth in grace, pious death and joy thereafter. Margaret Austin concluded: 'I see there is a great work to be wrought still in my soul: but he that has begun the work will surely finish; he that is the author will be the finisher.' It is a telling metaphor: God as the author who will finish his work, who will complete the 'life' in the double sense of the written narrative and the living experience of the author.

This is the way the gospel actually went to work to shape early evangelical narrative identity. But again, this larger story (of creation, fall, redemption and new creation) was explored within the deeply personal narrative of 'my' life, since the story-tellers had the vivid sense that the story had to do with themselves. The pattern offered an opportunity for men and women to locate themselves personally in a kind of spiritual and moral space and to explore the way in which their story uniquely reflected common themes.

So, was this identity constructed like a modern identity, or bestowed like a pre-modern identity? It was a bit of both. Arminians and Calvinists alike spoke of a certain number of 'ordained means of grace', such as preaching, holy communion, the reading of scripture, prayer, and Christian conversation and friendship. These were given things, received and not constructed. But it was in the midst of these shared practices that one experienced the travail of new birth and discovered a uniquely personal faith. The truth lies in the irony of realizing that a whole group of people was singing, 'His blood can make the foulest clean, His blood avail'd for *me*.'

In 1804, nearly 60 years old, James Lackington wrote another autobiographical book which is less well known. It was called *The Confessions of James Lackington* and it was a retraction of his earlier *Memoirs*.[40] He had turned back again to the Methodists and renewed his evangelical faith. He wrote, 'When I look into my memoirs, I shudder to see what I have done. I have wantonly treated of, and sported with the most solemn and precious truths of the gospel. O God, lay not this sin to my charge.' Michael Mascuch sees this as just one more act of self-revisioning, one more indication that Lackington was master of his own identity, able to remake himself once more at the end of his life, and he dismisses the *Confessions* as more or less unimportant.[41] This is almost certainly too hasty. Within his own lifetime James Lackington came to realize that the modern self was insupportable. Given the many voices today calling for the decentring, deconstruction or death of the self, and given the rejection of any essentialist notion of the self, it is surely significant that Lackington as a pioneer of the modernist identity shuddered back from the brink, and reposed in the community of faith and the word of the gospel.

Conclusion

To sum up, the rise of the laity within evangelicalism in the eighteenth century owed much to the appearance of a new individualism in modern society, but at the same time the self-identity of evangelicals contrasted sharply with the secular individualist self which has often been taken as the normative development of the Enlightenment.

It remains to make a few observations linking this distinctive evangelical self-understanding to the appearance within evangelicalism of an active and vocal laity. The narrative identity of evangelicals expressed through stories of conversion was embraced by a wide spectrum of society, including women as well as men, laity as well as clergy, and all orders from the lowest to the highest in social rank. If we take into view contexts such as Sierra Leone at the end of the century, we can add that this narrative identity included people of different races as well. Conversion was a central emphasis within evangelicalism and the genre of conversion narrative is correspondingly and surprisingly broad in its sociological reach. One of the implications is that the concept of the laity within evangelicalism, under the impetus of conversionism, became something more like the apostle Paul's use of the term *laos* to refer to the whole people of God, comprehending both clergy and nonclergy. In the eighteenth century this came into focus in certain debates about call to the ministry, ordination and what constituted a legitimate ministry. As Jerald Brauer writes, 'The moment one argues for the illegitimacy of a minister because he has not had a genuine conversion experience, one opens the possibility of ministry to any who have had such a conversion experience.'[42] Thus, the narrative identity of evangelicals, expressed through stories of conversion, led not only to lay membership but also to lay ministry. The confidence engendered by a coherent narrative led to the projection of a life lived in grateful obedience and service. One woman who wrote to Charles Wesley recorded what was true to so many after their conversion: 'I was filled with love as well as joy so that I prayed for all and I wept to see so many dead people in the streets. I could hardly get home without telling them so.'[43] Likewise, Thomas Cooper, when at last he found peace with God, wrote, 'I now found love to all the world and could not help declaring to all I met with what the Lord had done for my soul that they might feel the same.'[44]

Wesley asked each of his lay preachers to write an account of their conversion, and these were published at intervals in the *Arminian Magazine* and then later collected in editions by Thomas Jackson and John Telford. The plot of each of these narratives typically drives first towards the crisis of a guilty conscience and its relief under faith in the promises of God, and then towards a second crisis of spiritual vocation and the decision to forsake all to preach the gospel. The index to John Telford's edition of the lives of these preachers normally contains only three sub-entries: 'conversion', 'enters itinerancy' and 'other'. The process of entering an itinerant lay ministry is treated as following naturally from the conversion-centred identity, while the travail of preaching on trial and looking for spiritual responses that could be counted as 'seals' to their ministry, is seen as corresponding in emotional and narrative shape to the crisis of conversion. Entering ministry is a second conversion, likewise dependent upon grace rather than works, and upon charism rather than office. Whether in Methodism or beyond, the laypeople that emerged from the Evangelical Revival and the Great Awakening were converted individuals with a strong sense of personal identity and a zeal which would express itself in countless initiatives in the great age of the missionary society.

Notes

1 D.W. Bebbington, *Evangelicalism in Modern Britain*, London: Unwin Hyman, 1989, pp. 10–12, 42–50.

2 Several recent studies, such as Brian Young's monograph, *Religion and Enlightenment in Eighteenth-Century England*, Oxford: Clarendon Press, 1998, have emphasized the uniquely conservative experience of Enlightenment in England – that Enlightenment goals such as criticism, the focus upon experience or faith in progress were pursued in England, as often as not, within the context of religious piety and ongoing theological debate.

3 I. Kramnick (ed.) *The Portable Enlightenment Reader*, New York: Penguin Books, 1995, p. xv.

4 J. Telford (ed.) *Wesley's Veterans. Lives of early Methodist preachers told by themselves*, 7 vols, London, 1914, vol. 4, p. 1.

5 Sarah Middleton to Charles Wesley, 25 May 1740, ms. letter, Early Methodist Volume, John Rylands Library, Manchester (abbreviated EMV-JRL hereafter).

6 W.M. Jacob, *Lay People and Religion in the Early Eighteenth Century*, Cambridge: Cambridge University Press, 1996, p. 227.

7 J. Barry and K. Morgan (eds) *Reformation and Revival in Eighteenth-Century Bristol*, Bristol, 1994, p. 103.

8 Sarah Middleton to Charles Wesley, 25 May 1740.

9 Margaret Austin to Charles Wesley, 19 May 1740, ms. letter, EMV-JRL.

10 Ibid.

11 J. Burckhardt, *The Civilization of the Renaissance in Italy*, 2 vols, New York: Harper & Bros, 1958, vol. 1, p. 143.

12 G. Gusdorf, 'Conditions and limits of autobiography', in J. Olney (ed.) *Autobiography: essays theoretical and critical*, Princeton, NJ: Princeton University Press, 1980, pp. 29–30.

13 P. Burke, 'Representations of the self from Petrarch to Descartes', in R. Porter, (ed.) *Rewriting the Self: histories from the Renaissance to the present*, London: Routledge, 1997, pp. 17–18.

14 Martha Claggett to Charles Wesley, 24 July 1738, ms. letter, EMV-JRL. See also *The Journal of the Rev. Charles Wesley*, ed. T. Jackson, 2 vols, London, 1849, passim, for references to Martha Claggett and her daughters. Martha Claggett later became a Moravian and, indeed, a Moravian Eldress. See further, D. Benham, *Memoirs of James Hutton*, London, 1856, pp. 93, 96–7, 100n. Martha Claggett also figures largely in the archives of the Fetter Lane congregation; e.g. 'Fetter Lane Congregation Diary', bound mss., vol. 1, 1742, Moravian Church House, London.

15 R. Fletcher, *The Conversion of Europe*, London: HarperCollins, 1997, pp. 11–12.

16 T.J. Heffernan, *Sacred Biography: saints and their biographers in the Middle Ages*, New York: Oxford University Press, 1988, pp. 130–2, 157, 165.

17 R. Porter, *Mind-forg'd Manacles: a history of madness in England from the*

Restoration to the Regency, London: Penguin Books, 1990, pp. 66–7, 72–3, 80, 265, 279.

18 F.E Stoeffler, *The Rise of Evangelical Pietism*, Leiden: Brill, 1965.

19 J.C. Brauer, 'Conversion: from puritanism to revivalism', *Journal of Religion* 58, 1978, 227–43.

20 C. Taylor, *Sources of the Self: the making of the modern identity*, Cambridge: Cambridge University Press, 1994, p. 206.

21 Thomas Cooper to Charles Wesley, [1741], ms. letter, EMV-JRL.

22 Taylor, *Sources of the Self*, pp. 105–6.

23 Olney, *Autobiography*, p. 6.

24 M. Mascuch, *Origins of the Individualist Self: autobiography and self-identity in England, 1591–1791*, Cambridge: Polity Press, 1997, p. 23.

25 Ibid. p. 73.

26 Cf. J.C. Hilson, M.M.B. Jones, and J.R. Watson (eds) *Augustan Worlds: essays in honour of A.R. Humphreys*, Leicester: Leicester University Press, 1978, pp. 189–203.

27 W.R. Ward and R.P. Heitzenrater (eds) *The Works of John Wesley, Vol. 18, Journals and Diaries I (1735–38)*, Nashville: Abingdon Press, 1988, p. 250.

28 F. Hildebrandt and O.A. Beckerlegge (eds), with J. Dale, *The Works of John Wesley, Vol. 7, A collection of hymns for the use of the people called Methodists*, Oxford: Clarendon Press, 1983, p. 323.

29 M. Foucault, *The Order of Things: an archaeology of the human sciences*, English trans. London: Tavistock Publications, 1970, pp. 340–3.

30 Porter, *Mind-forg'd Manacles*, pp. 66–7, 72–3, 80, 265, 279.

31 Bebbington, *Evangelicalism*, pp. 50–74.

32 Mascuch, *Origins of the Individualist Self*, p. 2; J. Lackington, *Memoirs of the First Forty-Five Years of the Life of James Lackington . . . written by himself in forty-six letters to a friend*, London, 1792.

33 Ibid. p. 186.

34 Ibid. p. 243.

35 H.S. Stout, *The Divine Dramatist: George Whitefield and the rise of modern evangelicalism*, Grand Rapids: Eerdmans, 1991, p. xvii.

36 T. Jackson, *The Lives of Early Methodist Preachers*, 3rd edn, 6 vols, London, 1865–6, vol. 2, p. 59.

37 *The Olney Hymns*, London, 1779, p. 234.

38 J.M. Lloyd Thomas (ed.) *The Autobiography of Richard Baxter*, London: J.M. Dent & Sons, 1931, p. 11.

39 N. Frye, *The Great Code: the Bible and literature*, London: Routledge & Kegan Paul, 1982, p. 198.

40 J. Lackington, *The Confessions of J. Lackington, Late Bookseller . . . in a series of letters to a friend*, London, 1804.

41 Mascuch, *Origins of the Individualist Self*, pp. 208–9.

42 Brauer, 'Conversion', p. 242.

43 S. Hirsont to Charles Wesley, 23 May 1740, ms. letter, EMV-JRL.

44 Cooper to Wesley, [1741].

Chapter 6

A spiritual aristocracy

Female patrons of religion in eighteenth-century Britain

Helen M. Jones

It is an old adage that behind every successful man there is a woman. In many eras and societies it has been believed that the proper place for female power and influence is behind the scenes. In eighteenth-century Britain the importance of having a successful woman behind a man who himself wished for success, prosperity and happiness was well recognized. Conduct literature, which largely confined women of the leisured ranks to the home, nonetheless also carved out for them a sphere of importance and considerable authority within that area. The educational writer Fénelon argued that women's education needed far more attention than was customarily given to it, explaining that women, 'who have the direction of all domestic affairs . . . consequently decide the greatest concerns of all mankind'.[1] In 1799 Hannah More agreed that women should tend to domestic cares, where their influence was vital, but stressed that the impact of that influence also spread far beyond the home itself:

> The general state of civilized society depends more than those are cus-
> tomarily aware who are not accustomed to scrutinise into the springs of
> human action, on the prevailing sentiments and habits of women and on
> the nature and the degree of estimation in which they are held.[2]

The influence of women over men was vital to the success of the latter, to the health and happiness of the nation and its economic, social, political and moral welfare.

At the same time, the age regarded with suspicion women who adopted more overtly public roles. Hannah More continued: 'I am not sounding an alarm to female warriors, or exciting female politicians: I hardly know which of the two is the most disgusting and unnatural character.'[3] Charlotte Lennox, who began her *Lady's Museum* of 1760 with a call for better education for women, went on to insist that she would not 'wish to see assemblies made up of doctors in petticoats who would assail us with Greek and the systems of Leibnitz', and that 'there is nothing more disgustful than those female theologians'.[4] Many who advocated change in the way women were educated or regarded felt the need to add an apology or insistence that they were not suggesting the ending of female propriety, and were themselves suspicious of women who overstepped the mark. This suspicion, together with the praise lavished on women who were more properly influential from behind the scenes, meant that it was women who adhered to these boundaries and attempted to use their influence in legitimate ways who could achieve significant power and authority.

The mid-eighteenth century, the first period of evangelical revival in Britain, saw certain women able to exercise an apparently unprecedented degree of authority in religious affairs, yet without overstepping the accepted boundaries of women's influence. The most famous was Selina, Countess of Huntingdon, who founded her own religious connexion. Lady Betty Hastings was also known and respected for her practical support of 'godly' clergy and for her moral authority and example. Two Scottish peeresses, Lady Darcy Maxwell and Willielma, Viscountess Glenorchy, like Lady Huntingdon, built chapels for their own chosen clergy to preach in and expected to control these without the interference of the established church of which the buildings were nominally a part.[5]

Lady Betty Hastings was the earliest of these aristocratic patrons, her life ending as the Evangelical Revival began. Her role, as the most traditional of the group, fell within the puritan tradition of the previous century, when it was common for ladies of rank, particularly those who owned or controlled estates, to patronize individual clergymen. They occasionally possessed the right to present clergy to benefices on their estates; they often chose their own private chaplains and determined the style of worship within their own chapels.[6] Lady Betty was careful to choose those she regarded as godly clerics for her private chapel and the benefices which she controlled. She tended to the moral and religious well-being of servants and tenants, and had a high standard of personal piety. Money while she lived and bequests when she died were granted for philanthropic ends and the support of students training for the priesthood.[7] These activities were all appropriate and proper functions of a female aristocrat in control of her own fortune. Her biographer makes it clear that she was in every way a proper woman and did nothing which could be called masculine or immodest. Even the household prayers, which she had ordered to be said every day, were led by a Church of England cleric or, in the absence of such a person, by a male upper servant.[8] This is symbolic of Lady Betty's religion and exercise of patronage for religious ends. Significant moral authority lay in her hands and she used it to advance that style of piety in which she believed. But she would not usurp the male position of ministry even within an assembly so apparently 'private' as her own household.

Later in the century, Ladies Glenorchy and Maxwell in Scotland achieved exactly the same distinction, although the patronage of both extended beyond the limits of their own estates. Unusually for Scottish aristocrats both were evangelicals. Lady Maxwell was a follower of Wesley and Lady Glenorchy a Calvinist evangelical. Both were responsible for building chapels, Lady

Maxwell in Bristol and Lady Glenorchy in Edinburgh, and both exercised – and were prepared to challenge the local church authorities in order to exercise – complete authority over the incumbents and preachers who staffed those chapels. Apparently, neither patron was ever tempted to preach herself or even to lead public prayers. Again, even within their own households, prayers were conducted by an ordained minister or, in his absence, a male upper servant.

Both women believed that, in patronizing chapels of their own building that were fully under their control, they were exerting no different kind of authority from the patronage which female aristocrats had always exercised with propriety and as of right. Lady Glenorchy in 1775 informed the Edinburgh Presbytery that she intended her chapel to serve several hundred poor people of that city whom she felt were not adequately catered for by the present church system. The next year, she wrote to them after they made some objections to her choice of chaplain:

> I have already acquainted the Presbytery that the chapel is private property, and was never intended to be put upon the footing of the Establishment, nor connected with it as a chapel of ease to the city of Edinburgh . . . Having built the chapel wholly at my own expense for the accommodation of my family and numbers of poor people who at present are deprived of the best, and to many of them, the only means of being instructed in the principles of our holy religion, I think myself entitled to name the minister thereof, especially as no person is under any obligation to join with him in his ministrations, but such as shall voluntarily choose to do so.[9]

She thus made it abundantly clear that her zeal, position and, above all, wealth were in themselves sufficient to grant her the authority to control in effect her own small parish within Edinburgh, in which the poor people she mentioned – and anybody else who cared to attend – would receive such religion as she herself saw fit to provide through her chosen minister. At that point she became embroiled in the patronage issue, which troubled the Church of Scotland intermittently throughout the eighteenth century. Because of the general distaste of the Popular (or Evangelical) party for the principle of patronage, it is unusual to find a Scottish aristocrat exploiting the possibilities of patronage in order to further evangelical religion. The presbytery in Edinburgh, which contained many influential members of the Moderate party, felt serious unease at Lady Glenorchy's combination of evangelicalism and social influence. Although she stated in the same letter of 1776 that nothing was further from her mind than 'to promote any interest in opposition to the Church of Scotland', she was clearly well aware of the fear that was troubling them. Edinburgh, like many eighteenth-century British cities, suffered from severe church shortages as the cumbersome business of parish division and church building failed to keep pace with sharp rises in population. Lady Glenorchy had in 1775 explicitly rebuked the Edinburgh Presbytery over the failure of the establishment to cater for the religious needs of the city's poor. Her chapel was intended to address those needs and was, despite her arguments, a rival to the existing parish churches. And, although herself neither preacher nor priest in her chapel, she could be regarded as equivalent to a bishop, or overseer, at least in the exercise of some of the supervisory and authoritative functions of that office.

It was by buying the land on which to build a chapel that Ladies Glenorchy and Maxwell were able to claim the right to religious authority over the building, because this accorded with the authority over private chapels which had always been legitimately exercised by female aristocrats. The Countess of Huntingdon used the same argument to justify the building of many chapels in which she retained the right to appoint clergy of her own choosing, arguing that she was merely appointing private chaplains. That Lady Huntingdon's argument finally collapsed, obliging her to remove her connexion from the Church of England and license her chapels as Dissenting places of worship, was due to the greater scale of her religious activity in comparison to other female patrons. But it is significant that she avoided this outcome for so long. Her first chapel was built in 1761, but only in 1783, when she possessed over 60 places of worship, was she finally forced into separatism.[10]

Although the building and patronage of chapels in her own religious connexion may appear the most significant way in which Lady Huntingdon acted as a religious leader, less controversial religious activities also allowed aristocratic women to exercise influential patronage and moral authority. It was in an overtly domestic context that Lady Huntingdon's function first appeared episcopal to George Whitefield. In 1749 he wrote to a friend saying that she had been receiving preachers and those who wished to listen to them into her own home, Ashby Place. This, a secondary estate of her husband's family, was certainly not a purpose-built preaching station. 'Good Lady Huntingdon', he wrote,

> goes on acting the part of a Mother in Israel more and more. For a day or two she has had five clergymen under her roof, which makes her ladyship look like a *good archbishop* with his chaplains around him. Her house is a Bethel: to us in the ministry, it looks like a college. We have the sacrament every morning, heavenly conversation all day, and preach at night.[11]

Nor were those few days singular; all her life Lady Huntingdon attracted 'godly' preachers and laity around her as she deliberately opened her home for the spread of the gospel. In Scotland Lady Darcy Maxwell was to do exactly the same. Her diary in August 1770 records: 'In the evening, I attempted to bring some to the knowledge of God, by having the Gospel preached to them in the house: they flocked to hear, and the word seemed to fall with power on some.'[12] In this case, although the activity of preaching the gospel was undertaken by an unnamed clergyman, the effective agency, at least in Lady Maxwell's view, was very much her own. Neither Huntingdon nor Maxwell ever considered preaching themselves, although female preaching was becoming evident in the Methodist movement by the 1760s. Lady Huntingdon, though occasionally exhorted to preach by some of her friends, maintained her distaste for female preaching to the end of her long life on the grounds that it was unscriptural. She confined her moral and religious advice to the accepted female methods of private conversation and extensive correspondence.

It is clear that such individuals were able to exert authority in religious matters, even over leading male clergy, precisely because they did not step outside the bounds of propriety which circumscribed female activity. There was nothing which could draw suspicion upon the heads of ladies who appointed private chaplains of their own choosing, opened their homes in a spirit of charity to those who wished to hear good preaching, or paid for students of a godly character to train for the ministry. Whilst the public–private dichotomy is too inadequate a model to represent entirely the realities of any woman's life in the eighteenth century, its language can in some measure elucidate what was happening here. These women were pursuing private activities in a public way – using private spaces, such as their own chapels and homes, for what became public gatherings: in other words, making the private, public.

One reason why certain women were able to exploit this distinction and thereby gain such substantial religious authority was, quite simply, the force of their personalities. There is no doubt that it took intelligence and education, courage and will power, immense self-confidence and a deep-rooted and assured piety for women to become such religious leaders. These patrons were exercising power despite, and in some ways even through, the domesticity and behind-the-scenes influence which the mores of their society enforced. In other words, they were using precisely those things which were meant to limit their authority in order to exert influence. To a certain extent they were exploiting loopholes in their society's mores. They were not necessarily doing so deliberately, or at least not in any Machiavellian way. Each was motivated primarily by a strong personal religious belief. But no rhetoric which legitimizes a society's customs and structure can ever be watertight, however deeply it has penetrated the minds of the population. It is unusual and strong personalities that, when custom attempts to hem them in, will generally find ways to reassert themselves. When such personalities are combined with the fervour born of deep religious beliefs this is even more likely. It was the strength of personality these patrons showed which enabled them to adopt leadership roles in a society which did not regard women as natural leaders.

Strong personalities combined with deep religious fervour – was there something particular about the religious beliefs of these women, or the religious tenor of the times, which made the exertion of their authority easier? Certainly, some aspects of the religion of the Evangelical Revival made peculiarly possible the exercise of religious and moral authority by individuals who might not normally have aspired to such leadership. Evangelicalism stressed the religion of the individual at the expense of that dictated by the establishment – although the established clergy were nonetheless still recognized and respected as part of God's ministry. But the Reformation emphasis on the individual's faith, relationship with God and right to read and interpret scripture was renewed at this time. Educated women of high station were amongst those who could most easily take advantage of that renewal. Evangelical religion, moreover, was often described as a religion of the heart: highly emotive rather than rational or dogmatic.[13] Such religion was generally believed to appeal strongly to women and to lead to a stress, in the character of the ideal Christian, on those features often associated with the female, such as sensitivity, warmth and benevolence. Whilst modern thinking may challenge this linking of virtues to gender, the eighteenth-century mind tended to accept the connection.[14] Circumstances were conducive, then, for moral authority to be adopted by women to whom such virtues were believed to come naturally.

In an era of female domesticity, moral authority and the control of religious thought and personnel by women, in order to be acceptable, had to be exercised from the home. Evangelicalism was peculiarly a religion of the home. It placed a stress on domestic virtues and family religion. Conversion, as a central feature of the new tradition, was frequently experienced in the home, often by individuals in their private rooms. The regular practice of private and communal prayer, Bible-reading, religious conversation and exhortation led to some of the deepest personal experiences of God taking place in the domestic environment. Such a religion could and did lead to an enhancement of the role and moral authority of the women whose domain the home was. Evangelical women, whose religion led them to exercise philanthropy, generally did so from their own homes or those of local people.[15] The opening of one's home for religious purposes was by no means, however, confined to the aristocracy; many evangelical women, especially Methodists of all ranks, used their homes to host religious talks, classes, exhortations and prayer meetings. At such gatherings their religious authority was enhanced by their function as host, the control they exercised over those invited and, on occasion, by their own speaking role.

While the religious authority granted to women of lower ranks might not have matched that of the aristocratic patrons, it was still worthy of note. Examples might include Mary Bosanquet Fletcher, of gentry origin but never wealthy once her parents had all but cast her off because of her religious ideas. She was amongst the most influential of early Wesleyan Methodist women, gaining much moral authority over men and women by the time of her death through her lifelong labour in the work of Methodism and her charismatic, intelligent and courageous preaching.[16] Hannah More might also be mentioned. As the daughter of a schoolteacher, she became recognized throughout the country as a moral authority, particularly in the areas of female education and behaviour, care and education of the poor, and through her writing and work with charity schools.[17] There were undoubtedly new opportunities for laypeople in the Evangelical Revival that could be exploited by women other than the most rich and powerful.

For these lower-ranking women, also, it was through indirect influence, and the domestic roles which were seen as proper female functions, that opportunities were created or exploited for expansion into more direct fields of action. Although Bosanquet Fletcher became renowned for her preaching, she began to preach only after a long career involving more accepted roles, such as supervising her own charity school and holding religious classes in her home. Hannah More detested the very idea of female preaching. She achieved moral authority through the proper female activities of patronizing charity schools – institutions in which she took a direct interest but never taught – and writing exemplary literature for women and the poor. Direct influence or activism was born for many women gradually out of the exercise and unchecked expansion of what were regarded as their proper feminine roles. Once again, we see the public emerging from a particular use of the private. Such development of roles was not without long-term consequences, even upon the wider development of a feminist consciousness and the slow creation of equal opportunities for the sexes.

However, there are limits to the extent to which the religious authority of female patrons can be ascribed solely to the Evangelical Revival. The life and moral authority of Lady Betty Hastings, who died in 1739, shows the existence of a pre-evangelical tradition of female religious patronage and influence upon which later aristocratic women were to build. And if evangelicalism provided new opportunities for women in some ways, in others it reinforced the status quo in which women's authority was limited and indirect. The stress laid by evangelicalism on domesticity may have enhanced the roles available to women in the short term, but in the long run it may have served to keep women within domestic bounds for longer than might otherwise have been the case. The very fact of women exercising active religious roles within their traditional domestic sphere rendered any arguments that they should be allowed more public or institutional church roles at best needless and at worst irreligious. The Evangelical Revival brought about no official change in the role of women in the church. Although women of especially strong character were able to exploit loopholes in society's restrictions, those restrictions continued to limit the roles and opportunities open to the majority of their sex.

What else did these unusual women share which allowed them so to circumvent the restrictions usually placed on women that they exercised certain quasi-episcopal functions? They shared the all-important virtues of rank and wealth. These were crucial characteristics in the exercise of religious authority by female patrons. Patronage inevitably operated from a higher towards a lower rank in society. Only a woman of high social status could patronize a clergyman. The importance attached to exalted rank when it came to circumventing restrictions can be demonstrated by comparing any of these aristocrats with Hannah More, who just attained the lower ranks of the gentry. Although she achieved considerable moral authority through her own efforts, the opposition she faced was greater than anything Ladies Huntingdon or Glenorchy had to endure. The Blagdon controversy of 1800–3 was a serious challenge by a Church of England clergyman to More's attempt to appoint her own schoolmaster within his parish on no authority but her own. It demonstrates the difficulty which a woman of lesser rank faced when she tried to exercise the kind of religious authority that Lady Glenorchy defended with such panache against the Edinburgh Presbytery.[18]

As for wealth, its practical importance is self-evident. The Countess of Huntingdon was able to establish a connexion out of her many private chapels only because she had the money to build and maintain the premises. Similarly, she could appoint clergymen of her choosing because she was able to pay their salaries, and ensure a supply of preachers who suited her beliefs by paying for them to be educated in the college which she founded and maintained at Trevecca. The same arguments can be used for the other female patrons of religion. Money allowed Lady Glenorchy to argue for the right to appoint her own minister to her chapel in Edinburgh. Money built Lady Darcy Maxwell's chapel in Bristol. Money from the will of Lady Betty Hastings paid for the education of evangelical ordinands in Oxford. This was a society in which money was the principal building block for the creation of any kind of network of influence and activity. In a society which prized rank highly, the money attached to an old family of respect and title was especially influential. In a society which believed that the social hierarchy was dictated by God, the combination of rank and wealth was especially suited to the attainment of religious ends. There can be no doubt that these patrons believed that God had placed them in the circumstances of affluence and influence that they enjoyed because he wished them to use these privileges in the furtherance of his kingdom. In 1773, Lady Glenorchy wrote: 'I have thought it my duty to employ part of that substance with which God has been pleased to entrust me, in building a chapel . . .'[19] Who could doubt the religious authority of one who, woman or otherwise, had been placed by God himself in high social position and in command of the purse strings?

It would be wrong to conclude, however, that only the great and wealthy gained real spiritual authority from their religious activities, and that only because of their wealth. First, the work of lower-ranking evangelical women was also of real long-term significance, although they are not the principal focus of this chapter. Second, the religious authority of aristocratic female patrons was not solely due to their wealth, nor was it without long-term consequences for the women who came after them. Precedents were established, most importantly for women's activity beyond the home. These individuals may have worked largely behind the scenes, but their influence spread far beyond their immediate families. They exercised traditional domestic roles but used them to exert authority outside their own homes. Ladies Huntingdon and Glenorchy differed from pre-evangelicals such as Lady Hastings in taking their religious patronage beyond the boundaries of their private estates. The distinction between the public and the private spheres was in some ways breaking down, and it was their activities in making the private, public, which furthered this process. Lady Huntingdon's nineteenth-century biographer makes this apparent paradox explicit. He notes that, 'over the *connexion as a religious body* she had no *legal* control: nor is there any evidence that she aimed at this'. Rather was her authority moral, her control of her preachers being 'but the voluntary homage of free minds to a soul of a superior order'. In other words, hers was a private, personal influence. Yet he claims in the same paragraph: 'The publicity of her character, as the patroness of every good work, and especially of the extensive preaching of the gospel, caused the application from all quarters to be made directly to her rather than to any other person.'[20] Thus this most remarkable of women created a public space from the private home, making indirect influence as public and powerful as direct control.

Moving from the theoretical to the more concrete, and from Lady Huntingdon in particular to active religious women in general, precedents were also being set in terms of female moral authority and autonomy. Through the activities of such aristocratic figures, women as a whole were increasingly respected as being able to form their own judgements on religious matters, to hold well-thought-out doctrinal positions which affected the way they lived their lives, to be sources of moral influence over others than just their children and servants, and to have demonstrable administrative and organizational skills. They were a long way as yet from being bishops. George Whitefield likened the Countess of Huntingdon to a bishop only in the sense of overseer. It was a practical, administrative and, admittedly, powerful role, but not a sacramental one. The priesthood of all believers was not a doctrine which conferred sacramental functions upon laywomen. But more than ever before women began to assume some of the duties and responsibilities which had traditionally belonged to the clergy, and this was neither a negligible nor a reversible development. If it was rank and wealth which in the immediate term facilitated the real and widespread extension of female religious authority, subsequent generations of Christian women had reason to be thankful that those who possessed these benefits used them as they did.

Notes

1 François de Salignac de la Mothe Fénelon, *Instructions for the Education of a Daughter*, trans. G. Hickes, London, 1707, p. 4.

2 Hannah More, *Strictures on the Modern System of Female Education*, London, 1799, p. 2.

3 Ibid. p. 5.

4 Charlotte Lennox, *The Lady's Museum*, London, 1760, p. 11. I have been unable to identify a particular group of female theologians to whom Lennox's criticism might have applied. A general distaste for female involvement in doctrinal debate was typical of the age.

5 The primary sources for the lives of Ladies Huntingdon, Glenorchy and Maxwell are their nineteenth-century biographies, which include substantial extracts from their subjects' papers. See Anon., *The Life and Times of Selina, Countess of Huntingdon, by a member of the House of Shirley and Hastings*, 2 vols, London, 1839–40; T.S. Jones, *The Life of the Right Honourable Willielma, Viscountess Glenorchy*, Edinburgh, 1822; J. Lancaster, *The Life of Darcy, Lady Maxwell, compiled from her Life and Correspondence*, 2nd edn, London, 1826. The short biography of Lady Hastings was written soon after her death: T. Barnard, *An Historical Character Relating to the Holy and Exemplary Life of the Rt. Hon. the Lady Elizabeth Hastings*, Leeds, 1742.

6 See A. Laurence, *Women in England 1500–1760: a social history*, London: Weidenfeld & Nicolson, 1994, for an examination of female patronage of the clergy in the seventeenth century.

7 Barnard, *Lady Elizabeth Hastings*, pp. 28–30, 39–41, 54–5.

8 Ibid. pp. 11, 30.

9 Jones, *Willielma, Viscountess Glenorchy*, p. 377.

10 For details of the dispute which led to this move, see B.S. Schlenther, *Queen of the Methodists: the Countess of Huntingdon and the eighteenth-century crisis of faith and society*, Bishop Auckland: Durham Academic Press, 1997, ch. 11.

11 Quoted in *Selina, Countess of Huntingdon*, vol. 1, p. 163.

12 Lancaster, *Darcy, Lady Maxwell*, p. 61.

13 For an overview of the character of evangelical religion, see D.W. Bebbington, *Evangelicalism in Modern Britain*, London: Unwin Hyman, 1989.

14 Abundant eighteenth-century conduct literature details the domestic, soft and benevolent virtues believed to be the hallmark of true femininity. See, for example, Hester Chapone, *Letters on the Improvement of the Mind*, Edinburgh, 1780, pp. 67–70, 114; also Thomas Gisborne, *An Enquiry into the Duties of the Female Sex*, 3rd edn, London, 1798, p. 264. Jean-Jacques Rousseau, whose works were very influential in England, expounded a similar gender-linking of virtues: see his *Émile*, trans. B. Foxley, London, 1911, Book V, 'Sophy: or Woman'.

15 See F.K. Prochaska, *Women and Philanthropy in Nineteenth-Century England*, Oxford: Clarendon Press, 1980. No comparative study of eighteenth-century female philanthropy has yet been made, although there is considerable primary and biographical literature on individual female philanthropists.

16 See H. Moore, *The Life of Mrs Mary Fletcher, consort and relict of the Rev. John Fletcher . . . compiled from her Journal, and other authentic documents*, 2 vols, 2nd edn, London, 1817–18.

17 See Hannah More, *Works*, 8 vols, London, 1801; W. Roberts, *Memoirs of the Life and Correspondence of Mrs Hannah More*, 4 vols, 3rd edn, London, 1835.

18 See letter of 1776 from Lady Glenorchy to the Edinburgh Presbytery quoted in the text of this chapter at n. 9 above. For More and the Blagdon Controversy, see M.G. Jones, *Hannah More*, Cambridge: Cambridge University Press, 1952.

19 Jones, *Willielma, Viscountess Glenorchy*, p. 338.

20 Anon., *Selina, Countess of Huntingdon*, pp. 491–2.

Chapter 7

Taming the Spirit
Female leadership roles in the American Awakenings, 1730–1830[1]

Marilyn J. Westerkamp

Evangelicals yearned for the breath of the Holy Spirit. While most Christians had some vision of divine grace, for evangelicals the Spirit played an active, vital role in directing personal journeys of faith. Evangelicals sought out and recognized persons gifted with charisma, marvelled at the power of their speech and followed them as divinely appointed leaders, but they also found promise in the ability of ordinary persons to reach God. They revelled in the hope of that astonishing moment when God would touch their lives and infuse their souls with grace. This conviction of the individual soul's ability to experience God stood at the centre of their strength. They focused upon their personal relationships with God, venerating the work of the Spirit in the encouragement and promotion of the godly community.

Paradoxically, evangelicals also responded to demands to establish order amidst the swirling chaos of society and sin. Whether that order was grounded in the Enlightenment system of natural philosophy or a vision of separate spheres, women were consistently placed in a subordinate position to men. Male religious leaders remained committed to patriarchal structures based upon an understanding of gender that regarded women as physically, intellectually and emotionally inferior.

In other words, this value placed upon order (and its reward of male power) competed with an ethos that embraced the sacred potential of all individuals, women as well as men. For centuries Christians had believed that God moved in arbitrary, unpredictable ways, often gifting the least powerful while ignoring the most able. The voice of the Spirit was so authoritative that the only way male leaders could maintain their patriarchal headship was to silence, or at least limit, that voice. Despite their efforts women continued to overcome their social disabilities through the intervention of the Holy Spirit. If such individuals were seen as acting under divine commission, whether they were poor, ignorant or female, no earthly church institution could justify countermanding their actions or controlling their speech.

This chapter seeks to explore the spiritual careers of American evangelical women during the late-eighteenth and early-nineteenth centuries. The first appearance of evangelicalism during the Great Awakening of the eighteenth century was followed by the arrival and prosperity of Methodism, particularly on the western frontier, and the appearance of a less dramatic form of evangelical religion in the eastern states. As the evangelical movement developed and changed from 1730 to 1850 the leadership of women changed as well. In the earlier decades women led small prayer groups and, in some communities, served on lay committees directing congregational affairs. During the early decades of the nineteenth century a few women, including several especially gifted African-Americans, followed the Spirit's call and built reputations as lay preachers and exhorters. Although socially and politically subordinate, they experienced the immediate power of the Holy Spirit and discovered in it their own charismatic authority.

Beginning in the 1720s and continuing until interrupted by Revolutionary fervour in the 1760s, a Great Awakening swept British America. The first stirrings appeared in the mid-Atlantic colonies with the new immigrants and itinerant preachers. From there the spiritual vitality spread north and south. Communal rituals of intense, emotional revivalism, with their animated, frightening preachers and shrieking, weeping, fainting participants appeared everywhere. Throughout the colonies clergymen took sides for or against the Awakening. Its supporters, the New Lights, saw the essence of true faith as holy love – a religion of the heart. They believed the revivals to be the work of the Holy Spirit and understood the extreme physical manifestations as natural outcomes of an enlightened soul responding to the real threat of damnation.

The culture of the Great Awakening represented the first appearance of the evangelicalism that came to shape Protestantism in the United States. This culture grew out of two roots, blossoming into a single harvest. From the puritan and Congregationalist side came the emphasis upon the spiritual journey and conversion of the individual and the deeply emotional, sometimes passionate, but always personal, connection with God. Through the Scots-Irish Presbyterians were added communal rituals, understandings and language that facilitated those individual journeys. The intensity of the believer's personal relationship with God was acted out at a group level so that all could witness and appreciate (or decry) the excessive tribulations and joy experienced by the truly saved.[2]

Converts told of fears of hell, self-disgust and despair in their depravity. Evangelicals used intimate, often erotic language to describe their relationship with God. Irene Shaw reported that she 'felt ravished with the Love of God', while Hannah Heaton saw a 'man with his arms open ready to receive me his face was full of smiles . . .' Sarah Osborn

> could utter no other language but, 'Come in, Lord Jesus, take full possession; I will come to thee, thou art mine, and I am thine.' . . . surely my heart reached forth in burning desires after the blessed Jesus. O, how was I ravished with his love![3]

Women and men accepted God and experienced the ecstatic joy the encounter brought.

By the 1750s and 1760s a radical, revitalized Baptist movement was claiming its place in the leadership of evangelicalism. New England Baptists traced their history to the early seventeenth century, and throughout decades of persecution as well as toleration they had maintained their concentration upon the gifts of grace and the centrality of personal experience.[4] So, prepared to bloom, they were overwhelmed by the Spirit during the Awakening and their experiential focus led them to grant extraordinary spiritual authority to laypeople. In their struggle against structured, hierarchical establishments they found that the Spirit's clear gifts to individuals empowered the entire community. Extant congregations attracted new members. New congregations were formed throughout the north-east and the Baptist movement moved south. By 1790 about 750 Baptist churches crossed the nation, extending south to Georgia and west to the frontier.

Building upon the groundwork of the Presbyterians in the south, Baptists recruited extensively among the lower and middling classes. They rejected the ostentatious displays and entertainments of gentry culture that represented and reinforced the social hierarchy and embraced instead an egalitarian anthropology expressed through pietistic rituals. They replaced balls, races and extravagant hospitality with communions, baptisms and footwashings. Extemporaneous prayers were appreciated, read liturgies decried and inspired lay witnesses valued above learned clergy.[5] For Baptists such erudition was useless at best and could be a temptation to arrogance and elitism.

Baptists were among the few ideologically prepared and equipped to pursue the unchurched and appeal to society's dispossessed. All souls were of equal importance before God, and evangelical itinerants worked ceaselessly among settlers on the edge of survival: struggling frontier farmers and urban labourers, those deprived of the world's favours and excluded from the concern of most. This conviction that salvation was equally available to all was reflected in a somewhat egalitarian polity that crossed not only class but racial boundaries, regarding African-Americans along with European-Americans as souls in direct relationship with God. In fact, Baptists experienced the first significant successes in converting African-Americans to Christianity.[6]

This work, begun in the 1750s, first realized its rewards after the turn of the century. As late as 1800 no more than 5 per cent of all African-American adults in the southern states had joined one of the evangelical churches.[7] However, in a region stridently stratified by race, the presence of any significant numbers of African-Americans pushed churches to move beyond abstract promises to concrete demonstrations of their egalitarian theological principles. Questions were raised concerning slavery and many congregations worked to ensure black worshippers enjoyed as much spiritual authority as their callings allowed. Black men of high spiritual attainment were placed upon disciplinary committees investigating both black and white members, occasional black men were recognized as preachers, and white church members, including masters, were sometimes called to account for sinful dealings with their enslaved or free black men and women. Moreover, in their acceptance and even encouragement of black preachers evangelical churches were implicitly (if not explicitly) encouraging the formation of smaller prayer and study groups among, and sometimes led by, African-Americans. By the nineteenth century these separate networks and communions led by community members would serve as a source of personal strength and spiritual and political power for African-American Christians.

Within this climate of increasing lay authority women arose as active participants in New Light communities. They formed their own private groups where they found extraordinary spiritual counsel and nurture. The poet Phillis Wheatley maintained a correspondence with her friend Arbour Tanner, confiding her religious hopes, worries and pleasures, while Esther Edwards Burr and Sarah Prince kept up a three-year correspondence through which they admonished and encouraged one another. Sarah Osborn found a true spiritual companion in Susana Anthony, while Deborah Prince joined a female society 'for the most indearing Exercise of social Piety'. In Philadelphia it was reported that after Whitefield had first preached there 'four or five godly women in the city, were the principal counsellors to whom awakened and inquiring sinners used to resort, or could resort, for advice and direction'.[8]

The strength discovered in female evangelical networks sometimes empowered women to claim and exercise spiritual authority within their larger church communities. Most of these communities did not recognize women's equality. In fact, many evangelicals strenuously opposed any acknowledgement of women's authority. Nevertheless, the circumstances of the eighteenth century combined with a theology that resisted artificial hierarchies, like class and education, to open spiritual opportunities to women and justify their presence in the public forum of the church. In her book *Disorderly Women* Susan Juster cites several examples of both men and women voting in church affairs. While such examples are scarce, she persuasively argues that the absence of gender-identifying language in church records, the explicit use of gender-related language in the early nineteenth century and these few references, together suggest that church governance was a responsibility often shared by all church members, male and female.[9]

Women also raised major questions about speaking publicly: about witnessing, voicing their concerns and criticisms, preaching and joining the ranks of leaders. Throughout this era women refused to attend particular churches, railed against them and called them to account, and while evangelical leaders may have felt gratified when a Hannah Heaton criticized established clergy they were less pleased when they found themselves the subject under discussion. Isaac Backus was quite distressed when Ann Dellis rebuked him for his condescending attitude. Lois Adams was censured by the Canterbury Separate church for 'usurp[ing] authority over the Chh in that she Did in a Chh meeting autharitivey teach and admonish the house Church which is contrary to the word of God'.[10]

Few challenged the ability of godly women to arouse spiritual instincts and lead their female friends, children, servants, and even husbands, to God. The controversy surrounded not women's guidance over private lives, effected in private homes, but their role in addressing larger audiences in the public space of the church. If the leadership tried to pacify conservative elements by denying women's authority they might lose key female members. In Lyme, Connecticut, for example, seven women were cited for 'usurping the authority over the church and for neglecting the public worship of God in this place and church meetings and for building up a meeting hild by our admonished members'. Two years later two more women joined them.[11] In other words, evangelicalism often gave women a voice, but when they exercised that voice many were judged to be the founders of scandal and divisions.

As some evangelical churches opened the door to women's exhortation, some women, inevitably, were led to challenge their communities directly. In his diary David Hall noted a 'troublesome' woman who insisted upon singing while others prayed, and who disrupted his sermon with 'panting fits'. Isaac Backus described one Mrs Chase who spoke so loudly that various worshippers moved outside to escape her. She merely followed them outside and continued to address them. In their radical acknowledgement of the power of the Spirit, the Separate Congregationalist and Separate Baptist churches were far more open than most of their contemporaries to women moving beyond the occasional outburst to taking on the role of exhorter or even preacher. In Virginia, Martha Stearns Marshall developed a strong reputation as a lay exhorter: a woman of 'good sense, singular piety, and surprising elocution' who could melt 'a whole concourse into tears by her prayers and exhortations'. Sarah Wright Townsend, an outstanding exhorter, apparently delivered formal sermons on texts. She preached at Sunday meetings of a Separate Baptist community on Long Island from 1759 until at least 1773. When a segment of the congregation proposed uniting with the Regular Baptists, a move that would have restricted Townsend's opportunities, she and her followers left the church yelling, 'Babylon! Babylon! Babylon!' Her faction must have held the power balance, however, because the community did not join with the Regular Baptists until 1789, nine years after her death.[12]

Explorations of the Great Awakening always return to questions of power. The Awakening's proponents, like seventeenth-century puritans and Presbyterians, venerated the work of the Spirit but, unlike their forebears, the eighteenth-century evangelicals had lost the balancing emphasis upon learning. Those who emphasized erudition rejected evangelicalism entirely and, while individual ministers like Jonathan Edwards or Gilbert Tennent were certainly well educated, their understanding of spiritual progress focused upon the actions of grace within the heart. The futility of intellectual study as a spiritual method led New Light preachers to highlight the simple yet intense piety of the child as a model for faith. In the thinking of the new Enlightenment, bound by traditional assumptions about gender and race, the attainments of the adult mind were associated with European men, while women and African-Americans were judged to be simpler. In their childlikeness both the woman and the African-American came to represent the quintessential spiritual convert. In Edwards' *Faithful Narrative* his two examples of Awakening converts were the young, unmarried Abigail Hutchinson and the irritating four-year-old Phebe Bartlet, who spent most of her time praying, listening to ministers and instructing other children.[13]

In respecting heart above mind and love over reason, evangelicals opened the doors of authority to the dispossessed. The emphasis upon spiritual achievements allowed members of the lower and middling classes to become preachers or lay leaders. Racial boundaries were sometimes crossed, and the talents of a spiritually-gifted slave might well be recognized by the evangelical community. The third difficult boundary was, of course, gender, yet even here evangelical women organized their own spiritual networks and provided guidance to others. In some congregations women were involved in administrative and disciplinary decisions, and a few singular women found within the power of the Spirit a voice and authority all to themselves. Sarah Osborn, leader among the New Lights of Newport, Rhode Island, described herself and her calling with the confident humility of the gracious convert. She was:

> a Servant that Has a Great work assignd Him and However unworthy and unequal he may think Himself, and others may think Him, and However ardently He may wish it was in Superior Hands or that His Master would at Least Help Him, yet if He declines He dares not tell Him, well if you dont do it your self it shall go undone . . . the Harvest truely appears to be Plenteous but the Labourers are few.[14]

As the century turned, the new evangelicalism inherited not only the light and excitement of the Spirit, but also the disruptive problems of the Spirit's authority.

By 1800, Enlightenment optimism over human capacity had infiltrated theology. Many evangelicals now turned away from passively awaiting divine grace towards an active seeking after God. Salvation was now connected to effort and anyone with the will to turn to God could be saved. For settlers, whose lives demonstrated daily their capacity to control their environment and build families, farms and towns in the wilderness, a theology that acknowledged some measure of human control was extremely attractive and eminently reasonable.

During this era new groups arose including the 'Christian Connection', a movement of men and women who abhorred denominational divisions and promoted an anti-institutional, egalitarian vision. The absence of ordination procedures and examination committees opened the way for several women preachers. Nancy Mulkey, the daughter and sister of popular Christian preachers, became widely known for her brief exhortations.

> She would arise with zeal on her countenance and fire in her eyes, and with a pathos that showed the depth of her soul, and would pour forth an exhortation lasting from five to fifteen minutes, which neither father nor brother could *equal*, and which brought tears from every feeling eye.[15]

Nancy Gove Cram enjoyed four years of preaching in fields and barns on the New York frontier and published her own collection of hymns and poems before she died in 1815. One Christian Connection leader claimed that at least seven active ministers were converted under her influence. One of her converts, Abigail Roberts, founded four churches.[16] A third Nancy, Nancy Towle, dreamed that she was called to preach, and subsequently embarked upon an itinerant ministry that took her over 15,000 miles through the north-east, the south, Canada, Ireland and England. She described encounters with women preachers among Christians, Freewill Baptists, Universalists, and Methodists, and called for more women to join the preaching work.[17] Among the Christians and Freewill Baptists, historian Catherine Brekus has counted at least 41 women preachers. In addition to preachers, literally hundreds of women could be found as exhorters at camp meetings as well as regular parish gatherings. They were encouraged and praised by clergymen for their 'melting exhortations', 'ardent prayers' and 'powerful testimonies'.[18]

During the first decades of the new republic a new denomination arose to promote Arminian, or 'pick yourself up by your bootstraps', evangelicalism – the Methodist Church. Methodists began preaching in the colonies during the 1760s, and in 1771 John Wesley appointed Francis Asbury 'Superintendent of the American Colonies'. A brilliant organizer and indefatigable worker, Asbury structured a network, recruited preachers and inspired their labours.

Methodist preaching appealed with equal success across regional and racial lines. In addition to the European-American urban dwellers and farmers in both the coastal east and the expanding frontier, Methodists converted a considerable number of African-Americans, both slave and free. They organized a highly successful system of circuits and conferences in which preachers were assigned to serve one circuit of stations serving small groups or classes. This system was well suited to the dispersed population of the new nation, particularly the west. The tight organization combined with rhetorically skilful preachers, a fiery message of threatened damnation and promised salvation, and a commitment to individual spiritual authority and the reward of effort, provided the basis for amazing growth. Beginning with less than

1,000 members in 1771, the Methodist churches by1850 had more than 1,000,000 members – the largest evangelical network in the United States.[19]

Methodism arose in and migrated from England. John Wesley, the son of an Anglican clergyman Samuel Wesley, planned to follow his father as a respectable Anglican priest, but he soon found himself following his mother Susannah's intense piety instead. Critical of the Anglican Church for its self-absorption and spiritual emptiness, Wesley followed a call to the poor and working classes, among whom he enjoyed great popularity. Additionally, he established a support system of lay leaders that could continue his work while he moved on to preach elsewhere. In 1744 he held a conference of lay preachers that later became an annual meeting and would form the foundation of the separate Methodist Church.

From the beginning women played an important role, though it was with some ambivalence that Wesley faced this question. Against his conviction that women had no appropriate public role sat the example of Susannah Wesley, known throughout her neighbourhood for piety and wisdom. She held herself in subjection to her husband yet, when he was away (which he was a great deal), she led family prayers and directed scriptural study. Her audience could grow quite large, though she humbly explained that the increase was accidental, implying, of course, that it was the Spirit at work. She proclaimed that her efforts fell within the private world of women, under the protective umbrella of domesticity.

Wesley matured within a household structured around a woman's spiritual leadership and, as he grew more aware of women's potential, several factors made it easier for him to accept women's preaching. The movement was growing at a remarkable pace and leaders of both genders and all classes were needed. Women were among the most important patrons of the new movement, with many providing meeting houses, paying itinerants' expenses and holding services in their homes.[20] Most important, however, was Wesley's own understanding of calling, as he wrote to one of his most gifted preachers, Mary Bosanquet: 'I think the strength of the cause rests there: on your having an extraordinary call. So, I am persuaded, has every one of our lay preachers, otherwise, I could not countenance his preaching at all.' Wesley saw the movement as the work of the Spirit – as 'an extraordinary dispensation of His providence'. 'Therefore,' he continued, 'I do not wonder if several things occur therein which do not fall under ordinary rules of discipline.'[21] Female leaders themselves recorded internal struggles and they too grounded their work in the personal experience of God.

The American Methodist Connection was far less open to women's leadership than Wesley. Women were certainly important in the building of the early Methodist community. Barbara Ruckle Heck is credited with initiating the first Methodist class in New York in 1760. She and her husband organized a string of Methodist groups in upstate New York and in the St Lawrence River valley. Prudence Gough of Maryland has been immortalized as the quintessential godly mistress, serving her domestic congregation, leading her husband – planter Henry Gough – to conversion, and providing hospitality to Asbury and his circuit riders.[22] There were also active pastors' wives, such as Fanny Newell, who travelled with her circuit-rider husband in Maine and became known for her public prayers. She granted that she had a call to preach, but shrank from it because of female weakness; she referred to this calling as her 'cross'. Despite her own belief that she lacked gifts of eloquence (a perception not shared by her hearers) she began exhorting congregations after her husband had finished his sermon. She justified herself saying, 'Whatever may be said against a female speaking, or praying in public, I care not; for when I feel confident that the Lord calls me to speak, I dare not refuse.' Her husband accepted her efforts, comparing himself and his wife to Moses and Miriam.[23]

In his book *Women of Methodism* Abel Stevens identified 15 women deeply involved in the early movement. They hosted preachers, organized classes in their homes or neighbourhoods and accompanied Asbury on his journeys. Yet, by entitling one chapter 'Asbury and his female friends' Stevens revealed much about the limitations of women's authority.[24] These women were not like Nancy Towle. Their activities were restricted to the domestic, private realm and, while their influence may have spread far, they rarely enjoyed a public voice beyond the local class meeting.

Why did white Methodist women in the United States rarely appear as preachers? Lay preaching, the core of the Methodist network, was an important symbol of the common-man ministry that denied special status to education and wealth. The Methodist agenda had built within it the potential for women's activity. Who better to call women than women preachers? What of women's extraordinary calls? Asbury and his successors did not generally recognize such calls to women. His system of order was tied to his concern about 'fraternity' among his preachers. A circuit rider himself, he built the church upon itinerant ministries and did not really approve of settled pastors. Families represented competing loyalties that would divert preachers from God's work. As Russell Richey argues, 'it was commitment to Christ and to one another that mattered. The hedges around that commitment – celibacy, whiteness, maleness, mobility – only reinforced the primary commitment.'[25] Essentially, Asbury gathered around himself at one time or another literally thousands of young, unmarried men willing to withstand the rigours of weather, terrain and the risks of solitary travel. It was a life Asbury did not make available to women. Most white Methodist women who felt a call either translated that call into domestic leadership, that is as Christian housewife, or took on the lesser, local roles of testifier or class leader.

The problem was not restricted to Methodists. Baptists were also retracting their earlier promises. When Presbyterian James Carnahan of upstate New York denounced itinerant preacher Martha Howell and the Baptist churches saying, 'They suffer that woman Jezebel which called herself a prophetess, to teach and to seduce the servants of the Lord', the Baptists responded that Howell only witnessed to her own experiences and faith, and that she did not preach or teach.[26] Susan Juster has observed that by the end of the eighteenth century most Baptist men judged that women had no authority to preach, teach or pray aloud – an 'unlimited' prohibition. As one man concluded:

> I conceive it to be unscriptural for them to speak in the church *at all*, not only by teaching, or by prayer, leading the devotions of the church, but by professing their repentance toward God, and faith in the Lord Jesus Christ, or their future contrition and confidence; by imparting necessary information on any matter; in giving testimony to confirm any fact; in asking or answering any question; or by verbally assenting to or dissenting from, any proposition there . . .

As Baptists moved from ad hoc groups addressing problems on a case by case basis to standing committees, women were systematically excluded. Moreover, when women did speak they were silenced or labelled 'disorderly'.[27]

Both Methodists and Baptists were in part experiencing the polarization that follows institutional growth. Just as Asbury created an itinerant ethos that in its very conceptualization excluded women, so Baptists in their search for respectability enhanced their status by assimilating the nation's views on women and gender difference. Yet if the issue was respectability why were class boundaries still crossed? For many clergymen of the old school – Presbyterians, Congregationalists, Episcopalians – maintaining class, racial and gender differences provided the foundation of order. Evangelicals set themselves apart by crossing class divisions even as they found maintaining gender difference to be essential to their identities. This assignment of women to subordinate roles, despite a language that deeply respected the spiritual call, reflected a changed meaning of and lesser import given to the concept of spiritual calling. If all depended upon divine grace there would have been a continued recognition of women's potential equality. That women were usually not perceived as equal participants reveals that the basis of common-man ministry no longer lay entirely in the actions of God, but now owed some debt to the actions of men. This reflected the changing theology that placed more responsibility upon the shoulders of believers and denounced passivity, a feminine characteristic, as a viable pathway to salvation. In short, the crossing of class boundaries had less to do with a faith in the Spirit than with changing perceptions of human nature and human capacity.

In this sense the answer lay beyond the parochial world of preaching and congregations in the changing social and intellectual climate. This gender and class counterpoint was neither contradiction nor coincidence. Rather, these two ideological constructions combined with other beliefs and circumstances to constitute the popular, democratic ethos that would characterize turn-of-the-century politics and insinuate itself into religion. As Gordon

Wood has argued, the American Revolution transformed the ideological framework within which individuals were judged and the boundaries around which their relationships were formed.[28]

In the Revolutionary world framed by the Enlightenment any assumption that some were born to join the elite while others remained fixed among the masses was no longer uncontested. The phrase 'all men are created equal' was not mere rhetoric but the expression of a commitment to a basic equality of nature before circumstances interfered. Physician Benjamin Rush noted that,

> Human nature is the same in all ages and countries, and all the differ-ences we perceive . . . in respect to virtue and vice, knowledge and ignorance, may be accounted for from climate, country, degrees of civi-lization, forms of government, or accidental causes.[29]

He and others believed not in a levelled human condition but in a range of talent and intelligence that appeared across the spectrum of classes. What was necessary was that opportunities were available for all men to test their mettle and pursue their goals for the good of the men themselves and the good of the nation.

As the first national leaders soon discovered, they did not agree on key government policies and, as competing programmes and philosophies cap-tured competing interests, political parties appeared. In order to serve the nation leaders had to win elections, and in order to win they needed votes. In their campaigns the parties touted men's natural abilities to choose gover-nors and make political decisions. The franchise expanded ever outward and a strikingly anti-intellectual tone overarched much of the political debate, as if education, manners and taste could weaken an individual's innate abilities and common sense. Human equality was reconstructed with a levelling thrust: the equality of all men was assumed in their natural human condition.

Theories of humanity, grounded not in political theory but in natural phi-losophy, appealed to Enlightenment minds rejecting the privilege of birth, and to ordinary minds unwilling to grant others any right to rule over them. Their rhetoric empowered the socially inferior by denying either the reality or the significance of differences. Nevertheless, the language used did not need to eradicate all differences; it could, by naturalizing key distinctions, dis-count entire classes of persons. Race, for example, became a prime target of debate. Africans provided much food for discussion since, as some writers like Benjamin Rush argued, the inequalities and constrictions of slavery could easily account for any supposed intellectual or moral inferiority. Gender, however, was an easier target. Women's essential difference from and inferi-ority to men was hardly debated by male intellectuals, merely assumed as transparently obvious and invoked to rationalize the continued subordination of women.

The new rhetoric of citizenship was a white, masculine language. The social and economic needs of the white moneyed classes, north and south, resulted in a 1787 constitution (and its 1791 bill of rights) that, amidst all its discussion of representative government and individual liberties, implicitly excluded African-Americans from that government and explicitly protected the institution of slavery. The racial inferiority of African-Americans was judged to make them mentally and emotionally unfit for citizenship.

In similar fashion women were made dependants within the republic. Just as wives enjoyed no legal identity under coverture, but had their being subsumed under their husband's, so women had no political personhood apart from the men who supposedly represented them. As in the case of African-Americans, this was explained in terms of women's natural mental and emotional unfitness to participate in government. In both cases the concept of childlikeness was invoked, implying that women and African-Americans were not complete adult persons. It was not that the lives of women or African-Americans had changed. Their circumstances had not changed, and that fact pointed up the progress that had been made by non-elite white men in the cause of republican liberty.[30]

In opening the political arena to all white men regardless of class or wealth, participation in government at any level, from holding national office to voting in local elections, became a marker of manliness. Debating politics, organizing parades and running for office were performances of civic duty and, by extension, of masculinity. Slaves, free African-Americans and white women might enjoy patriotic celebrations and election parades but they were the audience for the public performance of white masculinity and citizenship. In the new republic all free white men were citizens, employing their talents for the good of the nation; women (white women) were represented (and praised) as producers of citizens – as republican mothers.[31]

This Enlightenment language of the natural equality of men, the increased popular participation in elections and the flattering language used by candidates to attract support, infected religious discourse. Nathan Hatch writes of the 'democratization' of American Christianity, arguing that these cultural and political forces undermined the significance of class and education as ideological organizers of society. The rising emphasis upon human ability reflected this new reluctance to set apart an 'elect' community of saints, while the common-man ministry accompanied the increasingly anti-intellectual bias of a nation that sometimes sneered at learning and taste as foppish and effete (i.e. as feminine). This perception of education as irrelevant, or even dangerous, was also apparent in a growing faith in a man's ability to interpret the Bible for himself. The educated ministry, like the virtuous citizenry, now merited significantly less respect and deference.[32]

Evangelicals considered themselves children of the Spirit; they were, in fact, children of the Enlightenment and the democratic revolution. In granting the role of human activity in spiritual fulfilment, evangelicals followed the guidance provided by eighteenth-century culture. They no longer respected as natural the ranks of birth, wealth and education, but they did understand women to be by nature essentially different from and inferior to men. The new democratic ideology and the solidifying denominational structures could easily account for the new opportunities offered to lower- and middling-class white evangelical men, as well as the closing down of similar options for African-Americans and women. However, the insistent appearance of women and African-Americans as preachers reflected a legacy, however grudgingly recognized, of the continuing work of the Holy Spirit among the people of God.

Methodists experienced extraordinary success among African-Americans, enslaved and free, although just how much is not known. Albert Raboteau believes that as late as 1820 the majority of slaves 'remained only minimally touched by Christianity', with evangelical religion having made its greatest strides among house servants, artisans and urban slaves. Gary Nash, on the other hand, has argued that in Philadelphia the membership of the African evangelical churches represented at least a third of the black population and probably much more.[33] But as early as 1800 race politics appeared to destroy the simple equality presumed by the evangelical ethos. In response African-Americans built their own separate churches, including Richard Allen's African Methodist Episcopal Church (AMEC).

From the time that African-Americans joined evangelical churches black women felt called to preach. The black male leadership was at best ambivalent. For example, Richard Allen had once discouraged Jarena Lee, explaining that, 'as to women preaching . . . our Discipline knew nothing at all about it – that it did not call for women preachers'. Yet Allen allowed Lee to hold meetings and exhort as she felt called. Eight years later an inspired Lee stood and preached extemporaneously in Allen's church, and he gave her unqualified support. In 1850 at the annual meeting of the Philadelphia AMEC conference women preachers were so numerous that they formed an organization. That association did not last and at the 1852 general conference a resolution to license women preachers was defeated by a significant majority of delegates, all of whom were male.[34]

How many women attempted a preaching ministry cannot be known, nor is there a clear sense of how many rose to be local leaders. Still, the number of black women who developed serious reputations as preachers remains astonishing. These women, converted in a flash of light, heard voices that summoned them to the preaching desk and felt irresistible impulses to embark upon the itinerant trail, sometimes into great danger. Two of the earliest black female preachers, Jarena Lee and Zilpha Elaw, were members of the AMEC. A third woman travelling among the Methodists was a generation older than Lee and Elaw. She published her story under the simple name of Old Elizabeth.

Elizabeth, born a slave in Maryland in 1766, was freed at the age of 30 and began preaching at 42. Her brief tale chronicles a successful career as a preacher who frequently toured the northern states and travelled as far west as Michigan and back again to Pennsylvania when she was 87. She lived at least 10 more years. Both Jarena Lee and Zilpha Elaw were born to free parents on the mid-Atlantic seaboard. Both were drawn fairly early to the Methodist Church and felt the commission to preach years before embarking upon their first missions at the age of 30.

Two themes dominate the stories of all three women. First, each emphasized the work of the Spirit in her heart. Their exceptionally strong connection with the supernatural first exhibited itself in personal experiences of conversion and sanctification. Elaw experienced conversion while milking a cow:

> I turned my head, and saw a tall figure approaching, who came and stood by me. He had long hair, which parted in the front and came down on his shoulders; he wore a long white robe down to the feet; and as he stood with open arms and smiled upon me, he disappeared.

She originally thought that the vision might only have been in her mind, except that the cow 'bowed her knees and cowered down upon the ground'.[35] Elizabeth had the far more terrifying experience of having been left 'standing upon the brink of this awful pit . . . Still, I felt all the while that I was sustained by some invisible power.' She struggled and cried for mercy until she felt herself being raised higher. 'Then I thought I was permitted to look straight forward, and saw the Saviour standing with his hand stretched out to receive me . . . I felt filled with light and love.' Granted a glimpse of heaven's door, she saw 'millions of glorified spirits in white robes'.[36]

The voice of the Spirit became most insistent in its charge to preach, speaking in direct, verbal instruction as well as in signs. Lee heard a voice say, 'Go Preach the Gospel . . . I will put words in your mouth'; Elaw reported that at a camp meeting, 'the Lord opened my mouth in public prayer'.[37] Elizabeth opened a Bible to the text, 'Gird up thy loins now like a man, and answer thou me. Obey God rather than men.' Many told her that nothing in scripture sanctioned women preaching and that the labour was too difficult for women, yet as she struggled, 'there seemed a light from heaven to fall upon me . . . and I was enabled to form a new resolution to go on to prison and to death, if it might be my portion . . .'[38] They read the success of their meetings as signs of divine approval; when they failed to follow God's will they suffered physically and emotionally. Elaw especially seemed a nineteenth-century Jonah, enduring several long periods of illness, which she interpreted as God's response to her failure to answer his charge.[39]

A second resonating theme was the importance of women's encouragement. When Elizabeth sought for a place to speak, the Spirit sent her to the home of a widow who happily gathered a meeting. At another point, when she was feeling demoralized by the elders' criticism, she met 'an aged sister, [and] found upon conversing with her that she could sympathize with me in this spiritual work'. Elaw was urged towards her call by her sister Hannah who, before her death, had 'seen Jesus . . . in the society of angels' who had instructed Hannah to tell Zilpha 'that she must preach the gospel'. As Elaw continued to resist she received a visit from a female minister who urged her on, believing that 'god has provided a real work for thy employment'. Even after Allen had encouraged her call Jarena Lee remained uncertain until the Spirit directed her to the house of a sister who had gathered a small meeting.[40]

None of these women challenged traditional feminine roles. Elaw wrote rather heatedly about woman's proper place:

> The boastful speeches too often vented by young females against either the paternal yoke or the government of a husband, is both indecent and impious – conveying a wanton disrespect to the regulation of Scripture . . . That woman is dependant on and subject to man, is the dictate of nature; that the man is not created for the woman, but the woman for the man, is that of Scripture.[41]

Yet all of these women travelled unencumbered by family responsibilities. Elizabeth was unmarried and childless. Both Elaw and Lee were young widows and each left her children in the care of others so that she could travel. Lee told of travelling 30 miles from home even though her son was extremely sick.[42] In the very public nature of their labour they overturned traditional expectations.

Perhaps the most astonishing evidence of their spiritual authority was the vast number of white men and women that came to hear them and was moved by the experience. Both Elizabeth and Elaw preached in slave states, risking capture and resale into slavery. After surprising people that 'a coloured woman can preach', Elizabeth directly confronted injustice, so that 'they strove to imprison me because I spoke against slavery'.[43] Lee recorded the success of 'a poor coloured woman' through whom the Spirit poured forth: 'Though, as I was told, there were lawyers, doctors, and magistrates present, to hear me speak, yet there was mourning and crying among sinners . . . The Lord gave his handmaiden power to speak . . .'[44]

These preachers laid all responsibility for their labour and success upon the Holy Spirit; all problems or shortfalls were attributed to their own failure to follow God's will. They presented themselves as vessels through which the Spirit poured unlimited grace, and in their very passivity they gained power, 'for as unseemly as it may appear now-a-days for a woman to preach . . . nothing is impossible with God'.[45] But they were not trance speakers and, fighting for their right to preach, they demonstrated a personal power of their own. They blamed the human actions that denied them a pulpit, and, perhaps inadvertently, displayed themselves as women actively following the call of grace. In direct response to someone's citation of the Pauline position, Elaw engaged in a knowledgeable, perceptive scriptural discussion:

> It is true, that in the ordinary course . . . Paul laid it down as a rule, that females should not speak in the church, nor be suffered to teach, but the Scriptures make it evident that this rule was not intended to limit the extraordinary directions of the Holy Ghost, in reference to female Evangelists, or oracular sisters.

This assertion was followed by a catalogue of female evangelists, including Phebe, Tryphena, Priscilla, the sisters of Nereus, the mother of Rufus, and the four virgin daughters of Philip. She noted the prophecy of Joel that God would pour out his Spirit upon his servants and handmaids. In the book of Acts Peter said that this prophecy was fulfilled at Pentecost, and if this was so, she argued, then 'the Christian dispensation has for its main feature the inspirations of the holy prophetic Spirit, descending on the handmaids as well as on the servants of God'.[46]

It is important to remember that while female evangelical preachers might have been recognized, they were permitted to travel and speak only as unpaid evangelists, leading isolated meetings or delivering haphazardly scheduled sermons. There was no question of accepting these women into the ordained ranks; they were not permitted to serve as delegates to the regional conferences. Their relationship to the AMEC leadership was similar to the relationship of black deacons and preachers to the Methodist conferences. Black deacons were recognized as spiritually gifted and were permitted to do a lot of work, but they were not paid and they had no place in making policy. After its separation from mainstream Methodism, the AMEC opened the doors more widely to female preachers but it provided no recognized status. It certainly did not ordain women.

The activity, authority and success of these early African-Americans raises again the question of white women. The male leadership of the AMEC behaved no differently from that of white Methodist men, but many black women who heard the call of the Spirit to preach did so, while white women accommodated themselves to the white male leadership. While there may have been differences in the way women and men, white and black, understood evangelical religiosity, it is likely that the answer lies in republican ideology and the gender politics of the early republic. White women lived in a world enmeshed in a habit of obedience to male authority. The rule of fathers and husbands was generally unchallenged and it was reinforced by a sharply gender-differentiated political culture that rewarded women for their own peculiarly female contributions to the citizenry – that is, the bearing and raising of male citizens. From the perspective of white women, white men were their masters. They accepted that reality. They found fulfilment in domestic roles and republican motherhood, and they exercised influence through household leadership.

The paradoxical epitome of this kind of domestic leadership was the missionary wife. As early as 1810 women realized a ministry in the mission field through marriage. Although most looked towards providence as the path by which they entered the field, the deliberation with which many women set themselves up for whirlwind courtships with missionary hopefuls, and the sheer number and brevity of those courtships, reflected a determination and world view that countermands any twentieth-century understanding of 'passive vessel'.

African-American women lived in a world in which their fathers and husbands had no social or political authority. Power lay in the hands of white masters or the white elite. The manhood of citizenship had no meaning for African-Americans, for black men were explicitly excluded from the citizenry. In this bifurcated society black men and women knew that white men held the power, but they did not grant the justice of that authority, for theirs was a relationship of force rather than consent. African-Americans split off from white evangelical churches, first into separate congregations within denominations and then, when excessively controlled, into separate denominations. Once separate the AMEC established its own lines of institutional hierarchy, with male leaders claiming the same privileges exercised by white men and accepting as given patriarchal assumptions about church networks. Women were expected to be domestic leaders. But, from their habit of distrusting authority, many black women, who as urban labourers themselves did not experience the thrills of domesticity, countered those assumptions. Men only were ordained and controlled the reins of church power but women were called as preachers. They preached and were greatly respected. Men as well as women discovered that the Spirit would not be denied, and soon black preaching women were criss-crossing the nation and the ocean carrying the gospel message.

When did women first consciously speak in their own voices rather than as mere channels of the Spirit? It once seemed to the author that this did not happen until the early twentieth century. Ellen Gould White, founder of the Seventh Day Adventists, for example, was a mystic whose visions led her to establish a spiritually based health reform movement. Mary Baker Eddy crafted her theology out of the inspiration of the Holy Spirit. Only in the twentieth century, or so it appeared, when Aimee Semple McPherson dressed as a police officer rode her motorcycle onto the stage of her vaudeville cathedral, did a woman dare to deliver her own sermons in her own words.

But this impression was wrong. In the 1840s, a 40-something emancipated slave named Isabel embarked upon a preaching career as she had been directed by the Spirit. First, however, she renamed herself Sojourner Truth.[47] She preached a millennialism that promised damnation as well as salvation in the last days that were coming soon. She railed against the sins of the time, by which she meant slavery and the subjection of women. Within the empowerment realized through the Holy Spirit, Truth denounced spiritual and political evils in her own voice. She may have been filled with the Spirit, but by the very act of naming herself Truth proclaimed herself an actor. And the action she took was the advocacy of rights: the rights of African-Americans and of women. Ironically, the inspiration of the Spirit prepared this uneducated woman to challenge the republic within the framework of natural philosophy and the republican paradigm. Human equality and natural rights became her language and the focus of her activism, albeit framed by the fiery millennial vision of evangelicalism. To read Sojourner Truth is to understand that the power of the Spirit was indeed an unpredictable, subversive, even dangerous force.

Notes

1 The interpretations outlined in this essay, along with historical references and text were originally published in M.J. Westerkamp, *Women and Religion in Early America, 1600–1850: the puritan and evangelical traditions*, London: Routledge, 1999. See ch. 1, 'Women, the Spirit, and the Reformation', pp. 6–8; ch. 5, 'Witnesses to the new light', pp. 86–102; and ch. 6, 'Gender, revolution, and the Methodists', pp. 109–26. I am grateful to Routledge for permission to draw on that material in this chapter.

2 On puritan spirituality, see C.L. Cohen, *God's Caress: the psychology of puritan religious experience*, New York: Oxford University Press, 1986; C.E. Hambrick-Stowe, *The Practice of Piety: puritan devotional disciplines in seventeenth-century New England*, Chapel Hill: University of North Carolina Press, 1982; A. Porterfield, *Female Piety in Puritan New England: the emergence of religious humanism*, New York: Oxford University Press, 1992. On the community rituals of the Awakening, see M.J. Westerkamp, *Triumph of the Laity: Scots-Irish piety and the Great Awakening, 1625–1760*, New York: Oxford University Press, 1988; L.E. Schmidt, *Holy Fairs: Scottish communions and American revivals in the early modern period*, Princeton, NJ: Princeton University Press, 1989.

3 S. Juster, *Disorderly Women: sexual politics and evangelicalism in Revolutionary New England*, Ithaca, NY: Cornell University Press, 1994, pp. 65, 63; S. Hopkins, *Memoirs of the Life of Mrs. Sarah Osborn*, Catskill, NY, 1814, p. 32. See also B.E. Lacey, 'Women and the Great Awakening in Connecticut', unpublished thesis, Clark University, 1982, p. 135.

4 On seventeenth-century Baptists, see C.G. Pestana, *Quakers and Baptists in Colonial Massachusetts*, New York: Cambridge University Press, 1991.

5 R. Isaac, 'Evangelical revolt: the nature of the Baptists' challenge to the traditional order in Virginia, 1765–1775', *William and Mary Quarterly* 31, 1974, 345–68; C.L. Heyrman, *Southern Cross: the beginnings of the Bible Belt*, New York: Alfred A. Knopf, 1997, pp. 3–27.

6 Among books that address this question of the relative evangelical success in proselytizing among African-Americans are A.J. Raboteau, *Slave Religion: the 'invisible institution' in the antebellum south*, New York: Oxford University Press, 1978, pp. 128–50; M. Sobel, *The World They Made Together: black and white values in eighteenth-century Virginia*, Princeton, NJ: Princeton University Press, 1987, pp. 178–203; J. Butler, *Awash in a Sea of Faith: Christianizing the American people*, Cambridge, MA: Harvard University Press, 1990, pp. 129–63.

7 Heyrman, *Southern Cross*, p. 44.

8 Phillis Wheatley to Arbour Tanner, 19 May 1772, in J.C. Shields (ed.) *The Collected Works of Phillis Wheatley*, New York: Oxford University Press, 1988, p. 164; C.F. Karlsen and L. Crumpacker (eds) *The Journal of Esther Edwards Burr, 1754–1757*, New Haven: Yale University Press, 1984; Thomas Prince, 'The sovereign God acknowledged and blessed . . . a sermon occasioned by the decease of Mrs Deborah Prince' (1744), in R.R. Ruether and R.S. Keller (eds) *Women and Religion in America*, 3 vols, New York: Harper & Row, 1983, vol. 2, p. 344; 'Obituary of Mrs Hannah Hodge', General Assembly's Missionary Magazine (1806), in Ruether and Keller, *Women and Religion*, vol. 2, p. 346.

9 Juster, *Disorderly Women*, pp. 41–2.

10 Ann Dellis to Isaac Backus, 26 April 1772, as quoted in Juster, *Disorderly Women*, p. 83; Lois Adams, as quoted ibid. p. 82.

11 Ibid. p. 88.

12 C.A. Brekus, *Strangers and Pilgrims: female preaching in America, 1740–1845*, Chapel Hill: University of North Carolina Press, 1998, pp. 47, 60, 62.

13 J. Edwards, *A Faithful Narrative of the Surprising Work of God*, 1737; Grand Rapids: Baker, 1979, pp. 85–93.

14 Sarah Osborn to Joseph Fish, 28 February–7 March 1767, in M.B. Norton (ed.) '"My resting reaping times": Sarah Osborn's defense of her unfeminine activities, 1767', *Signs* 2, 1976, 528–9.

15 J. Thomas, 'The life of the pilgrim Joseph Thomas' (1817), as cited in N.O. Hatch, *The Democratization of American Christianity*, New Haven: Yale University Press, 1989, pp. 79–80.

16 N.G. Cram, *A Collection of Hymns and Poems: designed to instruct the inquirer . . .*, Schenectady, NY, 1815; Gilbert McMaster, 'An essay in defence of some fundamental doctrines' (1815), as cited in Hatch, *Democratization of American Christianity*, p. 78; Brekus, *Strangers and Pilgrims*, pp. 194–7.

17 N. Towle, *Vicissitudes Illustrated, in the Experiences of Nancy Towle, in Europe and America*, Portsmouth, NH, 1833.

18 Brekus, *Strangers and Pilgrims*, pp. 132–54.

19 C.C. Goss, *Statistical History of the First Century of American Methodism*, New York, 1866, pp. 109–10; S.E. Ahlstrom, *A Religious History of the American People*, New Haven: Yale University Press, 1972, pp. 436–7.

20 G. Malmgreen, 'Domestic discords: women and the family in East Cheshire Methodism, 1750–1830', in J. Obelkevich, L. Roper and R. Samuel (eds) *Disciplines of Faith: studies in religion, politics, and patriarchy*, London: Routledge & Kegan Paul, 1987, pp. 57–8, discusses the importance of female patrons in one Methodist region. See also J.R. Tyson, 'Lady Huntingdon's reformation', *Church History* 64, 1995, 580–93.

21 Quoted in Malmgreen, 'Domestic discords', p. 58.

22 F.A. Norwood, 'Expanding horizons: women in the Methodist movement', in R.L. Greaves (ed.) *Triumph Over Silence: women in Protestant history*, Westport, CT: Greenwood Press, 1985, pp. 151–5; Ruether and Keller, *Women and Religion*, vol. 2, pp. 358–61.

23 Fanny Newell's 'Memoirs' as cited in C.A. Brekus, '"Let your women keep silence in the churches": female preaching and evangelical religion in America, 1740–1845', unpublished thesis, Yale University, 1993, pp. 122–3.

24 A. Stevens, *The Women of Methodism*, New York, 1866, pp. 213–53.

25 R.E. Richey, *Early American Methodism*, Bloomington: Indiana University Press, 1991, pp. 1–20, citation 18.

26 As cited in M.P. Ryan, *Cradle of the Middle Class: the family in Oneida County, New York, 1790–1865*, Cambridge: Cambridge University Press, 1981, pp. 71–3.

27 Juster, *Disorderly Women*, pp. 122–35, citation 130. Heyrman, *Southern Cross*, pp. 167–8 notes the same exclusion of women from Baptist positions of authority.
28 G. Wood, *The Radicalism of the American Revolution*, New York: Alfred A. Knopf, 1992. See especially pp. 229–43, 271–87, 305–25.
29 As quoted in Wood, *Radicalism*, p. 236.
30 S. McCurry, 'The two faces of republicanism: gender and proslavery politics in South Carolina', *Journal of American History* 78, 1992, 1245–64.
31 L. Kerber, *Women and the Republic: intellect and ideology in Revolutionary America*, Chapel Hill: University of North Carolina Press, 1980; M. Ryan, 'Ceremonial space: public celebration and private women', in idem *Women in Public: between banners and ballots, 1825–1880*, Baltimore: Johns Hopkins University Press, 1990, pp. 19–57.
32 Hatch, *Democratization of American Christianity*, especially pp. 3–46; see also Juster, *Disorderly Women*, pp. 108–44.
33 Raboteau, *Slave Religion*, p. 149; G. Nash, *Forging Freedom: the formation of Philadelphia's black community 1720–1840*, Cambridge, MA: Harvard University Press, 1988, pp. 132–3.
34 R. Allen, *The Life Experience and Gospel Labors of the Rt. Rev. Richard Allen*, Nashville: Abingdon Press, 1960; C.V.R. George, *Segregated Sabbaths: Richard Allen and the rise of independent black churches, 1760–1840*, New York: Oxford University Press, 1973, pp. 128–9; J. Lee, 'The life and religious experience of Jarena Lee' (1836), in W.L. Andrews (ed.) *Sisters of the Spirit: three black women's autobiographies of the nineteenth century*, Indianapolis: Indiana University Press, 1986, pp. 36, 44–5; Andrews, 'Introduction', in idem *Sisters of the Spirit*, pp. 6–7.
35 Zilpha Elaw, 'Memoirs of the life, religious experience, ministerial travels and labours of Mrs Zilpha Elaw, an American female of colour' (1846), in Andrews, *Sisters of the Spirit*, pp. 56–7.
36 'Memoir of Old Elizabeth, a coloured woman' (1863), in W.L. Andrews (ed.) *Six Women's Slave Narratives*, New York: Oxford University Press, 1988, pp. 5–6.
37 Lee, 'Life and religious experience', p. 35; Elaw, 'Memoirs', pp. 67–70, 75.
38 'Memoir of Old Elizabeth', pp. 9–10.
39 Elaw, 'Memoirs', pp. 81–2, 87.
40 'Memoir of Old Elizabeth', pp. 10, 13; Elaw, 'Memoirs', pp. 73–5; Lee, 'Life and religious experience', pp. 43, 45.
41 Elaw, 'Memoirs', p. 61.
42 Lee, 'Life and religious experience', p. 45.
43 'Memoir of Old Elizabeth', p. 17.
44 Lee, 'Life and religious experience', pp. 45–6.
45 Ibid. p. 36.
46 Elaw, 'Memoirs', p. 124.
47 On Sojourner Truth, see N.I. Painter, *Sojourner Truth: a life, a symbol*, New York: W.W. Norton, 1996, an outstanding biographical and cultural study. Truth tells her own story in *Narrative of Sojourner Truth*, ed. M. Washington, New York: Vintage Books, 1993.

Part III

Tensions surrounding an active laity

Chapter 8

Lay leadership, establishment crisis and the disdain of the clergy

Deryck W. Lovegrove

In 1652 there appeared in print the quintessential portrayal of the ideal parish clergyman. In George Herbert's prose masterpiece *The Country Parson* the reader is offered an attractive image of a devout, learned and self-giving religious leader, who cares deeply for even the humblest of his parishioners:

> The Country Parson upon the afternoons in the weekdays, takes occasion to visit in person, now one quarter of his Parish, now another. For there he shall find his flock most naturally as they are, wallowing [i.e. engaged] in the midst of their affairs.[1]

The parish clergyman was one who in Herbert's view should expound the most profitable texts of scripture to his parishioners, use regular catechizing to instil 'a competent knowledge of salvation', dispense charity, comfort and advice, and above all set before them a model of Christian living. While this patriarchal ideal exerted its benign influence in the Anglican setting, the writings of Knox and the Scottish reformers envisaged a similar resident ministry providing all that was necessary for the spiritual care and education of those living within a given territory. In practice, the ideal was rarely achieved and, in disregard of earlier warning signs, the end of the eighteenth century found the territorial ministry on both sides of the England–Scotland border in a less than healthy condition. In 1801 an article in the *Scots Magazine* suggested that 'the established Clergy of Scotland [had] lost a great part of that reverence and popularity among the lower classes, which distinguished their order at no very distant period'.[2] The previous year Bishop Samuel Horsley in a visitation charge to the clergy of his Rochester diocese sternly warned them against running 'the eternal round of giddy pleasure', as if entertainment rather than professional duty was the focus of their lives. He reminded them that the clergyman would only earn his parishioners' respect if he demonstrated true spiritual care.[3]

Though in structure and worship the Episcopalian establishment of England and Wales differed markedly from its Presbyterian counterpart in Scotland, the two churches shared a common exposure to eighteenth-century social mores, to agrarian and urban–industrial change and to the rising tide of popular discontent or, at least, indifference. The Anglican Church, in spite of its hierarchy, was a highly decentralized body with each incumbent to all intents and purposes the arbiter of local policy and practice. By contrast the Church of Scotland, especially during the second half of the eighteenth century under the leadership of the Moderate party, exercised strong centralized control over its parishes and clergy. The General Assembly, meeting in Edinburgh, governed a tiered system of regional synods, presbyteries and, at the lowest level, kirk sessions, all composed of ministers and elders.

By the latter part of the eighteenth century the Anglican Church was beset by practical difficulties which seriously compromised the parochial ideal. The 26 bishops were as much political functionaries operating in the House of Lords as they were spiritual leaders of the clergy in their dioceses. They exhibited the vices and virtues of the eighteenth-century aristocracy with whom they were associated. At the local level many parishes suffered from the loss of all or part of their tithe income while parsonage houses were frequently in ruin. As a result of these material deficiencies pluralism and non-residence were rife, with parochial duties entrusted to impecunious stipendiary curates, some of whom were compelled by circumstances to serve more than one parish. Even though the picture is far from uniform and recent work by Mark Smith on the industrializing areas of Oldham and Saddleworth has cast doubt on the conventional picture of a static church served by a neglectful clergy, there were numerous weaknesses in the system.[4] Notwithstanding the exemplary performance of some clergymen, the provision of services in many rural parishes tended towards the minimum requirement and in so doing fell far short of the Herbertian ideal. Triennial visitation returns reveal that in some parishes as few as 1 in 10 of the adult population were regular communicants.[5]

Scottish rural parishes appear to have enjoyed a more even performance of clerical duty. Under the Presbyterian system stipendiary substitutes did not exist, pluralism of the English type was not permitted and long-term non-residence was unknown. As in England, however, both extremes of clerical attention to duty were apparent. In the Highland parishes of Tongue and Urquhart William MacKenzie and Charles Calder respectively were renowned for their pastoral and evangelical diligence.[6] By contrast Patrick Nicolson, minister at Thurso, was described as keeping a good table and standing high in the favour of the gentry, but as being remiss and indolent in the discharge of his pastoral duties.[7] As in the rural parts of England so also in Scotland many of the country clergy were involved in farming, to a degree at times that, in the eyes of their critics at least, interfered with their professional responsibilities. One of the contributory factors was the relative meanness of clerical stipends. The need for augmentation forms a repeated theme of late eighteenth-century records, with individual ministers compelled to take grudging heritors to court in order to secure even a modest increase.[8]

In both countries the growth and movement of population associated with the rise of industrial centres presented yet another set of problems for the territorial establishment in the form of increasingly inadequate church provision for the new sector comprised of the urban poor.

Not surprisingly, given the indifferent performance of the two established churches and the climate of toleration that prevailed during the later years of the eighteenth century, religious alternatives began to claim a significant popular following. Since the 1770s Methodism had been growing rapidly in many parts of England and Wales among marginalized or emerging and often tightly knit occupational groups. Its acceptance was most pronounced in communities that stood outside the normal deference structures of the eighteenth century. Its combination of active membership, vernacular enthusiasm and optimistic theology appealed to those who rejected in a non-political manner the traditional values and institutions of the English ruling classes and sought to throw off the shackles of religious uniformity.[9] During the same period the older and more introspective Dissenting bodies underwent a transformation as they adopted expansionist strategies and applied them to their own inherited system of Calvinistic belief. In Scotland by the turn of the century the various groups of Presbyterian Seceders together numbered 200,000, or approximately 1 in 5 of the population.[10]

The developing crisis for the established clergy that was inherent in these changes in popular religious allegiance was merely accentuated after 1789 by repercussions from the political developments in France. Over the following years tension mounted as republican and anticlerical ideas began to spread through the more politically aware sections of the urban working and middle classes. The overt enthusiasm for French constitutional innovations displayed in 1790 by the London Dissenting minister Richard Price and two years later by rioting crowds in Dundee and Perth, gave way as the decade unfolded to a more sinister, clandestine circulation of republican ideas and anticlerical pamphlets.[11] By 1797 the threat of invasion by France and the reality of landings in Wales and Ireland put Anglican and Presbyterian clergy, as representatives of a beleaguered establishment, firmly onto the defensive.

As part of the developing confrontation during the Revolutionary years between popular belief and established conventions a new phenomenon seared itself into the consciousness of those who sought to defend the status quo. Penetrating even the remotest rural communities came the figure of the lay preacher wielding a Bible and religious tracts, delivering a simple and direct message, if necessary in the open air, and, in some cases, bringing with him an entourage of supporters. Lay-led Sunday schools and cottage meetings sprang up with the result that by the end of the century few villages were completely unaffected by the new wave of aggressively conversionist evangelicalism. The use of itinerant lay preachers was by no means new. In a minor way it had formed part of the English Dissenting tradition since the middle years of the seventeenth century. From the 1740s it had become a central feature of Methodism, but a combination of the geographical limitations of that movement during its earliest phase, the inertia of traditional Dissent and the absence of a political crisis had lessened its impact upon the consciousness of those who supported the establishment. In spite of sporadic mob hostility and the opposition of individual clergy and magistrates there was little sign of general concern about the spread of lay activity before the 1790s.

Traditionally, the employment of lay preaching by English Dissenters for the purposes of evangelism had been extremely limited. Theological constraints and the effects of geographical isolation had confined the energies of most pastors to the spiritual needs of their own congregations. But from the 1770s the influence of Calvinistic Methodism, especially as mediated through the Countess of Huntingdon's college at Trevecca, produced a new concern for evangelism. The model of Trevecca spawned a series of seminaries for the training of men who would unite care for a specific congregation with a continuing ministry to the unchurched in surrounding communities.[12] As a new generation of pastors schooled in itinerant preaching entered the ministry in the 1780s and 1790s, so they in turn encouraged suitable members of their congregations to establish regular preaching stations in neighbouring villages. In this manner centres such as Salisbury and Bedford were reported by the end of the century to be sending out upwards of 50 lay preachers every Sunday. In addition to this local effort, national and regional organizations came into being in most parts of the country with the explicit purpose of financing and promoting the new wave of popular evangelism. This was the largely unsung domestic counterpart of the explosion of interest in overseas missions seen in the years after 1792.

Although Calvinistic Methodists, Independents and Baptists were often prepared to make common cause or display at least some degree of cooperation, the practical separation between them and the followers of Wesley was almost absolute. Nevertheless, the distinction between Arminian and Calvinist preachers was lost upon most critics of the movement. For all practical purposes the two parallel streams of lay activity, with their geographically complementary penetration of the English countryside, coalesced into a single movement. By the turn of the century it offered a significant proportion of the rural population a viable alternative to the clerical services of the established church.

In terms of the new orientation towards the laity Scotland lagged well behind its southern neighbour. This was due in large part to the absence of any tradition of non-Presbyterian Dissent and to the virtual monopoly in northern Calvinism enjoyed by the convention of clerical leadership. Scottish Presbyterianism, with its long tradition of parochial schools, had, even in its dissident forms, laid great emphasis on ministerial education and the formal process of ordination, in a manner that was quite alien to English Dissent. The eighteenth-century Scottish Seceders knew nothing of the fluid pattern of pastoral leadership found in the south, whereby men from even artisan occupations, with little formal education, could occupy a pastoral role while supporting themselves by their own industry. The influence of the southern expansion of lay activity entered Scotland from 1793 onwards through the pages of the London-based *Evangelical Magazine*, closely followed by reports published in its Edinburgh counterpart the *Missionary Magazine*. As letters from southern leaders such as David Bogue, John Newton and George Burder echoed these reports, the first signs of lay evangelism began to appear north of the border. During the spring of 1797 John Campbell, an evangelical ironmonger in Edinburgh's Grassmarket, laid the foundations of a network of Sunday schools that were explicitly independent of the established church. Later the same year an exploratory preaching tour to the North of Scotland was mounted by James Haldane, a wealthy East India merchantman captain, in company with John Aikman, a former colonial businessman. This in turn led to a more permanent commitment to lay evangelism with the creation in January 1798 of the Society for Propagating the Gospel at Home (SPGH), an undenominational body designed to promote preaching and catechizing.[13]

The clerical reaction to the upsurge of lay preaching, though sharp and outspoken, was largely confined to polemics and attempts to influence politicians. It was also surprisingly short-lived. A flurry of episcopal charges sounded the alarm in several English dioceses. In 1798 John Douglas's visitation at Salisbury prompted a bitter local pamphlet war; a three-sided debate between Anglican clergy, orthodox Dissenting ministers and a Unitarian clothier.[14] Elsewhere a number of clerical tracts maintained the atmosphere of crisis whilst George Pretyman, bishop of Lincoln, attempted unsuccessfully to secure restrictive legislation. Other reactions were purely local, consisting of efforts to hamper individual preachers in the execution of their self-appointed tasks. In Scotland the more centralized character of the established church produced a more concerted reaction. As with Pretyman's initiative, leading clergymen including William Porteous of Glasgow and George Hill of St Andrews sought to persuade politicians of the need to act. More significantly, however, the General Assembly took action in response to anxious overtures received from regional synods. Having debated the matter at length it passed a Declaratory Act in May 1799 closing its pulpits to unlicensed preachers. At the same time it issued a *Pastoral Admonition* to be read out in every parish church warning of the activities of unauthorized lay missionaries. Finally, it initiated a thorough enquiry into the qualifications of those involved throughout the country in the teaching of the young. The actions of the Assembly prompted an exchange of tracts and drew into the discussion representatives of most shades of Protestant opinion.

At the heart of the clerical complaint about lay preaching lay the conviction that it affected vital principles of Christian belief and practice. This was expressed in two different but essentially related allegations: the creation of schism and the undermining of church order. Anglican polemic against the intruders turned repeatedly to the accusation that by coming uninvited into parishes the itinerants brought schism to the heart of Christian society. The charge of schism did not simply imply the introduction of divisions into the church, it also embraced the concept of a valid ministry. It was no coincidence that most of the Anglican strictures against village preaching issued from high churchmen. For them, even in the days prior to the Oxford Movement, any departure from a strict respect for apostolic ordination represented a fatal compromising of the church's integrity. In a sermon delivered in 1792 in four of the Oxford churches, Edward Tatham, rector of Lincoln College, warned against the contemporary spate of ignorant and self-ordained teachers 'who, under the appearance of religion, would disturb our happiness in this world by undermining the Church which is apostolical' and who 'instead of a Catholic faith uniformly professed, would introduce Heresies and Schisms'.[15] Elaborating on this theme Richard Mant, rector of All Saints, Southampton, noted the irony that Methodists with their sensitivity over matters of doctrine could be so callous in causing schism.[16]

Though the Scottish Presbyterian clergy lacked the same emphasis on apostolic succession and rarely mentioned the term schism, they believed strongly that lay preaching struck at the heart of church order. In its conventional expression this was simply the conviction that those who assumed clerical duties without being regularly ordained were undermining accepted norms, flouting ecclesiastical authority and challenging the hegemony of the established church. For those holding evangelical views, however, the issue was more theological. John Jamieson, a leading Edinburgh Antiburgher, and John Robertson, the assistant parish minister of Cambuslang, both regarded a formal call to ministry and ordination as indispensable to a church that was constituted on biblical lines. Both were at pains in their refutation of lay preaching to deny that any general sanction for the practice could be found in the apostolic church. Where it had occurred it had been validated by exceptional gifts imparted by the Holy Spirit.[17] In Robertson's eyes the New Testament laid great importance on the work of the ministry. It linked the government of the church to those who preached.[18] Consequently, any concession to the practice of lay preaching undermined the biblical basis of church order. Both men operated with a model of the church that was essentially static, and in that respect differed markedly from champions of lay itinerancy such as Rowland Hill. They believed that the peripatetic Anglican minister of London's Surrey Chapel was advocating a perpetual revolutionary government in the church that, by overthrowing the office of public teacher, would prompt a return to arbitrary authority and ultimately lead to unbelief.[19]

The opposition of the Scottish evangelical clergy to the new populist evangelicalism and its lay agents was unusual and not mirrored in England by the Clapham Sect. Whereas Wilberforce used his influence in 1800 to prevent

Pretyman's proposed restrictive legislation, and others such as John Newton, the venerable rector of St Mary Woolnoth in the City of London, had long encouraged lay preaching, the members of the Popular party, the Scottish evangelicals, voted unanimously with their Moderate counterparts in 1799 to condemn and oppose the new phenomenon. Their failure to support those who most closely shared their understanding of the faith was roundly castigated by Rowland Hill as reminiscent of the disciples of Jesus who in his hour of danger forsook him and fled.[20]

Disregard for church order and for the apostolic requirement of ordination seemed to issue all too often in what opponents of the home missionary movement regarded as unwarranted and outrageous criticism of the regular clergy. Frequent repetition of this point by spokesmen for the latter suggests a peculiar sensitivity to the idea that men of uncertain provenance should take it upon themselves to question the validity of their ministry. In referring to those who 'set up in opposition to the "dumb dogs" and "blind leaders" of the Church of England' Richard Mant preserved two of the more common epithets used by the lay missionaries.[21] Samuel Horsley expanded a little on the same subject when he suggested that despite their divisions the preachers agreed in abusing the established clergy for being 'negligent of their flocks, cold in their preaching, and destitute of the Spirit'.[22] During the Salisbury controversy John Malham, one of the more outspoken Anglican disputants, took issue with Henry Wansey, the Unitarian defender of itinerancy, for caricaturing the clergy as hunting, shooting, swearing and drinking pluralists who performed their duties perfunctorily and spent their weekdays 'equipt like a jockey in a velvet cap, a huntsman's belt, or buckskin breeches, or a scarlet coat, or some dress quite in the kick of the fashion'.[23]

The Scottish clergy were no less sensitive to criticism but with the onset of lay itinerancy they faced a different type of attack. What distinguished the northern preachers from their southern counterparts was their practice of commenting adversely in public on the doctrinal content of parish sermons. The custom had been initiated by James Haldane in July 1797 when he had commenced an open-air address in the market place at Kirriemuir by contradicting the parish minister. He had proceeded to employ the same approach elsewhere.[24] But by the time the SPGH was founded the following year the practice had been abandoned as counterproductive.[25] By then, however, the damage had been done. Such gratuitous criticism afforded a convenient stick with which to beat the missionary preachers, and unsurprisingly the official voice of the clergy as expressed in the *Pastoral Admonition* accused them of 'studying to alienate the affections of the people from their own pastors'.[26] Pluralism and clerical negligence were one thing; those faults could scarcely be gainsaid. Doctrinal differences were quite another. Given that good men could disagree over doctrine, who were these new arrivals to criticize those who had undergone years of study in theology? As the anonymous but probably clerical author of an imaginary dialogue made his hero say:

> You think if the Word of God contains already all that God has thought fit to make known, the Clergy of the Church of Scotland must not only be as well able to preach it as those whom you call Gospel preachers, but so much the more so as they are men of better education, and have applied themselves more to the study of it.[27]

With tracts as unsympathetic to the church and its clergy as Thomas Paine's *Age of Reason* in wide circulation, and by 1797 readily available even in the smaller Scottish burghs, it is not difficult to see why the regular clergy would associate the criticisms of the preachers with the contemporary growth of anticlericalism.

One of the unavoidable themes of the clerical polemicists is the disdain in which they held their lay rivals. Their criticisms ranged from the alleged self-authorization of the preachers to their wild enthusiasm and lack of learning. When Samuel Horsley applied the derogatory term 'non-descripts' to the hearers gathered by the itinerants he indicated the reason why so many polemicists raised the question of authority. Both audiences and speakers appeared to fall outside any of the existing churches and it was not unreasonable, therefore, to assume that those who conducted the religious assemblies were the assessors of their own vocations. While Anglican high churchmen treated their lack of authority as axiomatic, support for that position came from more surprising quarters. Both orthodox Presbyterians like Jamieson and strict Calvinistic Dissenters such as the English Particular Baptists were inclined to reject the preachers on exactly the same ground: namely, the lack of an explicit call from a church to the work of the ministry.[28] Even the General Assembly referred scornfully to those

> who, assuming the name of missionaries from what they call the Society for Propagating the Gospel at Home, as if they had some special commission from Heaven, are at present going through the land, not confining themselves to particular stations, but acting as universal itinerant teachers, and as superintendents of those who are established the teachers of religion by the Church.[29]

Whether or not the polemic accorded with reality, the style of the preachers was variously described as 'enthusiasm', 'fanaticism' and 'speaking in the power of the Holy Spirit'. No explanation of these terms was offered but, from the use of the word 'ranting' and the emphasis on the preachers' lack of learning, an unfavourable image was created. The impression given was that of wild figures working their hearers into a state of emotional excitement and claiming in the process to be speaking with the freedom and inspiration of the Holy Spirit. William Bowen, one of the Salisbury controversialists described such pretended inspiration as blasphemous.[30] Showing no more sympathy than his clerical contemporary, Richard Mant lumped together with earlier extremists those he referred to as 'the Wesleyans, Whitefieldians, Revivalists, New-itinerants, Swedenborgians, Zinzendorfians, Jumpers, Swadlers, and what not of the methodistical age'. 'London', he added uncharitably, 'is now, as heretofore, the hotbed of these prolific maggots.'[31]

When it came to reviewing the preachers' claim to learning and, therefore, to a possible alternative source of authority, their clerical opponents betrayed a strong sense of professional jealousy. Great emphasis was laid on the lengthy preparation undertaken by the regular clergy and their mastery of the biblical languages – factors that were assumed automatically to undermine claims that they failed to preach the gospel. By way of contrast the lay preachers were represented as ignorant and in some cases almost illiterate. They were described collectively as showing an antipathy towards learning and as having a low level of understanding. In pointing up this difference the clergy believed that no rational observer could fail to see that they constituted the only reliable spiritual and moral guides. In the contest for the allegiance and trust of the rising generation there was only one possible winner: the publicly ordained religious teacher who had traditionally been entrusted with the people's welfare.[32]

As far as the clergy were concerned those who engaged in lay preaching were the wrong sort of people. Though they admitted the existence of pious well-intentioned individuals there were others of an altogether different character. Their very background pointed to their unsuitability. How could artisans successfully transform themselves on a weekly basis into public expositors of the scriptures? Resorting to ridicule John Malham pointed to what he regarded as the ludicrous ostentation of the many working-class preachers in and around the city of Salisbury:

> So numerous are the horses wanted for the purpose of mounting these self-created and self-sufficient preachers, that the regular Ministers are frequently disappointed, if they do not keep horses of their own (which, in these times, very few of the Country Curates can afford); and it is no unusual thing to see the latter trudging through mire and dirt, whilst these Village preachers sally forth and canter along the roads, compelling all before them to make way. Who, indeed, are half so important as themselves! Confined in the week to the shop-board or the lap-stone, or whatever may be their respective occupations, we behold them on the Sunday morning dressed out cap-a-pee, in pantaloons, with shining boots, and glittering spurs, issuing from their retirements to dispense THE WORD, in the villages to which they have been respectively appointed for the day.[33]

The essence of Malham's argument, and of those like him who heaped scorn upon the lowly origins of the preachers, was that by assuming this role in Christian leadership they were flouting the well-established conventions of eighteenth-century society. If any active role were possible for the lay Christian it was simply that of promoting true religion in the station in life in which God had placed them.

Behind the social derision lay the fear of more sinister influences. Legislation had progressively outlawed suspect political activity, but how could those with a vested interest in maintaining constitutional stability be sure that the emerging networks of village preaching and Sunday schools were not being used as cover for the dissemination of republican and atheistic ideas? Across a broad swathe of clergy from English high churchmen such as Tatham and Horsley to the General Assembly, and even to those like Porteous within the Popular party, deep suspicions were entertained. A number of writers suggested that among the preachers disaffected elements were working to dissolve the traditional bonds of social cohesion. They despised the king, sought to destroy patriotic feeling and hoped ultimately to overturn the government. In 1799 both the *Pastoral Admonition* and the rector of Chislehurst in Kent voiced the fear that Samuel Horsley was to develop the following year in his pastoral charge to the clergy of the Rochester diocese: the belief that the associational structure to which many of the preachers belonged was a device to foster subversion and connect apparently innocuous religious gatherings with the world of clandestine politics.[34] In one or two Anglican clerical outpourings there was even a further suggestion that the popular preaching of the 1790s was an atavistic development reminiscent of the 1640s.[35] As the advocates of puritanism had done away with Charles I so the new religious dissenters contemplated the ending of the monarchy. The onslaught on the clergy was simply the prelude to a wider attack on the ancien régime, as the recent events in France suggested. However, despite the efforts of the pamphleteers and attempts by individual English and Scottish churchmen to influence politicians, their arguments failed to carry the day. The power of the church was fading and the lay preachers were seen by most people for what they really were: at times uncouth and ill-educated, frequently given to a more emotional version of Christianity than the higher social classes found appealing but, as far as the future of the country was concerned, essentially harmless.

The response to the clerical onslaught was conducted in what was, for the main part, a quiet and dignified manner. However, one or two of the apologists adopted a more robust attitude, while the maverick Anglican clergyman Rowland Hill, as befitted someone whose social background had never equipped him for deference, contributed his own unique blend of sarcasm, barbed humour and penetrating insight. Most of the apologetic, as might be expected, came not from the lay preachers themselves but from the pens of Dissenting ministers who sympathized with them and in most cases took part in similar activity. Though the itinerants undoubtedly made uncomplimentary references to individuals, it was left to the apologists to construct a coherent case against the parish clergy. That case went far beyond the general apportioning of blame. Niel Douglas, a Relief Church minister from Dundee, was dismissive of those Argyllshire clergy he encountered during a missionary tour of the western Highlands in the summer of 1797. Though they performed their duty, it was undertaken in a lifeless manner that did little to quell popular dissatisfaction. Describing the clergy as hirelings, he referred to the preaching of barren, moralizing discourses and to prayers that the parishioners knew by heart.[36] There were, however, two complicating factors affecting this assessment. As a Seceder with strong democratic leanings, he lacked any real sympathy for established religion and its close ties to the landed aristocracy. Second, while most of the inhabitants of Argyll spoke Gaelic, his own native tongue, the majority of the established clergy lacked even a basic fluency in the language and, as creatures of their landed patrons, had little basis for rapport with their parishioners. Not surprisingly, when shortly afterwards the SPGH sent one of its preachers into the area, the nucleus of a thriving Dissenting congregation was soon established.

At the opposite end of the country a similar criticism of the many sermons that were purchased commercially was voiced by the Salisbury clothier, Henry Wansey. Such meagre fare, he suggested, would not satisfy those who were hungry for the bread of life. The clergy were presented as a body of men who increasingly preferred their leisure pursuits to their duties and sought to turn the work of God into a sinecure.[37] In typically outspoken manner Rowland Hill replied to Samuel Horsley's slur on the political loyalty of the new undenominational Sunday schools by suggesting a radical solution to the church's exodus of worshippers. He argued that the bishop would do better to replace the '*dapper bucks and blades*', who were 'whipt through [the] universities [and] against their wills . . . thrust into the church', with some of the 'pious, rational, prudent young men' who staffed the Sunday schools. All they required was a little further education to fit them for office.[38]

In one case, that of the inflammatory sermon against itinerant preachers delivered in Oxford by Edward Tatham, the author was taken to task quite bluntly by a Wesleyan minister, Joseph Benson. The Methodist, incensed by Tatham's clerical arrogance and unwarranted allegations of political disloyalty, took particular exception to his prostitution of the ministerial character in stirring up mob violence against a peaceful congregation of Dissenters within the city.[39] But strong personal comment of that type was the exception rather than the rule. More typical of the general run of apologetic was the attitude to the clergy adopted by William Kingsbury, minister of Above Bar Independent church in Southampton. Recognizing the extent of clerical deficiency, he attributed the weakness of the Church of England to the sharp discrepancy between the sermons preached by its clergy and the articles and homilies of the church. Quoting contemporary bishops in support of his analysis he suggested that the church must return to the doctrinal preaching of leaders like Bishop Jewel. When pure doctrine was once again heard from the parish pulpits and was matched by consistent clerical behaviour, popular respect would return and the village preachers would disappear.[40] Rowland Hill made a similar point in his reply to the bishop of Rochester. He perceptively pointed out that very few people ever became Dissenters by conviction.[41]

Believing, as he did, that the real problem confronting the two established churches was not the external threat posed by lay preachers, but rather the existence of many unconverted and unspiritual clergy within their own ranks, Hill proposed a new concept of Christian ministry, one that would comprehend the lay itinerants. He rejected the contemporary process of ministerial education and selection, seeing it as responsible for producing men who were bred to the work of the ministry as to a trade. Such individuals, he believed, were bound to prove unsatisfactory. Instead, selection and ordination needed to be seen as a human ratification of a prior, divine appointment. Those who possessed the Holy Spirit's gifts for ministry were those whom the church should call. The old professional attitudes and jealousies had no place in such a view of gospel ministry. Rather, all potential pastors should first be encouraged to try out their gifts in an informal manner as village preachers.[42] This was the authentic voice of the new movement. It made no attempt to undermine the concept of a settled pastoral ministry or to decry its importance. But it rejected the essential distinction between clergy and laity. Both categories were regarded as united scripturally and indissolubly in the work of ministry. James Haldane in principle rejected the term 'laity' as a popish distinction, though for practical purposes he continued to use it, since its meaning was so widely understood.[43]

Where the critics of the lay movement spoke of self-appointment and self-authorization, defenders emphasized the careful manner in which preachers and catechists were chosen. Classically, the selection of an individual for such a task was made by the pastor and members of the congregation and involved a careful trial of gifts. The new itinerant societies took equal care in their choice of personnel, formulating rules for continuing supervision. As the movement progressed, a pattern developed whereby selection for village preaching was linked to a period of training at one of the new evangelical seminaries. In this manner the students who received a basic biblical and homiletic education in the series of academy classes sponsored by Robert Haldane in Glasgow, Edinburgh and Dundee between 1799 and 1808 provided the personnel for the extensive network of preaching and catechizing mounted by the SPGH. In this respect the slurs of the critics were unjustified. But it would not be possible to suggest that lay preachers never acted in a self-authorized capacity. One surviving tract indicates that it was by no means unknown for individuals to neglect to seek the authorization of their local congregation.[44] Those involved often appear to have been upwardly mobile self-improvers and, in an age when older congregations tended to be affected by a legacy of introspection, it would not be surprising if in some cases the allegations of self-selection were justified.

One of the most strenuously resisted of the clergy's claims was that the preachers were prompted by political motives. Almost every apologist sought in some way to refute this allegation. When the bishop of Salisbury suggested that the village preachers were responsible for spreading the false but prevalent philosophy of the times, Henry Wansey insisted that he had chosen the wrong target; that infidelity and atheism were deeply entrenched within the established church. Though he assured the bishop that he had no wish to see the contemporary prosperity of religious dissent founded upon the ruins of the Church of England, he allowed himself the provocative observation that there was as much vital religion in Revolutionary France as there had been during the previous century.[45] William Kingsbury, from his more orthodox evangelical perspective, emphasized the benevolent and wholly religious character of village preaching. Contrary to the accusations made by William Bowen, one of the Salisbury clergy, the village preachers had no secret agenda to subvert the established church or to deceive the populace with covert political designs. Nor was the attempted historical parallel with seventeenth-century regicide a sustainable one. It had been Parliament and not the early Dissenters who had determined the fate of Charles I.[46] In Scotland the SPGH and its promoters repudiated the political charge vigorously. Under the rules of the society lay agents were expressly forbidden to speak on political matters.[47] Apart from one incautious speech by Robert Haldane in 1792 during the early, constitutional stages of the French Revolution, and before his own association with evangelical religion, there was never any evidence of political involvement by those involved in village preaching in Scotland. In his response to the *Pastoral Admonition* Rowland Hill implied that the General Assembly had used the political smear as a tactical device for hitting back at a movement that posed a challenge to its religious control.[48] Responding later to Samuel Horsley's suggestions of secrecy surrounding the new itinerant societies and Sunday schools, Hill commended the transparency employed by the agents of evangelicalism. Nothing was done secretly. The meetings were open to any that wished to attend. The associations simply existed to defray the inevitable costs. The true Christian remained aloof from politics, believing that mere political revolution would accomplish little.[49]

In place of the static understanding of the church shared by the established clergy, Dissenters and Seceders, the apologists were proposing a dynamic model that was equipped to deal with a changing and increasingly irreligious society. The new concept was unashamedly pragmatic. Neither William Kingsbury nor his Chippenham colleague Samuel Clift regarded the use of laymen as preferable to evangelism carried out by trained ministers. Both merely noted that the scale of operations required was far beyond the physical capabilities of the latter. In their apologetic they were at pains to point out that the focus of the lay preachers was the genuinely irreligious sector of society. Their aim was to promote vital religion rather than Dissent, and therefore they looked for converts rather than proselytes. With that in mind,

Clift argued that there was no permanence about the preaching; he would be happy if, as a result of the work, the parish churches revived. Accordingly, the bishop was invited to examine the moral revolution already under way in the villages.[50] Of course, such arguments were misleading. Territorial churches and their clergy by nature admitted no rivals. Equally, as converts were made, meetings for preaching and prayer assumed a life of their own. During the confrontation between the clergy and the preachers, principle came into conflict with practical necessity.

Given the ephemeral nature of many of the organizations that supported lay preaching and the brevity of the period in which itinerancy dominated ecclesiastical relations, it is necessary to ask whether the confrontation between clergy and laity amounted to anything more than a passing phenomenon. How far was the upsurge of clerical anxiety a reaction to the social and political tension of the Revolutionary period? Alternatively, to what extent did it reflect permanent adjustments in the ecclesiastical landscape? Samuel Clift had declared with undoubted sincerity his own willingness to see the converts of village preaching find a home within a revitalized parish-church network. Both he and Kingsbury had suggested that the ultimate beneficiary of the preachers' labours would be the Church of England. In practice, as far as England and Wales were concerned, the period of village preaching at the turn of the century witnessed the foundations laid for the vast nineteenth-century expansion of Nonconformity. Only in Scotland might the efforts of the preachers be judged to have had relatively little permanent effect. Having commenced with a flourish and fielded over the course of 10 years the extraordinary number of 300 preachers, the SPGH ceased its work in an inglorious climate of personal recrimination in 1808. At that point an evangelistic movement, which had penetrated some of the remotest rural communities and overcome the linguistic barrier of the Highlands, declined into the relative obscurity of modern Scottish Independency: a persistent but minor tradition within the Scottish church. As with Methodism in southern France, evangelical Dissent failed to flourish in the Scottish setting because the available social crevices for alternative forms of religion were either too narrow or unreceptive. The dominant form of Protestantism in Scotland, namely Presbyterianism, flourished in both established and non-established forms. By contrast the Independency of the village preachers was an exotic plant which failed to thrive in the way that it did south of the border.[51]

If it has been established that the appearance of the lay preachers signified anything more than a temporary response to a political and social crisis, the nature of that significance has still to be determined. Contemporary clerical commentators noted the importance of the territorial clergy in maintaining the structure and integrity of the ancien régime. As the old order faded and with it the unitary Christian state, new opportunities for the individual expression of church allegiance presented themselves. The spirit of democracy and the questioning of the priestly role led to a profound re-evaluation of the relationship between clergy and laity and the limits of their respective spheres. It is significant that over the decades following the lay-preaching controversy the traditional powers of the established clergy were progressively eroded. In this period, even within the established churches, the influence of the laity grew stronger as opportunities multiplied for the adoption of an active role.

Although the apologists were at pains throughout the most sensitive period of activity to emphasize the benign character of the village preachers and their readiness to support those clergy that faithfully performed their duties, there is a sense in which their opponents had always been correct. The rise of lay preaching, by virtue of its intrusion into the territory and prerogatives of the clergy could be regarded, albeit within the religious sphere, as a manifestation of the contemporary spirit of anticlericalism.

Notes

1 J.N. Wall (ed.) *George Herbert The Country Parson, The Temple*, London: SPCK, 1981, p. 75.
2 *Scots Magazine* 63, 1801, 389.
3 S. Horsley, *The Charges of Samuel Horsley LL.D. F.R.S. F.A.S. Late Lord Bishop of St Asaph, delivered at his several visitations of the dioceses of St David's, Rochester and St Asaph*, London, 1830, pp. 108–9.
4 M. Smith, *Religion in Industrial Society Oldham and Saddleworth 1740–1865*, Oxford: Clarendon Press, 1994, pp. 32–62.
5 For example, the 1794 return for the parish of Kenninghall in the Norwich diocese records a quarterly celebration of communion attended by between 20 and 30 parishioners. The parish consisted of 128 houses with none of the inhabitants being members of any other religious body than the Church of England. Norfolk County Record Office VIS/35d.
6 J. MacInnes, *The Evangelical Movement in the Highlands of Scotland: 1688 to 1800*, Aberdeen: University Press, 1951, p. 118.
7 D. Sage, *Memorabilia Domestica; or, parish life in the North of Scotland*, Wick, 1889, p. 53. According to James Haldane, a vociferous lay critic of Nicolson, the 2,000 parishioners of Thurso in 1797 had not been catechized by the parish minister during the previous 40 years. J.A. Haldane, *Journal of a Tour through the Northern Counties of Scotland and the Orkney Isles in Autumn 1797. Undertaken with a view to promote the knowledge of the gospel of Jesus Christ*, Edinburgh, 1798, p. 74.
8 See, for example, *Edinburgh Evening Courant*, 7 Aug. 1797, 3 Mar. 1798, 11 Feb. 1799. The heritors or lesser landowners of a parish were responsible for paying the minister's stipend and maintaining church buildings. Eighteenth-century presbytery records record numerous disputes between minister and heritors over the non-fulfilment of their financial obligations.
9 A.D. Gilbert, 'Religion and political stability in early industrial England', in P.K. O'Brien and R. Quinault (eds) *The Industrial Revolution and British Society*, Cambridge: Cambridge University Press, 1993, p. 89; D. Hempton, *The Religion of the People: Methodism and popular religion c. 1750–1900*, London: Routledge, 1996, p. 26.
10 M. Fry, *The Dundas Despotism*, Edinburgh: Edinburgh University Press, 1992, p. 182.
11 R. Price, *A Discourse on the Love of Our Country*, London, 1790, pp. 41–2; H.W.

Meikle, *Scotland and the French Revolution*, Glasgow: James Maclehose, 1912, pp. 96–7. Thomas Paine's Deist and anticlerical tract 'The Age of Reason', published in 1794–5, was in circulation in places such as Forfar in 1797. See Haldane, *Journal*, p. 40.

12 Two such examples would be the academy founded by David Bogue, the Independent pastor at Gosport in Hampshire, and the evangelical seminary at Newport Pagnell in Buckinghamshire, presided over by William Bull.

13 For the details of its founding and objectives, see *An Account of the Proceedings of the Society for Propagating the Gospel at Home, from their commencement, December 28. 1797, to May 16. 1799*, Edinburgh, 1799.

14 D.J. Jeremy, 'A local crisis between Establishment and Nonconformity: the Salisbury village preaching controversy, 1798–1799', *Wiltshire Archaeological and Natural History Magazine* 61, 1966, 63–84.

15 E. Tatham, *A Sermon Suitable to the Times*, London, 1792, p. 15.

16 R. Mant, *Puritanism Revived; or Methodism as old as the great rebellion*, London, 1808, p. 7.

17 J. Jamieson, *Remarks on the Rev. Rowland Hill's Journal, &c. in a letter to the author: including reflections on itinerant and lay preaching*, Edinburgh, 1799, pp. 51–2; J. Robertson, *Lay-preaching Indefensible on Scripture Principles; being remarks on the sacred history of the apostles. With a view to ascertain what principles of church government are therein contained; and who have a right to preach the gospel*, Glasgow, 1800, pp. 51–2.

18 Robertson, *Lay-preaching Indefensible*, p. 70.

19 Ibid. pp. 90–1; Jamieson, *Remarks*, p. 86.

20 R. Hill, *A Series of Letters occasioned by the late Pastoral Admonition of the Church of Scotland*, Edinburgh, 1799, p. 42.

21 Mant, *Puritanism Revived*, p. 32.

22 Horsley, *Charges*, p. 104.

23 A Country Curate [John Malham], *Remarks on a Letter to the Bishop of Salisbury, on his late Charge to the Clergy of his Diocese: by H.W. of Salisbury, a Dissenter. With some cursory hints in defence of the inferior clergy*, Salisbury, 1798, pp. 20–1.

24 Haldane, *Journal*, pp. 39–40 and passim.

25 SPGH *Account*, p. 82.

26 *Acts of the General Assembly of the Church of Scotland 1638–1842*, Edinburgh, 1843, p. 871.

27 Anon., *Tabernaclism; or, a dialogue between a country gentleman and one of his work-people, who had been led away from the church, under the pretext of hearing the gospel and attending evangelical preachers*, Glasgow, 1802, p. 8.

28 Jamieson, *Remarks*, pp. 49, 52–3; J. Edwards, *Stubborn Facts; or, a plain statement of the proceedings of a Particular Baptist church with respect to two of their members, who were found guilty of praying, reading and expounding the scriptures, in the villages, under the patronage of the London Itinerant Society, without a regular call to the work of the ministry*, London, 1808.

29 *Acts of the General Assembly*, p. 871.

30 A Clergyman in the Diocese of Salisbury [W. Bowen], *An Appeal to the People on the Alleged Causes of the Dissenters' Separation from the Established Church: to which are subjoined a few cautionary observations, in respect to their present political views*, Salisbury, 1798, p. 5.

31 Mant, *Puritanism Revived*, p. 3.

32 Anon., *Tabernaclism*, pp. 13–14.

33 J. Malham, *A Broom for the Conventicle: or, the arguments for village preaching examined, and fairly discussed*, Salisbury, 1798, p. 54.

34 *Acts of the General Assembly*, p. 871; F. Wollaston, *A Country Parson's Address to his Flock, to caution them against being misled by the wolf in sheep's cloathing, or receiving Jacobin teachers of sedition, who intrude themselves under the specious pretense of instructing youth and preaching Christianity*, London, 1799, pp. 29–31; Horsley, *Charges*, pp. 102–5.

35 Bowen, *Appeal*, pp. 33–5; Mant, *Puritanism Revived*, pp. 32–4.

36 N. Douglas, *Journal of a Mission to part of the Highlands of Scotland, in Summer and Harvest 1797, by appointment of the Relief Synod*, Edinburgh, 1799, p. 14.

37 H. W[ansey]., *A Letter to the Bishop of Salisbury on his late Charge to the Clergy of his Diocese*, Salisbury, 1798, pp. 4–5.

38 R. Hill, *An Apology for Sunday Schools*, London, n.d. [c. 1801], p. 42n.

39 J. Benson, *A Defence of the Methodists, in five letters, addressed to the Rev. Dr Tatham*, 2nd edn, London, 1793, pp. 37–8.

40 W. Kingsbury, *An Apology for Village Preachers*, Southampton, 1798, pp. 32–5.

41 Hill, *Apology*, p. 33n.

42 R. Hill, *Journal of a Tour through the North of England and parts of Scotland with . . . some remarks on the propriety of what is called lay and itinerant preaching*, London, 1799, pp. 139–61.

43 Haldane, *Journal of a Tour*, p. 5n.

44 Edwards, *Stubborn Facts*, p. v.

45 W[ansey]., *Letter*, pp. 2–3, 23–4.

46 Kingsbury, *Apology*, pp. 23–9.

47 SPGH *Account*, p. 14.

48 Hill, *Letters*, pp. 8–9.

49 Hill, *Apology*, pp. 36, 40–1.

50 Kingsbury, *Apology*, pp. v–vi, 11, 31, 51–4; S. Clift, *An Incidental Letter, Addressed to the Lord Bishop of Sarum, August the 9th, 1798, the day of his visitation held at Chippenham, Wilts. With some observations and reflections in favour of village preaching*, Chippenham, n.d. [1798], pp. 4–7, 12.

51 Cf. Hempton on Methodism in France: *Religion of the People*, pp. 20–1.

Chapter 9

National churches, gathered churches, and varieties of lay evangelicalism, 1735–1859

Mark A. Noll

For introducing the complex situation of the laity within Anglo-American evangelicalism during the eighteenth and nineteenth centuries, it is useful to begin with a series of specific incidents. A handful of such snapshots cannot establish reliable generalizations for a religious movement that appeared in many different shapes throughout the many different localities of the North Atlantic region. Yet a few incidents can underscore the fact that questions about the role of the laity were central to the unfolding course of evangelical history.

In February 1749 Jonathan Edwards informed his church – the congregational 'Church of Christ' in Northampton, Massachusetts – that he was reversing the church's long-standing policy of permitting all respectable members of the community, even those who had not made a profession of saving faith, to come to the Lord's supper and present their children for baptism.[1] Even before the cooling of revival fires in the early 1740s, Edwards had begun to question the wisdom of this traditional practice. And so he announced a change: only those who could make a convincing profession of having been acted upon by God's grace, with the pastor (Edwards himself) as the judge of what was convincing, would be admitted to full membership and be allowed the use of the sacraments for themselves and their children. In response Edwards's congregation was enraged. They resented the monopoly he claimed for himself in deciding who was convincingly converted. They resented even more their loss of the right to baptism, which almost all members of the community had sought for their children. In June 1750, after a council of neighbouring ministers judged that differences between Edwards and his church were irreconcilable, the congregation voted by a 10 to 1 majority to dismiss him as their pastor.

The cross-currents in this situation were poignant. This was the Jonathan Edwards who in 1737 had published *A Faithful Narrative of the Surprising Work of God in the Conversion of Many Hundred Souls . . .*, a report on revival in his Northampton parish during late 1734 and early 1735 that was one of the first important books of modern evangelicalism. It was the same Jonathan Edwards whose numerous theological treatises during the 1740s had provided the most discriminatingly effective apology for the evangelical Great Awakening. But in 1750 the laity of Northampton, acting to defend what they considered the time-honoured privileges of an inherited religion, unceremoniously dismissed as their pastor the leading theologian of early evangelicalism.

A second incident illustrates a similarly complex situation. On 8 May 1807 the approximately 110 students who attended the opening session of the summer semester at the College of New Jersey in Princeton were summoned to hear a stern speech. Six weeks earlier a clamorous student riot had led to the suspension of over half the student body and a temporary closing of the college. The man who addressed the students at the start of the new session was Elias Boudinot (1740–1821), whom a biographer has justly described as 'without a peer . . . the foremost Christian layman of the United States'.[2] Boudinot, an influential lawyer, governmental official and Christian philanthropist, had been baptized by George Whitefield. He earned renown in the struggle for American independence by serving as George Washington's chief officer for the care and exchange of military prisoners. He became a mainstay in New Jersey's delegation to the U.S. Congress and later served for 10 years as the Director of the United States Mint. Boudinot's religious and philanthropic activities were even more notable than his political accomplishments. He was a long-serving trustee of the College of New Jersey at a time when Princeton was known for its evangelical commitments. He was active in his own Presbyterian denomination, but also avidly supported religious and benevolent projects sponsored by the broader religious community. In 1816 he became the first president of the American Bible Society. In his will he designated benefactions for Princeton College, Princeton Theological Seminary, the Presbyterian Church, the New Jersey Bible Society (to buy spectacles for the elderly), several local agencies for the poor, Magdalen societies in New York and Philadelphia, the American Board of Commissioners for Foreign Missions, the Moravian Indian mission, and a number of Indian schools. As an older man he ventured into print with several works, including a vigorous rebuttal of Tom Paine's rationalism entitled *The Age of Revelation: or the Age of Reason shewn to be an age of infidelity* (1801).

To the students in 1807 this active Christian layman spoke a message of inflexible subordination:

> In your Situation therefore, beloved Youths! submission is honor – not submission to despotism, which you need not apprehend, but deference to authority, exercised under the guardianship and controul of those, who in the place of your natural Parents, regard your improvement, as essential to their happiness; and as Patriots connect your acquirements with the dearest interests and highest destiny of our Country . . . The only reward we look for next to the approbation of our consciences and our God, is a love of Order on your part, a respectful deference to lawful Authority . . .[3]

In 1807 at evangelical Princeton, lay status signalled nothing about social outlook or attitudes towards democratic procedure. In that place and moment it was as easy for the layman Elias Boudinot to enforce social stratification and deference to a prescribed structure of authority as it once had been for Christian clerics throughout the European world.

The next incident concerns two of Ontario's great religious leaders of the nineteenth century – the Methodist Egerton Ryerson (1803–82) and the Anglican John Strachan (1778–1867).[4] Strachan, who eventually became the bishop of Toronto, was Ontario's most active proponent of an Anglican establishment as the necessary vehicle for creating a Christian civilization in the Canadian wilderness. Ryerson came to public attention in 1826 when he published a fierce rebuttal to a statement of such principles from Strachan. During his funeral address for the first Anglican bishop of Quebec, Strachan had unleashed a few shafts at the Methodists, who were, in his opinion,

> uneducated itinerant preachers, who leaving their steady employment, betake themselves to preaching the Gospel from idleness, or a zeal without knowledge, by which they are induced without any preparation, to teach what they do not know, and which from pride, they disdain to learn.

Ryerson did not take this assault lying down. When he responded, he stated explicitly what was wrong with Strachan's idea of religion. 'Our savior,' wrote Ryerson, 'never intimated the union of his church with the civil polity of any country.' Anglican ritual, to Ryerson, was 'all pompous panegyric'. What Canadians needed was what a high and dry Anglicanism could not provide. They needed passionate 'preaching the gospel' for repentance and conversion. To Strachan the establishment of religion and control exercised by a selected hierarchy were interlocking keys for creating a Christian society. To Ryerson, by contrast, that goal was approached much more effectively through the camp meeting and the democratization of religious authority. It seemed, in other words, to be a classic stand-off between the older Protestant establishmentarianism and the newer evangelicalism.

Yet between the mid-1820s and the incident in question in the early 1840s significant shifts took place in Upper Canadian religion. As the Methodists grew rapidly and as a never-ending series of complications impeded Strachan's push for an Anglican establishment, tempers cooled and former antagonists began to drift closer to each other. Methodists, who once had built inconspicuous halls for their mostly uneducated circuit riders, now began to construct stately cathedrals that dominated the urban landscape. Increasingly they were presided over by ministers who enjoyed the privileges of elite higher education. For their part, Anglicans, who once had built churches resembling official government structures, now began to construct buildings that looked like parish churches from an idealized rural England.

For both Methodists and Anglicans the move was from a segregation of spiritual and secular forces towards their integration.

This confluence of Methodist and Anglican interests set the stage for the first face-to-face meeting between Strachan the hierarch and Ryerson the evangelical. It took place in February 1842 when Ryerson, returning from Kingston to Coburg, found himself unexpectedly thrown together in a coach with Bishop Strachan. As Ryerson and Strachan chatted during their long ride, they were surprised to discover how well they got along. And they did more than simply exchange pleasantries. The Methodists, under Ryerson's leadership, had just obtained provincial approval for transforming their denominational academy into Victoria College. During this journey, Strachan gave Ryerson some advice on how to tap proceeds from the Clergy Reserves, land that had earlier been designated for the support of Protestantism, to fund the Methodists' new college. Neither Strachan nor Ryerson wanted to give up the distinctive contribution of their respective traditions, but each found it relatively easy to integrate his own concerns with those of a former opponent, while together promoting the place of religion in Ontario society. After long service to the Methodist cause, Ryerson became the director of public education in Ontario where he strove to infuse the province's schools with a full measure of Protestant values. From a situation where Ryerson's red-hot evangelicalism had drawn the scorn of Strachan for its use of 'uneducated itinerant preachers', Canadian Methodism had evolved into a religion that now promoted its own version of educational and ecclesiastical hierarchy.

An Upper Canadian contemporary of Strachan and Ryerson was Isaac Buchanan, a Lowland Scot who in the 1830s emigrated to North America in order to pursue opportunities for economic betterment. Through a long and active Canadian business career he nonetheless remained an earnest practitioner of the evangelical Presbyterianism of his youth. Along with many Scots of his day, age, social location and religion, he looked upon Canada as an extension of Scotland and so transferred religious expectations easily from the Old World to the New. One of the pieces of ecclesiastical baggage that Buchanan brought with him from Scotland to Upper Canada was the conviction that church–state establishments were not only permissible but in fact essential for the well-being of faith and society. This conviction he maintained in the New World, even after the Canadian Presbyterian Church divided in imitation of the division in Scotland between Free and Kirk Presbyterians that took place in 1843. It was not until Buchanan, on trips back to the old country, heard arguments from members of the Scottish Free Church attacking church–state establishment, and not until he also applied to ecclesiastical life arguments absorbed in Britain about the virtues of free trade, that he changed his opinion on ecclesiastical establishments. To quote a fine doctoral thesis on Buchanan:

It was in Britain that he first spoke out against church establishment and argued for the complete financial separation of church and state. Only later did he suggest that the granting of financial assistance to religion was as incorrect in the Canadas as it was in the homeland.[5]

For the layman Isaac Buchanan, the impetus for ecclesiastical emancipation of the laity arose not from the democratic levelling of the New World but from the cantankerous church history of the Old.

For the northern, urban United States the 1857–8 'Businessmen's Revival' has been widely regarded as a breakthrough for the evangelical laity. A contemporary observer wrote in 1858 that, 'In all former revivals, the hidden aggregated power of a thoroughly awakened laity was not known.' By contrast, this awakening 'has been conducted by laymen. It began with them . . . Clergymen share in the conduct [of its meetings], but no more than laymen, and as much as if they were laymen.'[6] In fact, the fame of the 1857–8 American awakening, reports of which played a role in sparking the memorable Ulster revival of 1859, lay partially in reversing earlier stereotypes. Those stereotypes featured women and clergymen as the chief agents of spirituality and the world of business as indifferent to faith. Now, however, laymen were leading prayers at noontime meetings within the business districts, while women and clergymen mostly watched from the sidelines. For a history of the laity within evangelicalism an intriguing exchange was taking place. Previously quiescent laymen found their voice but the cost was the silencing of laywomen. Although as many women as men attended the public meetings of the 1857–8 revival, and although during these years more women than men joined the churches that most actively promoted revival, both conductors of public meetings and later historians mostly excluded the women. In New York City and several other sites of well-covered activity, women were prohibited altogether from speaking before mixed audiences as a way of avoiding one of the 'controverted points' that divided American evangelicals of the time. Popular histories of the revival likewise focused almost exclusively on the laymen who came to the fore during its unfolding and left the many women who participated out of the account. The evangelical revival of 1857–8 thus witnessed a dramatic expansion of lay activity but also a considerable contraction.

The final incident comes from outside evangelicalism. Orestes Brownson (1803–76), after a long search through many of the United States' religions and philanthropies, entered the Catholic Church in 1844. Some of the stages he passed through in that pilgrimage were evangelical but, once he entered the Catholic Church, he became a fixed critic of evangelical practices as both deficient in religion and harmful to civilization. To be sure, during the American Civil War he championed the northern cause as compatible with both civilization and true religion. Yet afterwards he came to doubt the compatibility between American civilization and the principles of the Catholic

Church. Brownson's disillusionment with American society eventually became severe, but that disillusionment also reflected his first-hand experience of the evangelical and reformist faiths that had flourished so strikingly in the United States. In 1870 he wrote,

> I defend the republican form of government for our country, because it is the legal and only practicable form, but I no longer hope anything from it. Catholicity is theoretically compatible with democracy . . . but practically, there is, in my judgment, no compatibility between them. According to Catholicity all power comes from above and descends from high to low; according to democracy all power is infernal, is from below, and ascends from low to high. This is democracy in its practical sense, as politicians & the people do & will understand it. Catholicity & it are as mutually antagonistic as the spirit & the flesh, the Church and the World, Christ & Satan.[7]

For Orestes Brownson, wide experience with lay-energized, egalitarian, and freedom-loving forms of evangelical religion demonstrated their evil effects on society, even as they highlighted a contrast between the false faith of democratic evangelicalism and the One True Church.

Although all of these incidents come from North America, it would have been possible to select a similar range of episodes from Britain that not only revealed the reality of expanded lay activity in evangelical history, but also the complexity of that lay religion.[8] As suggested by these incidents, connections between the rise of the laity and the rise of evangelicalism were never simple nor predictable. Yet these phenomena were nonetheless twin developments in Anglo-American religion from the early eighteenth century to the mid-nineteenth. Evangelical impulses played a large role in several religious transformations that measurably expanded the place and function of lay-people in the churches. Evangelical understandings of the church and of Christian work likewise opened extensive fresh opportunities for the expansion of lay agency. Evangelicals also successfully adapted themselves to major transformations in secular society that further promoted the activity of the laity.

Notwithstanding these multiplied connections, the relationship between evangelical history and the history of the Protestant laity in North Atlantic societies was never entirely simple. New exhorters, managers, secretaries, itinerants, agents and preachers – like new presbyters of a previous century – could act in ways remarkably similar to old priests. Vibrant evangelical expansion sometimes occurred under the direction of autocratic church aristocrats. Laywomen experienced the transformations of religious life differently from laymen. Opportunities for lay initiative rose and fell in response to local conditions as well as to widely spread general trends in religion and theology.

The general movement of evangelicalism as a whole between the awakening of Jonathan Edwards's Northampton congregation in 1734 and the widely noticed revivals in Ulster and the northern United States at the end of the 1850s was, indeed, from national churches towards gathered churches. Evangelicalism, which began as a series of interconnected renewal movements within state–church European Protestant regimes, was being transformed into a series of interconnected denominations defined by the free actions of those who made up those denominations. That movement, however, did not proceed uniformly; nor did it entail foreordained consequences with respect to the place of the laity. As a partial explanation for those complexities it is important to sketch the emphases within evangelicalism that helped to redefine the church, even as they also redefined the nature of lay religion. Along the way will be mentioned briefly some of the evangelical adaptations to eighteenth- and nineteenth-century Anglo-American culture that assisted those redefinitions. In conclusion, some of the reasons will be revisited for suggesting why the general synergy between evangelicalism and the rise of the laity was always variable, often complex, and even occasionally ironical.

It is axiomatic that the personal religion of evangelicalism pushed in the direction of heightened lay involvement. Three of the four characteristic marks of evangelical religion that have been helpfully codified by David Bebbington markedly expanded the role of the laity.[9] First, the evangelical stress on conversion reflected a high regard for individual choice, individual responsibility and individual dignity. Second, evangelical attention to the Bible as supreme religious authority could, in fact, lead to new forms of clerical domination – discovered by searching the scriptures. Yet, especially in an age of growing literacy and a burgeoning of print, it usually enhanced the importance of personal Bible reading by individual laymen and laywomen. The modern evangelical movement probably witnessed more intense lay engagement with the Bible than any previous expression of Christianity. Third, the evangelical energy unleashed in active evangelism, active benevolence and active missionary service could be observed among both lay and clerical elements in the movement, but perhaps most of all in the new breed of evangelicals who functioned as both quasi-lay and quasi-clerical members. Lay preachers, professional managers and local agents of benevolent societies may have looked a little like ministers, but their prominence spoke much more to an expansion of the laity. Of Bebbington's four pre-eminent characteristics, only the stress on the cross of Christ as the heart of essential Christianity left ambiguity about lay empowerment. Theologies stressing vicarious substitution, representation by the many in the one, the grace of God appearing as the other side of the law of God, or the hope of perfection by the power of the Spirit in the resurrected Christ could operate to nerve even the least auspicious layperson. At the same time, they could also be used to justify the God-given dignity of special offices in church, home and society, or to undergird principles differentiating between equality before God and social differentiation on earth.[10]

Still other characteristic aspects of evangelicalism pointed even less ambiguously towards lay engagement and the expansion of lay activity. Evangelicals more or less invented hymnody as a broadly-practised means of simultaneously catechizing, creating fellowship, personalizing the Christian faith and expressing heartfelt religious sentiment.[11] Hymnody and its effects have been understudied in the history of evangelicalism, in part because the sheer breadth, diversity and depth of attachment to hymns defies the comprehension of any single scholar. Yet on both sides of the Atlantic, in black as well as white evangelical movements, among formalists and antiformalists, hymn-singing was noted as an activity that worked above all to inspire the laity. The momentously important promotion of the new evangelical hymnody by John and Charles Wesley was far from the least of the contributions by these elitist establishmentarians to the laicizing of evangelical faith.

Evangelicals by no means invented the personal religious narrative but much of the effect of this religious movement has always depended upon the convincing 'testimony'. The lay contribution has always been significant to the stream of evangelical spiritual narratives. As in so many areas of evangelical development, Methodism was the pacesetter in making the personal testimony a constitutive part of lay evangelical religion.

The self-discipline of lay individuals and groups has also been a widely shared feature of evangelicalism. Evangelical self-discipline was both a response to altered social conditions and an expression of inner religious motivation. The American historian Daniel Walker Howe has written with special insight about the importance of lay self-discipline in the century following the Great Awakening:

> The 'watch and ward' that lay members exerted over each other represented, within their voluntarily constituted communities, a substitute for the hierarchical subordination that maintained order in traditional society. It was a part of the Protestant programme for empowering the laity.[12]

In many different ways, then, evangelicalism has been a religion drawing upon lay resources, aimed at lay mobilization and working at its best when taken up by the laity. The implications of evangelical religion for the history of the laity, however, go well beyond the personal. Almost as soon as evangelical movements could be identified as such in the mid-eighteenth century, new practices respecting the church were present as well. Some of those practices came directly from evangelical religion, some were produced when evangelicals adjusted to seismic social changes. Some were political in the broad sense and affected the distribution of power. Together, they combined to create something like an evangelical ecclesiology that regularly created expanded opportunities for the laity. Among the most important of these practices were itinerancy, voluntary association and disestablishment.

Itinerancy

John Mason Peck was a pioneering Baptist preacher in the American Mississippi River valley at a time when it had become obvious that the formal American denominations – Congregationalists, Episcopalians and Presbyterians – were largely failing to keep up with the expanding American population. Yet what Peck concluded about the need of the hour spoke for realities in the settled portions of the American east as well as in much of Great Britain. On 6 December 1818 Peck preached a charity sermon in St Louis and then took up what he thought was the first collection for the support of itinerant missionaries in Missouri. As he did so he commented on the mistaken notion spreading among his fellow Baptists that 'none but pastors . . . are the instrumentalities God has appointed to extend the borders of his kingdom'. The way things should go was indicated rather by the Methodists:

> *A system of itinerant missions*, or 'circuit-preaching', as our Methodist friends call it, is the most economical and successful mode of supplying the destitute, and strengthening and building up feeble churches, that has been tried. It is truly the apostolic mode; and if the finger of Divine providence ever pointed out a method adapted to the circumstances of new and sparsely-settled districts, it is itinerating or circuit missions.[13]

It is no exaggeration to say that Methodist 'circuit missions' were already by 1818 remaking the face of American religion.

As they did so, however, they were only expanding the ecclesiastical effects of a system of religious dissemination that had received a new birth in the eighteenth-century evangelical awakenings and that had continued as a powerful force in evangelical reconceptualization of the church. George Whitefield was not the first paradigm-breaking itinerant in Christian history, nor was he the only evangelical to make steady use of itinerancy in the early days of the movement. Yet his spectacular success as a travelling preacher of the gospel both spoke to and precipitated an altered sense of the church.

A series of recent historical works have underscored how important the form of itineration became for the substance of evangelical ecclesiology. In Harry Stout's biography of Whitefield, itineration served as the means by which evangelical religion acknowledged a new social world of competitive free markets as well as a new world of urgent faith:

> An outdoor Whitefield would no longer be competing with the churches so much as with the merchants, hawkers, and stage players of the

world . . . In economic terms, religion would compete in the marketplace for its own market share. In religious terms, it would be going out to the hedges and highways to convict sinners.[14]

In the American context itinerancy was one of the forces that loosened Old-World restraints. Timothy Hall, in a fine general study, has suggested that,

> the element of choice in religious life highlights another enduring effect of the vast cultural transformation in which itinerancy played a role: the relaxation of cultural constraints which had fixed the self in a particular station within a deferential, bounded community.

As Hall notes, the momentum of itinerancy was matched by the movement of other social forces – land scarcity in settled regions, new prospects of abundance on the frontier, fresh opportunities for entrepreneurial creativity and accelerating impetus for egalitarian values. Itinerancy, in Hall's phrase, provided 'an avenue for a tradesman to become a preacher' and so promoted the conviction that 'the same Spirit which elevated lay preachers above unconverted ministers could similarly imbue their hearers with superior spiritual insight'.[15]

Itinerancy interacted with social developments differently in Britain than in America and also differently in different eras. Early Methodist itinerations during the mid-eighteenth century took place against a somewhat less tumultuous political background than did the itinerations that began to transform the older Dissenting denominations at the end of the century. For the latter group, as Deryck Lovegrove has shown, itineration sparked both 'Established alarm' among some Anglicans and 'undisguised pleasure at the growth of public interest in religious worship' among evangelical Dissenters.[16]

The constant in both America and Britain, however, was the opening up of the church to greater choice and the increase in people actively exercising those choices. Itineration did not necessarily translate into greater control by the laity over the details of religious observance, for itinerants could wield great power of their own. But the very presence of religious alternatives presented by travelling preachers – in Britain outside the establishment, in North America where perhaps no religious option of any kind had existed before the itinerant appeared – moved evangelical laypeople closer to control over their own religious practice.

Voluntary societies

By the early years of the nineteenth century evangelicals had adopted another new form of religious organization that also opened up avenues of service for the laity. The voluntary society had originated late in the seventeenth century when high-church Anglicans founded broad-based agencies like the Society for the Propagation of the Gospel and local associations for promoting disciplined spirituality. Methodist co-option of the form built a bridge to evangelicalism. In Britain the Baptist (1792), London (1795), and Church (1799) Missionary Societies, the Religious Tract Society (1799) and, supremely, the British and Foreign Bible Society (1804) offered Americans well-publicized examples for how rapidly, how effectively and with what reach lay-influenced societies could mobilize to address specific religious and social needs. A few small-scale voluntary societies had been formed in America before the turn of the nineteenth century, but it was only after about 1810 that voluntary societies – as self-created vehicles for preaching the Christian message, distributing Christian literature and bringing scattered Christian exertions together – fuelled the dramatic spread of evangelical religion in America. Many of the new societies were formed within denominations and a few were organized outside the boundaries of evangelicalism, like the American Unitarian Association of 1825. But the most important ones were organized by interdenominational teams of evangelicals for evangelical purposes. Charles Foster's helpful (but admittedly incomplete) compilation of 159 American societies from this era finds 24 founded between 1801 and 1812, and another 32 between 1813 and 1816, with an astounding 15 in 1814 alone. After a short pause caused by the Bank Panic of 1819, the pace of formation picked up once again through the 1820s.[17] The best funded and most dynamic societies – like the American Board of Commissioners for Foreign Missions (1810), the American Bible Society (1816) and the American Education Society (1816), which aimed especially at education for ministerial candidates – were rivalled only by the Methodists in the effectiveness of their national outreach.

In the United States context voluntary societies provided a compelling response to the intimidating challenges posed by disestablishment and the vigorous competition of a rapidly expanding market economy. Observers at the time took note of the innovation. Rufus Anderson, an early organizer of the American missions movement, wrote in 1837 that, 'The Protestant form of association – free, open, responsible, embracing all classes, both sexes, all ages, the masses of the people – is peculiar to modern times, and almost to our age.'[18] Later historians, especially Andrew Walls, have described in more detail 'the immense impact on Western Christianity and the transformation of world Christianity which (through its special focus in the missionary society) it [the voluntary association] helped to effect'.[19] In other words, where British evangelicals led, American evangelicals followed. Through voluntary organizations, opportunities for cooperation between laypeople and clerics multiplied, the tasks opened up to lay involvement expanded rapidly and publicity aimed at lay audiences transformed the evangelical press.

Transformations occasioned by lay participation in evangelical voluntary societies had a particular meaning for women. The sisters Sarah (1792–1873) and Angelina Grimké (1805–79) can serve as only two of many examples.[20]

The Grimkés were raised as slave-holding Episcopalians in early national South Carolina, but when the family moved to Philadelphia and the sisters joined the Quakers, who were coming under strong evangelical influence at the time, they began to speak out against slavery and other social ills. Angelina Grimké's tract arguing for the end of slavery, *An Appeal to the Christian Women of the South* (1836), won her immediate recognition in the new abolitionist movement, but also led many in both north and south to consider her a dangerous radical. Later both sisters became public speakers for the American Anti-Slavery Society. When such speaking in public by women was attacked, Sarah responded with a biblically-based defence in her *Letters on the Equality of the Sexes, and the Condition of Women* (1838). The avenue for service provided to the Grimké sisters by voluntary associations under evangelical influence was an avenue opened up for many other women who had earlier performed religious tasks only in private.

Disestablishment

The practice of ecclesiastical life was changed in the early history of evangelicalism not only by itinerancy and the voluntary societies, but also by new realities for the legal status of churches themselves. Among those realities, disestablishment marked the sharpest divide from the past. Again, the subject is approached from an American angle. Yet it could also be argued that one of the reasons that American forms of evangelicalism eventually rivalled British forms of evangelicalism in the world history of Christianity is that the American experience of disestablishment connected more directly to post- and anticolonial situations where Christian establishments were out of the question than did British experience where church establishment always loomed large for Nonconformists as well as Anglicans and Scottish Presbyterians.

As the expansion of evangelical churches in Britain and Canada demonstrated, the legal separation of church and state was not essential for the flourishing of evangelicalism. In the new American republic, however, creative exploitation of institutionalized disestablishment was a significant factor in rapid evangelical growth.[21] For Catholics, Jews, and some sectarian Protestants, religious freedom did not advance nearly as rapidly as for the evangelicals. Yet in a situation where, at least by 1800, evangelicals of all sorts were effectively free of all the legal connections between church and state that had so recently simply been taken for granted, the effect was as far-reaching upon the nation as upon the churches.

From the perspective of American experience, it could even be suggested that a natural affinity existed between key evangelical convictions and a polity of disestablishment. To hold that the new birth was a product of the Holy Spirit's action seemed irresistibly to trivialize the importance of institutions once widely held to mediate regeneration. Similarly, to exalt the converted person's use of the Bible as the most important religious authority was implicitly to devalue the elaborate edifices protecting scriptural interpretation that prevailed in all the historic European churches, Protestant as well as Catholic. The institutions compromised by such logic included established churches defined as authoritative communicators of divine grace through word and sacrament, institutions of higher learning monopolized by the establishment in order to protect intellectual activity from religious as well as rational error, and the monarchy as the primary fount of godly social stability. British Protestant Dissent moved somewhat more cautiously in this direction. But even after the rise of Methodism and the reinvigoration of the older Dissenting traditions, the strength of evangelicalism among British establishmentarians never permitted the kind of thoroughly voluntaristic ecclesiology that prevailed in the United States.

On questions of establishment, post-Revolutionary American evangelicalism marked a distinct development from the colonial period when the most important evangelical leaders had spoken with opposing voices. Some, like Charles Wesley, whose hymns were being used in America from the 1740s, remained fervent defenders of the status quo. Some, like George Whitefield, gave up establishment in practice but without ever addressing the social implications of such a move and without being troubled by occasional relapses into establishmentarian behaviour. Some, like the Baptists in America from the 1750s, renounced establishment with a vengeance and became ardent proponents of disestablishment across the board. Some, like the American Presbyterian Gilbert Tennent, eagerly threw establishment away in the enthusiasm of revival, only later to attempt a partial recovery after enthusiasm cooled. Some, like John Wesley, gave up establishment instincts reluctantly, even while promoting religious practices that others regarded as intensely hostile to establishment. Some, like Francis Asbury, the leader of American Methodists, gave it up without apparent trauma. Many, like Jonathan Edwards and the leading evangelical laymen of the Revolutionary era – John Witherspoon, Patrick Henry and John Jay – never gave up the principle of establishment, even though they came to feel more spiritual kinship with evangelicals who attacked established churches (including their own) than they did with many of their fellow establishmentarian Protestant colleagues who did not embrace evangelicalism. By the late 1780s, except in New England, this mixed attitude towards formal church and state ties had been transformed into a nearly unanimous embrace of disestablishment. Even in Connecticut and Massachusetts, where evangelical support of the Congregational establishments could still be found, the tide was running strongly away from mere toleration towards full religious liberty.

Methodism was an especially interesting variety of evangelicalism since its connectional system retained characteristics of an establishment (especially the human authority of Wesley, or the bishops who succeeded Wesley). But when Methodism eventually took institutional shape – under John Wesley's guidance but in opposition to his early intentions – it did so as an alternative to church–state establishment. Methodism's great energy, therefore, also contributed to moulding evangelicalism as a movement of disestablishment since, by the 1790s in Britain and even earlier in the new United States, Methodists were clearly committed to the choice against mediated religion and the traditional church exercise of formal control over society at large.

As an important comparative standard against which to measure American developments, it is helpful to remember that many of the key evangelicals outside the United States in the early nineteenth century remained firmly establishmentarian. This distinguished roster included the Anglicans Hannah More, Charles Simeon and William Wilberforce, Scottish Presbyterian Thomas Chalmers, Irish Presbyterian Henry Cooke, and even the Canadian Methodist Egerton Ryerson. In Canada the contrast is especially revealing, since some of the Methodists and Presbyterians, whom Anglicans struggled to keep out of the establishments they were trying to create, were themselves eager to share in establishmentarian privileges. When noting the singularity of the situation for American evangelicals, however, it is important to remember that large differences existed in degrees of enthusiasm for disestablishment. It is also important to realize that, for most white American evangelicals, a willingness to give up the establishment principle did not mean giving up life in society. It meant, rather, renouncing the traditional mechanisms by which Christian churches (including almost all the European Protestant churches of the eighteenth century) still protected their social prerogatives and inculcated their traditions. In place of this formal mechanism came informal moral, spiritual and voluntary ways of exerting social influence that did not require a formal establishment.

For laypeople, movement towards disestablishment meant an assumption of more direct responsibility for the maintenance of ecclesiastical property, programmes and personnel. It meant that self-created and voluntarily sustained institutions became central in religious life. It meant the necessity to create, rather than just to pass on, the structures of religious influence.

From the mid-eighteenth century to the mid-nineteenth century, evangelicals executed a series of adaptations to broad forces in Britain and North America that, generally speaking, pushed against an understanding of social cohesion defined by deference to inherited authority, respect for local hierarchies and accommodation to historical precedent. Instead, they pushed towards social cohesion defined as the product of individual choices linked to national and international networks that they themselves had created. Prominent among those adaptations that reoriented the course of evangelical ecclesiology were itinerancy, voluntary organization and disestablishment.

And yet, the expansion of the laity was not always an inevitable by-product of the expansion of evangelicalism. As the initial incidents suggested, the leaders of evangelicalism, even lay leaders, could make almost as much of the elitist prerogatives they had constructed for themselves as clerics under former circumstances had made of inherited prerogatives. In addition, as many students of evangelicalism have noted, egalitarian, sectarian and anti-establishment instincts of one generation quite easily become elitist, conformist, and quasi-establishmentarian instincts in the next generation. The history of Methodism is the prime example of that process. The careers of the American Nathan Bangs and of the English Wesleyan Jabez Bunting followed the path that the Canadian Egerton Ryerson also pursued, which was a path from democratic beginnings to establishment-like maturity.[22] The transformation of American Methodism from opposing slavery when the movement was in its initial charismatic phase to accepting slavery when Methodists became respectable is only the most obvious example of evangelical development, checking, as well as expediting, the emancipation of the laity.[23] Even itinerancy, especially when its practitioners had gained a measure of success, could work to restrain as well as to liberate lay initiative. As Deryck Lovegrove has pointed out, within English Dissent itinerant pastors regularly came to see themselves as 'exemplars and organizers' concerned with 'careful supervision . . . over those who took part in village preaching'.[24] The point is not to deny that new evangelical practices did liberate the laity. It is rather to suggest that liberation of the laity was never the only, or even sometimes the primary, effect of evangelical activity. As a former evangelical, Orestes Brownson was able to see more clearly than some evangelicals that the tension was between preserving historic Christian faith and expressing that faith in a modern individualistic world.

Nowhere was the complexity between lay and evangelical history more sharply experienced than among female evangelicals.[25] In the intensity of the revivals for which evangelicalism was best known, differences between men and women, as well as between clerical and lay status, regularly receded from prominence. 'The gendered self', as Catherine Brekus has concluded, 'became meaningless at the moment of union with Christ.'[26] Close cooperation between male and female evangelicals – as, for example, the early support provided by women for Methodist itinerants – also testified to the way that shared religious purpose could manoeuvre around gender divisions. At the same time, evangelical Christianity almost always meant something at least slightly different to the men as against the women who embraced it.

During the First Great Awakening, when the paradigmatic language of evangelical experience was taking shape, men and women tended to describe conversions with different vocabularies. Where conversion liberated women from the entanglements of oppressive relationships and bestowed personal agency, for men it provided a countervailing liberation from the excesses of agency and opened the possibilities of relational being.[27] Likewise, conversion for women was more likely to free from inherent corruption; for men it freed from the guilt of sinful actions. These contrasts in the experience of conversion were doubtless related to the widespread conventions of the eighteenth and nineteenth centuries that pictured women as both more inherently licentious and more potentially spiritual than men.[28]

After revival fires cleared away the forests of sin, however, gender distinctions of a different sort reasserted themselves. As the experience of women in the Businessmen's Revival suggests, the same evangelical religion that was revolutionary in the boundlessness of regeneration contributed significantly to the stiff boundaries of the gender-separated spheres that came to prevail in the nineteenth century. Evangelical attention to structural personal holiness and systematic social benevolence occurred at different times and in different ways among different groups. It was always in the forefront of consciousness for formalist Congregationalists, Presbyterians and Episcopalians. For antiformalists these concerns became more important as the urgent faith of democratic revivalism cooled (or matured) into steady-state religious concern for the future. Whether formalist or antiformalist, when white evangelicals turned to consider the religious needs of children, the sanctifying influence of stable families, the desirability of higher education for clergy, or the creation of institutions to meet far-flung or long-standing needs, they invariably promoted gendered ideals of mature spirituality. Men would speak and so clarify the gospel; they would lead and so mobilize church and home for action. Women would cultivate the passive fruit of the Holy Spirit – love, joy, peace, longsuffering, gentleness, meekness, temperance – and so build the godly households without which the Christian faith – as well as an orderly society – would flounder.[29] Especially in the decades after 1830, it became much harder for evangelical women, even from the most egalitarian traditions, to exercise the gifts of public unction and prophetic exhortation that were witnessed in surprising profusion during the first three decades of the nineteenth century.[30] When in that later period such attempts were made, they regularly involved a much more laboured rationale for female public activity than in the first years of the century.

The experience of evangelical women does not mean that the spread of evangelicalism reasserted a new kind of clerical control. It does show, however, that the movement from national churches to gathered churches – a movement that evangelicals did so much to inspire and that took place with such a genuine expansion of lay opportunity – was a complex movement. As in earlier and later periods of evangelical history, so also in the first generation of modern evangelicalism, the priesthood of all believers was a powerful ideal. That it remained as well an elusive ideal cannot obscure the powerful impetus that evangelical religion and lay Christianity offered to each other in the years between the revivals of the 1730s and the revivals of the 1850s.

Notes

1 See the full account in 'Editor's introduction', in D.D. Hall (ed.) *The Works of Jonathan Edwards, Vol. 12, Ecclesiastical Writings*, New Haven: Yale University Press, 1994, pp. 1–90.

2 G.A. Boyd, *Elias Boudinot, Patriot and Statesman, 1740–1821*, Princeton, NJ: Princeton University Press, 1952, p. 261.

3 Transcribed in M.A. Noll, 'The response of Elias Boudinot to the student rebellion of 1807: visions of honor, order and morality', *Princeton University Library Chronicle* 43, 1981, 19. On Boudinot's Christian philanthropy, see also Noll, *Princeton and the Republic, 1768–1822: the search for a Christian Enlightenment in the era of Samuel Stanhope Smith*, Princeton, NJ: Princeton University Press, 1989, pp. 93–7, 254–5.

4 Quotations from Strachan and Ryerson in this paragraph are from W. Westfall, *Two Worlds: the Protestant culture of nineteenth-century Ontario*, Kingston, Ont.: McGill-Queen's University Press, 1989, pp. 24–6. This follows Westfall also in the account of Anglican–Methodist convergence. On the coach ride, see J.W. Grant, *A Profusion of Spires: religion in nineteenth-century Ontario*, Toronto: University of Toronto Press, 1988, p. 93.

5 H. Bridgeman, 'Three Scots Presbyterians in Upper Canada: a study in emigration, nationalism and religion', unpublished thesis, Queen's University, Ontario, 1978, p. 345.

6 Samuel Irenaeus Prime, 'The power of prayer, illustrated in the wonderful displays of divine grace at the Fulton Street and other meetings', New York, 1858, p. 57, as quoted in K.T. Long, *The Revival of 1857–58: interpreting an American religious awakening*, New York: Oxford University Press, 1998, p. 68. This paragraph depends upon Long, *Revival of 1857–58*, pp. 68–76. On connections to the Ulster revival of 1859, see D. Hempton and M. Hill, *Evangelical Protestantism in Ulster Society, 1740–1890*, London: Unwin Hyman, 1991, p. 149.

7 From 'The Brownson-Hecker correspondence', p. 291, as quoted in J. Hennesey, *American Catholics: a history of the Roman Catholic community in the United States*, New York: Oxford University Press, 1981, p. 197. For context, see P.W. Carey (ed.) *Orestes A. Brownson, Selected Writings*, New York: Paulist Press, 1991.

8 My understanding of evangelicalism outside the United States depends heavily upon the following outstanding general works: D.W. Bebbington, *Evangelicalism in Modern Britain: a history from the 1730s to the 1980s*, London: Unwin Hyman, 1989; Hempton and Hill, *Evangelical Protestantism in Ulster*; N.M. de S. Cameron (ed.) *Dictionary of Scottish Church History and Theology*, Edinburgh: T. & T. Clark; Downers Grove, IL: Inter Varsity Press, 1993; G.A. Rawlyk (ed.) *The Canadian Protestant Experience, 1760 to 1990*, 2nd edn, Kingston, Ont.: McGill-Queen's University Press, 1993; D.M. Lewis (ed.) *The Blackwell Dictionary of Evangelical Biography, 1730–1860*, 2 vols, Oxford: Blackwell, 1995; M.R. Watts, *The Dissenters, Vol. 2, The Expansion of Evangelical Nonconformity, 1791–1859*, Oxford: Clarendon Press, 1995; and G.A. Rawlyk (ed.) *Aspects of the Canadian Evangelical Experience*, Montreal & Kingston, Ont.: McGill-Queen's University Press, 1997.

9 Besides the extended treatment in Bebbington, *Evangelicalism*, pp. 2–17, see the more recent refinements in Bebbington, 'Towards an evangelical identity', in S. Brady and H. Rowdon (eds) *For Such a Time as This: perspectives on evangelicalism, past, present and future*, London: Scripture Union, 1996, pp. 37–48; and Bebbington, 'Of this train, England is the engine: British evangelicalism and globalization in the long nineteenth century', in M. Hutchinson and O. Kalu (eds) *A Global Faith: essays on evangelicalism and globalization*, Sydney: Centre for the Study of Australian Christianity, 1998, pp. 122–39.

10 The evangelical theology featured in B. Hilton, *The Age of Atonement: the influence of evangelicalism on social and economic thought, 1785–1865*, Oxford:

Clarendon Press, 1991, seems to have been more at home with elitist clericalism than lay democracy.

11 The importance of hymnody for evangelical movements is well treated in several outstanding books, including L. Adey, *Class and Idol in the English Hymn*, Vancouver: University of British Columbia Press, 1988; J.R. Watson, *The English Hymn: a critical and historical study*, Oxford: Clarendon Press, 1997; and I. Bradley, *Abide With Me: the world of Victorian hymns*, London: SCM Press, 1997.

12 D.W. Howe, 'The market revolution and the shaping of identity in Whig-Jacksonian America', in M. Stokes and S. Conway (eds) *The Market Revolution in America: social, political, and religious expressions, 1800–1880*, Charlottesville: University Press of Virginia, 1996, p. 270. See also Howe, 'The evangelical movement and political culture in the north during the second party system', *Journal of American History* 77, 1991, 1216–39; and Howe, 'Religion and politics in the antebellum north', in M.A. Noll (ed.) *Religion and American Politics: from the colonial period to the 1980s*, New York: Oxford University Press, 1990, pp. 121–45.

13 R. Babcock (ed.) intro. P.M. Harrison, *Forty Years of Pioneer Life: memoir of John Mason Peck, D.D.*, Carbondale: Southern Illinois University Press, 1965 [orig. 1864], p. 124.

14 H.S. Stout, *The Divine Dramatist: George Whitefield and the rise of modern evangelicalism*, Grand Rapids: Eerdmans, 1991, p. 68. For a similar judgement, see F. Lambert, *Pedlar in Divinity: George Whitefield and the transatlantic revivals, 1737–1770*, Princeton, NJ: Princeton University Press, 1994, p. 61: 'To the evangelical, sinners were everywhere and required his "going out into the highways and hedges and compelling poor sinners to come in." Like the new merchants, Whitefield envisioned a much greater demand for his "product" than did the clergy.'

15 T.D. Hall, *Contested Boundaries: itinerancy and the reshaping of the colonial American religious world*, Durham, NC: Duke University Press, 1994, p. 136.

16 D.W. Lovegrove, *Established Church, Sectarian People: itinerancy and the transformation of English Dissent, 1780–1830*, Cambridge: Cambridge University Press, 1988, p. 147.

17 C.I. Foster, *An Errand of Mercy: the evangelical united front, 1790–1837*, Chapel Hill: University of North Carolina Press, 1960, pp. 275–9.

18 R. Anderson, 'The time for the world's conversion come' (1837–8), as reprinted in R.P. Beaver (ed.) *To Advance the Gospel: selections from the writings of Rufus Anderson*, Grand Rapids: Eerdmans, 1967, p. 65; with discussion in A.F. Walls, *The Missionary Movement in Christian History*, Maryknoll, NY: Orbis, 1996, pp. 223–4, 242–3.

19 Walls, *Missionary Movement*, p. 241.

20 See K.D.P. Lumpkin, *The Emancipation of Angelina Grimké*, Chapel Hill: University of North Carolina Press, 1974; and G. Lerner, *The Grimké Sisters from South Carolina: rebels against slavery*, Boston: Houghton Mifflin, 1967.

21 For a perceptive statement of the dynamics at work in the United States early in the history of disestablishment, see R. Finke, 'Religious deregulation: origins and consequences', *Journal of Church and State* 32, 1990, 609–26.

22 On Bangs, see N.O. Hatch, *The Democratization of American Christianity*, New Haven: Yale University Press, 1989, pp. 201–4; and J.H. Wigger, *Taking Heaven By Storm: Methodism and the rise of popular Christianity in America*, New York: Oxford University Press, 1998, pp. 189–90. On Bunting, see D. Hempton, *The Religion of the People: Methodism and popular religion, c. 1750–1900*, London: Routledge, 1996, pp. 91–108; and more generally, Hempton, *Methodism and Politics in British Society, 1750–1850*, London: Hutchinson, 1984.

23 See D.G. Mathews, *Slavery and Methodism: a chapter in American morality, 1780–1845*, Princeton, NJ: Princeton University Press, 1965; C.L. Heyrman, *Southern Cross: the beginnings of the Bible Belt*, New York: Alfred A. Knopf, 1997, pp. 155–6; and C.L. Lyerly, *Methodism and the Southern Mind, 1770–1810*, New York: Oxford University Press, 1998, pp. 177–84.

24 Lovegrove, *Established Church, Sectarian People*, p. 162.

25 An excellent, rapidly growing literature has well documented those experiences. See, as exemplars, D.G. Mathews, *Religion in the Old South*, Chicago: University of Chicago Press, 1977, pp. 101–24; D.M. Valenze, *Prophetic Sons and Daughters: female preaching and popular religion in industrial England*, Princeton, NJ: Princeton University Press, 1985; A.G. Schneider, *The Way of the Cross Leads Home: the domestication of American Methodism*, Bloomington: Indiana University Press, 1993; S. Juster, *Disorderly Women: sexual politics and evangelicalism in Revolutionary New England*, Ithaca, NY: Cornell University Press, 1994; S.R. Frey and B. Wood, *Come Shouting to Zion: African American Protestantism in the American South and British Caribbean to 1830*, Chapel Hill: University of North Carolina Press, 1998, pp. 101–10, 121–8; C.A. Brekus, *Strangers and Pilgrims: female preaching in America, 1740–1845*, Chapel Hill: University of North Carolina Press, 1998; and Long, *Revival of 1857–58*, pp. 68–92. It is worth recording that virtually all accounts show that women almost everywhere made up a majority of evangelical adherents.

26 Brekus, *Strangers and Pilgrims*, p. 42.

27 Juster, *Disorderly Women*, pp. 46–74; Brekus, *Strangers and Pilgrims*, pp. 39–43; Mathews, *Religion in the Old South*, pp. 104–5.

28 Brekus, *Strangers and Pilgrims*, p. 41; Mathews, *Religion in the Old South*, p. 113.

29 Schneider, *Way of the Cross*, p. 173.

30 Brekus, *Strangers and Pilgrims*, pp. 267–306; Valenze, *Prophetic Sons and Daughters*, pp. 275–7.

Chapter 10

Methodist New Connexionism

Lay emancipation as a denominational raison d'être

Timothy Larsen

Unless they happen to have exhibited particularly exotic or quixotic traits, historians usually do not have much time for small, defunct, religious denominations. The Methodist New Connexion, founded in 1797, made the mistake of championing fairly innocuous and sensible ideas, which later became ubiquitous throughout Methodism, and has paid the penalty of having its history neglected. For example, even a volume with such a promising title as, *Conflict and Reconciliation: studies in Methodism and ecumenism in England, 1740–1982*, manages to ignore the Methodist New Connexion altogether.[1] The few modern discussions of this denomination that have been produced are all around 13 pages or less in length.[2] Nevertheless, an examination of this largely forgotten movement has the potential to provide a uniquely illuminating case study of the relationship between evangelicalism and the rise of the laity.

No one was more likely to raise the question of the Methodist New Connexion's denominational raison d'être than its own champions and leaders. William Cooke, a prominent New Connexion minister, noted in a sermon in 1847:

> We are members of the Methodist New Connexion. We exist apart from the Parent Body; there must be a cause for this . . . the most fastidious need not murmur if we give a reason for our Denominational existence, and our distinctive principles.[3]

The *Methodist New Connexion Magazine* argued in 1850 that, 'Every member ought, especially in the present day, to understand our system, and be able to give to every man a reason why he prefers it to other systems of Methodism.'[4] Some ministers would even adopt a catechetical style on this point: 'But if we are so much like the Wesleyans, why are we not one body? I will tell you.'[5] This was a denomination with a sense of its own mission and fidelity to truth.

The notion of 'emancipation' was central to this self-perception. The words 'freedom', 'liberty' and 'rights' are littered throughout New Connexion writings. A review in the denominational magazine of a memoir of Alexander Kilham, the most prominent founder of the denomination, claimed that the book would be treasured by 'every lover of religious liberty' and that its subject laboured 'in the cause of Christian freedom'.[6] The marble monument at Kilham's grave declared that he was 'a zealous defender of the rights of the people'.[7] The preface to the denomination's jubilee volume looked forward to the day when 'the church [would] be emancipated from priestly assumption', the point being that the Methodist New Connexion was in the vanguard of this movement and from its happy position could not resist extolling the joys of liberation.[8] In 1854 there was a widespread movement to change the denomination's name on the grounds that their connexion could no longer be considered 'new' with accuracy. One of the most popular alternatives proposed was 'The Methodist Free Church'. Some people felt that this might be invidious, but William Cooke argued that they need not be ashamed to proclaim their emancipated condition: 'The truth is we believe ourselves to be "*Free*." We are "*Free*," not only in doctrine but "*Free*" in every branch of our polity.'[9]

The Dissenting community as a whole placed a high value on taking a stand on principle, and the New Connexion prided itself on existing solely in order to assert and exemplify great principles.[10] It is a matter of public record that at the denomination's jubilee tea party in 1846 the faithful consumed 1,000 pounds of currant bread, 1,000 pounds of plain bread, 130 pounds of butter, 50 pounds of tea, 300 pounds of coffee, 47 gallons of cream, and 300 pounds of lump sugar.[11] Nevertheless, they did not live by currant bread alone, and we are assured that at this same event 'the benignant and scriptural principles of the New Connexion were fully appreciated; and it is only proper to say that there never was a time when they were so ardently admired, or so warmly espoused, as at the present day'.[12] *The Methodist New Connexion Magazine* could wax eloquent on this subject: 'Yet God has been graciously with us. He has given us to see that our principles are immortal, and become fresher with age.'[13] It even went so far as to note solemnly that 'those who know, and understand, and prize our pure, scriptural principles, should hold by them to the death'.[14] The core members of the New Connexion held to their principles sincerely and tenaciously and were determined to exist as a denomination for as long as it was left to them to maintain this witness.

So, what was it that they thought they had been emancipated from and what were the principles they espoused? The jubilee volume defined the principle that was the denomination's raison d'être as: 'That the Church itself is entitled, either collectively, in the persons of its members, or representatively, by persons chosen out of and by itself, to a voice and influence in all the acts of legislation and government.'[15] Fifty years later, in the centenary volume, the relevant passage included more details of the denomination's constitution:

The office of the ruling elder in the Methodist New Connexion is the distinguishing feature between it and the Parent Body. The admission of an officer so called to the exercise of power alongside the teaching elder, so as to give ministers and laymen equality of authority in all deliberative and legislative assemblies, is the sole point remaining out of the many causes of dissension and final rupture in the struggle for Methodist reform one hundred years ago. This indeed was the main cause of difference then . . .[16]

This principle was often referred to more succinctly as 'lay representation'. The denomination's magazine spoke of 'their distinctive principle – lay representation'.[17] The specific formula used to enact this principle was an equal number of ministers and lay representatives at all levels of collective decision-making including, most particularly, the highest one, Conference itself. Those governed by it were reminded that: 'The Conference was formed on the principle of admitting an equal number of preachers and lay representatives, freely chosen by the people from amongst themselves.'[18]

This principle was grounded in various arguments, with the biblical one not necessarily being pre-eminent. The jubilee volume could happily slip it into the middle of a list: 'truth, reason, scripture, and justice, required this concession to the people'.[19] An article published in 1847 listed four major reasons for embracing it:

1   We think it *reasonable* and *just* . . .
2   We find the principle is recognized in the New Testament . . .
3   The principle of Lay-representation was maintained in the ancient Church *after* the times of the Apostles . . .
4   The principle of Lay-representation enters into the economy of all Protestant denominations . . .[20]

Indeed, its 'reasonableness' was often the first apologetic offered, and denominational writers seemed to take a particular delight in finding this practice reflected in the church government of other denominations and in the writings of the early church fathers. Notably, the jubilee volume (mainly by inserting sizeable extracts from other books), felt a need to ground the polity of liberal Methodism in references to Clement, Ignatius, Polycarp, Tertullian, Cyprian, Origen, Ambrose, Augustine, and 'the Rev. Dr. Buchanan's account of the Syrian Christians'.[21] Nevertheless, such material was invariably coupled with a careful sifting of the relevant biblical clues. The New Connexion used as a kind of motto to encapsulate the rightness of lay emancipation a quotation from Matthew's gospel: 'one is your Master, even Christ; and all ye are brethren' (Matthew 23.8). Moreover, to set these arguments in competition with each other is to defy how the members of the denomination themselves actually perceived their interrelationship: 'On this subject, as on every other of practical importance, Reason and Revelation are seen – not in hostile attitude, employed in the demolition of each other's work, but harmoniously uniting.' In terms of theological reflection, the principle of lay representation was said to be an expression of the Protestant notion of the priesthood of all believers. The *Methodist New Connexion Magazine* claimed in 1872, 'When the royal priesthood of believers – of *all* believers – is understood, this question will be happily settled.'[22] It was routinely argued that Methodism as a whole had emancipated laymen to works of service such as local preaching and that then to thwart them with the other hand by excluding them from rule was unjust, vexatious and untenable. The Wesleyan body, however, as several modern scholars have ably shown, was by the early Victorian period articulating a rival principle that asserted the rights and dignity of the pastoral office.[23]

Notwithstanding its championship of lay rights the New Connexion was not crudely anticlerical. The assessments in the centenary volume perhaps owed something to the respectability to which the denomination aspired in the late Victorian era rather than faithful historical perspective, especially when they claimed that the New Connexion 'was established not more to vindicate the proper standing of the laity in the Church, than to obtain for the ministry its proper functions and prerogatives' and that the Connexion sought 'to emancipate the preachers'.[24] Nevertheless, such claims were grounded in incontrovertible historical facts. Kilham began his career as a reformer by publishing a pamphlet in which he argued that Methodist preachers should be allowed to administer the Lord's supper. The Wesleyan Conference disapproved of his actions and sent him to Aberdeen as a punishment.[25] Nevertheless, he continued to campaign for the preachers to be granted full ministerial rights. Moreover, a tone of respect for the ministry can be found throughout the history of the New Connexion. In 1854, for example, the *Methodist New Connexion Magazine* published a long discourse entitled, 'Loving esteem for ministers'.[26] The Connexion saw the maintenance of a perfect balance between the rights of ministers and laymen as part of the genius of its system. In 1839 the magazine included an article entitled, 'The Wesleyan, Congregational, and Methodist New Connexion systems compared'. With the term 'compared' acting as a euphemism for 'contrasted', the article set out to demonstrate that its own polity achieved the golden mean:

> Our Conference, the governing assembly of the connexion in all general matters, being constituted of an equal number of Preachers and Lay-representatives, must necessarily lend its aid, to prevent the ministry being trampled upon, as complained of under the congregational system; and, as necessarily, [unlike Wesleyanism] it must act for the general benefit of the people, in accordance with their properly expressed wishes.[27]

Whatever views it might hold of Congregationalism, the New Connexion's witness against the Wesleyan system was much more germane to its raison d'être. Simply put, it justified its existence on the grounds that while Methodism was a good and necessary thing, the principle of lay representation was sufficiently important to make continuance within a denomination which did not recognize it an unacceptable compromise. The jubilee volume justified the denomination's existence with a rather sharp analogy:

> Popery necessitated Protestantism, and so long as the Church of Rome cleaves to its errors and corruptions, so long must Protestantism be perpetuated, both as a witness against it, and as a means of reforming it. And so long as the Wesleyan constitution and government remain unaltered, so long must the New Connexion remain a system of antagonism.[28]

When someone suggested in 1854 that the denomination's name be changed to the 'Wesleyan Free Church', a correspondent spoke for many when he claimed, 'to call us "Free Wesleyans," would be about as incongruous as to speak of . . . free bondmen'.[29] Even as late as 1875 abusive language was still in order:

> The Wesleyan Conference . . . has a spice of the arrogance of ecclesiasticism. It prides itself in its pastoral prerogatives and its clerical separateness. It has a pharisaic consciousness (not to say boastfulness) of these things, and it robes itself with hauteur respecting the validity of its ecclesiastical superiority which contrasts rather strongly with its professed spiritual humility.[30]

One hundred years after the bitter fights that occasioned the first secession from Wesleyanism the wounds were only just healing.[31]

The Wesleyans, equally, were not above hurling abuse at the opposite camp. A favourite technique was to attack Kilham. Repeatedly articles appeared in the *Methodist New Connexion Magazine* that were prompted by Wesleyan aspersions on the most eminent of the denomination's founders: for example, 'The Wesleyan Magazine and Mr. Kilham' (1843); 'The character of the Rev. A. Kilham and of our Connexion defended' (1848); and 'The Rev. Alexander Kilham defended against the malignant slanders of the "Watchman"' (1854).[32] On the positive side the magazine deemed it necessary in 1851 to reprint a sympathetic obituary of Kilham from the supplement to the *Gentleman's Magazine* for 1798.[33] Notwithstanding their habit of vindicating their ancestor, New Connexion apologists were sensitive about the denomination being too strongly identified with Kilham. They did not wish to defend him in such a way that might be construed as denominational devotion to an individual. The following is a typical disclaimer: 'It has been a prevalent impression that our body originated in *personal sympathy* with Mr. Kilham . . . But the impression is not correct. The Connexion did not origi-nate in personal sympathy, but in *principle*.'[34] The article even goes on to argue that Kilham was not the founder of the New Connexion – he was only one of the founders and not the one who became its first president. The habit of referring to members of the New Connexion as 'Kilhamites', which is indulged in by some modern Methodist historians (most of whom sympa-thize with the Wesleyan view of the ministry championed by Jabez Bunting), would have appeared to those concerned as inaccurate, insensitive and unfairly partisan.[35] The New Connexion was ready and willing to engage in a vigorous debate about principles and resented being confronted instead with *ad hominem* attacks.

Members of the New Connexion always hoped that disgruntled Wesleyans would not establish a new denomination but would consider the New Connexion their natural haven. Although they missed the big catches, this expectation was reasonable enough to cause a great deal of flirtation. One of the hazards of becoming a self-declared home of freedom is that it constitutes an open invitation for rivals to emerge who claim to offer even greater liberty. Following abortive negotiations for a union between the New Connexion and the Wesleyan Methodist Association in 1837, Robert Eckett, the domi-nant figure in the Association, began to champion a new principle, 'circuit independency', boasting of the superior freedom it secured. When the next crop of reformers emerged in the late 1840s and the first half of the 1850s, the New Connexion again tried to direct the traffic towards itself. In a notice in the *Methodist New Connexion Magazine* concerning a pamphlet by a Wesleyan Reformer, which advocated union with the New Connexion, the reviewer suggested that 'our lay friends should purchase copies by hundreds and thousands for gratuitous circulation'.[36] Robert Currie has noted that during 'times of agitation in Wesleyanism the New Connexion Book Room's output increased by 25–50 per cent'.[37] Eckett, who was busily fishing in the same pool, responded by repeatedly attacking the New Connexion without worrying too much about whether his actions gave the impression of being animated by malice. The *Methodist New Connexion Magazine* probably devoted more space in 1850 to refuting and counter-attacking Eckett than to any other subject.[38] By the time the jubilee volume was in circulation, Eckett's judgement was viewed in New Connexion circles as so perverse as to be the exception that proved the rule: 'It will, however, gratify our friends to learn that every review or notice given by editors of other publications has been of a decidedly favourable character, except that written by Mr. Eckett.'[39] Nevertheless, his actions appeared to bear fruit: the Reformers ultimately decided to join forces with the Association, thereby creating the United Methodist Free Churches. The New Connexion was repeatedly hampered in such negotiations by its tendency to view the proceedings as a takeover rather than a merger. No longer the vanguard in the cause of Methodist freedom, the New Connexion was left emphasizing that there were evils on the left as well as the right. The magazine quoted approvingly the disillusioned Reformer who claimed that his body was 'degenerating into the wildest notions of ultra-democracy'.[40] Even the irenic Primitive Methodists were attacked for alleged imperfections in their polity, which was said to lean to the opposite extreme from that of the Wesleyans. As late as 1897, by which time ecumenism was very much in the air, Primitive Methodist church government was summarized in this combative manner: 'Its features are ministerial disability in relation to the Conference, legal predominance to lay officialism, and the absence of provision for the direct representation of the Church.'[41]

The propaganda of certain Wesleyans notwithstanding, Kilham and the early members of the New Connexion cannot justly be accused of having been Jacobin revolutionaries.[42] A more plausible charge might be that the New Connexion sought to import the secular values of liberal democracy into the church. This accusation presumes that these two forces ought to be incompatible. Many people, however, would shrink from the extreme expression of this opinion made famous in Jabez Bunting's dictum that, 'METHODISM [was] as much opposed to DEMOCRACY as to SIN.'[43] For better or worse, New Connexion apologists unashamedly argued that the spirit of the age was correct in its liberal tendency and that they were proud to be in step with it in this regard. They did not even blush to tell the church that it ought to catch up with the British constitution: 'The representative system of government, which, as Britons, we hold so dear, and on which alone, as we have been made to feel, our civil liberties can securely rest, is equally adapted to religious society . . .'[44] Such comments are ubiquitous in New Connexion literature. If the charge of Jacobinism had to be endured, the counter-charge was also hurled that the Wesleyan powers were 'ecclesiastical tories'.[45] The New Connexion was dimly aware that some would argue that it was undignified and corrupting for the church to borrow its beliefs from the body politic: 'Civil government, we are told, is earthly . . . but the Christian church is a purely Divine institution.' It answered this objection with the claim that 'great principles and modes of procedure may exist which are equally applicable to both'.[46] For those who were still uncomfortable, the eye of faith might just be able to discern the process happening in reverse: 'The method of government practised in the Apostolic Churches in many respects resembles that embodied in the civil constitution of England.'[47]

The suspicion that the New Connexion was flowing with broad currents of British social and political thought rather than simply being propelled by the abstract logic of great principles is reinforced by its failure to emancipate lay-women. Even though the laity was represented in all the decision-making bodies of the denomination, only laymen were eligible to be representatives. Even classes comprised entirely of women were required to find a man to represent them.[48] In 1869, when a plan to unite with the Bible Christians had reached the stage at which all potential obstacles needed to be addressed, the

New Connexion was reassured on the issue of women preaching: 'It was stated to the Committee that this usage was gradually passing away, there being now only one female preacher among the Bible Christians.'[49] The jubilee volume included a section on 'The usefulness of females', but the problematic nature of the role of women was amply illustrated by the wistful reflection that it was unfortunate that Methodist women were unable to become nuns.[50] The charge that unreformed Methodism emancipated the laity when it came to works of service but thwarted it when it came to the exercise of power would have been even more apt if it had been applied to the situation of laywomen.[51]

The New Connexion was always a small body in comparison to both Wesleyan and Primitive Methodism: it began in 1797 with around 5,000 members, had around 10,000 in 1822, 30,000 by the end of the century and ended its separate existence as a denomination in 1907 with approximately 40,000 members.[52] Currie has noted Methodism's general 'sensitivity to statistics', and in demonstration of this the New Connexion was clearly embarrassed by its failure to mushroom into a great force. A recurring feature of its literature is interminable statistical articles attempting to prove that, although significantly smaller than many other denominations in absolute terms, its rate of growth was equal to or greater than that of the larger bodies.[53] One such article, entitled 'They say we don't get on: is it true?', having browbeaten would-be critics with an impressive mathematical barrage, proceeded to an anticlimax with the words: 'all we want now is cordiality, prayerful exertion, and strong faith in the promises, and soon the little one shall become a thousand, and the small one a strong nation'.[54] This sensitivity, together with a predictable interest in the wider cause of its raison d'être, encouraged the New Connexion to take a great deal of vicarious pleasure in witnessing the spread of the principle of lay representation amongst other Methodist bodies. It would patiently rehearse the intricacies of the constitutions of every body from the Bible Christians to the Primitive [i.e. Church] Methodists of Ireland, noting how each embraced the principle of lay representation, and it never tired of noting: 'that the Methodist New Connexion is the Leader of Liberal Methodism. All the other Bodies of Methodists, apart from the Old Connexion, *have adopted its distinctive principle* . . . they have not adopted a *new principle*.'[55] Moves towards increased lay participation in Methodist bodies were tracked with the keenest interest. The following comments on events in the Methodist Episcopal Church of America in 1859 typify the New Connexion's triumphalist attitude to this matter:

> The above resolution shows that the principles for which our forefathers in the New Connexion struggled and suffered are rising to the ascendant; for if the above resolution be adopted by the General Conference of America, as recommended, the great principle which fifty years ago had no advocates in Methodism, except among our own people, will be

incorporated by four out of every five of the whole Methodist people: and, in fact, our friends of the British Conference, and those under its care, will be the only residue, forming a small minority, who refuse its adoption; and even of these we see no reason for despondency. *The Truth is mighty, and must prevail.*[56]

Concomitant with such optimism was the question of Methodist union: if the denomination's distinctive principle was no longer distinctive then the question of its continuing separateness needed to be reopened. From the 1830s onwards, the New Connexion sporadically flirted with the idea of union with various other Methodist bodies. Nevertheless, as the original standard-bearer for Methodist reform, it could smugly argue that it was the task of the newer denominations to explain what distinctive principle they espoused that kept them from throwing in their lot with the New Connexion. A more fundamental question concerned the implications of favourable moves that were evident in the parent body. Already in 1847 Cooke, commenting on changes that had allowed Wesleyan laymen onto various committees which served Conference, observed that,

> since Lay-men are taken to the very doors of Conference, it can scarcely be expected they will not, ere long, be taken a little further. We hail these advances, and should rejoice to see the day when such further advances will be made in the economy of Wesleyanism, as will annihilate all remaining distinctions, and prepare the way for all the branches of the Methodist family . . . to become identically one . . .[57]

From 1878 onwards Wesleyan laymen were represented in Conference itself. Members of the New Connexion claimed that the structure of this concession (notably a ministerial 'upper house') and the restrictions that hedged it round contradicted any assumption that the Old Connexion now embodied their own distinctive principle, but this alteration undoubtedly indicated that for any subsequent generation sufficiently inspired to pursue union the barriers would not be found to be insurmountable.

The movement towards union became complete when the Methodist Church was formed in 1932, a body that embraced the principle of lay representation and that merged the Wesleyans and the Primitive Methodists with the United Methodist Church. The United Methodists were themselves the product in 1907 of a merger between the United Methodist Free Churches, the Bible Christians and the Methodist New Connexion.[58] Thus the triumph of the New Connexion's distinctive principle had deprived it of its raison d'être, thereby signalling its extinction as a separate body and its relegation to historical obscurity. If it could never boast that it had enlisted vast numbers of people into its ranks, it could justly take pride in having fought and won the battle for the emancipation of Methodist laymen. Moreover, it also appears to have possessed the gift of prophecy. The centenary volume of 1897 had predicted:

> Our witness to the rights of the laity in the government of the Church will not be forgotten. But there is less need of that testimony to-day than at any period in the past, and as other Churches continue to travel on the same lines as ourselves the need will diminish still more and more as time advances. Bearing such testimony is therefore likely to be a matter whose importance will recede until it reaches the vanishing point, and whose principal interest will be for the student and the historian.[59]

Notes

1 J.M. Turner, *Conflict and Reconciliation: studies in Methodism and ecumenism in England, 1740–1982*, London: Epworth, 1985. Mention is made, however, of the controversies in Wesleyan Methodism that led to the secession that created the New Connexion.

2 Notably, E.A. Rose, 'The Methodist New Connexion, 1797–1907. Portrait of a church', *Proceedings of the Wesley Historical Society* 47, 1990, 241–53; and R.E. Davies, E.G. Rupp and A.R. George (eds) *A History of the Methodist Church in Great Britain*, 4 vols, London: Epworth, 1965–88, vol. 2, pp. 280–94.

3 *Methodist New Connexion Magazine* [hereafter *MNCM*] 50, 1847, 15–16.

4 *MNCM* 53, 1850, 72.

5 *MNCM* 53, 1850, 455.

6 *MNCM* 41, 1838, 29–31.

7 [J. Blackwell], *Life of the Rev. Alexander Kilham*, London, 1838, p. 394.

8 *The Jubilee of the Methodist New Connexion: being a grateful memorial of the origin, government, and history of the denomination*, London, 1851, p. iv.

9 *MNCM* 57, 1854, 48.

10 For the importance of the notion of principle in this milieu, see T. Larsen, *Friends of Religious Equality: Nonconformist politics in mid-Victorian England*, Woodbridge: Boydell, 1999, pp. 105–8.

11 *Jubilee*, p. 190.

12 *MNCM* 49, 1846, 472.

13 *MNCM* 50, 1847, 23.

14 *MNCM* 63, 1860, 567.

15 *Jubilee*, p. 73.

16 G. Packer (ed.) *The Centenary of the Methodist New Connexion, 1797–1897*, London, 1897, p. 30.

17 *MNCM* 75, 1872, 292.

18 *MNCM* 53, 1850, 457.

19 *Jubilee*, p. 56.

20 *MNCM* 50, 1847, 18–20.

21 *Jubilee*, pp. 121–9.

22 *MNCM* 75, 1872, 292.

23 The fullest treatment of this theme can be found in J.C. Bowmer, *Pastor and People: a study of church and ministry in Wesleyan Methodism from the death of John Wesley (1791) to the death of Jabez Bunting (1858)*, London: Epworth, 1975. See also W.R. Ward, *Religion and Society in England, 1790–1850*, London: Batsford, 1972; and J.H.S. Kent, *The Age of Disunity*, London: Epworth, 1966.

24 Packer, *Centenary*, pp. 28, 224–5.
25 [Blackwell], *Kilham*, pp. 125–79.
26 *MNCM* 57, 1854, 417–26.
27 *MNCM* 42, 1839, 223–4.
28 *Jubilee*, p. 204.
29 *MNCM* 57, 1854, 52.
30 *MNCM* 78, 1875, 611.
31 Packer, *Centenary*, p. 67.
32 *MNCM* 46, 1843, 341; 51, 1848, 427; 57, 1854, 168.
33 *MNCM* 54, 1851, 75.
34 *MNCM* 50, 1847, 16.
35 For example, Bowmer, *Pastor and People*, p. 132; Ward, *Religion and Society*, p. 275.
36 *MNCM* 57, 1854, 626.
37 R. Currie, *Methodism Divided: a study in the sociology of ecumenicalism*, London: Faber, 1968, p. 60.
38 *MNCM* 53, 1850, 215–20, 375–85, 438–9.
39 *MNCM* 54, 1851, 484.
40 *MNCM* 58, 1855, 433.
41 Packer, *Centenary*, p. 207.
42 For a discussion of the origin of the New Connexion set within the wider political context, see D. Hempton, *Methodism and Politics in British Society, 1750–1850*, London: Hutchinson, 1984, ch. 3. According to his biographer, Kilham's politics were 'of the reforming Whig character, the same as those held by Earl Grey, Lord Erskine, Mr Fox, &c'. [Blackwell], *Kilham*, p. 340.
43 Currie, *Methodism Divided*, p. 43.
44 *Jubilee*, p. 144.
45 *MNCM* 57, 1854, 50.
46 *Jubilee*, p. 146.
47 Packer, *Centenary*, p. 51.
48 *Jubilee*, p. 75.
49 *MNCM* 72, 1869, 738.
50 *Jubilee*, p. 229.
51 The laywomen of some Congregational and Baptist churches, by way of contrast, enjoyed a measure of emancipation, even during the first half of the nineteenth century. T. Larsen, '"How many sisters make a brotherhood?" A case study in gender and ecclesiology in early nineteenth-century English Dissent', *Journal of Ecclesiastical History* 49, 1998, 282–92.
52 Packer, *Centenary*, pp. 92, 174; Rose, 'Methodist New Connexion', 252.
53 Currie, *Methodism Divided*, p. 13. See, for example, *MNCM* 44, 1841, 412–14.
54 *MNCM* 53, 1850, 460.
55 *Jubilee*, pp. 200–1.
56 *MNCM* 62, 1859, 84.
57 *MNCM* 50, 1847, 21.
58 For Methodist union, see Currie, *Methodism Divided*; Kent, *Age of Disunity*; and H. Smith, J.E. Swallow and W. Treffry (eds) *The Story of the United Methodist Church*, London: Henry Hooks, 1932.
59 Packer, *Centenary*, p. 250.

Part IV

Missions and the widening scope of priesthood

Chapter 11

The missionary movement
A lay fiefdom?

Andrew F. Walls

In *Mansfield Park* Jane Austen describes the final interview between a young lady of the smart London set and the earnest young clergyman to whom she has become attracted. The occasion is the news of a scandalous affair involving her own brother and the clergyman's sister. The young clergyman expresses his disapprobation of their moral conduct. Mary's reaction is:

> A pretty good lecture, upon my word! At this rate, you will soon reform everybody at Mansfield and Thornton Lacey, and when I hear of you next it may be as a celebrated preacher in some great society of Methodists, or as a missionary into foreign parts.[1]

For the London smart set in Jane Austen's day, there was only one step on the ladder of enthusiasm higher than that of Methodist preacher and that was foreign missionary. Edmund, to whom the words quoted were addressed, was a beneficed clergyman of the Church of England. In 1811, when *Mansfield Park* was being written, not a single beneficed clergyman had become, in Mary's meaning of the words, 'a missionary into foreign parts'.

Forty years later, another country parson's daughter was writing about the style of life she knew. In Charlotte Brontë's *Shirley* the heroine is struggling with her responsibilities towards the institution known variously as 'the Jew basket' or 'the missionary basket'. The author explains:

> The 'Jew basket' and 'Missionary basket' . . . are willow repositories, of the capacity of a good sized family clothes basket, dedicated to the purpose of conveying from house to house a monster collection of pin-cushions, needle-books, card racks, workbags, articles of infant wear, etc., etc., etc. made by the willing or reluctant hands of the Christian ladies of a parish, and sold per force to the heathenish gentlemen thereof, at prices unblushingly exorbitant. The proceeds of such compulsory sales are applied to the conversion of the Jews, the seeking up of the ten missing tribes, and to the regeneration of the interesting coloured population of the globe. Each lady-contributor takes it in her turn to keep the basket

a month, to sew for it, and to foist off its contents on a shrinking male public. An exciting time it is when that turn comes round; some active-minded women, with a good trading spirit, like it, and enjoy exceedingly the fun of making hard-handed worsted spinners cash up, to the tune of four or five hundred per cent above cost price, for articles quite useless to them; other feebler souls object to it, and would rather see the prince of darkness himself at their door, than that phantom-basket, brought with 'Mrs. Rouse's compliments, and please, ma'am', she says 'it's your turn now'.[2]

These sound like words from the heart. One suspects that the missionary basket was a bane of Charlotte's life at Haworth parsonage. But its inescapable presence shows the middle classes of small town and rural England in the 1840s mobilized in support of overseas missions, with the women at their head. The menfolk, even if far from devout themselves, are systematically laid under tribute. The missionary basket releases entrepreneurial gifts among people who could have few other outlets for the skills that realize a profit of 500 per cent. And even those who tremble at the basket's arrival cannot avoid taking their turn. That they cannot do so has nothing to do with the church or the clergyman. It is lay peer pressure – and female lay peer pressure at that – that drives the missionary basket on its way.

The two passages well illustrate the change in social attitudes over the 40 year period that separates Jane Austen from Charlotte Brontë. The difference was noted by contemporary observers. Edward Steane, preaching the fiftieth anniversary sermon of the Particular Baptist Missionary Society in 1842, comments on the remarkable change in public opinion about missions since William Carey began his work:

> Where at the present day are the statesmen who would prohibit the missionary from setting his foot on any shore that owes allegiance to the British crown? Where are the writers who affect to treat his self-denying labours with contempt? Where are the wits and reviewers who turn them into ridicule . . . And where is that large portion of the public who gratified their impious merriment at the expense of methodism and missions? . . . Men enriched with the noblest intellectual endowments are found among [the missionary cause's] advocates; senators extol it in parliament . . . it moulds much of the current literature of the day, and tinctures more. It has even created a literature of its own. The popular feeling has turned almost entirely in its favour, so that you shall hear it spoken of in terms of commendation in almost all circumstances into which you can go.[3]

Allowing the usual discount for the eloquence of the pulpit, Steane is pointing to a genuine transformation in the attitudes expressed in society at

large. Within half a century, missions passed from being one of the enthusi-
asms of the evangelical to a cause supported by earnest churchmen of every
strand of opinion. Whereas at one time a concern for missions might give rise
to a suspicion of religious fanaticism or even political disaffection, the time
came when the secretary of the Church Missionary Society, if burdened by
government action or inaction in Africa, could be sure of a sympathetic
hearing from his brother-in-law, the Under Secretary for the Colonies.

Part of the change, of course, is due simply to the general rise in the public
significance and general respectability of evangelicalism in British life. By the
beginning of the Victorian period evangelical norms were adopted by all
sorts of people who were not evangelicals. But it is necessary to make certain
qualifications. For one thing, general approbation of the missionary project
did not translate into general participation in that project. The missionary
basket might pass round middle-class households, but throughout the nineteenth century the active promotion of missions remained the concern of a
minority. Financial embarrassment dogged mission agencies throughout the
century. In the very period of general approbation we have mentioned, the
Wesleyans dismissed their most high profile missionary, a man who had
opened up untold new possibilities for missions, essentially because he was
spending too much money.[4] The entire income of all the Bible and missionary societies, says Thomas Chalmers in 1819, would not maintain one ship of
the line for a year.[5] By the end of the century the insignificance of missionary
contributions in comparison with expenditure on luxury goods and posi-
tively harmful products becomes a preacher's commonplace.[6] Until the 1880s,
missions were also generally short of missionaries. Sometimes the shortage
was chronic: the Church Missionary Society spent its first five years without
a single missionary on the field. A prime reason for the widespread recognition given in mid-century to the policy of self-governing, self-supporting,
self-propagating churches was that there were simply not enough missionaries for the dual task of maintaining existing churches and founding new ones;
nor could the agencies envisage that there ever would be, nor that they would
be able to support them if there were. The Victorian churches appropriated
the missionary movement, but never saw it as more than marginal to their
principal concerns. However fervently they sang 'From Greenland's icy
mountains', domestic concerns concentrated the minds of English and
Scottish churchmen far more than how to deliver other lands from error's
chain. And those domestic concerns which so absorbed them could wreak
havoc on the mission field. The Scottish Disruption, for instance, occurred
just at the point where the Church of Scotland's India mission (its first and
then only mission) might be regarded as soundly established. All the missionaries declared for the Free Church; all their buildings and facilities
remained the property of the Church of Scotland. The work was relocated
but it was also duplicated, because, with the whole of the subcontinent before
them, both Auld Kirk and Free Kirk found it necessary to continue what they

saw as *their* mission. Unions could be still more destructive than schisms. The union of the Free Church of Scotland with the United Presbyterian Church in 1900 produced such a vast array of overseas commitments that the emergent United Free Church reduced the range, and the Japan field was given up. Union produced retrenchment rather than the expansion to be expected from combining resources. Worse was to follow when the House of Lords settled the resultant property dispute in favour of the remnant of the Free Church which did not join the union. The mission budget of the United Free Church went into crisis just at the time when there was an increased demand for missionaries, for instance in West Africa where the Calabar mission was no longer confined to its creeks.[7]

Further, general approbation of the missionary project was not to be permanent. Paradoxically, at the end of the century, when missionary enthusiasm reached its peak, when the numbers of British missionaries achieved unprecedented levels, when the upper levels of society and the privileged educational institutions linked with them began to produce missionary candidates in significant numbers, the signs of change appeared in the intellectual climate. Even good churchmen were now beginning to argue that for lower races Christianity might be too difficult; perhaps Islam was better fitted to raise Africans in the scale of civilization.[8] In 1842 Steane could believe that no official of a British government would dare to exclude missionaries from British territory. By the end of the nineteenth century, however, Queen Victoria had become the world's leading Islamic ruler and in her name missions were excluded from more than one territory. Queen Victoria kept missionaries out more effectively than the Sultan of Turkey had ever done. For all the militant enthusiasm of missionary literature in the late nineteenth century, the note of embattlement is evident. The heyday of the empire, which ought to have given missions their greatest opportunity, was bringing disappointment, frustration and inhibition. And the intellectual and literary worlds, apparently so favourable in the 1840s, had become even less friendly to missions than the political.[9]

If, therefore, we take the concept of the laity to comprehend the whole professing Christian body of the nation ('Remember', says another of Jane Austen's characters, 'that we are English, that we are Christians'[10]), and its opinion-forming and decision-making classes in particular, there was a relatively short period when overseas missions were, in this special sense, a lay fiefdom. But full commitment to the cause of missions was in practice always an elite movement, and there were good reasons why it should be. The reasons require a digression on the origins of the missionary movement and the nature of western Christianity.

The peoples of northern and western Europe accepted Christianity, in the course of a long, painful process, by adopting it into their customary law and making it the basis of that law. In its essence, western Christianity is tribal religion, and tribal religion is fundamentally more about acknowledged symbols, and custom and recognized practice, than about faith. At the same time it can be a powerful constituent of identity ('Remember that we are English, that we are Christians'). The circumstances of the conversion of Europe created Christian communities which were notionally subject to the law of Christ. The political development of Europe ensured that the western experience of Christianity would be in territorial terms. On one side lay Christendom, Christian territory, the assembly of Christian princes and their peoples, subject to the law of Christ, territory in which idolatry, blasphemy and heresy could have no place; on the other side lay heathendom, the world outside. The fact that the only substantial non-Christian entity known to Christendom directly made an analogous distinction between Dar al-Islam and Dar al-Harb could only strengthen the habit of mind. The long and troubled story of relations with the Islamic world also suggested crusade as the natural model for encounter with the non-western, which was also the non-Christian, world. Crusade was the attempt to extend the territory within which the law of Christ was observed. It was the model adopted in the Middle East and North Africa, where it generally failed; it was adopted in Granada, where it succeeded. It was extended by the Spanish into the Americas, where at first (if deceptively) it appeared to succeed. But it had not the slightest chance of succeeding in the vast territories of Asia and Africa in which the Portuguese were granted the papal monopoly. It was a situation in which the crusade model was not only inappropriate but impossible to apply that forced the creation of a new model for the spread of Christian allegiance. In this model the representatives of Christendom were to commend, demonstrate and illustrate the gospel: to persuade without the instruments to coerce. To undertake this task implied a readiness to enter someone else's world instead of imposing the standards of one's own. It meant learning another's language, seeking a niche within another's society, perhaps accepting a situation of dependence.

This is the origin of the missionary movement. It was a model of Christian activity entirely foreign to the mainstream of European experience. In consequence, it needed new structures to express it. In Catholic Christianity, where the movement began, there were already institutions which could be adapted to serve the new purpose, and the religious orders developed new forms and functions. A Protestant missionary movement emerged in due course. Protestant concepts of Christendom were not basically different from Catholic, and the sixteenth-century Reformation left the foundational assumptions of European Christianity essentially untouched. But the structures to give effect to the missionary movement took much longer to develop. The Catholic movement had been able to develop on the basis of the religious orders, but the Reformation had slain the goose that laid that particular golden egg.

Missionary activity needed three preconditions, and the absence of one or more of these factors accounts for the long periods in which Protestants did not establish missions, even though they sometimes desired to do so. The first necessity was a body of people with the degree of commitment needed to live on someone else's terms, together with the mental equipment for coping with the implications. Such commitment was in turn most likely to arise in the wake of powerful religious influences. Times of religious renewal were necessary for the recruitment of a sizeable company of such people, and the maintenance of a succession of them. A tradition of mental training, however, was also needed; charismatic inspiration alone would not suffice, and indeed the plodder might succeed better with a new language and a new society than the inspired preacher.

The second need was for a form of organization which could mobilize committed people, maintain and supply them, and forge a link between them and their work and the wider church. Since in the nature of things both their work and the conditions in which they carried it out were exceptional, the necessary structures could not readily emerge in very rigid regimes, whether political or ecclesiastical. They needed tolerance of the exceptional, and flexibility. The third factor necessary to overseas missions was sustained access to overseas locations, with the capacity to maintain communication over long periods. This implies what might be called maritime consciousness, with maritime capability and logistical support.

All three factors were present in the first, Catholic, phase of the missionary movement. The Catholic Reformation released the spiritual forces to produce the committed worker, the religious orders offered possibilities of extension and adaptation which produced the structures for deploying them, and the Portuguese enclaves and trading depots provided the communication networks and transoceanic bases. When in the course of the eighteenth century the Catholic phase of missions began to stutter, it was partly because the three factors were no longer fully in place.

The Protestant movement developed as the Catholic movement weakened. It began, not at the end of the eighteenth century (that is a purely British perspective) but at the end of the seventeenth; not in England, but in Germany and Central Europe. Its main motors were in Halle and Herrnhut, though, just as German Pietism drew on the English puritan tradition, it had a puritan prologue. William Carey's *Enquiry*[11] did not initiate it; the object of that famous tract was rather to urge English Baptists to become involved in a work already well established at the hands of others.[12] But the awakening of missionary interest in Britain which the *Enquiry* represents did have a profound effect on the Protestant movement. It greatly enhanced the second and third of the prerequisites we have noted, the organizational and the logistical. The political and economic situation in Britain (and, as soon became plain, still more in the USA) favoured the development of what was to become the most potent instrument of the Protestant missionary movement, the voluntary society. British maritime consciousness and capability opened vastly expanded possibilities to a missionary movement that had hitherto been based in the Continental land mass.[13] Pietism in its various branches had already helped to fulfil the first prerequisite by providing the spiritual dynamic and the intellectual fibre capable of producing a corps of qualified mission workers. The evangelical movement in Britain and North America increased the flow, slowly at first, eventually in a flood.

The logistical prerequisite does not particularly concern us here, but the other two have some relevance to the theme of the rise of the laity.

The first prerequisite, the recruitment of a corps of competent personnel, leads us to the western understanding of the proclamation of the gospel. Western Christianity, being essentially territorial in conception, had always operated on a territorial understanding of Christian ministry. That understanding was also monarchical: the ordained pastor in his parish. Inheriting this understanding, the Protestant missionary movement took for granted that the missionary, as a preacher of the gospel, would be an ordained minister. The early promoters of mission therefore considered recruitment of missionaries in terms of the sources from which the home ministry was recruited.[14]

Evangelical Anglicans of the 'regular', Simeonite type, committed to Anglican liturgy and discipline, were accordingly in particular difficulty. They were pledged to honour the monarchical ordained parish ministry and were sensitive to accusations of Methodist freewheeling. The official mechanism for the maintenance of the Church of England overseas, the Society for the Propagation of the Gospel, did not reflect an evangelical understanding of mission; the London Missionary Society, with its boldly ecumenical pretensions, did not reflect an Anglican understanding of the church. These difficulties were circumvented by the creation of a new organization, the Church Missionary Society, with the structure of a voluntary society but a commitment to Anglican principles and formularies.[15] The implication was that its missionaries would be episcopally ordained clergymen. But for a long time episcopally ordained clergymen simply did not offer for missionary service. Charles Simeon's circle of pious young students, the nursery of so many evangelical clergy, did not produce a single volunteer.[16] Soon the fathers of the CMS ceased to expect such recruits. 'It is hopeless to wait for missionaries,' growled Simeon. 'Send out catechists.'[17] And John Venn drafted for the society a memorandum on the advantages of recruiting lay catechists for service overseas. The memorandum was full of references to the practice of the early church and pointed out that in the early church catechists, whose duties included teaching Christian truth and instructing new converts, were sometimes ordained if they proved themselves worthy. Here was excellent precedent for the CMS to appoint for missionary service pious laymen whose social and educational background were obstacles to their ordination.[18]

The proposal provoked a notably hostile reaction from the circle of regular evangelical clergy who formed the society's backbone. How could people whose identity lay in uniting evangelical doctrine and Anglican discipline institute a process so flagrantly at variance with that discipline? The catechist proposal was quickly dropped; missionaries must be ordained clergy. Venn had previously toyed with the idea of a special ordination for overseas service, which would be justified on the ground that preaching to people at a low stage of civilization did not demand the social and educational attributes necessary to the place the clergy held in English society. But the counter was obvious: a person ordained for overseas service could not be prevented from returning to an English benefice. The mission field would then become an open invitation to social climbers.

It was for this reason that the CMS took five years to get its first missionaries to the mission field.[19] The office of missionary was a clerical one, not to be filled by a layman. But neither the clergy, nor the sources from which the clergy came, were able to supply the mission field. There was, everyone recognized, a lay constituency able and willing to do so, but there was no way of utilizing this supply without ordination and little prospect of that ordination from a largely hostile episcopate.

The CMS was only able to square this circle with the help of German Pietism. Rescue came through a link forged by C.F. Steinkopf, German pastor in London, with Johannes Jänicke of the Berlin Seminary. From its foundation in 1799 to the end of the Napoleonic Wars the society sent out 24 missionaries. 17 of the 24 were Germans. Most of these were already in Lutheran orders.[20] This took care of the ordination question and, it was quietly observed, provided for future ordinations on the field without involving the English bishops, while the nationality of the missionaries removed the fear of the mission field becoming a short cut to an English benefice. Of the seven Englishmen in the list only three were ordained and all of these were sent out during the last year of the period, 1815. Only one of them was a university graduate. Of the four English laymen one was sent briefly to Sierra Leone as a schoolmaster under an arrangement with the colonial government to provide schoolmasters as well as clergy for every village. Two were artisans sent to New Zealand as 'lay settlers'. This was really another version of the catechist idea, but defended on the theory then being advanced by Samuel Marsden that the Maori could be prepared for Christianity by the introduction of 'civilization', that is, western arts and technology. They were later joined by a more educated man, Thomas Kendall, a schoolmaster who was intended to supply the arts.[21] The situation improved for the CMS after 1815, partly through a greater degree of sympathy among the bishops, partly, as will be argued later, because the development of a mass membership system increased the pool of potential candidates. But it was a long time before the society's dependence on Germany (and some other parts of Continental Europe) faded completely. In the period up to 1830 the missionary roll rose to 166 and of these, 49, or something approaching a third, came from Continental Europe. In the whole period up to 1850 more than one fifth of the missionaries, sent out by a society that had come into being to represent the missionary concerns of the regular evangelicals of the Church of England, came from outside England or Ireland.[22]

In Scotland missionary activity before 1829, when the Church of Scotland began its own mission, was mainly conducted through voluntary societies based in Edinburgh and Glasgow on the ecumenical model of the London Missionary Society.[23] This involved less the bridging of denominational divides than the uniting of Presbyterians of diverse affiliation, holding together members of the established church with those of the various voluntarist seceding bodies. (The strain eventually became too much for the Glasgow Missionary Society, which split into establishment and voluntarist sections.) Both societies adopted a rule that their missionaries should have completed the procedures for ordination in their respective churches before being sent out. The rule proved impossible to implement; most of the early offers of service were from artisans, and few of the early missionaries completed the course of study for the ministry. The results of the early commissions were not uniformly encouraging: one missionary turned slave trader, another returned to promote atheism in Scotland. The Glasgow society decided to send no more artisans; the Edinburgh society decided to establish its own hall for training missionaries. The society had been in existence 25 years before the hall was set up.[24]

William Carey's Particular Baptists started on a modest scale: the basis was a ministers' fraternal and initial finances of a little over £13. They had some marked advantages, however. They began with two offers of service, one of them from Carey, the principal architect of the project. He was himself of artisan background, but this was not uncommon among ministers of his denomination. A formidable autodidact, he had combined in varying proportions the roles of shoemaker, schoolteacher and pastor. The tract that he wrote clearly envisages that missionaries would be self-supporting: he even lists the equipment they would need to take for shooting and growing their own food. In view of the subsequent history, in which his society disconnected him, this self-reliance was just as well. And for most of his long career Carey was self-supporting: in his early days as an indigo plantation overseer, later as a teacher in government service at the College of Fort William. Partly from the special vision and position of their leading missionary, partly through their own basis in the lower ranks of English society, the Particular Baptists managed the matter of missionary recruitment better than most.[25]

By contrast, the all-embracing Missionary Society, established in 1795 and soon identified as the London Missionary Society, started with a flourish. It had the support of many prominent Dissenting ministers, of the expatriate Scottish community in London and of such notable, if irregular, Anglicans as Thomas Haweis and Rowland Hill. In an inaugurating sermon Haweis made it clear that the missionaries they should expect would come from the shop or the forge rather than the normal sources of the ministry. Their deficiencies in formal education would not be inhibiting, since a knowledge of the dead languages was not necessary to the communication of the truth in living ones, and their practical skills would be a positive advantage. And find them they did; not less than 30 missionaries, with some wives and children, went off to the Pacific together in 1796. Four were ordained as ministers, one was a surgeon, most of the rest were artisans or labourers. One was so anxious to go that he worked his passage on the ship and was accepted as a missionary on arrival. The voyage took eight months, so the group naturally formed a gathered congregation on board ship (and had the sadness of having to excommunicate some of their number on doctrinal grounds). A short period in the islands produced a drastic thinning of the ranks by death and desertion, though one of the labourers went on to devote 48 years to the service of the mission and one of the artisans to give 45. Another group of 23 missionaries was sent to the Pacific in 1798 but never got there, being intercepted by a French warship.[26] By 1799, the year that saw the foundation of the CMS, the London Missionary Society had already sent out 67 missionaries.[27]

This total had included one person who represented a new class of missionary. Johannes Theodorus van der Kemp was a doctor of medicine, a former dragoon officer, a former rationalist philosopher, an established author and already 50 years old. Furthermore, while missionary candidates routinely bewailed the misspent periods of their youth, van der Kemp's sins really had been as scarlet.[28] He and his colleague Kicherer were the first LMS recruits from the Netherlands. The Dutch missionaries with the LMS, while not occupying the place that the Germans did with the CMS, were to be a significant factor for many years.

But van der Kemp and Kicherer were exceptions. Typically, early LMS missionaries had been pious artisans and, while some proved splendid successes, there was a disproportionate number of casualties – physical, mental, moral, spiritual. The experience of the Scottish societies had been similar; only Anglican principle and prejudice, and the resources of German Pietism, had kept the CMS from the same outcome.

The early missionary societies had proved that the missionary vocation could attract numbers of lay volunteers. But the societies were not interested in lay volunteers as such; they were trying to tap non-traditional sources for the ministry. The disappointments led them to attempt to bring the average missionary candidate closer to the general standards expected of the ministry. The LMS appointed David Bogue, a substantial Scots theologian, to superintend the training of their candidates. The CMS set up a college in Islington to bring candidates without the education and social graces for immediate presentation to a bishop to at least the level tolerated of ordinands in the province of York.[29] Islington had an impressive record and produced missionaries of scholarly attainment; yet even in the 1860s Henry Venn, the

CMS secretary, was saying that the college would not be necessary if the society could get enough candidates from the universities. Even at that late point the missionary vocation was seen as essentially belonging to the sphere of the ordained ministry, even though it was manifest that the ordinary sources for supplying that ministry could not fulfil it.

Ministerial status remained the missionary norm until the last third of the nineteenth century. In some missions it was hard to envisage any other pattern. The Scottish church missions in India concentrated on higher education as the main missionary tool and took for granted the full Scottish university course in arts and divinity as the teacher's essential equipment. The Wesleyans, subject to a connexional committee rather than a lay-dominated society, were perhaps the most resolutely clerical of all. This is not to say that there was no place at all for lay participation in the mission field; the CMS, the LMS and, in their early African undertakings, the Scottish church missions, all continued to send laymen, particularly artisans, but these were seen essentially as auxiliaries working under the direction of clerical missionaries. Sometimes, as in the Scottish missions in Africa, laymen were appointed specifically for industrial or agricultural functions. (In the Scottish missions not only salary but rations for artisan missionaries were calculated according to their rank in Scottish society, while those of clerical missionaries reflected their ministerial status.)[30] Sometimes, especially in areas of acute personnel shortage, such as faced the CMS in West Africa, good service as a layman could be recognized by subsequent ordination,[31] just as John Venn had intended with the abortive scheme for catechists.

Three discrete factors gradually eroded the clerical norm of the missionary. All three had begun before the middle of the nineteenth century; their cumulative effect was not fully felt until towards the century's end.

The first of these was the rise of medical missions. Medical training was from the beginning a frequent part of missionary preparation. A surgeon was, as we have seen, among the large LMS party for the Pacific in 1796; many early missionaries routinely gave medical attendance and some held formal medical qualifications.[32] But their medical function was long seen as purely ancillary to the irregular, that is, their ministerial, duty. Medical missions in the strict sense, that is, missions directed primarily at medical practice by missionaries whose primary ministry was medical, first arose in China. They were the fruit of a situation in which antiforeign feeling was so intense that missions on the traditional pattern were severely limited in what they could accomplish. The first medical missionary is usually identified as the American, Peter Parker.[33] The first British medical missionary was probably William Lockhart of the LMS, appointed to China in 1838, who established his hospital in Shanghai in 1843. Thereafter medical missions burgeoned, especially in China and India. They were not universally adopted: Henry Venn, for instance, was distinctly cool on the subject and the CMS was slow to develop them. But where they were established they sometimes proved a Trojan Horse for mission-field organization. The missionary doctor was often, though not always, a layman, but he could neither be treated as an ancillary worker nor fitted into the clerical command structure.

This was ensured by the professionalization of medicine in the middle of the nineteenth century; indeed, before that time western medicine probably had little, at least outside of the field of surgery, to offer the rest of the world. (Many of the missionaries who died in the 'white man's grave' of West Africa must have been offered on the grisly altar of medical science.)[34] Early mission hospitals were simple affairs, often in the missionary's house, but they rapidly developed into large and ambitious institutions. Their equipment was equally ambitious; medical missionaries were frequently young, recently trained with the latest and best facilities and they coveted the latest and best facilities for their own hospitals.[35] Hospital staffs increased the numbers of personnel in the service of the missions exponentially and became increasingly specialized: nurses, dressers, dispensers, cleaners, watchmen – and evangelists and catechists, for the mission hospital was an evangelistic and pastoral institution as well as a medical one. There were services on its premises, there was interaction with patients and ex-patients at various stages of sickness and recovery. The medical, evangelistic and pastoral functions must be harmoniously integrated and the only person who could do this, the only person who could hold together the spider's web of hospital staff and make decisions in what could be life-threatening situations, was the medical superintendent. No ministerial senior could meaningfully overrule him or question his judgement in his own field and the ordained chaplain, if there was one, must work under his direction.[36] We have hitherto spoken of the medical missionary as 'he'; when, as in due course occurred, the medical missionary was a woman, the capacity of the Trojan Horse was increased.[37]

There were those who were not content with an arrangement made on pragmatic grounds. The China Missions Conference held at Shanghai in 1907 produced a particularly interesting statement on medical missions, for which the lead paper was prepared by Dr Dugald Christie of the United Free Church of Scotland mission in Manchuria (the founder of the Mukden Medical College). Christie had come to China specifically as a medical missionary, insisting on his own hospital. He had later received ministerial ordination from the Presbytery of Manchuria. Far from holding up his own experience as a model, Christie argues in his paper that the office of medical missionary is a ministry of the church which continues the healing ministry of Christ. It should therefore be marked by a special sort of ordination and commissioning parallel to that which marks the ministerial office.[38]

Through the door opened by the doctors the other non-ministerial professions were able to enter. The lay schoolteacher had been on the mission field since early days but had so long been the lowly auxiliary of the ministerial missionary that it was hard even for the new breed of trained educationists to break free. At the World Missionary Conference of 1910 there were still complaints that in some locations the headship of any educational institution had to be held by a minister, however pedagogically unqualified, even when there were abundantly qualified teachers on the staff. But the process set on foot by the doctors was inexorable. A range of missionary specialists, their specializations professionalized by developments mirroring those in medicine and education, came to the mission field in the wake of the Student Volunteer Movement.[39] The clerical conception of the missionary office, which had been a feature of the Protestant missionary movement from its early stages, was radically altered. And one of the principal contributing factors was the social transformation of the mission field brought about by the student volunteers and other young people of the middle and higher echelons of British society, so different from the homespun missionary material characteristic of the earlier days of the movement.[40]

The second, and still more transformative influence, was the steadily increasing indispensability of the woman missionary. As with so many aspects of the Protestant missionary movement, the woman missionary happened by accident; no one planned her or developed her concept as a strategic instrument. Even leaving out of consideration such wholly exceptional figures as the extraordinary Hannah Kilham, exercising her Quakerly concerns in West African education, linguistics and agriculture in the early nineteenth century (and one might add equally extraordinary Roman Catholic women such as La Mère Anne-Marie Javouhey) it is hard to identify the first female missionary. From the earliest times wives of missionaries, regarded by the missionary societies as present essentially for their family role, regularly undertook missionary duties. Many early missionaries commenced schools; their wives frequently commenced schools or classes for girls and extended their responsibilities into other aspects of the women's world, still envisaged as an extension of their husbands' activity. Every so often, wifely enterprise would blossom into a significant institutional commitment and in such cases a crisis might arise on the death or departure of the lady or her husband, which could only be resolved by appointing a female replacement. This was happening at least from 1820.[41] No one was intending to create a category of women missionaries, nor questioning the assumption that a 'real' missionary was an ordained minister of the gospel; they were simply seeking a means of maintaining the valuable work begun by the late excellent Mrs Jones. Then it became clear that India in particular had whole areas of life shut off from male view; only women could ever have any hope of entering those areas. So in India, and then in England and Scotland, societies for female education emerged, to recruit Christian teachers to reach women and girls. It was some time before these societies, often the result of the concern of devout residents of India, came formally within the orbit of the missions, but they usually worked in relation to missions and (sometimes to the dismay of their organizers) their teachers often married serving missionaries. It took some time for the missions to realize how important, and how nearly autonomous, women's work had become, in both its home and its overseas organization.[42]

In the 1860s the newly-formed China Inland Mission, which challenged many of the orthodoxies of mission practice, took actions which clarified the position. It not only accepted women as missionaries in their own right, but assigned them, usually in pairs, to work as field missionaries independently of resident male oversight. By the end of the nineteenth century women had changed the whole face of the Protestant missionary movement by sheer force of numbers. The proportion of women in the medical profession in Britain remained small; the proportion of women among medical missionaries was much larger. By the First World War, Britain was giving place to North America as the main source of missionaries, and both during and after the war the number of women in the British missionary force came first to equal and then to outstrip that of men.[43] It became a commonplace among those who appealed to university audiences for recruits for the mission field that, by contrast with its great days of the student volunteers, the response of the young men of the day to the missionary call had become, 'Lord, here am I; send my sister'. If we are thinking of its personnel, the missionary fiefdom had become not only lay but female.

But there is another way of considering the missionary fiefdom, which takes us to the third of the transformative factors of the nineteenth-century missionary movement. It also takes us to the second of the prerequisites identified early in this essay, the development of effective organizational structures capable of recruiting, maintaining and supplying missionaries and linking their work with that of the wider church. This is not the place to speak at large about the voluntary society, the main organizational engine of the Protestant movement, nor of the way in which, when applied to the missionary movement, it subverted all the traditional European forms of church government.[44] All these forms of government had arisen in the setting of territorial Christianity; they had mostly proved impotent for the presentation of the gospel outside the territorial context. But while the voluntary society subverted church structures it did not always or necessarily declericalize or laicize them. The voluntary society certainly gave the potential for lay involvement. By its means Miss Pym of the Mission to Lepers could exercise quasi-episcopal functions and within it the services of many a captain of industry were called on to assist in computing the cost of many a projected tower. Nevertheless, some missionary societies managed to keep their inner counsels resolutely clerical, assisted in so doing by clerical assumptions about the missionary's office. The CMS, however, eager to maintain loyalty to Anglican formularies and polity, could only defend itself from predatory bishops by the assertion that it was a lay society, even on occasion unconvincingly claiming a status analogous with that of a lay patron.[45] After 1829 the Church of Scotland might claim to have integrated church and mission,

but a glance at the origins of the various missionary operations of the
Scottish churches reveals a patchwork of private initiatives.[46] The most substantial laicization of the inner counsels of the missionary movement took
place with the second wave of voluntary societies that followed in the wake of
the China Inland Mission and took a great part of missionary activity outside
the denominational churches altogether. That is a story needing separate
treatment.

But a form of laicization, while not necessarily taking control of the inner
counsels, nevertheless brought new life to the missionary societies of the first
wave. To see its significance we must return to Charlotte Brontë's missionary
basket and the ladies who sewed and sold for it.

The origin of such activity probably lies in a development initiated by the
British and Foreign Bible Society and copied by missionary societies, including the CMS, of establishing local auxiliaries. The local Bible societies had a
dual function: they distributed the Bible in their own localities by arranging
easy-payment subscriptions and enrolled those who already possessed a Bible
to contribute to making it available elsewhere in the world – both at home and
overseas. In Scotland, where a higher proportion of households than in
England already had Bibles, there was little scope for the first function but
plenty for the second, and in both England and Scotland the second function
was readily applied to overseas missions. It was a new sort of society, for,
while its leadership was inevitably dominated by clergy and local bigwigs, its
membership straddled a vast range of income and social standing, since the
subscription could be as little as a penny a week. Subscription was encouraged and sustained by a flow of information, information from and about
lands with which the subscribers had hitherto had nothing to do, but in
which by their subscriptions they were now personally involved. Thomas
Chalmers in 1819 reflects on the educational function of such societies, their
capacity for enlarging minds by up to date reporting from every continent.
Characteristically, he also assesses their socio-economic effect. He had been
deeply impressed to come upon an Aberdeen Female Servants' Society for
Distributing Scriptures among the Poor, where the subscription was only a
halfpenny a week. This meant that female domestic servants, who were at the
very bottom of the earned income scale, could contribute to the improvement
of the lot of people who were poorer still. It led Chalmers to consider 'the
influence of Bible Societies on the temporal necessities of the poor'.[47] Bible
and missionary associations, he argued (and much to the dismay of some
Bible Society committee members he wanted to amalgamate the two),[48] were
a bulwark against pauperism. There could be no surer form of social and economic insurance than to raise the dignity of poor people to the level of their
social superiors by recognizing them as donors in their own right.

The missionary societies followed the Bible Society example. We have
already seen how long the CMS waited in vain for English missionary
candidates. From its beginning it was a voluntary society, but in its early

years essentially a clerical society, a network of evangelical clergymen who kept up a correspondence based on their knowledge of their own parishes and congregations. Around 1812 the society began to develop local auxiliaries with a penny-a-week subscription. Not only was there an increase in finances, the society began to receive applications from viable candidates of whom the members of the clerical circle had never heard, and this at a point when missionary work was being identified with the 'white man's grave' and heavy mortality.

The broadened base of support, the approach to something like mass membership, necessitated a broader literary appeal. A whole new literature appeared along the trail first blazed by the Baptist *Periodical Accounts*.[49] Missionary literature got beyond the formal reports intended for clergy and the middle-class subscribers of guineas; it produced 'missionary intelligence' from all over the world that could be read aloud in church meetings or in groups, as well as quietly at home. A new middlebrow readership was created and the *Missionary Register* and its Scottish counterpart reached a broader spectrum of homes than the *Edinburgh Review* or the *Quarterly Review* ever did.

On one occasion Henry Venn noted with satisfaction the news from West Africa that the attack by the king of Dahomey upon the city of Abeokuta, the centre of CMS activity in Yorubaland, had been repulsed. The news, he said, caused many to rejoice, from Her Majesty's ministers to the humble collectors of a penny a week. To a high proportion of even the educated British public (and perhaps even to some few of Her Majesty's ministers) the king of Dahomey must have been a shadowy figure, hardly to be distinguished from the queen of Sheba. But to the collector of a penny a week, who had been following the missionary intelligence and sharing with other subscribers the news of the perilous attack, with all its dread potential, the slave-raiding king of Dahomey was a clearly defined personage. Chalmers' vision of a nation transformed and made prosperous by the universal presence of Bible societies may not have materialized, but at least he was right about the cultural impact of the missionary movement on a section of the public that had hitherto had little reason to think of the world outside.

Enthusiasm for missions remained for the most part the concern of an elite group in churches which were busy mainly about other things. Few in ecclesiastical leadership had the remotest idea that the so-often struggling movement was to be instrumental in the transformation of the demographic and cultural composition of the Christian church. A movement that arose in the heart of Christendom helped Christianity to survive the death of Christendom. A project that was soaked in the Enlightenment helped to produce a Christianity whose strength now lies in its independence of the Enlightenment. An expression of Christianity that arose from interaction with deep currents in European culture has helped to foster a Christianity which will depend for its future on its critical interaction with the ancient cultures of Africa and Asia.

The elite group kept alive the movement that had such epoch-making significance. It was not entirely a socially elite group, but rather mixed and fairly representative of active Protestant Christianity. It held seigneurial rights to a lay fiefdom; its symbolic figure was the penny-a-week collector reading a missionary magazine.

Notes

1 Jane Austen, *Mansfield Park*, vol. 3, ch. 16 of the original edition.
2 Charlotte Brontë, *Shirley* (first published 1849), ch. 7.
3 The sermon is reprinted in the collection *Missionary Sermons*, London: Carey Press, 1924.
4 Thomas Birch Freeman superintended the Wesleyan mission in the Gold Coast from 1838 to 1857. His journeys to Ashanti, Yorubaland and Dahomey and his negotiations with African rulers there attracted much attention, but he was in constant disputes with his home committee from at least 1844 about escalating expenses. In 1848 the committee declined to honour some of his bills; by 1856 his resignation was inevitable. See T.B. Freeman, *Journal of Various Visits to the Kingdoms of Ashanti, Aku, and Dahomi, in Western Africa*, 3rd edn, introduction by H.M. Wright, London: Frank Cass, 1968; A. Birtwhistle, *Thomas Birch Freeman*, London: Epworth, 1950; P. Ellingworth, *Thomas Birch Freeman*, Peterborough: Foundery Press, 1995.
5 T. Chalmers, *The Influence of Bible Societies on the Temporal Necessities of the Poor*, Edinburgh, 1819.
6 See the Student Volunteer Missionary Union conference reports *Make Jesus King!* London, 1896 and *Students and the Missionary Problem*, London: SVMU, 1900.
7 For the background of the examples quoted, see A.F. Walls, 'Missions', in N.M. de S. Cameron (ed.) *Dictionary of Scottish Church History and Theology* [*DSCHT*], Edinburgh: T. & T. Clark, 1993; on the Calabar question, see G. Johnston, *Of God and Maxim Guns: Presbyterianism in Nigeria 1846–1966*, Waterloo, Ont.: Wilfred Laurier University Press, 1988.
8 On the debate sparked by Reginald Bosworth Smith's lectures on *Mohammed and Mohammedanism: lectures delivered at the Royal Institution of Great Britain*, London, 1874, see A. Walls, 'Africa as the theatre of Christian engagement with Islam in the nineteenth century', *Journal of Religion in Africa* 29, 1999, 155–74.
9 Cf. E. Stock, *History of the Church Missionary Society: its environment, its men and its work*, 3 vols, London, 1899, vol. 3, ch. 77 'Controversies from within and attacks from without'. See also W.H. Temple Gairdner's paper in E.M. Wherry, S.M. Zwemer and C.G. Mylrea (eds) *Islam and Missions*, New York: Revell, 1911, pp. 195–203.
10 Jane Austen, *Northanger Abbey*, vol. 2, ch. 9 of the original edition. Henry Tilney is making clear to the young heroine the folly of believing that English landowners can routinely murder their wives.
11 W. Carey, *An Enquiry into the Obligations of Christians to use Means for the Conversion of the Heathens . . . in which the religious state of the different nations of the world, and the success of former undertakings, and the practicability of further undertakings, are considered*, Leicester, 1792.
12 See A. Walls, 'The Protestant missionary awakening in its European context', in B. Stanley (ed.) *The Missionary Movement and the Enlightenment*, London: Curzon Press, 2000.

13 Even before the British movement developed, the Halle-inspired branch of the Continental movement was relying on British logistical support. The inspiration, and all the missionaries, for the Danish-Halle mission throughout the eighteenth century came from Halle Pietism, but for a variety of reasons it was convenient to organize the mission under the Society for Promoting Christian Knowledge. The solid high churchmen who formed the basis of the London society endeavoured from time to time during the century to place English church missionaries in what was theoretically an English mission. They never found any. See W.K. Lowther Clarke, *A History of the SPCK*, London: SPCK, 1959; also D.L. Brunner, *Halle Pietists in England: Anthony William Boehm and the Society for Promoting Christian Knowledge*, Göttingen: Vandenhoeck & Ruprecht, 1993.

14 So even Carey: 'And this [living in native style] would only be passing through what we have virtually engaged in by entering the ministerial office. A Christian minister is a person who in a peculiar sense is *not his own* . . .', *Enquiry*, pp. 71–2.

15 Stock, *Church Missionary Society*, vol. 1; C. Hole, *The Early History of the Church Missionary Society for Africa and the East to the end of AD 1814*, London, 1896.

16 Stock, *Church Missionary Society*, vol. 1, p. 74.

17 Stock, *Church Missionary Society*, vol. 1, p. 64.

18 See M. Hennell, *John Venn and the Clapham Sect*, London: Lutterworth Press, 1958, ch. 4.

19 The Society for Missions to Africa and the East was founded in 1799. Its first missionaries Melchior Renner and Peter Hartwig, recruited from Germany as indicated below, were accepted in 1802 and began 15 months of study at Clapham. They left for Sierra Leone in 1804. For the first two years Renner served as Colonial Chaplain, so that until 1806 Hartwig, whose career was brief and colourful, was, strictly speaking, the society's only missionary. See *Register of Missionaries (Clerical, lay and female) and Native Clergy from 1804 to 1904*, London: Church Missionary Society, n.d.

20 On the question of Lutheran orders for Anglican missionaries and changing attitudes in England, see J. Pinnington, 'Church principles in the early years of the Church Missionary Society: the problem of the "German" missionaries', *Journal of Theological Studies* NS 20, 1969, 523–32.

21 On Kendall, see J. Binney, *Legacy of Guilt: a life of Thomas Kendall*, London: Oxford University Press, 1968.

22 Data and calculations in this paragraph are based on *Register of Missionaries* between 1804 and 1850.

23 See Walls, 'Missions', *DSCHT*. It should be noted that the society founded as the Edinburgh Missionary Society became generally known as the Scottish Missionary Society.

24 An account of the Scottish societies occurs in W. Brown, *History of the Propagation of Christianity among the Heathen*, 3 vols, Edinburgh, 1854, vol. 2. Brown was long the secretary of the Scottish Missionary Society. See also J. Kilpatrick, 'The records of the Scottish Missionary Society (1796–1848)', *Records of the Scottish Church History Society* 10, 1950, 196–210.

25 Carey's early views on missionary supplies ('a few knives, powder and shot, fishing tackle and the articles of husbandry') are indicated in his *Enquiry*, pp. 73–5. On the subsequent history, see E.D. Potts, *British Baptist Missionaries in India, 1793–1837*, Cambridge: Cambridge University Press, 1967.

26 On the early events, see R. Lovett, *History of the London Missionary Society 1795–1895*, 2 vols, London, 1899, vol. 1. See also A.F. Walls, *The Missionary Movement in Christian History*, Maryknoll, NY: Orbis; Edinburgh: T. & T. Clark, 1996, ch. 12.

27 Data in J. Sibree (ed.) *London Missionary Society: a register of missionaries, deputations, etc. from 1796 to 1923*, 4th edn, London: London Missionary Society, 1923.

28 On Van der Kemp's career, see I.H. Enklaar, *Life and Work of Dr J. Th. Van der Kemp, 1747–1811*, Rotterdam: Balkema, 1988.

29 See A. Hodge, 'The training of missionaries for Africa: the Church Missionary Society's training college at Islington, 1900–1915', *Journal of Religion in Africa* 4, 1971–2, 81–96.

30 The question needs fuller study. In the meantime, T.J. Thompson, *Christianity in Northern Malawi: Donald Fraser's missionary methods and Ngoni culture*, Leiden: Brill, 1995 offers a view of a Scottish mission at work.

31 For example, Henry Townsend, *Register*, no. 231, who became the patriarch of the Yoruba Mission, was appointed to Sierra Leone in 1836 at only 21 years of age after a brief spell at the Islington College. In 1844 he was ordained successively deacon and priest, and appointed to Yorubaland, where he had already carried out distinguished reconnaissance work.

32 Among well-known missionaries of the London Missionary Society, Robert Morrison, who took medical studies along with other forms of missionary preparation, is an example of the first category; David Livingstone, who was a licentiate of the Faculty of Physicians and Surgeons, of the second.

33 On Parker, see *The Life, Letters and Journals of the Rev. and Hon. Peter Parker, M.D., missionary, physician and diplomatist*, Boston, 1896.

34 See P.D. Curtin, *The Image of Africa*, Madison: University of Wisconsin Press, 1964, chs 3 and 5.

35 See Walls, *Missionary Movement*, ch. 16.

36 This is clear, for instance, in an address by Dr Herbert Lankester, secretary of the CMS medical committee to the Student Volunteer Conference of 1900. He recommends the appointment of evangelistic missionaries to busy hospitals, but clearly takes for granted the responsibility of the medical superintendent for the oversight of the whole work, medical and spiritual. See *Students and the Missionary Problem: addresses delivered at the International Student Missionary Conference, London, January 2–6, 1900*, London: SVMU, 1900, pp. 497–9.

37 The LMS appointed its first female medical missionary in 1889. It appointed another 15 up to 1921. Marriage sometimes complicated the structures of responsibility. The Revd George Kerr and his wife Dr Isobel Kerr jointly superintended the work of the Dichpali Leprosy settlement maintained in Hyderabad by the Wesleyan Methodist Missionary Society. See D. Monahan, *The Story of Dichpalli: towards the conquest of leprosy*, London: Cargate Press, 1949.

38 See *Records of the China Centenary Missionary Conference Shanghai 1907*, Shanghai, 1907; also D. Christie, *Thirty Years in Moukden. 1883–1913*, London: Constable, 1914.

39 The LMS list includes agriculturalist, architect, building superintendent, chemistry professor, engineer, marine [*sic*?], pharmacist and kindergarten [teacher], besides categories such as 'educational superintendent', 'lady superintendent' of a hospital and various grades of nurse. Artisans, teachers and printers had been on the mission staff much earlier.

40 See Walls, *Missionary Movement*, pp. 106–10.

41 See Church Missionary Society, *Register*, List II, p. 260, nos. 1–2.

42 A British equivalent is urgently needed to the comprehensive investigation by D. Robert, *American Women in Mission: a social history of their thought and practice*, Macon, GA: Mercer University Press, 1996.

43 For the Church Missionary Society the trend is visible early: in the 10 year period

1895–1904 the society sent out 391 male and 425 female missionaries. For the London Missionary Society parity was achieved in 1908, with 11 men and 11 women, but it was not until the First World War that the women came into their own. In the years 1915 to 1918 the LMS sent 14 men and 38 women. Even with the peace and the release of the male backlog, the women remained significant: 17 to 8 in 1920, 4 to 7 in 1921,10 to 11 in 1922 and, wartime distortion over, 14 to 9 in 1923.

44 On this question, see Walls, *Missionary Movement*, ch. 18.

45 See the detailed discussions in H. Cnattingius, *Bishops and Societies: a study of Anglican colonial and missionary expansion, 1698–1850*, London: SPCK, 1952; and T.E. Yates, *Venn and Victorian Bishops Abroad: the missionary policies of Henry Venn and their repercussions upon the Anglican episcopate of the colonial period 1841–1872*, Uppsala: Swedish Institute of Missionary Research, 1972.

46 A survey of the origins of the different fields of the missions of the Scottish churches reveals a variety of initiatives – by concerned nationals and expatriates in India, and by individuals and groups in various parts of Scotland. See Walls, 'Missions', *DSCHT*.

47 Edinburgh, 1814. An enlarged edition appeared in 1819.

48 'An old member' of the Bible Society committee wrote a refutation.

49 *Periodical Accounts Relative to the Baptist Missionary Society*, which appeared between 1800 and 1817, circulated widely outside Baptist circles, and the Serampore mission, especially its translation work, received support from many outside the denomination.

Chapter 12

Industry, professionalism and mission

The placing of an emancipated laywoman, Dr Ruth Massey 1873–1963

Clyde Binfield

The title of this book plays suggestively with the layers of ambiguity with which evangelical Christians shroud the shaping of call and response. The very concept of laity implies that not all are necessarily lay; but is any distinction between the laity and the rest one of status, even caste, or is it simply one of function? And if it is one of function, can that distinction always be quite as utilitarian as it sounds? When might the qualities needed for that function become special rather than particular? Such questions are sharpened by the concept of call, which implies response, by the context of social class, which entails distinction, and by the training, which gives effect to the call, conditions the responses and slips so easily into the expectations of social class.

This chapter considers the issues of call, response, class, and training in a missionary context at the turn of the nineteenth and twentieth centuries. It focuses on one woman, formed in Manchester, professionally trained in Edinburgh, certainly called, possibly ordained, although she must be categorized as a laywoman, who practised and therefore witnessed in Central China. Its sources are largely restricted to a small family archive.[1] This is a conscious restriction, because it illuminates how some intelligent homewatchers saw and followed their kinswoman's ministry: it looks at what was communicated to them and at how they placed it in context. It is, moreover, shaped as a narrative, for that is how homewatchers tended to see missionary endeavour. To them it was an exciting and, in God's good time, ultimately triumphant story. Mission history is now much more sophisticated than that, but it should neither ignore nor undervalue the narrative aspect of its historiography. The yarn contributes to its fabric. The chapter ends, however, where it has begun, with the ambiguity inherent in evangelical priesthood.

There was nothing romantic about Hankow. The London director of a large Sheffield steel firm visited the place in late autumn 1897 and wrote in his journal of a city

under water for three months in the year owing to the snow waters of the Yangtze being so great. The heat in those months June, July, August is terrific and the miasma arising from the water is most poisonous. Dr J.

said that till this year his garden has been so flooded that they have had to use a boat to get to the house. Mrs S. said she had often fished from their balcony . . . The weather had become very cold, but . . . they were all rejoicing in the rapid lowering of the flood waters – the mud was something terrible whilst I was there.[2]

That London businessman, Arnold Pye-Smith, had a name which resonated in Dissenting circles and his visit to Hankow was as much on missionary as on steel business, for its highlight was a fruitful fellowship with the city's London Missionary Society compound.[3] Dr J. was the pioneer missionary, Griffith John, who had been in Hankow since its opening as a treaty port in 1861.[4] Mrs S. was his daughter, Mary Sparham, whose husband had served in Hankow since 1885.[5] Hospitals and schools were integral to the LMS mission in Hankow and Pye-Smith's visit was the occasion for a significant gift to boost hospital extension at a moment of financial crisis. Hospitals and schools were also integral to the newer mission across the river in Wuchang where Pye-Smith noted a new chapel, two houses 'built by Mr Harris of Calne', and 'Mr Massie's hospital'. Harris and Massey, like Pye-Smith, were successful businessmen. Harris was a bacon-curer and Massey, whom Pye-Smith was shortly to meet in Bangalore, was an engineer. Massey, Harris and Pye-Smith had Congregationalism, missionary enthusiasm, and successful business interests in common. They also had daughters. Two of Harris's daughters had come out to Central China to find vocation, husbands and – one of them – an early grave.[6] Now Mr Massey's daughter, Ruth, was preparing to come out to the hospital which her father had provided. Our concern is with her.

The Masseys were not, perhaps, as Congregationally pervasive as the Pye-Smiths, but they too managed to get everywhere: a network of kith and kin known to each other in Kent, Berkshire, Norfolk, and Gloucestershire; in Norwich, Liverpool, Sheffield and, above all, in Manchester, which meant Stretford, Openshaw, Rusholme, Bowdon, and Wilmslow. Religiously it chiefly meant Baptists and Congregationalists, a countrywide web of evangelical Dissent.

Their business, which they also regarded as God's, was hammers. 'We must depend upon Him and the Hammer', wrote the senior founding partner in his diary.[7] There were four generations of Congregational Masseys and there have been four generations of engineering Masseys. From 1861, the year of Hankow's opening to western investment, to the 1980s, latterly as part of a Sheffield-led conglomerate, their works were synonymous with Openshaw. Today no trace remains. Yet their rise coincided with what one of Manchester's most perceptive observers called the fourth change in Manchester's history:

the gradual settlement within the boundaries of the city of perhaps the greatest engineering interest in the world. The evening dispersal of the amalgamated engineers in Openshaw on the east and Trafford Park on the west in times of good trade is torrential. A main pipe of humanity might have burst![8]

B. & S. Massey, of Lees Street, Openshaw, fed that main pipe, balanced by Saxon's, the mill-engine manufacturers round the corner. There was another balance. Saxon's were the mainstays of Openshaw's United Methodist Free church; Massey's, of Lees Street Congregational church.

What made for industry and Dissent also, at least in Manchester's case, made for cosmopolitanism. Manchester at the turn of the twentieth century was England's most cosmopolitan city outside London, marked out for its grammar school, its university, its library, its collections of art and antiquities, its newspapers, politics, music and cricket, and for businessmen who, whether they made or sold, knew the world. In all these respects the Masseys were Manchester made and marked. They made hammers for tyre-welding, steel-fitting, stone-breaking and crank-bending. By the 1890s they had outlets in Europe from Belgium to St Petersburg and in the Americas from Canada down to Argentina. They supplied railways from India to Australia and had government contracts with arsenals from Woolwich to Venice. They exhibited in Paris and Philadelphia. While Arnold Pye-Smith was travelling the world in 1897–8, young Leonard Massey was in Russia and the United States, and his uncle Stephen was in India, having visited China back in 1893. Here were men whose mission was business.

Accompanying this, however, was another missionary dimension. The Masseys were proud of the fact that John Williams, the martyr of Erromanga, was a family connection.[9] Their Gloucestershire Baptist cloth-manufacturing cousins, the Barnards, with whom they kept close contact over the generations, produced an adventurous Kate (Norton), who went to Nice, started a school and married a pastor of the *Église Reformée* who, born a peasant, became governor of New Caledonia. Like many travellers and missionaries she attributed her health and longevity to homeopathic medicine. Another educationally adventurous Kate (Barnard) became governess to a Hohenzollern princess. These manufacturers saw both value and use in educated daughters. Stephen Massey stood squarely among them.[10]

From 1879 to 1912 he was senior partner in B. & S. Massey and for most of that time he was a member of Lees Street, the Congregational church next to the works. By 1912, however, he was a deacon at Wilmslow Congregational church. That was when he retired from the firm (a limited company now), striking what came to be seen as a ruinous deal. Irrespective of trade conditions he was to receive his full dividend, tax free. That was not greed. It was so that he could maintain his commitments to overseas mission.

For Stephen Massey, like Arnold Pye-Smith's wife, was a director of the London Missionary Society, and in 1896 he was its chairman. He maintained a rest bungalow for jaded missionaries at Kodaikanal, in Travancore; and throughout the 1890s he held LMS house parties at Keswick, to coincide with the Convention. A visitors' book survives, devoted solely to LMS visitors, covering the years 1893 to 1927: India, China, Africa, Madagascar, the South Seas, all furloughed with the Masseys at Keswick, Fairfield or Wilmslow. The first and the last names are those of women serving in China: Annie Pearson, Peking, October 1893; Dorothy McFarlane, Wuchang, October 1927. Annie Pearson, then in her lateish thirties, was shortly to marry a doctor.[11]

Benjamin Massey, the senior founding partner of B. & S. Massey, had two sons and a daughter. Those sons carried on the firm. Stephen Massey had no sons, but two daughters, Mary and Ruth. From 1893 to 1899 Ruth was in Edinburgh studying medicine and surgery at the Medical College for Women. While there she was active in the Student Volunteer Missionary Union. It cannot be coincidence that 1893 saw Stephen Massey in Hankow, the start of his hospital in Wuchang, the visit of Annie Pearson of Peking, and the commencement of his daughter's medical studies in Edinburgh. It was certainly not coincidence that Ruth figures with her sister and parents in group photographs at the Keswick missionary house parties, along with the Arnold Fosters, the Davenports, the Cousinses, all of Hankow and Wuchang, or the Muirheads, Brysons, Peills, and Curwens from elsewhere in China. These survive in a missionary archive collected by the family, volumes of greetings cards, cuttings, orders of service, annual reports, and letters: politics, society, church, hugger-mugger over the first 30 years of the twentieth century.

Ruth Massey went out when she was 26. It is important to stress that she went out from a society in which, while women knew their place, they also knew that their place could command considerable space. Even so, the responsibilities which she faced demanded more than a sense of command. One of her younger women cousins, an agnostic factory inspector, reflected on this years later: 'When she came home on leave, she lived with her parents in Wilmslow. She was affectionate and modest, and we were all very fond of her . . .', and then she added, 'she had an amazing lot of responsibilities in China, which she quite took for granted, and which would certainly not have come her way here.'[12]

This reflection from a woman factory inspector about a pioneer woman medical missionary, serves to bring home the extent to which, in the late nineteenth century, what might be called the 'private sector' aspect of overseas expansion acted, often literally, as a godsend to go-ahead young people with their way to make in the new, or reshaped, professions. They were the first generation of their sort. They were the first to be educated in more than a hit-or-miss way. They were the first to see the need and find the means for training. They were new. They were many. They were not too easily placed at home, in a society which liked above all things to be able to place its members. For these young people, commerce, industry, engineering, building, architecture, medicine, education, all beckoned abroad. It was the private sector which first beckoned. Government work followed. And while this should be seen as part of that new and pressing question of the age, the man question, it should also be seen as part of the woman question, for these men had sisters to whom similar pressures and opportunities applied.

Such people did not belong to army families; they were neither officers nor other ranks. They did not belong to great landed families, although a large number had farming stock lodged in their cousinhoods. Though many were solicitors and some were barristers, few were as yet likely to be judges. They were more likely to be town councillors than members of parliament, although their horizons were lifting. They certainly belonged to the wrong church to be bishops. On the whole they belonged to the wrong church to be heads of great schools or famous colleges. But they could be just as able, restless, ambitious, and inspired. They could write, paint, draw, administer, create. They could speak foreign languages, if not in tongues. They were mental artmen, and women. They produced their quota of spies, adventurers and confidence tricksters. Indeed we probably underestimate the extent to which they were all adventurers, for we too easily forget how religion, especially evangelical religion, can sanctify the venturing. Life at the turn of the century had more opportunities than ever it had. It was to be enjoyed. But can there be any enjoyment where there is no aim, and is there anything more truly enjoyable than a trust? The evangelical Christian's missionary imperative, that splendidly imperial and imperious concept, fitted this mentality like a glove.

By the 1890s this was clearly seen as an imperative for properly trained Christian women, and particularly for teaching and healing women. There were, of course, some things that only women could do for other women, but even those were more easily recognized overseas than at home; an instructive instance of out of sight out of mind. Thus there had been women doctors in Britain since the 1860s, but to become a woman doctor predicated a family which could afford to pay for a long training. It took a considerable breaching of barriers for that sort of family to do such a thing, and it took a second great breaching for that sort of family then to tolerate a daughter, who might have been a helpmeet, doing indelicate things to bodies, for money. A Sheffield family, for instance, the Wilsons, who were precious metal smelters related to the Pye-Smiths and known to the Masseys, bonded like them into support for the London Missionary Society, produced two pioneer women doctors. While one became Sheffield's first woman general practitioner the other seems not to have practised.[13] It was here that missionary work provided an answer. Missionary work was a response to a call, not just a profession. Missionary work could also be placed, not least by the unthinking and the conventionally minded. Missionary work was at once a lightning conductor for the timid and a motor for revolution for those determined to see beyond the next corner.

All this can be seen in the barrage of farewells which exploded around

Ruth Massey in 1899, justifying the six years of professional training which had confirmed her response to a missionary call. Ruth's mother had kept the landmarks of those years, telegrams from Edinburgh: 'Girls all through except Hilda Macfarlane praise the Lord' (July 1894); 'Coming tomorrow 10.15. Ploughed in Anatomy Probably other subject also' (March 1896); 'Massey Droylsden Through Ruth' (July 1899). At last she was Dr Ruth Massey MB, ChB, Edin., and it was a case of upward as well as onward, since this came one early September day from Fort William: 'From Britain's highest point we send our greetings joint Stephen Mary Ruth', father and daughters.[14]

She took her degree on 29 July 1899. Of 150 Edinburgh Bachelors of Medicine and Surgery that year, six were women. All were addressed by Professor Sir Henry Littlejohn. He congratulated them on how their medical school had improved.[15] No longer had the 'diseases of the eye, the ear, the throat, the skin, infectious diseases, diseases of childhood and insanity . . . to be studied in the Continental schools', for now 'all is changed'. Yet he still felt it good for the young doctor to experience a *wanderjahr*, a year of travel, that 'powerful adjunct in the cultivation of an intelligent and liberal spirit'. So he spoke of the relaxing, re-creative qualities of art and literature and music ('Of course I need not mention the higher considerations of religion'): the cultivation of all these was vital to their duty as citizens of 'one of the greatest empires the world has ever seen'.

No doubt Dr Ruth took that in her stride, although she planned for rather more than a *wanderjahr*, all of it subject to those barely mentioned higher considerations of religion. Even so, Sir Henry's address was defiantly masculine, even for those non-inclusive days: 'the medical man' should not be active in politics, other than those of public health, though, 'protected as he is by the ballot', he should 'in all circumstances record his vote'. There was little joy there for the medical woman, who had no parliamentary vote before 1918 and there was even less joy in his peroration: 'bear yourselves as gentlemen who have enjoyed the full benefits of a liberal university education'.

It was not like that at the valedictories. There were five of these, beginning the day after her degree congregation with a service in Edinburgh's Morningside Congregational church at which, as reported in the *Scotsman*, both Ruth and her father gave addresses.[16] They really got into the swing, however, in October. On the 18th there was the LMS valedictory in the Victoria Rooms, Bristol; on the 23rd, in London, those valedicted presented themselves to the full LMS board, 80 strong. One suspects that they looked with special interest at Ruth, since back in July, between hearing her results and getting her degree, the board had minuted: 'Mr. Stephen Massey had undertaken to support his daughter, Dr Ruth Massey, and to provide for her work, as a medical missionary in Wuchang.' On 24 October there was a second valedictory, this time in Kensington Chapel. On the 25th the action moved up to Lees Street Chapel, Openshaw, and on the 30th Mrs Stephen

Massey was 'at home', twice over, at 'The Willows', Fairfield, to friends wishing to say goodbye to Dr Ruth Massey.

The Bristol and Kensington valedictories were stirring occasions. Here the missionary endeavours of an entire denomination were focused on the world: China, India, Madagascar, Africa, New Guinea, Samoa. At Bristol, where 'the audience pleasantly whiled away the time listening to the strains of an excellent band', there were 16 missionaries or their wives returning to the field and 14 going out for the first time. At Kensington, of 23 missionaries, 15 were women and two of these were doctors. The rhetoric was of a type. In his address at Kensington Silvester Horne 'likened the missionaries to soldiers going into the field', while in Bristol Samuel Pearson, Annie Pearson's brother, 'spoke of the gathering as a great peace meeting. Where Christianity went the blessings of civilization followed close upon its heels. Let those who were going out remember that they had a vast army of friends who were the friends of God.' That was fighting peace talk, perhaps out of deference to the meeting's Quaker chairman, Joseph Storrs Fry.[17] His words should be noted too:

> He could no more imagine a living church being destitute of the missionary spirit than of a strong and healthy man spending his life in the coffin in which he was to be buried. When a church ceased to be a missionary church, the death warrant of that church had been signed in heaven.

And it was a matter of life and death. At least two of those valedicted were going out to die. One was Oliver Tomkins, who would fall in New Guinea with James Chalmers in 1901, one of that band of martyrs which ceased in old-style history with Alfred Sadd, 40 years on, although in fact that roll call will not end this side of eternity. The other was Winifred Bateman. Tomkins came of firmly Dissenting stock. Miss Bateman's was decidedly Anglican (it included Bishop Moule of Durham and Charlotte 'Just as I am without one plea' Venn Elliott), but she was off to Shanghai to marry the London Missionary Society's Dr McAll, before moving on to Wuchang. She too would die in 1901 and her husband would write in the family's *In Memoriam* card the extraordinarily suggestive words: 'Her passing was His Will; if Christ had not been there she had not died.'[18]

That was in the future, if only just. A present reality for all those watching this thin red missionary line was the women. Down in Bristol the reporter for the *Christian World* was understandably yet not too tiresomely sexist in his rhetoric:

> The Lady doctors, and it was difficult to associate so august a title with the slight, girlish forms that stood before the audience, met with a very cordial reception. Again and again came the testimony of home training in the missionary spirit.

The heart of that matter, however, was reached in Openshaw, for there the entire service was focused on three women: Bolton's Dr Alice Hawker, bound for North India; Openshaw's own Ella Sharp, bound for 'King Khama's capital in Central Africa' (Khama had been a guest at 'The Willows' a few years earlier); and Dr Ruth Massey.[19] Here a local church, in a genuinely working-class district, however much it was enlightened by paternalism, enlarged for the occasion by the countrywide fellowship of churches, concentrated at once on India, Africa and China, and on three young women.

'Farewell to Lady Missionaries at Openshaw', ran the local headline. This allowed for the display of some useful statistics (the London Missionary Society had 20 women missionaries, countless wives, 22 native Bible women and 356 other native women on its roll), some detailed descriptions of the mission field in Central China, South Africa, and North India, and some practical theology:

> Drs Massey and Hawker were going out to devote their knowledge in caring for the bodies and healing the bodies of women and children in China and India, and also at the same time healing the soul and the restoration of the whole person in Jesus Christ.

By far the most perceptive part of this valedictory, however, was the sermon. The preacher was at once a relatively local man and a Massey family connexion. He was the father-in-law of Ruth's cousin Harold Massey, the great Dr Mackennal of Bowdon Downs.

Alexander Mackennal, pastor, preacher, author, and ecclesiastic, was the most sympathetic of the late Victorian Free Church pulpit princes. Perhaps that is why he is one of the least remembered. Earlier that month he had written to Stephen Massey:

> My wife tells me you are a little anxious about my presence with you on Wednesday the 25th inst. I am fully hoping to share in the solemnity and joy of Ruth's ordination. It will be to me a service of love.[20]

'Ruth's ordination': loosely used no doubt, and consciously ambiguous too; perhaps it was simply a slip of the pen, although there is just as much reason to think that Mackennal meant what he wrote, since the text for his sermon was 'For the letter killeth, but the Spirit giveth life'. And as in an ordination his was a charge directly to the candidates, three young women trained in a human empire to capture souls for God's empire. It would be hard to imagine a better or more fitting charge for any ordination:

> And now the time has come when you who have been trained are to be trainers . . . Now it may be well for you three girls to remember that the Apostle Paul was the greatest of human missionaries, and that he was a

nervous man . . . at the time he was suffering from an attack of 'nerves' . . . Two of you girls are psychologists. You know perfectly well that the human beings you will have to deal with are body, soul, and spirit. So are you. Their claims upon you will be so heavy because of that complex human nature. For the most part I trust that your complex and rich human nature will serve them sufficiently; but I would also remind you that in virtue of that very ability to serve them you will be affected by them [for you too are subject to human nature] . . .

[And then there is the mystery of your work. In its course] you will come into intimate association with many, and you will love some more than others. But not always will those whom you love most be those who will be won. And those whom you do not love most you will reprove yourself for not loving as much as you ought . . . Oh! the self-torture which is possible to a Christian woman's soul. [But, always remember this,] He fitted you to be His servants . . . He stood by the student; He will stand by the missionary . . . In the old times when Christian men and women loved experimental hymns, I have heard people say, and it has almost always been a woman who spoke, in the midst of manifold perplexities, calling to mind the fidelity of God:

> His love in times past forbids me to think,
> He'll leave me at last in trouble to sink.
> Nor can He have taught me to trust in His name
> And thus far have brought me to put me to shame.

Out of the mouths of the poor, and the humble, the needy old woman, trembling, and knowing little except how to trust, and having little power of argument for her trust, God has perfected praise. And you, the successful students, the graduates, you have that faith to sustain you . . . as often times, perhaps, you may have little else . . . Problems? We shall have all Eternity to solve them in. You will not have the work of saving the heathen in all Eternity. A few years, how few, please to remember, it is for God to answer the question . . . Will you remember that the Apostle Paul said, 'Christ sent me not to baptise but to preach the Gospel'; and that the heart of the Eternal is most wonderfully broad . . . Answers may not come, but grace will come, fitness will come, for He has called you to be servants of the manifold grace of Christ.

'Servants of the manifold grace of Christ': the rhetoric there is more hand-maidenly than knightly, let alone kingly. It is not, perhaps, very far from that Victorian stereotype, so easily misunderstood, of woman as helpmeet. But Dr Mackennal's interpretation of that remains a sensitive one, aptly tailored to suit any ordination: hence his reflection that when Christianity first came to

Britain it spread 'by domestic and social association'. For 220 years Roman officials had come over with their wives and their households and their slaves. By the same token, it struck Mackennal, 'You are going to come into closer contact with the domestic life of South Africa, of India, of China, than the preaching missionary ever came.'[21]

One hopes that Ella Sharp, Alice Hawker and Ruth Massey were not too excited and edgy for these wise words to pass them by. Mackennal was speaking to their condition exactly as he had done, Sunday by Sunday, for over 20 years to what outsiders saw as one of Manchester's most cat's whiskers congregations, making of it one of Congregationalism's most usefully moving-and-moulding, active-citizen congregations. What spoke to their condition in the more humdrum circumstances of Lees Street, Openshaw, would certainly speak to their condition holed up in the small community life of a mission compound, or serving, in profound culture shock, the women and children of another world, and doing so when that other world was in chronic transformation. Mackennal's words were ripe for mission in perpetual motion, which is how it was throughout Ruth Massey's time in Central China.

Ruth Massey and Winifred Bateman sailed from Southampton a week after the Openshaw service, on the *Preussen*, a German steamer which sank a few years later off the Goodwin Sands. They arrived in Shanghai about a week before Christmas 1899 and Ruth at once wrote a letter to the Lees Street church, in time for it to be read or passed around on communion Sunday.[22] That vital, difficult, educational task of bringing to life both the reality of the mission field and what the homewatchers wanted to think was its reality, had begun.

In Ruth Massey's case that task was largely achieved. Her letters, balanced on the one hand by the reports of her hospital and on the other by newspaper cuttings, chiefly from the *Manchester Guardian*, make for strong narrative. The storyline is exciting. Its complexities, however, are never hidden. All are displayed: the imperatives of Christian mission and social service, the shaping and interweaving of personalities, the roles of women and youth, the birth of a new China and the chronic revolution which attended it, the practical needs of an increasingly sophisticated hospital, the tensions of race, class and creed. These were refracted through a relatively well-placed band of homewatchers, up to three generations of Nonconformist consciences, many of them with other missionary contacts of their own, their elders shaped by the Manchester School, wrestling with empire, fighting imperialism, all of them shouldering and some of them exploiting a changing world's burdens. These were not men and women for whom distance lent enchantment, but it could inspire.

The missionary's work is swiftly done, over and done with in the twinkling of an eye. Dr Mackennal had recognized that in his charge at Openshaw. But missionary work is never done. Ruth Massey's fifth furlough fell between spring 1921 and autumn 1922. That May she addressed the London Missionary Society's 128th annual public meeting in London's Queen's Hall, following 'with quiet force' a film about Canton. Her message was confident: 'If they took the opportunity the next generation of Christian women would capture the teaching, nursing and medical professions. But in any case Chinese girls meant to get education, Christian or non-Christian.'[23]

Towards the end of that decade, very early in 1928, although she had been back in England since spring 1927, she sent in her resignation. Her father, whose income had allowed her to remain an 'honorary' missionary, was reaching the close of his long life. Dr Gillison, who 31 years before had shown Arnold Pye-Smith the Hankow compound, wished Ruth Godspeed with a characteristic letter: 'were every foreign missionary to leave China tomorrow the gospel is firmly planted in this land – and Jesus Christ will not leave China'. Then, describing how five young Chinese officers of the southern army had worshipped with them the previous Sunday, he added: 'God is in this movement – the devil is very apparent too – but as one man said to me – "Where the devil is – there God is also!"'[24]

Those statements were never more intensely tested than between the late 1930s and the late 1970s. For most of that time Ruth Massey was in Wilmslow, to which her family had retreated from Fairfield. She became its Congregational church's first woman deacon.[25] And when, towards the end of her life, a cousin commented that she must find very depressing the way in which all her work had been undone, she replied: 'no – not in the least[.] I have sown a seed which will fructify in God's good time.' She had lived out the burden of Alexander Mackennal's ordination charge, her response to day-to-day events giving angels words they needed to cry out to us from heaven.[26]

That is not an extravagant sentiment. It is an accurate expression of the ecclesiastical polity through which she witnessed, and with this we return to those providential ambiguities with which this chapter began. The congregational polity, particularly as expressed by Baptists and Congregationalists, its ragged origins pulled into shape by the persistent interweaving of scriptural interpretation and contemporary politics, encouraged respect rather than hierarchy, order tempered by pragmatism. Its keynote was mutuality. It was grateful ground for professionalism. It was vulnerable to supposedly stronger systems because it could seem to be so systemless, but it stood on its own feet, and it was more genuinely, indeed instinctively encouraging of indigenous self-help than other mission-minded polities. Congregationalists had no licence to delegate their faith. Theirs was a polity tailor-made for emancipated laypeople. What then distinguished their ministries from other, more traditional forms?

That question underwrote a long and fruitful tension. Ruth Massey's was a professionally trained and disciplined life. Three generations later this Congregational laywoman would have been a prime candidate for ordination to the auxiliary or non-stipendiary ministry. Had she lived a decade longer and been rather younger, she could, as a deacon of Wilmslow Congregational church, have been ordained to the eldership when her church became part of the United Reformed Church. In both cases, though with varying emphases, the word 'ordination' was carefully, almost precisely, used. Such developments, sharpened while Ruth was in Wuchang by English Congregationalism's formal recognition of the ordination of women to the ministry of word and sacrament, were the natural accompaniments of constant concern over the nature and expression of ministry, that duty and privilege of all believers. So what of the minister, whom John Angell James, the famous Birmingham Congregationalist, had once called 'the highest type of Christian'?[27]

The challenge lay in recognizing the call of such Christians and shaping their training. In 1908 the general secretary of the Baptist Union, J.H. Shakespeare, took the high ground at the union's spring assembly, when he defended 'the greatness and sacredness of the ministerial calling . . . The call of the risen Lord to this office is through the Church as its most solemn function.'[28] Ten years later, in *The Churches at the Cross-Roads*, he intensified his conviction: a minister must suggest by his bearing the unseen and the eternal, have healing in his touch, mediate the mystical and the divine.[29] So should all Christians, and Shakespeare had been a notably successful pastor; but he had become a commanding ecclesiastic, latterly bewitched by dreams of organic unity. It is tempting to see in his language a shift from the higher pragmatism to a significantly evolving ecclesiology. Between formulating those two statements Shakespeare had collaborated with the Congregationalist, P.T. Forsyth, in a volume on Free Church unity.[30] Forsyth too had been a notably sensitive pastor, with a marked awareness of overseas mission, but now he was principal of a London theological college which, as it happened, was the direct issue of the Evangelical Revival.[31] Taking part in ordinations was therefore an occupational hazard of his calling. It was at this time, so 'A Baptist Layman' told the *Christian World* some years later, that Forsyth came to a south coast town for the ordination of its Congregational church's co-pastor. 'Baptist Layman' described how one speaker told the young minister:

> There were places where the main emphasis of the minister's work would be found in his teaching, in others it would be the prophetic note, in this town the main emphasis was laid upon his work as a priest, the way in which he had to stand with men and women before God.

Then Forsyth spoke, striking that point home: 'You will have to be a priest.' Disturbed by this, 'Baptist Layman' wrote in protest to Forsyth, who replied:

> Yes, every minister should realize he is a priest. We agree with the Anglicans, that he stands in a special way for the priestliness of the

Church. I wish our ministers were more priests than they mostly seem to be, and let the Anglican priesthood alone, or in much imitate them.

Hardly mollified, the Baptist pursued the correspondence. What of the New Testament's teaching of the priesthood of all believers? At which Forsyth expressed his gladness 'to have had a hearer so attentive', and referred him to the Free Church principal Lindsay's book on the church and the ministry. Recalling the exchange, the Baptist concluded:

> Evidently Dr Forsyth was a man of great attainments, high culture, and a leaning to High Churchism, and it is a matter of devout thankfulness that in the closing years of his life he was a firm believer in the Atonement.[32]

We might see in that exchange the tension built into evangelical Christianity since the Reformation, kept sharp and effective by that Congregational temper shown so strikingly by Ruth Massey in Wuchang, her father in Manchester, and those threading webs of Christian connection which sustained and explained the genuinely Congregational ministries of men like Alexander Mackennal but also of men like Shakespeare and Forsyth.

Notes

1 In gathering material for this chapter I have been indebted to Dr Sylvia Dunkley, Mr R. Morley Fletcher, Mr C.N. Massey, Mr K.F. Massey, Miss M. Massey, Miss G.M. Pye-Smith, Mr and Mrs R. Pye-Smith, Mr E. Alan Rose, Mr P. Walmsley, Miss J.H. Whitworth. The archive [hereafter Massey MS] is in the possession of the Massey family.

2 Arnold Pye-Smith MS Journal, in possession of the Pye-Smith family, to whom I am indebted for permission to publish these extracts.

3 Arnold Pye-Smith (1847–1933), grandson of Dr John Pye Smith (1774–1851), principal of Homerton College, was partner in Samuel Osborn and Co., founded 1852.

4 Details of London Missionary Society [hereafter LMS] missionaries are taken from J. Sibree (ed.) *London Missionary Society: a register of missionaries, deputations, etc. from 1796–1923*, 4th edn, London: London Missionary Society, 1923, with additional material from N. Goodall, *A History of the London Missionary Society 1895–1945*, London: Oxford University Press, 1954, Appendix III, pp. 595–625, and B. Thorogood (ed.) *Gales of Change: responding to a shifting missionary context. The story of the London Missionary Society 1945–1977*, Geneva: World Council of Churches Publications, 1994, Appendices A – C, pp. 258–324. Griffith John (1831–1912), Shanghai 1855–61, Hankow 1861–1912, 1888 elected chairman of Congregational Union of England and Wales (a unique recognition of a serving missionary) but declined.

5 Charles George Sparham (b. 1860) served in Hankow 1885–1918. In 1891 he married Griffith John's daughter Mary (b. 1863).

6 Pye-Smith's reference to Harris and 'Massie' unveils a far-flung Dissenting network. Mary Harris (1867–95), Hankow 1892–5, daughter of Thomas Harris JP (d.

1909), married James Walford Hart (1860–94), Chung King 1892–4; her sister, Elizabeth Mary Harris LRCP & S (Edin.), married Thomas Gillison MB (1859–1937), Hankow 1883–1918. Their brothers William James Harris MD, FRCS, (b. 1867), thrice mayor of Shaftesbury, Joseph Colebrook Harris (b. 1871), farmer in British Columbia, and Alexander Charles Harris (b. 1872), engineer in Leicester, were at Mill Hill School where contemporaries included Leonard and Harold Massey, nephews of and future directors with, Stephen Massey (1839–1930) of B. & S. Massey, Openshaw. Pye-Smith was not at Mill Hill, though his father, three brothers, and two sons were; and his grandfather was one of its founders.

7 H. Janes, *Sons of the Forge: the story of B. & S. Massey Limited 1861–1961*, London: privately published, 1961, p. 19.

8 W.H. Mills, 'Modern Manchester. A note of 1923', in *The M.G.C. Manchester Year Book*, Manchester, 1923, p. 7.

9 John Williams (1796–1839), LMS, South Seas 1816–39, killed Erromanga 20 November 1839. The connection was distant. The firm's senior partner, Benjamin Massey (1837–79), and his brother Richard (1832–1901), an Anglican parson, married Baptist sisters from Norwich whose mother was a Williams and on whose nursery wall 'there hung an unframed portrait painted on rough canvass – a dark eager young face which mixed itself with my dreams and we were told that is your cousin John Williams who was martyred at Eromanga'. Massey MS Lucy Massey, 'Memoires' 1918, copied 1979 by K.F. Massey.

10 Stephen Massey and his nephew Leonard (1867–1943) both married Sarah Barnards; the Barnards of Barnard, Bliss and Barnard, broadcloth manufacturers of Nailsworth, were traditionary Baptists and Radicals.

11 Annie Pearson (b. 1856), Peking 1887–94, married Dr Eliot Curwen (b. 1865), Peking 1894–9, chairman of LMS Medical Council 1909–22; Dorothy (Thorpe) McFarlane (b. 1889), Somerville College Oxford, Shanghai 1916–19, married Alfred James McFarlane (b. 1870), Merton College Oxford, Hankow 1899–1936.

12 Marian Massey to author, 5 and 18 December 1984.

13 Dr Helen Mary Wilson (1864–1951), JP (1920), LSA (1889), MB Lond. (1890), MD. Lond. (1894) and her first cousin Dr Ruth Wilson (1864–1940), trained at Edinburgh, were both immersed in social service. Both, perhaps perversely, were influenced by Christian Science; Ruth, who was warden of a Salvation Army home and joint superintendent of the Sheffield Women's Police Court Mission, became a Christian Science reader.

14 Massey MS 'Ruth's Book 1899'.

15 Ibid. Littlejohn (1828–1914) had been Edinburgh's Medical Officer of Health since 1862 and was Professor of Forensic Medicine 1897–1906.

16 The following section is drawn from cuttings from the *Scotsman*, 29 July 1899; *Christian World*, 26 October 1899; from undated cuttings and other material in 'Ruth's Book'.

17 Charles Silvester Horne (1865–1914), minister at Kensington and MP Ipswich 1910–14, was author of *The Story of the LMS 1795–1895*, London, 1894; Samuel Pearson (1842–1907), minister at Broughton Park, Salford, had missionary and doctor sons. Joseph Storrs Fry (1826–1913), perhaps contemporary Bristol's most traditional philanthropist, had been in charge of the family chocolate firm since 1886.

18 Oliver Fellows Tomkins (1873–1901), Papua 1900–1; James Chalmers (1841–1901), Rarotonga 1867–77, Papua New Guinea 1877–1901; Alfred Lionel Sadd (1900–42), South Seas 1933–42; Winifred Bateman (d. 1901) married Percy Lonsdale McAll (b. 1870), MB, ChB (Edin.), Hankow 1898–1917, in China to 1935. Winifred McAll was buried next to Mary Hart.

19 Dr Alice Mary Hawker (b. 1870), MB, BS (Lond.), India 1899–1935; Ella Sharp (b. 1874), Africa 1899–1933. Their service was markedly influential: N. Goodall, *London Missionary Society*, pp. 40, 260–1.

20 Alexander Mackennal, Beechwood, Bowdon, to Stephen Massey, 12 October 1899, 'Ruth's Book'. Harold Fletcher Massey (1871–1950) married Ethel Mackennal (1869–1938). For Alexander Mackennal (1835–1904) see D. Macfadyen, *Alexander Mackennal BA, DD. Life and letters*, London: James Clarke, 1905.

21 Undated cutting, 'Ruth's Book'.

22 Letter written in Shanghai, Sunday 17 December 1899 to Revd Robert Sutton, Openshaw, received 14 January 1900 and printed, undated cutting, 'Ruth's Book'.

23 Cutting of meeting 11 May 1922, 'The Book of Ruth and Things Chinese' Vol. III, November 1912–27.

24 Dr Thomas Gillison, Hankow, to Dr Ruth Massey, Wilmslow, 9 March 1927. 'The Book of Ruth'.

25 W. Lazenby, *Pleasant Pastures*, London: Independent Press, 1946, p. 93.

26 K.F. Massey to author, 28 January 1987.

27 This was recalled by an old missionary warhorse, Robert Dawson (1836–1906; Shanghai 1859–61) in 1901 at the dedication in Margate of Edith Calvert (b. 1877; Wuchang 1901–10, then in Papua after marriage to Robert Lister Turner b. 1875; Papua 1902–40). Cutting dated 26 September 1901, 'Ruth's Book'.

28 J.H. Shakespeare, *The Arrested Progress of the Church: an address to the spring assembly of the Baptist Union of Great Britain and Ireland*, London, 1908, p. 24, quoted in P. Shepherd, 'John Howard Shakespeare and the English Baptists 1898–1924', unpublished thesis, University of Durham, 1999, p. 120.

29 J.H. Shakespeare, *The Churches at the Cross-Roads*, London: Williams & Norgate, 1918, p. 92, quoted in Shepherd, 'John Howard Shakespeare', p. 191.

30 P.T. Forsyth and J.H. Shakespeare, *A United Free Church of England*, London: National Council of Evangelical Free Churches, n.d. [1911]. Forsyth's contribution was 'The United States of the Church'.

31 His mission consciousness was characteristically expressed in *Missions in State and Church. Sermons and addresses*, London: Hodder & Stoughton, 1908.

32 London, Dr Williams's Library, Congregational Library MS, P.T. Forsyth, 134.4: 'Dr Forsyth as a friend', in *Christian World*, 24 November 1921. Thomas Martin Lindsay (1843–1914), wrote *The Church and the Ministry in the Early Centuries*, London: Hodder & Stoughton, 1902.

Chapter 13

A foundation of influence

The Oxford Pastorate and elite recruitment in early twentieth-century Anglican evangelicalism

Mark Smith

Towards the end of 1895, the pages of *The Nineteenth Century. A Monthly Review* were briefly stirred by a minor religious controversy. In the October number, the Revd A.C. Deane produced an article on 'The religion of the undergraduate' in which he characterized the prevalent attitude to religion at both Oxford and Cambridge as one of easy-going agnosticism. The springs of this attitude, according to Deane, were to be found not in the undergraduates themselves, for 'a very little influence would suffice' to keep them within the faith, but rather in the nature of the influence to which they were subjected. Dons, and especially, 'the modern young Don who mixes freely with the undergraduates', were largely responsible for the spread of agnosticism – a bad influence compounded by the indifference of colleges to the spiritual welfare of their charges and the mischievous effects of compulsory attendance at college chapel.[1]

This indictment was immediately challenged by H. Legge in the November number of the *Review*. Whatever might be the situation at Cambridge, Legge asserted, Oxford men were not in the mass agnostic or irreligious, rather they were indifferent or non-religious – a condition that might ultimately lead them in any direction.[2] However, if Legge made an important distinction about the nature of the religious atmosphere at Oxford, he agreed with Deane about the causes. Just like Deane's 'agnosticism', Legge's 'indifference' was propagated by the academic body:

> One cannot help thinking, one only hopes wrongly, that many of the clerical Fellows are utterly indifferent to the spiritual welfare of men under their care, and do not in the least realise that they are responsible for them. How many of them can honestly say that they, as priests of the Catholic and Apostolic Church, have done their utmost for the young men under their charge?[3]

This situation was compounded by the often disgraceful services in college chapels and the useless examination in Divinity Moderations.[4]

It was in the context of this apparent decline in the vitality of Oxford

University's religious system and in the religious commitment of the under-graduate body that a group of leading Anglican evangelical laymen and clerics had met early in 1893, at the instigation of F.J. Chavasse, the principal of Wycliffe Hall, to plan a response. Their solution to indifference within the colleges was to provide an extra-collegiate chaplaincy to work in parallel with college chaplains and the clergy of the city churches – a plan that had already been adopted by the Tractarian founders of Pusey House. This chap-laincy was, moreover, to bear the distinctive stamp of their own tradition: it was to be, as its first appeal for funds made clear, 'AN EVANGELICAL PASTORATE FOR UNIVERSITY MEN AT OXFORD'.[5]

If the prevailing historiographical tradition is correct, then this initiative would seem, in at least two respects, to have been doomed to failure. In the first place, all commentators seem agreed that the evangelical tide, which had been at the flood in the middle of Victoria's reign, was on the ebb by the last decade of the century. The evangelicals were a declining force in English Christianity as a whole and in the Church of England in particular. According to Kenneth Hylson-Smith,

> By the time Edward VII ascended the throne they were quite seriously dispirited, uncertain of their role within the church and in society, and without that cohesion, purposefulness and energy which had character-ized them in the halcyon days of the past.[6]

This was a position from which it took them half a century to recover. Adrian Hastings concurred, citing Hensley Henson's claim that by the early twenti-eth century, 'the Evangelicals were exhibiting all the marks of a moribund party',[7] and asserting that 'Never was Evangelicalism weaker than in the 1920s – in vigour of leadership, intellectual capacity or largeness of heart'![8] Even the most sympathetic commentators have assumed that they are required to tell a story of decline. Randle Manwaring, for example, entitled his three chapters on Anglican evangelicalism between the First and Second World Wars, 'The defensive years', 'Through the waste land', and 'Continuing nadir'.[9]

The reasons given for this decline are various. They include an overenthu-siasm for foreign missions which creamed off the best evangelical leaders, a rather sectarian and increasingly introverted concentration on holiness focused by the Keswick Convention and the growing popularity of futurist pre-millennial eschatology, and over-reliance on stereotyped and obsolescent forms of revivalism. Perhaps more important still was the impression that the movement was primarily negative in character – obscurantist in its attitude to modern theology and spending much of its energy in opposing the ritual innovations of advanced high churchmen. This process culminated in the use, in 1928, of a Protestant majority in the House of Commons to throw out a revised liturgy, already approved by the church.[10]

Overall the impression is given that historians have taken Henson's famous characterization of evangelical opponents of the 1928 Prayer Book as 'an army of illiterates generalled by octogenarians',[11] as an epitome of Anglican evangelicalism as a whole. If one accepts the accuracy of this representation, it is difficult to imagine a form of religious life less likely to seize the imagination of the cream of England's educated youth gathered in a university, and least of all those gathered in the University of Oxford. For although an evangelical witness did persist there, two other religious influences seemed to dominate within the university.

On the one hand there was the continuing legacy of the Oxford Movement – perhaps at its most powerful in the late nineteenth century with its strongholds at Keble College and St Stephen's House, and the popular advanced ritualism of St Barnabas' church. It also possessed an active missionary centre at Pusey House, which was enjoying its greatest period under the influence of Gore and Darwell Stone.[12] On the other hand there was the influence of liberal Christianity, given powerful impetus earlier in the century by T.H. Green, whose 'method of regarding life and religion' was described by William Temple, writing in 1907, as still the dominant type of religious thought in Oxford.[13] Liberalism had been further reinforced in the 1880s by the introduction of Nonconformist theology into Oxford – especially from the pulpits of Mansfield and Manchester Colleges – and it issued (often in coalition with high-church interests) in a steady stream of active social work via college and university settlements, and ultimately in the Oxford branch of the Christian Social Union.[14] In this atmosphere university evangelicalism struggled for survival. It was organized primarily by the zealots of the Oxford Inter-Collegiate Christian Union (OICCU), whose 'shibboleths were terrifying, their narrowness a byword'[15] and whose chief claim to public notice was their willingness 'to incur the charge of folly by preaching at the Martyrs Memorial'. This was a form of religion which might be deprecated or admired for its intensity but which was unlikely to exercise much influence beyond its own isolated inner circle.[16]

It is against expectation, therefore, that throughout the period under consideration the *Annual Reports*[17] of the Oxford Pastorate record continuous, steady and sometimes spectacular success in its work among undergraduates. How was this success achieved and measured and how might it lead us to modify existing views about the nature of Anglican evangelicalism and its potential appeal to the educated laity in the early twentieth century? In order to answer these questions it is necessary briefly to consider the objectives of the Pastorate and then to investigate its methodology and its character.

The avowed aim of the Pastorate at its inception was to meet the need for spiritual supervision pointed to by Deane and Legge by introducing extra-collegiate chaplains. It also had a defensive purpose of preventing undergraduates from evangelical homes from drifting away from the tradition, and of encouraging an adequate supply of evangelical candidates for ordination.[18] However, quite rapidly, the Pastorate also became explicitly concerned with the wider influence of Oxford on the laity, as well as the clergy, as Francis Chavasse indicated in a statement of objectives published in 1897:

> It is the duty and wisdom of Evangelical Churchmen to safeguard a small but growing minority of undergraduates exposed to peculiar temptations in a University city. Every member of that minority will eventually have more or less influence as a clergyman, schoolmaster, barrister, country squire, merchant or Indian civil servant. Every man who drifts away is so much loss to the side of Truth. If Charles Simeon was accustomed to say as he saw *one* undergraduate enter Trinity Church, Cambridge, 'Here come 600 people', what shall be said of the value of hundreds now in residence in Oxford, all waiting to be shepherded?[19]

Similar statements constantly recur in the Pastorate's *Annual Reports*, increasingly combined with an expanded vision of the potential strategic importance of Oxford. 'The Cause of the Church at Home and of our Imperial Mission to the world', it was declared in 1900, 'is closely bound up with our older Universities.'[20] As the work began to grow, the defensive aims of the Pastorate also began to give way to an emphasis on active evangelism. In a statement of objectives prepared in 1913, for example, the safeguarding of undergraduates from evangelical homes came only third behind bringing 'the influence of personal religion to bear upon the men who are careless and irreligious', and work among 'that large section of men, who, without being indifferent to religion, are unwilling, for various reasons, to attach themselves to any of the recognised Christian bodies'.[21] There is certainly no sign here of any loss of confidence or of an assumption that the influence of evangelicalism would be confined to a narrow circle of enthusiasts. Instead, there is a clear expectation that it should be able to continue both to recruit the educated laity and to mobilize its recruits for active ministry. In the 1920s the Pastorate's Oxford Committee confirmed that its primary objective was 'to influence undergraduates *generally* in moral and spiritual matters'.[22] It had clearly established its role not as a university pastorate for evangelicals but as an evangelical pastorate for the university.

This recognition of the importance of influencing not only candidates for ordination but also the potential future leaders of society in general is a feature of British evangelicalism at least as old as More and Wilberforce. The Oxford Pastorate, however, was one of the earliest institutional embodiments of this strategy of elite recruitment, which seems to have played a vital role both in sustaining the position of Anglican evangelical churchmanship during the early twentieth century and in laying the foundations of its resurgent influence in the present. Historians have already noted the importance of the formation of the Inter-Varsity Fellowship in the 1920s as a vital factor in the advance of conservative evangelicalism after the Second World War.[23] Greater attention to the continuities in the policy of evangelicalism towards Oxford and Cambridge during its period of 'decline' is clearly overdue.

If the objectives of the Pastorate might have been predictable on the basis of long-standing evangelical tradition, its methodology seems rather unexpected. Shaped by the model of the college tutor, the methods adopted by the Pastorate chaplains were as far away from the popular revivalist image of turn of the century evangelicalism as can be imagined. 'We are naturally asked what methods we pursue', noted C.S. Woodward in 1914, reflecting on the previous five years spent as a Pastorate chaplain, 'the answer may be put in two words – personal influence.'[24] How was this influence brought to bear in practice? The intended approach was explained in detail in an appeal for public subscriptions in 1894:

> It is proposed to plant in the heart of Oxford two Clergymen of special gifts, whose single aim shall be to take up the spiritual side of the ideal Tutor's work, and by frequent and affectionate intercourse to seek to win to Christ, or to build up in Him, the large number of University men, who, at the present time, as is well known, are more than ready to welcome their help. Such spiritual advisers would form a centre round which Undergraduates may rally, and would be a source of inspiration and of guidance. They would be accessible at all times. They would be given to hospitality. They would act as the friends, advisers, sympathizers of those commended to their care or seeking their acquaintance.[25]

This pastoral and evangelistic approach, based on attempts to build relationships with undergraduates on an individual basis, remained the staple work of the Pastorate for at least its first 30 years. Thus, for example, the biographer of Temple Gairdner noted that during 1897, when he was a chaplain, his 'rooms became a storm-centre of religious life, a rallying point, a confessional. "So-and-so opened up" is a recurring phrase in his diary . . . One week he notes thirteen fresh names of men to be prayed for individually.'[26] The pastoral methodology also influenced the choice of chaplains. The first, and for over 30 years the senior chaplain, was H.H. Gibbon, a retired cavalry officer not remarkable for intellectual gifts or flamboyant evangelism, but possessing a remarkable capacity for cultivating the trust of undergraduates and, according to V.H.H. Green, 'a man of transparent sincerity and holiness'.[27] A system based on the development of friendships did not necessarily require the ministry of a clergyman, however, and while most of the chaplains were ordained, the Pastorate Council proved itself quite willing to employ laymen to work alongside Gibbon. Moreover, as the presence of female students became more prominent in the 1930s and 1940s, the Pastorate also took on a succession of laywomen – most notably Stella Aldwinckle who joined the staff in 1941.[28]

A comprehensive description of the chaplains' personal work in practice was given by Woodward in 1914:

> It is by the quiet work of making friends that the Pastorate justifies its existence, and may be said to be influencing the religious life of Oxford. Each year, as a new batch of freshmen arrives, the Chaplains come into touch with a few in every College: some inevitably fall off after a little, or remain on the outer circle of acquaintanceship; but even so, the opportunity is not wasted. It has more than once happened that men whom one had thought to have been entirely uninfluenced have come to one's house with moral and spiritual difficulties about which they sorely need help. The mere fact of inviting such men to an occasional meal, of sometimes seeing them in their own rooms, or meeting them by the river, may seem on paper a very little thing, but experience shows that even this casual intercourse may lead to large results later on. The day may come, and not seldom does, when it means a good deal to such men that there is a parson to hand whom they know, and believe that they can trust. But there is, of course, a very considerable number of men with whom the Chaplains are on far more intimate terms, with whom acquaintanceship has ripened into real and close friendship. They are men of very different kinds, with very different careers before them, with very different outlooks upon life, but it is not, we think, an exaggeration to say that they come to look upon the Chaplains as men to whom they would naturally go in time of need, for advice and spiritual help.[29]

Intensive work of this kind naturally imposed limits on the number of undergraduates each chaplain could befriend in the short space of an Oxford academic year. In 1913, for example, Woodward reported that some 1,600 men had been to his house for meals or coffee and that he was in touch with a total of 330.[30] Between 300 and 400 seems to have been the effective limit and, since lack of resources prevented the Pastorate from employing more than two or three chaplains at one time, this methodology did limit the scope of its work. In 1900, for example, the Council reported that the limits on its resources prevented the work from touching more than a fifth of the 3,000 undergraduates then in residence.[31]

The work of the Pastorate was not, however, restricted to making contact with undergraduates in Oxford. From an early stage the chaplains established links with the Children's Special Service Mission and the University Camps for Public Schoolboys and thus gained introductions to potential undergraduates before they reached the university.[32] Within Oxford, the chaplains supplemented their personal work with assistance to Bible-reading circles in colleges and the organization of occasional lectures, sermon series and discussions with prominent evangelical laymen.[33] No attempt was made, however, to organize any regular meetings or a society in which students associated with the Pastorate might gather, since it was felt that undergraduate activities in the university were best organized by the students themselves.[34] Nevertheless, the chaplains did seek to maintain good relations with the existing societies, especially the OICCU, and were sometimes called upon to advise their undergraduate leaders, as well as encouraging Oxford delegations to attend the summer camps associated with the SCM and with Keswick.[35]

Students linked with the Pastorate were also rapidly drawn into a second level of activity – a mobilization of the undergraduate constituency for active lay ministry. From the very beginning, undergraduates were encouraged to work as volunteers in Oxford parishes during term and outside Oxford in their vacations – sometimes in teams led by one of the chaplains.[36] However, much the most important outlet for undergraduate lay-ministry was vacation work at the Oxford Medical Mission in Bermondsey. Founded in 1897, and from its inception linked to the Pastorate, the Mission operated as a free medical service combined with a club for young men and boys. Both the medical and recreational parts of the work offered opportunities for pastoral and evangelistic activity and undergraduate volunteers were heavily involved in this.[37] The Pastorate clearly regarded the link with Bermondsey as a crucial part of its own work – especially with respect to its effect on the volunteers:

> They are learning there that the service of the poor, and self denial for the poor, is an integral part in the Christian life. We have noticed a distinct deepening of spiritual life and strengthening of character in many of the men who have been to work in Bermondsey.[38]

The fundamental organization of the Pastorate remained unchanged for nearly three decades. The 1920s, however, saw major changes which also influenced its methods of work. In July 1921 it was agreed, on the suggestion of the retiring rector of St Aldate's, one of the major evangelical churches in the city centre, that his successor might be appointed as a Pastorate chaplain. The Pastorate would provide a subsidy towards the rector's income and, in return, St Aldate's would provide an identifiable church base for the Pastorate.[39] The new rector, Christopher Chavasse (the son of the founder) was an enthusiast for the arrangement and turned St Aldate's into a major Pastorate centre with special sermon series and a range of meetings aimed at undergraduates, which became more elaborate over the subsequent decade.[40] This gradually changed the centre of gravity of the Pastorate's work and by 1936 the *Annual Report* could describe, in addition to the usual work alongside student-run societies, the development of a

> 'St Aldate's Fellowship' with its crowded Sunday morning congregations: its gatherings such as those at the Rectory on Tuesday afternoons; its

missions, evangelistic campaigns, and quiet week-ends; and all those Bible Study Circles which have lately sprung up in the Colleges.[41]

In 1942 this process was taken a stage further when the Pastorate finally took the step of organizing an undergraduate religious society – the Socratic Club. Initially founded by Stella Aldwinckle as a club for Somerville students, the Socratic rapidly developed into a mixed-sex university society with the orthodox Protestant C.S. Lewis as its president. Its aim was, according to the *Annual Report,* to bring undergraduates 'into touch with well-informed men and women of living faith who can understand and meet their intellectual difficulties, and lead them on into a personal knowledge of Christ'. It was also 'designed to challenge Christians to more radical realistic thinking about their Faith in the light of modern knowledge and thought so that they may be the better equipped as evangelists to meet educated pagans on their own ground'. The Club seems to have made a considerable impact during the 1940s. It had registered over 100 members by the end of its first year and by 1945 had begun to establish study groups and hold an annual conference.[42]

Although the bulk of the chaplains' time continued to be spent on making individual contacts, the development of church-based activities did allow larger numbers to be catered for. In 1935, for example, it was reported that numbers on the Pastorate list stood at 1,200: 'That is to say, fully a quarter of the University have some touch with St Aldate's and the Pastorate, and look to them in matters of spiritual guidance and inspiration.' In 1939 it was confidently asserted that, in the opinion of undergraduates, the Pastorate was rated as the strongest spiritual influence in the university.[43]

There was also an important change in the nature of the work in which the Pastorate sought to involve its undergraduate constituency – a gradual shift in emphasis from work at Bermondsey to involvement in evangelistic campaigns. The increasing concentration on missions, already apparent in the mid-1920s, clearly accelerated with the appointment of Bryan Green, himself a talented evangelist, as a chaplain in 1931. This activity included both undergraduate-led open-air services in local villages and missions to the university during term, and larger-scale campaigns elsewhere during vacations. It is important to note, however, that the campaigns did not take the form of the revivalist meetings centred on a star preacher usually associated with evangelicalism. Most of the preaching was undertaken by ordained ministers like Green himself, but much stress was also laid on the activity of the undergraduate teams. These were often large: 120 undergraduates were involved in the mission to Coventry in 1935, for example, and they took a central role not only in personal evangelism and visiting but also in the main mission meetings.[44] The Bournemouth Mission of 1933, in particular, was credited with introducing a new format in which instructional preaching by the clergy was supplemented by lay witnesses who gave personal testimony to their own experience of Christ – a development of an approach popularized by Frank

Buchman's Oxford Groups.[45] This systematic use of lay testimony in evangelism proved so successful that almost half the undergraduate population was attracted to a similar testimony meeting in the Town Hall in the subsequent term, and it was adopted as the standard pattern for future Pastorate missions.[46]

If the Pastorate in its methodology diverged from the stereotypes associated with evangelicalism, it was even further removed from those stereotypes in its character. Far from being negative, exclusive and oppositional, it represented an evangelicalism which, while definite about its own position, was positive, inclusive and constructive in its emphasis. The character of the Pastorate was, at least initially, determined by that of its founders, and especially of its leading light F.J. Chavasse. Chavasse eschewed Protestant extremism and aggressive campaigns against ritualism in favour of a more positive presentation of evangelical positions and dialogue with other groups within the church.[47] Although the importance of a distinctively evangelical Anglican witness continued to be stressed in the early twentieth century,[48] the combination of a firmly held evangelicalism with a broadly non-partisan attitude seems to have become a Pastorate tradition. Early chaplains like Archibald and Temple Gairdner while both being former presidents of the OICCU were also known for their broadness of outlook. Similarly, Woodward, at his interview with the Pastorate Council in 1908, declared himself to be in sympathy with 'the distinctively Evangelical and Protestant basis of the Pastorate' but also 'anxious to avoid partisanship of any kind'. Woodward's postwar successor Douglas Downes, who had developed an undergraduate ministry to tramps during his chaplaincy, left in 1922 to develop this work further and ended as the founder of the Franciscan order within the Church of England.[49] This tradition enabled the Pastorate to work with and, to some extent, to represent all the major strands within Anglican evangelicalism. Thus, in addition to the more conservative figures associated with Wycliffe Hall, E.A. Burroughs, a leading liberal evangelical, was closely associated with the Pastorate and was secretary of its Council until 1921.[50] Again, in the 1920s and 1930s, when a conservative evangelical OICCU split from the more eclectic SCM, the Pastorate was able to work cordially with both organizations.[51] The tradition was maintained during this period by Christopher Chavasse and Bryan Green, who have both been identified by David Bebbington (along with Max Warren who was offered a chaplaincy in 1934) as holding a centrist position within evangelicalism, wishing to hold together the liberal and conservative wings.[52]

The open and positive character of the Pastorate was not restricted to the various strands within Anglican evangelicalism. The lay activity of undergraduates at Bermondsey, in particular, proved attractive to a wider constituency. William Temple, for example, became involved with the Medical Mission as a student at Balliol and subsequently retained a close interest in it and in the organization of the Pastorate itself. One of the referees for his final, successful attempt to gain ordination in 1908 was H.H. Gibbon the Pastorate chaplain.[53] Perhaps the most spectacular example of the Pastorate's ecumenical tendencies, however, was the mission to Bournemouth in 1933. Led by Bryan Green and organized locally by Max Warren, the mission team comprised 12 clergy, including Miles Sargeant of Pusey House, two Mirfield Fathers and around 140 undergraduates of widely differing Anglican traditions (including, for example, Trevor Huddleston) all cooperating on the basis of 'an intense devotion to Jesus Christ'. The experiment seems to have produced a striking effect although it did alienate some of the Pastorate's most conservative supporters.[54]

There were limits, however, to the Pastorate's irenicism. Despite the assertion in its own official history that it never had an official attitude to the Oxford Groups, and the fact that one of its own employees H.J. Rose (chaplain 1926–32) was a leading light in Buchman's movement, the minutes of the Pastorate's Oxford Committee reveal an attitude of suspicion.[55] The committee seems to have sought to supervise Rose's work quite carefully and he was given permission to take a party on a campaign in South Africa in 1928 only on the understanding that the visit had 'no connection with Buchmanism'.[56] Christopher Chavasse, in particular, seems to have become concerned at what he regarded as the excessive subjectivism of the Groups and he encouraged the appointment of Rose's successor Bryan Green as a response – though, typically for the Pastorate, not so much to oppose Buchmanism as in the hope that he might be able to develop a positive counter-attraction to the Groups within Oxford.[57]

As the history of the Oxford Pastorate clearly demonstrates, to represent early twentieth-century evangelicalism as a negative and declining force is to omit an essential part of its story. Evangelicalism was a variegated phenomenon. It could be negative, sectarian and unattractive. It could also be open, innovative and successful. Even in the 1920s, Anglican evangelicals continued to demonstrate a capacity both to attract substantial numbers to their organizations and to find means to mobilize them for active social work and evangelism. If these positive elements had not played a significant role in shaping the character of contemporary evangelicalism it could not have sustained an effective mission within Oxford. That evangelicals both persisted and prospered in this attempt to influence the influential was a measure and also a foundation of their success.

Notes

1 A.C. Deane, 'The religion of the undergraduate', *The Nineteenth Century. A Monthly Review* 224, 1895, 673–80.
2 H. Legge, 'The religion of the undergraduate: a reply from Oxford', *The Nineteenth Century* 225, 1895, 861–9.
3 Ibid. 867.
4 Ibid. 869.

5 Oxford, Pastorate Collection, in the hands of the secretary, Dr H. Burd, advertisement bound with Council Minutes 30 April 1894.
6 K. Hylson-Smith, *Evangelicals in the Church of England 1734–1984*, Edinburgh: T.
   & T. Clark, 1988, p. 227.
7 A. Hastings, *A History of English Christianity 1920–1990*, 3rd edn, London: SCM,
   1991, p. 76.
8 Ibid. p. 200.
9 R. Manwaring, *From Controversy to Co-existence. Evangelicals in the Church of
   England 1914–1980*, Cambridge: Cambridge University Press, 1985, pp. 17–56.
10 The best account of evangelicalism in this period remains D.W. Bebbington,
   Evangelicalism in Modern Britain, London: Unwin Hyman, 1989, pp. 151–248. See
   also Hastings, *English Christianity*, pp. 76–90, 200–6, 453–4; Hylson-Smith,
   Evangelicals in the Church of England, pp. 227–66.
11 Quoted in Hastings, *English Christianity*, p. 206.
12 For the religious background at Oxford, see, for example, R.W. Gent, 'The reli-
   gious life', in J. Wells (ed.) *Oxford and Oxford Life*, London, 1892, pp. 120–38;
   'Religion in Oxford', *Church Quarterly Review* 109, 1902, 1–24; R.W. Macan,
   Religious Changes in Oxford During the Last Fifty Years, London: Humphrey
   Milford, 1917, pp. 11–34; V.H.H. Green, *Religion at Oxford and Cambridge*,
   London: SCM, 1964, p. 327; F.M. Turner, 'Religion', in B. Harrison (ed.) *The
   History of the University of Oxford, Vol. 8, The Twentieth Century*, Oxford:
   Clarendon Press, 1994, pp. 293–326.
13 W. Temple, 'The religion of the undergraduate', *Oxford and Cambridge Review* 1,
   1907, 45–56.
14 Ibid. 49–54; Turner, 'Religion', pp. 295–8.
15 C.E. Padwick, *Temple Gairdner of Cairo*, London: SPCK, 1929, p. 20.
16 'Religion in Oxford', *Church Quarterly Review* 109, 13.
17 *Oxford Pastorate Annual Reports* [hereafter *AR*], 1894–1945.
18 Advertisement bound with Council Minutes, 30 April 1894.
19 F.J. Chavasse, *The Evangelical Pastorate for Undergraduates at Oxford*, London,
   1897, pp. 1–2 (copy in Pastorate Collection).
20 *AR*, 1900, p. 11.
21 Statement bound with Council Minutes, 17 April 1913.
22 Oxford, Pastorate Collection, Minutes of the Pastorate Oxford Sub-Committee
   [hereafter Committee Minutes], 4 July 1921 (my emphasis).
23 Bebbington, *Evangelicalism*, pp. 259–61.
24 *AR*, 1914, p. 16.
25 Advertisement bound with Council Minutes, 30 April 1894.
26 Padwick, *Temple Gairdner*, p. 50.
27 Green, *Religion at Oxford*, p. 328.
28 G.I.F. Thomson, *The Oxford Pastorate. The first half century*, London:
   Canterbury Press, 1946, pp. 59–60, 154–8.
29 *AR*, 1914, pp. 18–20.
30 Council Minutes, 14 April 1913.
31 *AR*, 1900, p. 11.
32 See, for example, *AR*, 1899; E.M. Archibald, *Malcolm Archibald: a memoir*,
   London: privately published, 1923, pp. 13–16.
33 *AR*, 1899, p. 9; 1903, p. 8; 1905, p. 9.
34 *AR*, 1914, pp. 17–18.
35 *AR*, 1906, p. 9; Archibald, *Memoir*, pp. 15–16.
36 *AR*, 1895, p. 7; 1913, pp. 9–10.
37 Thomson, *Pastorate*, pp. 38–9, 45–50; *AR*, 1901, pp. 24–8.

38 Ibid. pp. 10–11.

39 Committee Minutes, 4 July 1921; *AR*, 1922, p. 3.

40 *AR*, 1922, pp. 3–4; 1930, pp. 4–6.

41 *AR*, 1936, p. 4.

42 *AR*, 1942, pp. 10–11; 1945, p. 10.

43 *AR*, 1935, p. 6; 1939, p. 6.

44 *AR*, 1926, p. 4; 1930, pp. 4–6; 1935, p. 4.

45 M.A.C. Warren, *Interpreters: a study in contemporary evangelism*, London: Highway Press, 1936, pp. 43–9, 136–40. For a discussion of the Oxford Groups, see Bebbington, *Evangelicalism*, pp. 235–40.

46 *AR*, 1933, p. 4; Thomson, *Pastorate*, pp. 117–18.

47 Chavasse to J.W.H. Inskip, 8 October 1902, Oxford, Bodleian Library, Chavasse Dep. 1, No. 124; J.B. Lancelot, *Francis James Chavasse, Bishop of Liverpool*, Oxford: Basil Blackwell, 1929, pp. 156–7; 'Religion in Oxford', *Church Quarterly Review* 109, 13.

48 See, for example, E.A. Burroughs, *The Oxford Pastorate and the Crisis in the Church*, Oxford: privately published, 1911.

49 Archibald, *Memoir*, pp. 10–16; Padwick, *Temple Gairdner*, pp. 34–9; Council Minutes, 18 December 1908; Thomson, *Pastorate*, pp. 93–5, 156.

50 Burroughs' liberal evangelicalism did not, however, reach its fullest stage of development until the 1920s. H.G. Mulliner, *Arthur Burroughs. A memoir*, London: Nisbet, 1936.

51 Thomson, *Pastorate*, pp. 151–4; *AR*, 1936, p. 4.

52 Bebbington, *Evangelicalism*, pp. 251; Committee Minutes, 7 November 1934.

53 F.A. Iremonger, *William Temple, Archbishop of Canterbury. His life and letters*, London: Oxford University Press, 1948, pp. 42, 122–4, 599; Council Minutes, 18 December 1908, 5 November 1912.

54 Warren, *Interpreters*, pp. 136–40; B. Green, *Bryan Green Parson-Evangelist*, ed. T.E. Yates, Thame: Bryan Green Society, 1994, pp. 36–7.

55 Thomson, *Pastorate*, pp. 99, 157; G.F. Allen, 'The Groups in Oxford', in R.H.S. Crossman (ed.) *Oxford and the Groups. The influence of the Groups considered*, Oxford: Basil Blackwell, 1934, pp. 1–41; I.M. Randall, *Evangelical Experiences*, Carlisle: Paternoster, 1999, pp. 238-68; Committee Minutes, 17 May 1930.

56 Ibid. 11 July 1928, 17 May 1930.

57 Green, *Parson-Evangelist*, pp. 35–9. However, Chavasse himself seems to have had some links with the Groups in the 1920s. Randall, *Evangelical Experiences*, p. 242.

The church of the laity

'The church itself is God's clergy'

The principles and practices of the Brethren

Neil T.R. Dickson

The Brethren movement was in part the product of increased participation by laypeople in nineteenth-century evangelicalism. It arose in the late 1820s in Dublin, quickly spreading to England and arriving in Scotland a decade later. After 1848 it divided into two sections: the Exclusive Brethren who followed the leadership of the ex-Anglican clergyman, John Nelson Darby, and the Open Brethren, a looser grouping of independent churches. There was, in addition, another schism within the latter in 1892–4, which gave birth to the Churches of God, a body governed by a hierarchy of elders.[1] Among those who joined the nascent movement there was considerable dissatisfaction with the institutional church and among the causes of discontent was the role of the clergy.[2] The Brethren retained the deeply rooted anti-Catholicism of their radical evangelical background:[3] for the young J.N. Darby the papacy was 'Satan's fiction' in answer to the true church.[4] Robert Beverley, a lawyer and Anglican turned Dissenter, who was for a while associated with the Brethren, judged other churches by the proximity of their ecclesiology to that of Rome. 'Any one with ordinary intellectual capacities', he pronounced dismissively, 'can weigh the Church of England in the gospel balances, and discover its deficiencies.'[5] He instanced a hypothetical evangelical vicar in a country parish, who had succeeded in reforming the manners of the village yet who, due to the power of the patrons, would be succeeded by either a 'rapacious cormorant' or a younger son of an aristocrat, 'a famous fox-hunter and an unerring shot'. The consequences for the village were 'inevitable'.[6] Evangelical clergy, he evidently felt, were compromised. Nor did Nonconformity as represented by Congregationalism fare any better, being embarrassed by the monarchical form of its ministerial office. The exaltation of one man could become an excuse for inactivity among the members.[7] The laity were marginalized, not emancipated.

In Ireland the problems of the evangelical clergy and their relations to the laity were acute and became one of the principal causes behind the formation of the movement there. After the union of 1801 the embattled Anglo-Irish community saw their task in the countryside as being one of religious conversion. Membership of interdenominational societies became an important marker of evangelical self-identity. After Catholic emancipation in 1829 evangelicals tended to become isolationists within the church.[8] By 1833 Darby was noting that the three contemporary characteristics of the religious scene in Ireland were the desires for preaching, scriptural knowledge and communion with one another.[9] It was out of small groups meeting to satisfy the last two of these concerns that the Brethren had grown.[10] Judging by the frequency with which he wrote about it, the first of these desires was also of importance for Darby in the impetus towards secession. This can be seen in the problems raised by the Irish Church Home Missionary Society. Founded in 1828 by an Anglican clergyman (probably Robert Daley, vicar of Powerscourt), it was an agency of the Church of Ireland for the itinerant evangelization of the country.[11] Darby considered most of the clergy to be unconverted: he calculated that two thirds of them did not preach the gospel.[12] Accordingly, lay preaching outside the church became of great importance.[13] Faithfulness to Christ meant that Christians should preach to those ready to perish and he was critical of those who restricted their evangelism in order not to offend their superiors.[14]

Darby had arrived at a characteristic Anglican dilemma between compliance with church order and loyalty to evangelicalism, and he was coming to the same conclusion that the pre-Simeonite evangelical Anglicans had reached before him: that the commission to preach the gospel made irregularity inevitable.[15] In addition he felt that because the established church was parochial and episcopal it existed for those who were already Christian. It failed as an evangelistic means and it was to supply this deficiency that the Irish Home Mission came into existence.[16] As a body the mission was opposed by the bishops because it violated church order. Having initially included lay preachers, its operations were eventually taken over entirely by the clergy because they refused to work with laymen in such a role. Darby cited one incident where no preacher had been available when, rather than send a godly layman, an empty carriage had been sent instead.[17] The work of the Home Mission, he felt, was shot through with inconsistencies. Paradoxically, laymen had sought official recognition from the system they were violating.[18] In a pamphlet published in 1833 he gave two examples of the contradictions into which the Home Mission clergy were led. An individual with a call from God would go to a parish with an ungodly clergyman in office. Though the itinerant was irregular he would be recognized by the Home Mission. The second example Darby gave, which he admitted was less common, was that of a layman preaching in countryside which was destitute of the gospel. Converts would be made, but the Home Mission would insist on them being handed over to the care of ungodly clergymen. The inevitable result of this case, Darby felt, would be schism.[19] Indeed he came to think that the essential tendency of the Home Mission was schismatic. It acted independently of the bishops by allowing irregular preaching by evangelical clergy and only recognized episcopal authority over the exclusion of laymen.[20] Yet, paradoxically, Darby noted, it was ministers of state – themselves laymen – who appointed the clergy to their office, making it ridiculous to talk of the 'heavenly-derived' character of episcopal control.[21] In 1834 he finally proclaimed in an article for the *Christian Witness*, a Brethren magazine founded that year, the 'Christian liberty of preaching and teaching the Lord Jesus Christ'. In a tract written about the same time and entitled *The Notion of a Clergyman Dispensationally the Sin against the Holy Ghost*, which he had printed but did not issue, he maintained that evangelical clergymen who condemned laymen for preaching the gospel and thereby committing the sin of schism, were themselves guilty of the sin against the Holy Spirit by calling the work of God sinful, that is, the work of Satan.[22] Darby's involvement in the evangelical missionary crusade to convert Ireland forced him to side with lay agency against the principles of the established church, thus making his secession inevitable.

The eighteenth-century Evangelical Revival had, in the words of W.R. Ward, 'impressively demonstrated the real force of that Cinderella of Protestant doctrines, the priesthood of all believers'.[23] The Irish Home Mission, which showed Darby the value of mobilizing the laity, was part of a growing movement that produced similar effects in the early nineteenth century. Spanning the two centuries were the itinerant evangelists Robert and James Haldane who introduced to their Edinburgh congregation an ecclesiology and patterns of worship similar to those which the Brethren were to adopt some 30 years later. It is not possible to demonstrate a direct influence of Haldaneite thinking on the Brethren, but influences emanating from the Haldanes undoubtedly made some impact. Arguments employed by James Haldane can be paralleled in Brethren writings,[24] and the phrase 'social worship', forming the title of one of his most influential books, was used by Henry Craik and George Müller when they were steering their Baptist church in Bristol towards Brethren practices. In subsequent years Craik continued to use the term.[25] In addition the Haldanes had affected Irish evangelicalism: the Home Mission was probably one product of their influence. Two Irish secessionist bodies of the period founded by Thomas Kelly and John Walker, which adopted a primitivist ecclesiology, were inspired by Haldaneite thinking and the Brethren were certainly aware of their existence.[26] Even if the Brethren were not reading the Haldanes, their arguments and vocabulary had passed into the milieu from which the Brethren emerged. There were also other movements among the laity in contemporary evangelicalism. Many of the small fellowship meetings in Ireland and England, the former having previously influenced the Haldanes, gave their followers a predisposition towards Brethrenism.[27] Lay agency was also promoted by two other influential Scots in the early nineteenth century: by Thomas Chalmers whose *Christian and Civic Economy of Large Towns*, published from 1819, enjoyed a wide readership and by David Nasmith who founded a number of city missions, including the London City Mission in 1835, which extended Chalmers'

Glasgow experiment with lay visitors who supported the work of the regular clergy.[28] The general upsurge in lay activity at the turn of the nineteenth century was a significant part of the background from which the Brethren movement emerged and grew.

In an American context Nathan Hatch has written of the democratization of Christianity in the early nineteenth century. Although Hatch believes that this was a peculiarly American phenomenon – seeing English Christianity as handicapped by gentility and compromised by its association with the social and political establishment – the trend he examines also had a considerable effect in Britain, constituting one of the streams which fed into the Brethren movement.[29] It can be seen in a figure such as John Bowes. Bowes, a native of Yorkshire, was a Primitive Methodist who left the denomination after a disagreement in 1828 between his circuit and the Edinburgh Mission to which he had been sent. After making attempts from Scotland to form a union with various Free Methodist bodies, he travelled south to Liverpool in 1837 where he heard of Craik and Müller at Bristol. Although he remained an ultra-independent, who differed on a number of points from what came to be accepted as orthodoxy within the emerging Brethren movement, he adopted its ecclesiology, forming and encouraging congregations mainly in the north of England and Scotland. A number of these became part of mainstream Brethrenism.[30]

Bowes was part of the reaction within Methodism to the central control of the Conference and as such represented a more lay-orientated, congregational perspective. It also produced for the Brethren William Trotter, who was expelled from the Methodist New Connexion along with Joseph Barker in 1841 after a dispute involving the Conference of that body. Trotter was a significant early influence on Brethrenism in Yorkshire.[31] He was among those who had renounced their ordination and whom Bowes hailed in a pamphlet entitled *A Hired Ministry Unscriptural*, written about 1843 shortly after Bowes came in contact with the Brethren. In this tract the author argued that the gift of teaching was 'not limited to one man in the church – to college educated ordained men'.[32] There were other ways also in which Bowes rejected contemporary orthodoxies by attacking professional interests. He advocated a healthy lifestyle, challenging the medical establishment by recommending cold-water baths and vegetarianism.[33] In his church order he empowered ordinary people, promoting mutual exhortation and even proposing questions from the congregation to the preachers.[34] He also dreamt of a new religious and social order. In his first book, *Christian Union* (1835), he expressed the hope that the unity of Christians would lead to the conversion of the world.[35] Soon after the collapse of Feargus O'Connor's land plan in 1847, Bowes developed one of his own in which he proposed an equitable distribution of the nation's resources funded out of money saved by abolishing the army and the clergy.[36] His was the 'blurring of worlds' which Hatch detects in the contemporary democratizing impulse, mixing Enlightenment rationalism with

Romantic sensibility.[37] Among early Brethren, R.M. Beverley, the former Anglican turned Dissenter, was perhaps the closest to Bowes, for he too possessed a polemical spirit which derided establishments, had social concerns and dreamt of a time when 'all the world will be our country, and all mankind our brothers'.[38] But generally those who shared Bowes' attitude of seeking for a more demotic church order were lower in the social scale than the pioneers of the Dublin–Plymouth–Bristol axis. Among those drawn into the Brethren over the first two decades were several who shared Bowes' aspirations.

Mid-Victorian revivalism, which had a marked effect on the growth of the Brethren,[39] also continued the mobilization of the laity and often circumvented institutional Christianity. When in 1866 Duncan Matheson, the leader of the Scottish revivalist network, advised two lay evangelists about their forthcoming visit to Renfrew, he told them that the town's ministers had closed the kirks against revivalists. Consequently, he sent them to a mission run by a woman.[40] Laymen were prominent in mid-Victorian revivalism and there was a further upsurge in lay preaching after the 1859 revival, which was known in Scotland as 'the laymen's revival'.[41] John Kent has described the evangelicalism which emerged from 1830 until 1850 as being

> lay in spirit, urban in concern, disaffected from the ministry, indifferent to denominational frontiers, expressing its distrust of traditional religious institutions by the formation of new ones, which were kept out of the control of the clergy as much as possible.[42]

The piety which the awakenings fostered led easily to Brethrenism. Perhaps less ecclesiastically radical than the earlier phase of democratization identified by Hatch, it nevertheless signified the rising of a more demotic Christianity. The two evangelists bound for Renfrew in 1866 were Brethren and a number of other itinerants and many of the converts found the movement congenial. Others prominent in the revivalist network, such as the publisher R.C. Morgan, who was in a Brethren assembly for a while, were deeply influenced by the thinking of the movement.[43] How easy it was for those touched by revivalism to become Brethren can be seen in the recollection by Robert McKilliam, an Aberdeenshire physician, of conversational Bible readings held in Old Meldrum following the visit of the lay preacher Reginald Radcliffe in 1859.

> We used to meet night after night in each other's houses, sit around the table with a Book in our hands, with our eyes up to Jesus, our Lord, and talk out to each other our thoughts as He gave them.[44]

The ethos was that of a Brethren meeting. McKilliam later left the Free Church of Scotland to found an undenominational congregation in Huntly, which subsequently united with the town's Brethren assembly.[45] When he moved to London in 1880 McKilliam himself entered the movement.[46] The lay spirit of the awakenings has perhaps been underestimated in histories of the Brethren as an important shaping force on its ethos. After 1859 the movement to some extent was remade, with Brethrenism inheriting not only the anti-establishment spirit of mid-century revivalism, but also its lay orientation.

The upsurge in lay activity was an important part of the evangelicalism from which Brethrenism emerged and tensions between clerical establishments and laypeople became a significant cause of accessions to the new movement. The Brethren developed their own thinking on the laity, but their principles and practices did not arrive fully fledged. The commemoration of the Lord's supper in Dublin to which Brethren origins are traced, initially had a set order of service, but it gradually came to allow spontaneous participation by attendants.[47] The mature thought of Darby, in particular, slowly evolved and, in addition, there were differences of emphasis among individuals, something which was to harden after the division of 1848. Also of significance was the denominational background of Brethren members, whether in Anglicanism or Nonconformity. The review offered here will attempt to take some account of these nuances of time, personality and experience.

The Brethren rejected the traditional division between clergy and laity. This was an important point for James Lampen Harris, a former Anglican clergyman who was one of the early Brethren leaders at Plymouth and editor of the *Christian Witness*. In the opening article of the magazine's founding issue in January 1834, Harris maintained that in Christianity the 'highest in office' has the same access to God 'as the merest babe'. Division of the church into categories was designed to 'give a pre-eminence in standing, as to nearness to God, to the clergy, and thereby setting at a distance the laity', thus obscuring the grace of God. In the true church all were equal before God, for 'The church is God's clergy (*kleroi*) (I Pet. v.3).'[48] This text was important for the Brethren, for it demonstrated that the English word was derived from the Greek for 'lot' or 'portion', signifying in scripture God's heritage. Darby defined the term 'clergy' as 'the elect body, or rather bodies of believers, as God's heritage, as contrasted with those who were instructors, or had spiritual oversight over them'.[49] It was not just by an appeal to the New Testament that the Brethren, especially those with an establishment background and anxious to avoid the charge of schism, were concerned to refute the charge of novelty in their rejection of the division into clergy and laity. When Charles Hargrove, an Episcopalian curate in Ireland, resigned his living in 1835, he gave the example of the Corinthian church as showing mutual cooperation within the one body with no division into clergy and laity. But, not surprisingly, he also quoted extensively from the first volume of Neander's church history to demonstrate that the primitive church did not have a class of priests. William Henry Dorman made the same point when he resigned in controversial circumstances as minister of Islington Congregational Chapel in 1838 and he also cited the opinions of Robert Browne and John Milton.[50] R.M. Beverley sought to show that Luther had realized the priesthood of all believers, liberty of ministry and the abrogation of the official priesthood, but had not judged it politic to insist on his views as part of the Reformation.[51] For Beverley, as for Harris, every true Christian was a priest 'in the gospel sense'. To divide the church into clergy and laity was to take away the glory of Christ who 'anoints all his elect servants to be kings and priests'.[52] If any ecclesiastical institution separated believers into two distinct categories 'then is the design of the gospel not answered'.[53] The division into clergy and laity was seen as a product of confusion between Judaism and Christianity.[54] Attacks on the Judaizing of Christianity were particularly marked among those with an Anglican background,[55] probably because the Old Testament example was used to defend establishment and church order. It was Darby who, in developing the scheme known as dispensationalism, which rigidly divided Judaism from the church, pressed the contrast furthest.[56] The radical implications which the Brethren saw in the New Testament led them to reject any division between members of the church.

High views of the Christian ministry were also rejected. One target here was the notion of ordination: Darby commented, 'derived authority from man I believe to be most evil'.[57] It was not ordination which proved the trustworthiness of the preacher, but doctrine and character.[58] James Patrick Callahan has recently drawn attention to the influence exerted by Anthony Norris Groves, a dentist from Exeter who subsequently became a missionary in Persia and India. Both George Müller and Robert Chapman, the Brethren pioneer in Barnstaple, derived their rejection of ordination from Groves.[59] He had intended to seek Anglican ordination before he entered missionary service, but abandoned the plan when he developed conscientious scruples over the thirty-ninth article on the bearing of arms. He renounced any dependence on human institutions, among which he regarded ordination, and attempted to demystify the conception of Christian ministry. In 1835 he gave a pragmatic illustration of the illogicality of attempting to trace apostolic succession to scripture. If Dr Andrew Bell, the recently deceased educational innovator, had appointed schoolmasters over every school, but among his papers had made no reference to either himself or his heirs having the sole power to do so, it would not be concluded that he had arrogated the power to himself. Moreover, if his extant letters referred to the character and qualifications of subsequent schoolmasters, but not to his power of appointment, then it would be deduced that he never intended to have that right inalienably. Groves applied this analogy to the New Testament in order to deny the concept of apostolic succession. 'Ordination' in scripture meant 'placed', or 'put': terms that might be used in connection with schoolmasters, but not in the modern ecclesiastical sense. Allied to his rejection of a high view of ministry was his disapproval of the meaning given to the laying on of hands in the contemporary church. For Groves it was a cultural matter. Modes of commendation differed: prayer meetings were the English practice whereas laying on of hands was Jewish.[60] Beverley also was critical of the practice in Congregational churches. Ordinary people, he maintained, either thought that the ministers had the power of conveying the Holy Spirit or believed they were a corporation admitting the candidate to their body.[61] A ministerial presence, the Brethren argued, was not needed for preaching, baptism, or commemoration of the Lord's supper.[62] Beverley was also scathing about what he saw as ministerial pretension in using the title 'reverend', a term used in scripture in connection with God.[63] The renunciation of separate or exalted status for any group within the church was a corollary of the levelling which the Brethren detected in Christianity.

Underlying the rejection of ordination and suspicion of laying on of hands was the belief that the call to ministry came from God, a conviction which was central to Brethren thought.[64] All were agreed that true ministry had a divine origin. For Groves, 'it is by Christ's appointment alone that any one becomes a minister of Christ'.[65] The more mystical Darby usually made the Holy Spirit the active agent. It was because the 'authority of man' had been substituted 'for the power and presence of that, holy, blessed and blessing Spirit, by which this dispensation is characterized' that he believed the notion of a clergyman in the Christian era constituted the sin against the Holy Ghost.[66] The sin of the Irish clergy was compounded in Darby's eyes by the exclusion of lay preachers from the Home Mission. By this action they had put themselves against those with a Spirit-given competency to preach.[67] Beverley provokingly argued that the Roman Catholic Church was nearer to the truth than Nonconformity on this point because it believed that in ordination it conferred the Spirit who gave validity to ministry.[68] It was the primacy given to the divine origin of ministry which made the Brethren downgrade the importance of education. 'The training of a university', warned Craik, 'or the humbler aid of a dissenting college, will be found miserable substitutes for the teaching of the Spirit, and the energy of His inward operations.' However, he added: 'First let there be the higher qualifications of simple faith . . . and then let all the helps, connected with mental attainments and diligent study of the Scriptures, be rendered available for the furtherance of the Gospel.'[69] The qualification was one that Brethren subsequently rarely, if ever, made.

The marked emphasis on the role of the Spirit in the church at the expense of human resources had particular implications for the commemoration of the Lord's supper. An early member of the Plymouth assembly, Percy Francis Hall, a naval officer who had resigned his commission on conscientious grounds, asserted that 'mutual edification' was practised by the Corinthian church at the Lord's supper in a manner which 'gave free power to the Holy Ghost in His presiding presence'.[70] Although 'open meetings' at which there was no pre-arranged preacher were used for a while, it was the Brethren breaking of bread, as the service came to be called among them, which preserved the spontaneous form of worship and constituted the most distinctive meeting of the movement. At Plymouth, and initially elsewhere, an elder presided over the exercise of ministry, which restricted worship to a degree,[71] but the pattern which came to prevail was that of open participation by the men as the Spirit moved them to take part. It was here that the Brethren model of equality in worship reached its fullest expression.[72] William Trotter, the former Methodist, recollected occasions in one unidentified assembly when the ideal had been achieved at the breaking of bread:

> When silence was broken, it was with a prayer that embodied the desires, and expressed the breathings of all present; or a hymn in which all could with fulness of heart unite; or a word which came to our hearts with power. And though several might be used in such hymns, and prayers, and ministrations, it was evidently one Spirit who guided and arranged the whole, as though a plan of it had been made before-hand, and each one had his part assigned. No human wisdom could have made such a plan. The harmony was divine. It was the Holy Ghost acting by the several members, in their several places, to express the worship, or to meet the need of all present.[73]

Not only was it God who gave the ability to minister, it was God who guided the ministry.

'Holy liberty and love is the only character of the gospel, and surely therefore of this service', Captain Hall maintained concerning the commemoration of the Lord's supper.[74] Openness to the Spirit led the Brethren to stress liberty of ministry and with the idea of liberty went an expanded idea of what 'ministry' was. For Harris 'ministry or service might be either teaching, or exhorting, or giving to the poor, or preserving order', while, he noted, there had been 'an undue coveting of serving in the Word, as if that was exclusively ministry'.[75] Beverley defined ministry as '*any service of the saints to God and to His church*'.[76] The lists of gifts in the New Testament epistles were scoured to compile a comprehensive concept of what 'ministry' included. In the diversity of gifts that might be expected in the church, once again the Corinthian church served as a model but, unlike Edward Irving, it was not expected that miraculous endowments would be restored to the church.[77] There was also criticism of the idea of confining all gifts to one individual, namely the minister.[78] Benjamin Wills Newton, sometime Oxford fellow and a leader of the Plymouth assembly, commented, 'this we know from scripture to be impossible: all are not prophets, all are not teachers, all do not interpret'.[79] Dorman, on the other hand, did not feel this to be impossible per se but doubted that 'such a concentration of gift was ever contemplated by the Spirit, as the invariable order of things. He still "*divides to every man severally as he will*"'.[80] The effect of confining all the gifts to one individual, it was agreed, was deleterious. 'He is teacher, minister, preacher, exhorter, ruler everything', wrote Bowes of the clergyman.[81] Instead of the domination of one man in the church, the Brethren maintained there should be a plurality of elders who would function in groups.[82] Darby and those who followed him, however, differed on this point. The church was in ruins, he believed, by which he meant not that it no longer existed but that 'the Church is not all in its normal state'.[83] Therefore, while gift might exist in the church, appointment to office, which was an apostolic function, did not and so elders should not be instituted in the contemporary church.[84] There was no successional authority in the church and no appointment to formal roles within the congregation. The Open Brethren argued there was no need to take human measures to supply teachers in individual churches – they would emerge as they waited upon God.[85] Even the Exclusive Brethren, conscious that the church was divided and an assembly might not comprehend all Christians with gifts in a given locality, maintained that the Spirit would supply the needs of the church.[86] The Spirit was sovereign and liberty of ministry expressed his sovereignty.

Brethrenism emancipated the laity. A product of the upper and middle classes in its initial phase, it had developed an ideology which allowed it to become downwardly mobile. Its spiritual democracy meshed with significant elements within the British working classes. It appealed to the literate, autonomous working-class individual for whom the autodidact, a phenomenon often nurtured by evangelicalism, was a figure of respect.[87] Thus it was in the 1860s that Brethrenism was transmuted, emerging as an almost wholly working-class and lower-middle-class sect, rooted in industrialized communities. Activism was a way of life for the Brethren. Laypeople were completely absorbed in the life of the church. Isaiah Stewart, a coal miner in Lanarkshire and a Brethren member from 1882 until his death in 1934, rose early to read the Bible before he started work at 5 a.m. and was prominent in his meeting for Bible teaching and participation at the breaking of bread. His constancy was remembered in a piece of doggerel describing the members of the Haywood Brethren written about the time of the First World War:

> Isaiah's name we'll here record
> It does deserve a place,
> For often do we hear his voice
> In ministry and Praise.[88]

Such working-class individuals possessed roles which were unimaginable in the contemporary denominational churches. The movement also produced a proportionately large number of missionaries. Harold Rowdon has stated that, in the United Kingdom at least, it would not be an exaggeration to claim that 1 per cent of the entire membership served overseas.[89] It has been calculated that in 1945 Brethren missionaries accounted for more than 5 per cent of all Protestant foreign missionary personnel.[90] The movement utilized the gifts of laypeople and allowed them scope for exercise of their talents.

The Brethren concept of the church was built around a number of princi-ples: the priesthood of all believers, liberty of ministry, diversity of gifts and the sovereignty of the Spirit. There were, however, a number of ways in which Brethren practice undercut these principles. It might be expected, given the radical way in which the Brethren stressed, in the words of J.L. Harris, the 'equal nearness, equal liberty of access' of all believers, that their practice would be democratic.[91] In addition, it was maintained that judgement of a teacher's doctrinal correctness should be made by the whole church. Groves went as far as to argue that in John's Second Epistle it was a lady and her chil-dren who were to be the judges. He concluded, 'we are *all* responsible – men, women and children – for the *exercise* of our judgment'.[92] Yet the Brethren were politically conservative. In 1844 Darby replied with evident pleasure to a Swiss detractor, who felt that religious radicalism led to social and political radicalism, that it was being reported in England that the new movement was attracting the aristocracy by way of reaction to the extreme democracy of English Dissent.[93] Darby disliked political democracy, deploring the effects of the 1832 Reform Bill,[94] and other Brethren shared his aversion. Newton accused Dissenters of self-will which was seen 'in the earnestness with which they contend[ed] for the democratic principle of elective and controlling power being vested in those who should be governed'.[95] Groves, recalling the church to poverty, stressed that in doing so he did not want to join those who would strip the established church of its power and wealth and encourage the spirit of insubordination.[96] What is perhaps surprising is that even after the mid-century revivals, when the Brethren became largely working and lower-middle class, the disapproval of democracy continued. Mainstream Brethren opinion represented a nineteenth-century conservative counterculture, which in the movement also meant an intense social and political conservatism.

Generally Brethren did not participate in politics, but their secular conser-vatism carried over into ecclesiology and they rejected Congregationalism. There was a strong desire for order in the church. One later Brethren member J. Albert Boswell, a leader of the Churches of God division within Open Brethrenism, cryptically wrote in 1888 that freedom in leaving 'the sects' (as the Brethren termed the institutional church) 'may only be the very worst of democracies because lawlessness in the very House of God'.[97] Men are not equal, asserted Beverley, anxious to avoid what he termed the 'absurdity' of the *Rights of Man*, but have varying values for the church.[98] Ministry and priesthood were different, for although all believers were priests, not all were ministers, but only those whom the Spirit raised up.[99] Just as despotism was the evil in popery, democracy was the evil in Congregationalism. It was a denial of the sovereignty of the Spirit.[100] This tenet was a principal article for the Calvinist Darby: 'the liberty of the believer', he wrote in 1834, 'is not the spirit of insubordination, but of entire subjection to the Spirit and the Church of God wheresoever they be found'.[101] With the stress on liberty went a strong emphasis on order. The Exclusive Brethren, who followed

Darby, had no formal offices in their congregations and retained a charismatic concept of ministry. But although within the local congregation decisions were arrived at collectively, the overall movement had one teacher who held a dominant position.[102] The lack of institutionalized procedures for appointing leaders left it open to abuse and led eventually to the eccentric and dictatorial policies of the 'universal leader' James Taylor Jnr, which were to have disastrous consequences for Exclusivism after 1959.[103] In the Open Brethren voting was rejected as a means of appointing elders.[104] Groves had believed that the evangelist who founded a church might be responsible for appointing the initial leadership, but this would only be an interim measure. Both he and Craik insisted that leadership required church approval.[105] But this view eventually disappeared. Some Open Brethren assemblies followed the Exclusive pattern of not appointing elders, being governed instead by a 'brothers' meeting', an informal group of the long-established male members.[106] But the concept of eldership which won general favour was that developed under Newton at Plymouth and accepted by Craik and Müller at Bristol in 1843 during a retreat to determine basic church principles. The Spirit was seen as appointing elders; the place of the church was to receive that choice by acknowledging those who clearly had the gift of eldership.[107] This theory combined a charismatic ministry with church order. Eventually it was accepted that the existing elders should be the ones who recognized those with the gift,[108] effectively ensuring the successional leadership of a self-appointing oligarchy.[109] Typically such an organization has an implicit conservative tendency which makes it reluctant to accept change. The Churches of God, horrified at what they termed the 'looseness' of Open Brethrenism, developed the power of the elders, a system of government residing in an ascending hierarchy of oversight groups which co-opted new members into its ranks.[110] Brethren ecclesiology often in practice negated the radical levelling of the priesthood of all believers. The democratization of Christianity did not always produce a democratic ecclesiology.

Initially a number of churches effectively had pastors. Among the names mentioned already were Craik and Müller at Bristol, Newton at Plymouth and Hargrove at Gower Street, London, and there were others.[111] The gradual disappearance of pastor-figures among the Open Brethren was probably due, in addition to anticlericalism, to the argument that ceasing from secular employment was not essential for Christian workers as the example of Paul demonstrated. Groves fully accepted this point, but added,

> If also a pastor be worth having, he is worth paying; and wherever there is much spiritual work to be done, it is a bad economy to let much of his valuable time be employed in mere labouring for his earthly substance.[112]

However, he felt that much damage had been done by offering financial inducements to the clergy, enticing the ungodly into the church by 'surrounding our holy ministries with the riches, rank and respectability of this world'.[113] John Bowes was stoutly opposed to the 'hireling minister'. *'The quiet people pay him for thinking and speaking for them'*, he argued, *'and therefore do not trouble themselves to think or speak much themselves.'*[114] Eventually full-time Christian workers attached to a particular congregation disappeared, but the Brethren continued to have itinerants. The pattern of support adopted for the latter and for foreign missionaries was that of 'living by faith'. This was the idea that Christian workers should not be paid a regular salary but should look to God for all physical subsistence. The concept originated with Groves, but its most famous exemplar was George Müller who with his German Pietist background trusted God to supply all the needs of the children within his Bristol orphanages. Consequently, he received no sponsorship and refused to make any financial needs known. The example was universally followed within the Brethren movement though 'living by faith' spread beyond it to the wider evangelical world, principally through the contacts enjoyed by Hudson Taylor.[115] Timothy Larsen in a recent article has argued that one effect of this doctrine was to reinforce the anticlericalism of the movement. This meant that leaders had to remain sensitive to the opinion of the people because they constituted the means of their support. It was, he wrote, 'fuelled both by a positive desire to liberate the people and a corresponding negative wish to curb the ambitions of the leadership'.[116] Paradoxically, Harold Rowdon has argued, the effect was to create an elite.[117] One reviewer of Rowdon's paper, who was himself raised among the Brethren, has noted that during his upbringing in the movement he 'encountered a theoretically egalitarian society ("the priesthood of all believers") rigidly structured in a hierarchical fashion. Missionaries "living by faith" were at the top of this structure as contrasted with the clergy in most other Christian traditions or with a spiritual elite based on "gifts."'[118] Perhaps the truth is that the acceptance of any full-time Christian workers, however financed, will inevitably produce classes of Christians. The crucial point is not the priesthood of all believers but the reality that some will have higher-status ministries than others. Thus what begins with spiritual equality becomes, to some extent, a hierarchy.

Women were much more restricted in their liberty to minister. As was often the case with evangelicalism, Brethrenism had offered them expanded roles. Theodosia, Lady Powerscourt, played a significant part in fostering the movement, holding at her house the prophetic conferences which were instrumental in its formation.[119] A number of other laywomen were prominent in the early development of the movement, but there were limits as to what they could do. Hargrove was typical of many early Brethren when he condemned the Catholic Apostolic Church for allowing women to minister in the church, the practice being expressly forbidden by scripture. However, he also reproved the same body for not allowing 'their labouring with them in the gospel, when in their place their labour is blessed indeed'.[120] Consequently, in the Open Brethren women members were encouraged to be Sunday school teachers, workers among women, hospital visitors, Bible women, and missionaries – principally tasks involving evangelism or nurture. There was one way, however, in which women could make their voice heard in church – through hymn-writing – and probably the most gifted in this respect was Frances Bevan.[121] Yet even with their hymns the female authors remained invisible. A more visible role for women within the Brethren movement arose in the revivalism of the 1860s. During this period, as part of the general increase in lay activity in the nineteenth century, women evangelists preaching to mixed-sex audiences emerged in Britain.[122] Some prominent Brethren encouraged or were at least sympathetic to this development.[123] In Scotland female evangelists were used within the movement and assisted in the formation of several new assemblies. Some Scottish Brethren were even prepared to argue that they might participate in church. But the phase of preaching to mixed audiences was relatively short-lived, reaching its zenith between 1863 and the mid-1870s, and finally ceasing in the 1880s.[124] Thereafter women reverted to the more confined roles typical of Victorian evangelicalism. Among stricter members of the Open Brethren and Exclusives opportunities for formal Christian service were severely limited or not permitted at all. Apart from a brief period, the priesthood of all believers did not mean public roles for women.

In the nineteenth century Brethren views contributed to mid-Victorian revivalism, and greater emancipation of the laity within the latter was due, in part, to its absorption of Brethren principles and practices.[125] Brethrenism has continued to exercise a broad influence on conservative Protestant evangelicalism. Within the movement itself the view of the church as God's clergy was shaped by a number of principles but, as their practice demonstrates, each principle did not have uncontrolled expression. Extreme views of the sovereignty of the Spirit discouraged the adoption of human structures and this sometimes left the movement open to abuse from unregulated power. Because of the tenet of uniformity of judgement, which Exclusivism adopted, this happened within the movement on an international scale. The independency of the Open Brethren tended to localize difficulties, but it did not stop leadership problems arising within the local congregation. Other principles also conflicted with those discussed in this chapter. Living by faith unintentionally reinstated a hierarchy, while the biblical literalism of the movement limited the roles available to women. The principles which the Brethren adopted underwent a sectarian hardening. 'Diversity of judgment on points of ecclesiastical polity', wrote Henry Craik concerning agreement among Christians of different denominations on cardinal issues, 'must not be allowed to interfere with this substantial agreement on matters of essential moment.'[126] It was not a sentiment which all later Open Brethren would have shared. The movement demonstrates the transmission of ideas across class and cultural lines, the paradox of radical spirituality and political conservatism, and the difficulty of giving adequate institutional expression to the priesthood of all believers. Even within a movement which made the doctrine a fundamental principle, the laity achieved only a qualified emancipation.

Notes

1 For the history of the movement, see H.H. Rowdon, *The Origins of the Brethren 1825–1850*, London: Pickering & Inglis, 1967, and F.R. Coad, *A History of the Brethren Movement*, 2nd edn, Exeter: Paternoster Press, 1976.
2 For a summary of these discontents, see Rowdon, *Origins*, Appendix 1, pp. 267–86.
3 Cf. J. Wolffe, *The Protestant Crusade in Great Britain 1829–1860*, Oxford: Clarendon Press, 1991.
4 [J.N. Darby], 'Considerations addressed to the Archbishop of Dublin and the clergy who signed the petition to the House of Commons' (1827), in W. Kelly (ed.) *The Collected Writings of J.N. Darby*, 34 vols, London, n.d., vol. 1, p. 8.
5 R.M. Beverley, *The Heresy of a Human Priesthood, traced in letters on the present state of the visible church of Christ, addressed to John Angell James, minister of the gospel in Birmingham*, 2nd edn, London, 1839, p. xv.
6 Ibid. pp. 13–14.
7 Ibid. pp. ii, 16–18, 30.
8 T.C.F. Stunt, 'Evangelical cross-currents in the Church of Ireland, 1820–1833', in W.J. Shiels and D. Wood (eds) *Studies in Church History* 25, 1989, pp. 215–21; T.C.F. Stunt, *From Awakening to Secession: radical evangelicals in Switzerland and Britain 1815–35*, Edinburgh: T. & T. Clark, 2000, pp. 147–81, 271–8.
9 [Darby], 'Thoughts on the present position of the Home Mission', in Kelly (ed.) *Collected Writings*, vol. 1, pp. 87–9.
10 Rowdon, *Origins*, pp. 37–47.
11 Ibid. pp. 21–2.
12 [J.N. Darby], 'Parochial arrangement destructive of order in the church', *Christian Witness* [hereafter *CW*] 1, July 1834, rpt, *Scripture Subjects and Truths for the Church of God*, Glasgow, 1882, pp. 272, 283.
13 [Darby], 'On lay preaching', Kelly (ed.) *Collected Writings*, vol. 1, p. 205.
14 [J.N. Darby], 'Christian liberty of preaching and teaching the Lord Jesus Christ', *CW* 1, 1834, 182–5.
15 C. Smyth, *Simeon and Church Order: a study of the origins of the evangelical revival in Cambridge in the eighteenth century*, Cambridge: Cambridge University Press, 1940, pp. 250–66.
16 [Darby], 'Home Mission', pp. 78–80.
17 [Darby], 'The notion of a clergyman dispensationally the sin against the Holy Ghost', Kelly (ed.) *Collected Writings*, vol. 1, pp. 65–7.
18 [Darby], 'Home Mission', pp. 81–2.
19 Ibid. pp. 91–2.
20 Ibid. pp. 84–5.
21 Ibid. pp. 99–100.
22 [Darby], 'Notion of a clergyman', pp. 59–60. For the history of this pamphlet see Kelly (ed.) *Collected Writings*, vol. 1, pp. 55–6, and Rowdon, *Origins*, p. 107 n. 99.
23 W.R. Ward, *The Protestant Evangelical Awakening*, Cambridge: Cambridge University Press, 1992, p. 353.
24 Cf. J.A. Haldane, *Observations on the Association of Believers; Mutual Exhortation; the Apostolic Mode of Teaching; Qualifications and Support of Elders;*

Spiritual Gifts, &c. in which Mr Aikman's Observations on Exhortation, &c. are considered, Edinburgh, 1805, p. 46; [Darby], 'Christian liberty', pp. 178–9n.; [Darby], 'On lay preaching', p. 202; R.M. Beverley, *An Inquiry into the Scriptural Doctrine of Christian Ministry*, London, n.d., pp. 8–9.

25 J.A. Haldane, *A View of the Social Worship and Ordinances Observed by the First Christians, drawn from the Sacred Scriptures Alone*, 2nd edn, Edinburgh, 1806; [G. Müller], *A Narrative of Some of the Lord's Dealings with George Müller*, 9th edn, London, 1895, vol. 1, p. 281; H. Craik, *New Testament Church Order*, Bristol, 1863, p. 68.

26 G. Carter, 'Evangelical seceders from the Church of England, c. 1800–1850', unpublished thesis, University of Oxford, 1990, pp. 108–63, 287–90.

27 Ibid. pp. 302–6.

28 J. Campbell, *Memoirs of David Nasmith: his labours and travels in Great Britain, France, the United States, and Canada*, London, 1844.

29 N.O. Hatch, *The Democratization of American Christianity*, New Haven: Yale University Press, 1989, pp. 5, 8. Hatch discusses Wesleyan Methodism but ignores Primitive Methodism which exemplified his democratized Christianity.

30 J. Bowes, *The Autobiography: or the history of the life of John Bowes*, Glasgow, 1872. For examples of his work in the north of England, see D. Brady and F.J. Evans, *Christian Brethren in Manchester and District: a history*, London: Heritage Publications, 1997, pp. 20–35; and for Scotland, see N.T.R. Dickson, 'The history of the Open Brethren in Scotland 1838–1999', unpublished thesis, University of Stirling, 2000, pp. 34–111.

31 Rowdon, *Origins*, p. 175.

32 J. Bowes, *A Hired Ministry Unscriptural*, Manchester, [c. 1843], p. 6.

33 [J. Bowes], 'Hydropathy or the cold water cure', *Truth Promoter* 1, 1849–51, 217–19; [Bowes], *Autobiography*, p. 185.

34 [Bowes], 'Modern preaching wrong', *Truth Promoter* 1, 1849–51, 7–8.

35 'An epitome of the faith, and an outline of the essential principles of the united Christian churches' (1835), in J. Bowes, *Christian Union: showing the importance of unity among real Christians of all denominations, and the means by which it may be effected*, Edinburgh, 1835, Appendix C, pp. 307–10.

36 [J. Bowes], 'The land: a lecture by J. Bowes, delivered in Bell Street Hall, Dundee, 7 mo. 28th, 1851, showing how every family of five persons may have fourteen acres of land', *Truth Promoter* 1, 1849–51, 233–6.

37 Hatch, *Democratization*, p. 34.

38 Beverley, *Human Priesthood*, p. 137.

39 J.E. Orr, *The Second Evangelical Awakening*, London: Marshall, Morgan & Scott, 1949, pp. 201–3; Coad, *Brethren Movement*, p. 169; D.W. Bebbington, *Evangelicalism in Modern Britain*, London: Unwin Hyman, 1989, p. 203.

40 W.H. Clare, *Pioneer Preaching: or work well done*, Glasgow: Pickering & Inglis, [c. 1925], pp. 64–5.

41 Anon. (ed.) *Reminiscences of the Revival of Fifty-Nine and the Sixties*, Aberdeen: The University Press, 1910, p. xiii.

42 J. Kent, *Holding the Fort: studies in Victorian revivalism*, London: Epworth Press, 1978, p. 101.

43 G.E. Morgan, *R.C. Morgan: his life and times*, London and Glasgow: Pickering & Inglis, 1909, p. 21.

44 [J. Radcliffe], *Recollections of Reginald Radcliffe by his wife*, London, [1896], pp. 71–4.

45 'Dr Robert M'Killiam, London', *Believer's Pathway* 36, 1915, 54–6; *Witness* 40, 1910, 55.

46 H. Pickering (ed.) *Chief Men among the Brethren*, 2nd edn, London: Pickering & Inglis, 1931, p. 176.
47 [J.G. Bellet], *Interesting Reminiscences of the Early History of the Brethren*, London, n.d., pp. 7–8.
48 [J.L. Harris], 'On Christian ministry', *CW* 1, 1834, 9.
49 [Darby], 'Notion of a clergyman', pp. 70–1.
50 C. Hargrove, *Reasons for Retiring from the Established Church*, 2nd edn, London, 1838, pp. xl–xlii; W.H. Dorman, *Principles of Truth on the Present State of the Church addressed to all Denominations: also reasons for retiring from the Independent or Congregational body, and from Islington Chapel*, London, 1838, pp. 46–52.
51 Beverley, *An Inquiry*, p. iii; cf. Beverley, *Human Priesthood*, pp. xiii–xiv.
52 Ibid. p. 14.
53 Ibid. p. 26.
54 A.N. Groves, *On the Liberty of Ministry in the Church of Christ*, Sidmouth, 1835, pp. 55–9.
55 J.L.H[arris]., *Jewish Bondage and Christian Freedom; or Jewish and Christian worship contrasted*, London, 1892, pp. 19–20.
56 [Darby], 'The character of office in the present dispensation', Kelly (ed.) *Collected Writings*, vol. 1, pp. 144–68. Judging from the position this article has in the *Collected Writings* it was written in the 1830s and therefore represents an early expression of developed dispensationalism.
57 Ibid. p. 168.
58 [Darby], 'Christian liberty', pp. 177–9; Groves, *Liberty of Ministry*, pp. 10, 17–18, 30.
59 J.P. Callahan, *Primitivist Piety: the ecclesiology of the early Plymouth Brethren*, Lanham, MD: Scarecrow Press, 1996, pp. 55–6.
60 Groves, *Liberty of Ministry*, pp. 12–13, 18–21, 26–7.
61 Beverley, *Human Priesthood*, pp. 16–17.
62 Beverley, *An Inquiry*, p. 19; Groves, *Liberty of Ministry*, pp. 32–3, 73–4; Dorman, *Principles of Truth*, pp. 35–6.
63 Beverley, *Human Priesthood*, p. 18.
64 H.H. Rowdon, 'The early Brethren and the ministry of the word', *Journal of the Christian Brethren Research Fellowship* 14, 1967, 16.
65 Groves, *Liberty of Ministry*, p. 30.
66 [Darby], 'Notion of a clergyman', p. 58.
67 [Darby], 'Home Mission', pp. 90–1.
68 Beverley, *An Inquiry*, pp. 23–4.
69 Craik, *Church Order*, pp. 21–2.
70 [P.F. Hall], 'Review of Mr Burgh's letter', *CW* 1, 1834, 65.
71 S.P. Tregelles, *Three Letters to the Author of 'A retrospect of events that have taken place amongst Brethren'*, 2nd edn, London, 1894, pp. 3–10.
72 N. Dickson, '"Shut in with Thee": the morning meeting among Scottish Open Brethren, 1830s–1960s', in R.N. Swanson (ed.) *Studies in Church History* 35, 1999, 276–89.
73 W.T[rotter]., *Five Letters on Worship and Ministry of the Spirit*, London, 1859, pp. 9–10.
74 [Hall], 'Review', p. 69.
75 Harris, 'Christian Ministry', p. 4.
76 Beverley, *An Inquiry*, p. 11.
77 Ibid. pp. 8–9.
78 [Darby], 'Christian liberty', p. 173; [Darby], 'On lay preaching', p. 203.

79 [B.W. Newton], 'Review of Mr Peter's letter', *CW* 1, 1834, 332.

80 Dorman, *Principles of Truth*, p. 33.

81 Bowes, *Hired Ministry*, p. 8.

82 [Newton], 'Mr Peter's letter', p. 332; Beverley, *Human Priesthood*, pp. ii–iii; Groves, *Liberty of Ministry*, p. 67; Dorman, *Principles of Truth*, p. 84.

83 [Darby], 'On the presence and action of the Holy Ghost in the church: in answer to the work of Mr P. Wolff, entitled, "Ministry as opposed to hierarchism and chiefly to religious radicalism"', Kelly (ed.) *Collected Writings,* vol. 3, p. 419.

84 [Darby], 'Scriptural views upon the subject of elders in answer to a tract entitled, "Are elders to be established?"', Kelly (ed.) *Collected Writings*, vol. 4, pp. 280–348.

85 Beverley, *An Inquiry*, p. 30.

86 T[rotter]., *Five Letters*, pp. 17–8.

87 J. Rose, *The Intellectual Life of the British Working Classes*, New Haven: Yale University Press, 2001, pp. 12–91, 300.

88 'Isaiah Stewart', *Witness* 64, 1934, 167; Writer's collection, James McCallum, 'The roll call', MS transcript of a poem [c.1914].

89 H.H. Rowdon, 'The Brethren contribution to world mission', in H.H. Rowdon (ed.) *The Brethren Contribution to the Worldwide Mission of the Church*, Carlisle: Paternoster Press, 1994, p. 38.

90 R. Cawston, 'The church and mission', *Christian Brethren Review* 40, 1989, 19–20.

91 H[arris]., *Jewish Bondage*, p. 24.

92 Groves, *Liberty of Ministry*, pp. 46–8.

93 [Darby], 'Holy Ghost', pp. 331–5.

94 [Darby], 'Progress of democratic power and its effect on the moral state of England', Kelly (ed.) *Collected Writings*, vol. 32, pp. 506–11.

95 [Newton], 'Mr Peter's letter', p. 331.

96 Groves, *Liberty of Ministry*, pp. 1–2.

97 J.A.B[oswell]., 'Holiness in the house', *Needed Truth* 1, 1888, 35.

98 Beverley, *Human Priesthood*, pp. vi–vii.

99 Beverley, *An Inquiry*, p. 36.

100 Ibid. p. 33.

101 [Darby], 'Christian liberty', p. 185.

102 Cf. T.C.F. Stunt, 'Two nineteenth-century movements', *Evangelical Quarterly* 37, 1965, 229, who describes the Exclusive Brethren as 'conciliar' within the congregation but 'papal' as a movement.

103 B.R. Wilson, *The Social Dimensions of Sectarianism: sects and new religious movements in contemporary society*, Oxford: Clarendon Press, 1990, pp. 87–102.

104 Craik, *Church Order*, pp. 50–5.

105 Groves, *Liberty of Ministry*, p. 30; Craik, *Church Order*, p. 54.

106 H. Rowdon, 'Orientation to the "Brethren" scene', in *Don't Muzzle the Ox: full-time ministry in local churches*, introduced by A. Batchelor, Carlisle: Paternoster Periodicals, 1997, pp. 83–4.

107 J.D. Burnham, 'The controversial relationship between Benjamin Wills Newton and John Nelson Darby', unpublished thesis, University of Oxford, 1999, pp. 168–9; [Müller], *Narrative*, vol. 1, pp. 276–80.

108 E.W.R[odgers]., 'The believer's question box', *Believer's Magazine* 60, 1950, 93.

109 Stunt, 'Two nineteenth-century movements', p. 229.

110 G. Willis and B.R. Wilson, 'The Churches of God: pattern and practice', in B.R. Wilson (ed.) *Patterns of Sectarianism: organisation and ideology in social and religious movements*, London: Heinemann, 1967, pp. 260–74.

111 See Rowdon, 'The early Brethren', p. 11, for a fairly comprehensive list of such ministries.

112 Groves, *Liberty of Ministry*, p. 51.

113 Ibid. p. 28.

114 Bowes, *Hired Ministry*, p. 8.

115 K. Fiedler, *The Story of Faith Missions*, Oxford: Regnum Books, 1994.

116 T. Larsen, '"Living by faith": a short history of Brethren practice', *Brethren Archivists and Historians Network Review [BAHNR]* 1, 1998, 89.

117 H.H. Rowdon, 'The concept of "living by faith"', in A. Billington, T. Lane and M. Turner (eds) *Mission and Meaning: essays presented to Peter Cotterell*, Carlisle: Paternoster Press, 1995, p. 352.

118 J. Ingelby, 'Reviews', *BAHNR* 1, 1998, 62.

119 Coad, *Brethren Movement*, pp. 109–10.

120 Hargrove, *Reasons for Retiring*, p. xxviii.

121 J.S. Andrews, 'Frances Bevan, translator', *Evangelical Quarterly* 34, 1962, 206–13; 35, 1963, 30–8.

122 O. Anderson, 'Women preachers in mid-Victorian Britain: some reflexions on feminism, popular religion and social change', *Historical Journal* 12, 1969, 467–84.

123 See, for example, *H.I.G., In Memoriam: Jessie McFarlane a tribute of affection*, London, 1872, pp. 23–4, 58–9; Mrs Gratton Guinness, *'She Spake of Him': being recollections of the loving labours and early death of the late Mrs. Henry Dening*, Bristol, 1872, pp. 195, 239–40.

124 N. Dickson, 'Modern prophetesses: women preachers in the nineteenth-century Scottish Brethren', *Records of the Scottish Church History Society* 25, 1993, 89–117.

125 Anderson, 'Women preachers', p. 475; Kent, *Holding the Fort*, pp. 126–7; Bebbington, *Evangelicalism*, pp. 157–9.

126 Craik, *Church Order*, p. 25.

Chapter 15

Changing Baptist concepts of royal priesthood
John Smyth and Edgar Young Mullins

Malcolm B. Yarnell, III

In this millennium of anniversaries let us remember William Heth Whitsitt. Whitsitt wrote *A Question in Baptist History* in 1896, challenging an historiographical fallacy called Baptist successionism or Landmarkism. Whitsitt, after careful research, discovered Baptist beginnings in seventeenth-century England, opposing the prevailing view that they could trace their history through an unbroken 'trail of blood' comprised of Lollards, Waldensians and Donatists to Jesus, John the Baptist and the Jordan River. In 1899, in reward for his careful research, he was forced out of the presidency of Southern Baptist Seminary, the oldest Southern Baptist educational institution, by the founder of Southwestern Baptist Seminary, now the largest seminary in the western world. Whitsitt concluded from this experience that, 'Baptist history is a department in which "the wise man concealeth knowledge."' [1] Painfully aware of this precedent, the author of this present essay is delivering a similar reckless revision as he takes up a position at Southwestern Seminary. [2]

The thesis is that in the doctrine of the royal priesthood modern Baptists differ significantly from their forefathers. That this thesis is true will be evident to dispassionate scholars; that it is not will be self-evident to many Southern Baptists, especially their scholars. Where early Baptists considered royal priesthood a third-tier metaphor descriptive of a certain Christology and ecclesiology, modern Baptists have elevated the doctrine to the centre and redefined it as rugged individualism. John Smyth (c. 1554–1612) will serve as our central seventeenth-century Baptist theologian while Edgar Young Mullins (1860–1928) will provide the same service for the twentieth century. In 1609 Smyth fathered what became known as the General Baptist churches, although the Baptist churches in America and England during the next two centuries are better defined by the Particular Baptists who arose during the English Civil Wars.

Mullins was president of Southern Baptist Seminary (1899–1928), the Southern Baptist Convention [SBC] (1921–4) and the Baptist World Alliance [BWA] (1923–8). Harold Bloom describes him as the 're-founder' of the SBC, as being comparable to Calvin, Luther or Wesley, and as 'the most neglected of major American theologians'.[3] His historical theology defined moderate Southern Baptist orthodoxy in the twentieth century while his penchant for hyper-individualism was heartily endorsed by the English Baptist John Clifford and codified in a BWA confession.[4] The SBC, with some 16,000,000 members, is today the largest American Protestant denomination and constitutes the largest bloc within the BWA. Its modern ranks include 'the Protestant pope' Billy Graham and such political luminaries as Newt Gingrich, Trent Lott, Al Gore and Bill Clinton, the last of these figures recently exemplifying Mullins's emphasis on 'soul competency'.[5] Its central budget, partly a creation of Mullins, annually garners $250,000,000; numbering its full-time missionaries requires five digits. Enough of hubris; we begin with an obscure Cambridge fellow.

John Smyth's 'kingly priesthood'

The first modern Baptist was tutored in the stridently puritan atmosphere of Christ's College, Cambridge, by the future separatist, Francis Johnson. His career took the classic puritan to separatist turn when his episcopal preaching licences were revoked. His view of royal priesthood reflects the Calvinist definition: *triplex munus Christi*, the threefold office of Christ as prophet, priest and king, as manifested in proclamation, worship and government. Calvinists conceived of Christ as dually present, eternally presenting his sacrifice and interceding before the Father, meanwhile establishing his kingdom through his saints upon the earth. Separatists went beyond puritanism by reifying Christ's authority within covenanted congregations, a radically political move based on a unique understanding of the early modern 'mixed polity' of Aristotle's political distinctions.

There has been some debate about the central theme of Smyth's theology. Barry White suggests that of covenant while Douglas Shantz points to the resurrected Christ as ruling king. James Coggins concludes both Shantz and White are correct: Christ is present as ruler within the gathered church.[6] Smyth wrote that 'the summe of the gospel' is, on the one hand, faith and repentance, and on the other, 'that Iesus Christ the Sonne of God, & the Sonne of Mary, is the only King, Priest, & Prophet of his Church'. The church manifests the work of Christ by 'governing, Sacrificing, making intercession, & prophecying after that holy manner & according to those rules which he hath prescribed in his Testament'.[7] Thus, Smyth mimics the separatist correlation of predestinarian soteriology and political ecclesiology.[8] Separatists parted from puritanism by identifying the ruling presence of Christ with the covenant.

Smyth began his ecclesiology with Matthew 18.20, 'For where two or three are gathered together in my Name, there am I in the middes of them' (*Geneva Bible*). Coupled with Christ's threefold mediatorial office, Smyth applied this verse to the covenantally-constituted visible church:

> Private persons separating from al synne, and joyning together to obey
> Christ their, king, priest and prophet, as they are bound, are a true visi-
> ble Church, and haue a Charter given them of Christ therto, being but
> two or three. Mat. 18,20.[9]

Smyth and his company constituted their first church by covenant, 'the Lord
assisting them'.[10] The visible church thus constituted was seen as the 'only
religious societie that God hath ordayned for men on earth'. This visible
church was Christ's kingdom simply because its resident king was Christ. The
form of the church consisted of an inward faith and an outward covenant:
that is, a mutual covenant with God and others. The properties of the church
were 'communion in Christ and His benefits' and 'the power of Christ' to
receive, maintain and reject. Christ as prophet, priest and king manifested his
powers in the marks of the church: word, sacraments and discipline. By
focusing on the third mark, so problematic for the Reformed, the separatists
created the visibly gathered purifying church, taking their cue from Matthew
18.[11]

In his second major work as a separatist, *The Differences of the Churches of
the Seperation* (1608), Smyth fully develops his conception of royal priesthood. The 'kingdom of saynts' is differentiated from the 'priesthood of
saynts'. Kingdom concerns the church's 'Leitourgie'; priesthood concerns
her 'ministrie'. On the one hand, kingdom actions are of 'opposition, difference, plea, & strif: as in admonition, examination, excommunication,
pacification, absolution, &c'. On the other, 'the saynts as Priests offer vp
spirituall sacrifices acceptable to God by Iesus Christ'. 'The actions of the
Church in dispencing the preisthood are actions of concord or vnion . . . spirituall worship properly so called.'[12] Smyth carefully defines ecclesial
priesthood in spiritual worship, giving paramount attention to ministers.

Smyth balances a high view of ministry with the possession of spiritual
gifts by all members. The Mosaic high priesthood typifies that of Jesus;
Mosaic priests typify New Testament elders. Church elders perform the works
of priesthood and kingdom. The work of priesthood is spiritual sacrifice:
prophecy, prayer, and psalms of praise and thanksgiving. Both elders and
brethren perform this service; however, they must do so 'in order' and in the
context of corporate worship:

> The office of the Eldership or the work of the presbytery is to lead &
> moderate the Church in these Spiritual Sacrifices . . . yet the brethren are
> interested in vsing their gifts for the performance of al these parts of
> Spiritual worship, & that when the whole Church is come together in one.

Similarly, in the works of the kingdom, elders 'lead & moderate the Church
actions & speeches', but the brethren are also 'interested in all the parts of
administration'.

Smyth's appreciation for ministry does not cloud his view of where church authority begins. 'The brethren joyntly have all powre both of the Kingdom & preisthood immediately from Christ & that by vertue of the covenant God maketh with them.' But in spite of the gift of this power to and its nominal retention by the congregation, elders normally exercise 'the publique actions of the Church, eyther of the Kingdom or preisthood' on its behalf. The only powers which elders may not exercise on their own are 'Elections & communication'. Moreover, 'the presbytery hath no powre, but what the Church hath & giveth vnto it: which the Church vppon just cause can take away'. In a doctrine later rejected by General Baptists, in the interim between elders, the church may preach the word and administer the sacraments on its own.[13]

In *Paralleles, Censvres, Observations* (1609), Smyth's primary concern lies in defending his new conception of church government. Interestingly, he refers often to the church as the seat of authority quite apart from any reference he makes to priesthood or kingdom. He is more concerned with the keys of binding and loosing in Matthew 18 than with the royal priesthood of I Peter. When he does mention our focal doctrine in this treatise, he dwells on the kingdom, which functions as a metaphor for the governmental aspect of corporate existence in Christ.[14]

In his Baptist phase, Smyth neither affirms nor denies the priesthood of the congregation. The spiritual kingdom created by covenantal baptism is affirmed, however. Baptist ecclesiology is defined in the following terms: 'The true constitution of the Chu. is of a new creature baptized into the Father, the Sonne, & the holy Ghost: The false constitution is of infants baptized.' He clarifies the meaning of 'covenants & seales'. The spiritual seal of the covenant is the Holy Spirit; baptism is the visible manifestation of that seal. 'They that are not actualy possessed of the promises or covenant, are not actually to be invested with baptisme.' The one, visible, common faith is the basis of communion. One submits to the 'rule of Christ' by being baptized and receiving congregational nourishment and discipline. Infants are unable to submit to Christ's kingship because they cannot consent to the contract or seal the covenant or 'be made disciples by instruction'.

Smyth was accused of arbitrarily baptizing himself, by which he earned the title, 'Se-Baptist' or self-baptizer. The pejorative term stuck, though it misrepresents his real position.[15] A more appropriate title would be 'Church-Baptist' since it preserves the visible and communal focus of his argument. He contended that the baptismal decision was made by the church corporately: 'it is Lawfull for a man to baptize himself together with others in communion'. Their decision was based on the authority of Christ inherent in the gathered church, not on Smyth's personal fiat; he was simply the agent of a congregational discovery of 'further light' and a congregational choice to reclaim the primitive form of baptism. 'For two men singly are no Church, joyntly they are a Church.' Indeed, baptism is 'a seale in the concrete', a visible expression of a divine, corporate and personal event. The divine character of this corporate commitment has been compared to a marriage. 'When a split came, it produced the rancor of a divorce because the covenant had all the force of a wedding vow.'[16]

Always desirous of order, Smyth joined the Waterlander Mennonites in recognition of their congregational and ministerial succession. In this phase, Smyth dropped both the term and content of royal priesthood, apparently in deference to Anabaptist sensibilities over the centrality of the ministry and difficulties presented by the violent sacrificial language of Münster. In his first submission to the Waterlanders, *Nomina Anglorum* (1609), Smyth failed to mention universal priesthood and kingdom by name but their role as source of priestly power was retained (art. 13). In his next submission, *Defence of Ries' Confession*, a rebuttal of a Reformed critique of *A Short Confession of Faith*, universal priesthood and kingdom as the seat of authority disappeared. The royal priesthood offered in its place had Cranmerian, Mennonite and Schwenckfeldian characteristics. In his final submission, *Propositions and Conclusions concerning True Christian Religion* (1611), he resurrected royal priesthood, but congregational authority was strictly qualified by a ministerial monopoly on preaching and ministration of sacraments (arts 30, 81, 82).

Baptist developments

As is well known, Thomas Helwys could stomach neither the Waterlanders' denial of Christian magistracy nor their avowal of a celestial flesh Christology. He forsook Smyth, returned to England, penned a revolutionary, apocalyptic tract and, like the true martyr, sent a copy to James I. His followers dropped his apocalyptic language, concentrating on survival instead. These small groups of General Baptists eventually found themselves in competition with the Particular Baptists. Research into their communal confessions and individual theological monographs yields a picture of Calvinist priesthood among both groups. Although there is not space here to elaborate, the trend of their thought may be summarized as a Trinitarian mutuality between Christ, church and person. Christ was at the centre of their thought; in dynamic relationship to him was the gathered church; and in the fold of the church were rightly related individuals.

The early Baptists generally agreed with both conformists and puritans in their understanding of Christ's priesthood. Christ is central to the divine economy and must be exalted.[17] His fully efficacious sacrifice was once-for-all made on the cross, but his presentation of that sacrifice continues eternally. Due to our unworthy prayers, he must continually intercede for us. Thomas Collier exalts Christ at length for his continuing priesthood. While Collier affirms human access to God, it is a 'privilege' and 'comfort' dependent on Christ rather than a pre-existent right of the soul. To drive this point home, he excoriates ten things in self, which Christ teacheth his [people] in som measure to deny, and to lay all down at his feet. There is; 1. Self sinful. 2. Self-righteous. 3. Self-wisdom. 4. Self-glorying and boasting. 5. Self-profit. 6. Self-pleasure. 7. Self-love. 8. Self-wil. 9. Self-strength and Self-sufficiency. 10. Self-ends.[18]

Not only is the self restrained in relationship to God by its sinfulness and lack of self-sufficiency, as evidenced by the Calvinistic penchant for total depravity and divine election, but it is also restrained by the divine community. Although early Baptists had an appreciation for the dynamic distribution of spiritual gifts, they strictly controlled their exercise. William Kiffin informed the scurrilous Daniel Featley that although Baptists did not require a university-trained ministry, they opposed unrestrained lay prerogative. Broadly, 'all who are gifted may preach the Word, and administer the Sacraments'. Specifically, 'none amongst us teach, but they have ordination; for they are elected, examined and proved'.[19] Though egalitarian in essence, they held to traditional vocational distinctions. This relative conservatism comes into focus in the detailed ecclesiological statements of the early confessions. In these confessions, they ground their ecclesiology in *triplex munus Christi*. Table 15.1 compares two Particular Baptist confessions with Luther's early, and radical-sounding, view of royal priesthood. From this it can be concluded that Particular Baptists were nowhere near as radical as the early Luther. The General Baptist *Orthodox Creed* is similar in content though it provides for a 'bishop' or 'messenger' over several congregations.[20]

The individual was prized by the early Baptists, but only within the context of the divine and the communal. There was a healthy respect for conscience, but what they meant by conscience was different from what we mean. The early modern conscience required shaping. Though not to be coerced, it could and must be persuaded. Leonard Busher agreed with James that heresy must be excised from society, but by the proclaimed word rather than the bloody sword.[21] Following the casuistry of William Perkins and William Ames, Baptists constructed and utilized vast collections of judgements on 'cases of conscience'.[22] Their business meetings were elaborate exercises in the communal examination and correction of individual consciences in preparation for communion.[23] Smyth viewed the conscience as one of the four parts comprising the regenerate soul: 'a sorowfull or consortable testimony answerable to the matter handled'. It convicted of sin and bound a person to membership in a visible church. Elders were to follow their conscience in determining discipline.[24] In the eighteenth and nineteenth centuries Daniel Turner and Andrew Fuller agreed that 'even *conscience itself* may be mistaken' and individual liberty may never be used to deviate from true ecclesial doctrine.[25] Baptists were proponents of voluntaryism, but the will of the church preceded that of the individual.

There is a growing tension in later Baptist thought between the fragmentary and the formative. The fragmentary can be seen in the incredible success

Table 15.1 Luther's theological position compared with Baptist confessions of 1644 and 1677

Luther (1523)	Baptist confession (1644)	Baptist confession (1677)
'the ministry of the Word is common to all Christians'	'such to whom God hath given gifts, being tryed in the Church, may and ought by the appointment of the Congregation, to prophesie' (45)	though primarily exercised by 'Bishops or Pastors', 'others also gifted, and fitted by the Holy Spirit for it, and approved, and called by the Church' (26.11)
'the second function, to baptize'	'the persons designed by Christ, to dispense this Ordinance, the Scriptures hold forth to be a preaching disciple' (41)	'these holy appointments are to be administered by those only, who are qualified and thereunto called' (28.2)
'the third function is to consecrate . . . This function, too, like the priesthood, belongs to all'		'the Lord Jesus hath in this Ordinance, appointed his ministers to Pray, and bless the Elements' (30.3)
'the fourth function consists in binding and loosing from sin'	'Christ has likewise given power to his whole Church to receive in and cast out' (42)	'so all that are admitted unto the priviledges of a Church, are also under the Censures and Government thereof, according to the rule of Christ' (26.12)
'the fifth function is to sacrifice'	'and all his servants are called thither, to present their bodies and soules, and to bring their gifts God hath given them' (35)	in the Lord's supper, 'a spiritual oblation of all possible praise unto God' (30.2)
'the sixth function is to pray for others'		'Saints by profession are bound to . . . performing such other spiritual services, as tend to their mutual edification' (27.2)
'the seventh and last function is to judge and pass on doctrine'	'every Church has power given from Christ for their better well-being to choose to themselves meet persons' (36)	'that he be chosen thereunto by the common suffrage of the Church it self . . . with imposition of hands of the Eldership' (26.9)

of Quakers in raiding General Baptist churches, whose emphasis on free will opened them to spiritualist thought.[26] It is also evident in the thought and practice of Roger Williams and John Leland. Williams established a minor strand of Baptist churches in New England, remaining with them for all of three months before heading into the woods to become a Seeker. His most recent biographer concludes that Williams was ever striving for exile. In his debate over sacraments with George Fox and the Quakers, he was nailed for his hypocrisy in defending that which he had abandoned.[27] John Leland, a Virginia Baptist, is best known for his flouting of establishment, once sending a 1,235-pound 'Mammoth Cheese' to President Thomas Jefferson bearing the motto, 'Rebellion to tyrants is obedience to God.' Leland viewed conscience as intellectual self-reliance. Coupling this with a rabid anticlericalism and an extreme localism, he stood against any efforts to centralize the Baptist churches, even for missions. He refused to administer the Lord's supper, as he had never seen it bring conversion, and as a result was disciplined by his association.[28]

The formative strand in Baptist thought can be seen among such American fathers as Richard Furman and Isaac Backus. Along with the powerful Philadelphia Baptist Association, they led the way to a connectedness among Baptists which stressed discipline and common effort for the advancement of the gospel. Among American Baptists, local churches and associations have long played the roles of church court and magisterium.[29] Only in the twentieth century did these roles come under successful attack, but with the recent controversy in the SBC they have seen a revival. The formative has ever battled against the fragmentary. Strangely, fragmentary theologians such as Francis Wayland have often been instrumental in forming supralocal organizations. They function as builders whilst their theology acts as a fifth column within the very movements they construct.[30]

The sociologists Ernst Troeltsch and Max Weber classified Baptists as 'sects'. Troeltsch categorized them under sect-type, midway between church-type and mystic.[31] A.C. Underwood, a prominent English Baptist historian, followed Troeltsch but conflated sect-type and mystic, substituting Troeltsch's definition of the latter under the name of the former.[32] Underwood's faux pas exemplifies how confused Baptists become when comparing their current atomism with their former sectarianism.[33] Thus, Ernest Payne was forced to add a chapter on 'spiritual discipline' in revising a book subtitled *Baptist thought and practice yesterday and today*.[34]

E.Y. Mullins's 'soul competency'

Mullins is the prime example of a sectarian fifth columnist. Born three centuries after Smyth, he redefined Baptist theology to meet twentieth-century concerns. The 'great state of Texas' in which he was raised is the modern Mecca of self-sufficient individualism – political, economic and religious.

This frontier of cowboys, vigilantes and entrepreneurs isolated in distant farmsteads gave Henry Ford every reason to develop that ultimate symbol of standardized individuality, the automobile. As Mullins matured, Protestantism dominated America. William Jennings Bryan roused farmers with his populist speeches of a 'cross of gold'. Woodrow Wilson proved southern gentility could once again lead the Democrat party and the nation. Following their manifest destiny and bearing their white man's burden, these proud Anglo-Saxons, populist and progressive, were pressured by non-white, non-Protestant advances. Their greatest opposition came from Catholic immigration and philosophical materialism. Their only hope for maintaining Protestant hegemony lay in denying Protestant diversity by reducing theological distinctions among Protestants to the bare minimum.[35]

Mullins completed his first theological degree at Southern Seminary under the Calvinism of J.P. Boyce, a seminal figure who brooked little deviance and embraced the principle of creeds. He soon moved north, taking pastorates in Baltimore and Boston, revelling in part-time courses at avant-garde Johns Hopkins University and mildly evangelical Newton Theological Institute. A dynamic speaker, he was awarded an honorary doctorate in divinity by Carson-Newman College of Tennessee in 1895. He preferred pastoring in the north, according to his wife, because of the 'artistic and intellectual setting' and the chance to preach 'with perfect freedom', and because 'there was wealth to be influenced, a thing never to be despised'.[36] He combined a natural penchant for emotional revivalism and Victorian poetry, in its most introspective expressions, with a delight in the experiential teachings of Bowne, James and Schleiermacher, classifying the last among the church fathers.[37]

Mullins's first book, a mild dispensational text, denounced the Roman Catholic Church as apostate. When the Landmarkers began their attack on Whitsitt, Mullins wrote several articles identifying them as 'a Roman Catholic Party Among the Baptists' bent on the destruction of free inquiry. He preferred the model provided by Roger Williams. Yet his articles were ignored. Paradoxically, when the trustees of Southern Seminary began to look for a compromise candidate, they turned to Mullins.[38] He was initially appointed to teach church history and his wife records his subsequent immersion in a self-taught crash-course in the subject, a course brought to a precipitate end by his chief opponent's resignation from the chair of theology, a chair to which he gratefully gravitated.[39] Two prominent historians of the day were Philip Schaff and Thomas Lindsay. Schaff considered universal priesthood to be one of the three dogmatic principles of the Reformation; Lindsay saw it as the basis of all Reformation doctrine.[40] Although Mullins probably consulted Schaff, the only historian to whom a reference has been found was Alexander Allen. Allen was a minor Cambridge scholar who found a thousand ways to denigrate Catholic sacerdotalism while praising Protestant mysticism and private judgement.[41] Mullins also garnered some knowledge of the Seeker Williams and the anticlericalist Leland; these relatively minor figures became lynchpins in his version of Baptist history.[42] He ignored early Calvinistic Baptists almost entirely. Following Allen, he said that Nonconformists stood 'for individualism, for soul freedom, for the spiritual and direct relation of the soul to God as against the ecclesiastical lordship of the established church'.[43] Like Wayland before him, who admitted his ignorance of history while making sweeping pronouncements on Baptist polity, Mullins was an amateur historian.

Mullins's first objective was to reconcile the warring parties among the Southern Baptists. His second was to reconcile Southern Baptists with mainline Protestantism. He accomplished his first task by appropriating the Landmarkist language of 'distinctives'. They used Baptist distinctives as a way of delineating themselves from their denominational rivals; Mullins accepted the term but filled it with new meaning. Where Landmarkers defined Baptist 'distinctives' in terms of a 'high church ecclesiology' centred on local churches, Mullins redefined the primary distinctive as 'soul competency', a concept for which he offered no biblical proof text.[44] This was a classic liberal move, using traditional language in a new way. It was also a pan-Protestant move, for Protestant personalism was now in its heyday, and Mullins invited other Protestants to join his logical consistency by becoming moderate Baptists.[45]

Although Mullins did not create the language of Baptist distinctives, he coined the term 'soul competency'.[46] Bloom and an anonymous Baptist scholar (probably Bill Leonard) could find no theological precursor for the term but noted the contemporary meaning of 'competency' as economic self-sufficiency.[47] Mullins defined soul competency as pre-existent, immediate access to God. In his influential work, honestly subtitled *a new interpretation of the Baptist faith*, he correlated it with a montage of Baptist principles or axioms, sometimes four, sometimes six in number, each a further expression of individual self-sufficiency.[48]

'Soul competency'

At the centre of Mullins's thought is his doctrine of soul competency. Soul competency colours his rendition of anthropology, Christology and ecclesiology, as well as his theories of communication and priesthood. He turns the early Baptists' Christocentric and dynamic relationship between person and community on its head.

Mullins exalts the individual soul. The soul is a diamond while Christ is more vaguely the sun, the kingdom of God a rainbow and the church a vacuous social expression of the rainbow.[49] The 'mother principle' of New Testament Christianity is 'soul competency': the individual soul's capability to deal with God without any tyrannical mediatory church or priesthood. Direct access to God is a 'right' for all souls. The soul or personality loves freedom and is prefigured in the Anglo-Saxon principle of individualism. It is comparable to Nietzsche's superman but with a difference: 'under Christ all is regenerated and spiritualized'. 'Self-realization' is the metaphysical end of life while 'self-assertion' is the definition of freedom. Even God is constrained in his dealings with the autonomous individual. Comparing the Divinity to a Master Bowler, he says God must necessarily elect the strategic or 'great men' of history as other souls will naturally follow them in great numbers. (Mullins's wife and colleagues ranked him accordingly.) Ironically, the precious diamond is also fragile. For God or man, more than mentioning salvation to a person at the appropriate time is 'doing violence to the will'.[50]

Mullins's Christ plays a supporting role. If the soul is an eagle, Christ is the atmosphere. He is the 'Sun of Righteousness' who can easily be 'eclipsed' by the human will. His primary work is bestowing autonomy. Christ is, moreover, slavishly dependent on scripture for human relevance. He is the monarch of the church but his authority cannot be localized. Where early Baptists emphasize the authoritative presence of Christ in the gathered congregation, Mullins is sure that Christ is only omnipresent. Such omnipresence implies absence. In his defence of the separation of church and state, he is adamantly opposed to any temporal rule by Christ. The believer is the pivot in the relationship between Christ and the brethren; the ontological unity of believers in Christ is anathema.[51]

Mullins's high anthropology and low Christology lead to an impoverished ecclesiology. Church and sacraments are lesser principles overemphasized by earlier Baptists. His church has the characteristics of the club of like-minded individuals described by Robert Bellah. The individual is the basis of the church. Mullins distinguishes between the formation of the church spiritually and temporally. The temporal church is 'sacerdotal and sacramental' and thus heathen. The true church is formed spiritually only in rare historical circumstances. This comes perilously close to the Docetic ecclesiology he elsewhere denies. If Baptists stand somewhere between Quakerism and Presbyterianism, the latter is in his opinion the greater danger. The invisible universal church is his preferred paradigm.[52] He allows local churches some power but vehemently denies any credal or juridical functions for associations of local churches. The absent Christ is the only authority in these 'administrative' supralocal gatherings. Mullins's ecclesiology encapsulates 'the principle of live and let live'. As for lay commitment to church activities, less is best.[53]

His impoverished ecclesiology indicates a hostile view of ministry and the mediation of faith.[54] He is somewhat contradictory at this point. On the one hand, any mediation, any priesthood is tyranny. On the other, 'associated souls may influence each other' and the gospel must be preached to be received. The emphasis, however, is on the evil nature of mediation. Soul competency indicates the capacity to deal with God directly:

Direct access to God through Christ is the law of the Christian life. It is a species of spiritual tyranny for men to interpose the Church itself, its ordinances or ceremonies, or its formal creeds between the human soul and Christ.

Succinctly, 'the voice of conscience is stifled by authority'. Such vehement assertions prevent him from carefully defining ministry and mediation. If anything, ministry is simply a 'convenience or expediency in the church'. He is also opposed to parental interference.[55]

Mullins's doctrine of priesthood is inconsistent. The priesthood is pagan in origin, not Christian. The priest is an 'exclusive manipulator of sacraments'. Roman Catholicism has propagated this pagan priesthood; its characteristic belief is the 'incompetency of the soul' to relate to God. But if John Henry Cardinal Newman's priesthood is Mullins's bête noire, John Calvin's is his brown beast. Christ's priesthood is primarily authorial and by implication discontinued. If the soul has the capacity to deal with God directly, then Christ's priesthood necessarily ceases to exist. Universal priesthood is a corollary of soul competency: 'the expression of the soul's competency on the Godward . . . side of its religious life'. Universal priesthood leaves no room for a particular priesthood. 'The social principle accents the priesthood of all believers against the claims of an exclusive priesthood, which means of course that there can be no priestly class in the church of God. All are priests alike.' Universal priesthood also means no priesthood. 'No human priest may claim to be mediator between the soul and God because no possible reason can be assigned for any competency on his part not common to all believers.'[56]

When we turn to Mullins's systematic offering, we find much the same. From where then did he gather his views of priesthood? There is little evidence that he ever read Leland or Williams; history functioned only as proof for his fragmentary theology. Instead, he read modernity. While critical of materialist philosophers, he drank deeply from the well of Immanuel Kant and Albrecht Ritschl. For his sustenance, however, he turned to Friedrich Schleiermacher, William James and Borden Parker Bowne. *Christian Religion in its Doctrinal Expression*, Mullins's theological summa, is an apology, a series of speeches to religion's cultured despisers which is highly dependent on religious psychology and idealistic personalism. He took these seminal thinkers and presented their conclusions in as orthodox a light as possible, except in his doctrine of priesthood.

With James, he agreed that religious experiences prove God's existence. One can imagine his ecstasy reading through case after case of personal access to the divine, often access apart from Christ, in what he describes as a 'notable work'.[57] With Bowne, he agreed that since individual humans are personal, the deity they conceive must be personal. This contributed to Mullins's high anthropology and fascination with a personalized God. 'The crown and goal of nature is its highest outcome, man himself'; indeed, 'the human will is, in a relative sense at least, a first cause'; moreover, 'man is self-determined'.[58] James and Bowne thus contribute to Mullins's intoxication with personal freedom and personal rights, 'even to the loss of the indispensability of society and social relationships for personal life'.[59]

Mullins builds on Schleiermacher's work but goes beyond him. With Schleiermacher, he considers institutionalization the corruption of religion. With Schleiermacher, he believes Roman sacerdotalism is the antithesis of Protestant individualism. Christ relates directly to the individual apart from the church; the church is a by-product of a previous reality. But against Schleiermacher, who synthesizes the two western movements, Mullins fails to read the German theologian dialectically and as a result demonizes Rome and completely atomizes the church.[60] With Schleiermacher, he regards religion as a feeling of absolute dependence, an internalized religious consciousness. Against Schleiermacher, he believes religion can be localized only in the personal experience of Christ. Mullins, scared by Schleiermacher's pantheistic tendencies, resorts to an exalted personalism which takes his anthropocentrism one step further. Therefore, (in contrast to the New Testament emphasis on the mutual indwelling of Christ and church) Mullins emphasizes the presence of Christ in the individual consciousness.[61] With Schleiermacher, he conflates Christ's priesthood with his sacrifice and puts an end to both. With Schleiermacher, he then provides a little room for Christ's continuing intercession, but its relation to his priesthood is vague. With Schleiermacher, he believes this eliminates any distinction between laity and clergy. Against Schleiermacher, however, he sees no need for the church to represent the world to God.[62] With Schleiermacher, he believes there are many means of experiencing God and the church is not primary amongst them; rather, religion proceeds from an innate human capacity: 'there is absolutely no barrier to the salvation of any, save their own wills'.[63] While for many of his views Mullins depends on Schleiermacher, on the subject of priesthood he stands even further to the left than the father of theological liberalism.

Conclusion

Mullins's *Axioms* and *The Christian Religion* were influential among Baptists. *The Christian Religion* replaced Boyce's Calvinistic system in 1917, remaining Southern's authoritative theological text well into the 1950s. *Axioms* was revised by 'the venerable' Herschel Hobbs, who collapsed all the axioms into 'self-determination in every area of life'.[64] Hobbs was instrumental in adding a prefatory caveat to the 1963 *Baptist Faith and Message* in which soul competency and 'the priesthood of the believer' may deny the confession any official value. Thus, a creed may be made creedless while creedlessness may be given credal status. The atomistic priesthood of the believer became central in

American Baptist thought, both northern and southern, and even found some echoes in Britain.[65]

With the recent controversy over academic freedom in the SBC, the doctrine scaled new heights in the efforts of the moderate party to counteract formative tendencies. Failing in their use of scripture, they resorted to history for a theological foundation. The 'historic' distinctive of the believer-priest allowed a new publishing house, anachronistically named 'Smyth & Helwys', to be launched; their current catalogue offers half a dozen monographs on the subject. Following Mullins, and indeed taking him further along the path of a vacuous individualism, they speak of an historic Baptist position that has little to do with events prior to 1908. The Baptist convention of churches in Mullins's home state, now led by a scholastic Mullinsite, recently created a Baptist Distinctives Committee devoted to maintaining the new theology, and is currently contemplating the creation of yet another fragmentary institution, the Convention of the Americas.

Having never read Smyth nor any other early Baptist, an amateur historian was able to create a new theology which claimed history as its foundation. 'The priesthood of *the* believer', a doctrine rejecting creeds, exalting individualism in the name of sole competency, denigrating both ministry and church and generally ignorant of the biblical teaching concerning the continuing priesthood of Christ, has displaced the traditional emphasis on 'the priesthood of *all* believers'. The latter is a doctrine founded in the priesthood of Christ and manifested in his covenanted church, which assumes a mutuality between ministry and laity. *The early Baptists were Christocentric churchmen; Mullins and his disciples are anthropocentric individualists – therein lies a world of difference.* Many modern Baptist scholars, whose raison d'être has come to depend on this supposed Baptist distinctive, fail to see the irony and will doubtless find the comparison humourless.

Notes

1 W.B. Shurden, *Not a Silent People: controversies that have shaped Southern Baptists*, Nashville: Broadman Press, 1972, p. 32.

2 After taking up his post at Southwestern Seminary in July 2000, the author of this chapter was appointed as Dean of the Faculty and Vice President of Academic Affairs at Midwestern Baptist Theological Seminary, Kansas City, Missouri.

3 H. Bloom, *The American Religion: the emergence of the post-Christian nation*, New York: Simon & Schuster, 1992, p. 199.

4 'A message of the Baptist World Alliance', in *Third Baptist World Congress. Stockholm 1923. Record of proceedings*, ed. W.T. Whitley, London: Kingsgate Press, 1923, pp. 223–8.

5 Concerning Clinton's equivocations, E.G. Hinson asserted, 'When the President told that his problems were between himself, his family and "our God", that was a very Baptist statement.' K.L. Woodward, 'Sex, sin and salvation', *Newsweek*, 2 November 1998, 80.

6 B.R. White, *The English Separatist Tradition: from the Marian martyrs to the Pilgrim Fathers*, London: Oxford University Press, 1971, p. 125; D. Shantz, 'The place of the resurrected Christ in the writings of John Smyth', *Baptist Quarterly* 30, 1984, 199–203; J.R. Coggins, 'The theological positions of John Smyth', *Baptist Quarterly* 30, 1984, 246–64.

7 *The Works of John Smyth, Fellow of Christ's College, 1594–8*, ed. W.T. Whitley, 2 vols, Cambridge: Cambridge University Press, 1915, vol. 1, p. 157; vol. 2, p. 471.

8 S. Brachlow, *The Communion of Saints: radical puritan and separatist ecclesiology, 1570–1625*, Oxford: Oxford University Press, 1988, pp. 21–76.

9 Smyth, *Works*, vol. 1, p. 267.

10 C. Burrage, *The Early English Dissenters in the light of recent research, 1550–1641*, 2 vols, Cambridge: Cambridge University Press, 1912, vol. 1, p. 230.

11 Smyth, 'Principles and inferences concerning the visible church' (1607), *Works*, vol. 1, pp. 249–68; Coggins, 'John Smyth', pp. 248–9.

12 Smyth, *Works*, vol. 1, pp. 270–5.

13 Ibid. vol. 1, pp. 307–8, 314–15. Cf. 'Conversion appertaineth not only to ministers', Ibid. vol. 2, p. 552.

14 Ibid. vol. 2, pp. 436–8.

15 W.H. Burgess, *John Smith the Se-Baptist, Thomas Helwys and the first Baptist church in England*, London: James Clarke, 1911.

16 Smyth, 'The character of the beast or the false constitvtion of the church' (1609), in *Works*, vol. 2, pp. 565, 574, 580, 585–6, 594, 603, 645, 652, 654–5, 660–3; J.R. Coggins, *John Smyth's Congregation: English separatism, Mennonite influence and the elect nation*, Scottdale, PA: Herald Press, 1991, pp. 117–20.

17 Robert Abbot, *The Exaltation of the Kingdome and Priesthood of Christ*, London, 1601; Tobias Crisp, *Christ Alone Exalted*, London, [1643], 1690, pp. 241–59, 563–654.

18 T. Collier, *The Exaltation of Christ in the Days of the Gospel. As the alone High Priest, Prophet, and King, of Saints*, 4th edn, London, 1651, pp. 51–67.

19 D. Featley, *The Dippers Dipt*, London, 1645, pp. 8, 12–13, 16–18, 28–9, 113.

20 *Luther's Works*, ed. J. Pelikan and H.T. Lehmann, 55 vols, St Louis: Concordia; Philadelphia: Fortress Press, 1955–86, vol. 40, pp. 3–44; M.B. Yarnell, 'Reformation development of the priesthood of all believers', unpublished thesis, Duke University, 1996, ch. 1; W.L. Lumpkin (ed.) *Baptist Confessions of Faith*, Valley Forge, PA: Judson Press, 1969, pp. 144–70, 235–334. Chapters and articles are in parentheses.

21 L. Busher, *Religions Peace*, London, 1614.

22 Thomas Grantham, *Christianismus Primitivus*, London, 1678, book 3.

23 E.B. Underhill (ed.) *Records of the Churches of Christ, Gathered at Fenstanton, Warboys, and Hexham*, London, 1854; R. Hayden (ed.) *The Records of a Church of Christ in Bristol, 1640–1687*, Bristol: Bristol Record Society, 1974.

24 Smyth, *Works*, vol. 1, pp. 256, 265, 276.

25 D. Turner, *A Compendium of Social Religion*, London, 1763; A. Fuller, *Complete Works*, London, 1831, pp. 829–31, 854–5.

26 T.L. Underwood, *Primitivism, Radicalism, and the Lamb's War: the Baptist–Quaker conflict in seventeenth-century England*, Oxford: Oxford University Press, 1997, p. 38.

27 E.S. Gaustad, *Liberty of Conscience: Roger Williams in America*, Grand Rapids: Eerdmans, 1991, p. 184.

28 N.O. Hatch, *The Democratization of American Christianity*, New Haven: Yale University Press, 1989, pp. 93–101, 236–9.

29 G.A. Wills, *Democratic Religion: freedom, authority, and church discipline in the*

Baptist south, 1785–1900, Oxford: Oxford University Press, 1997; J.L. Garrett, Jr., *Baptist Church Discipline: a historical introduction to the practices of Baptist churches*, Nashville: Broadman Press, 1962, revision forthcoming.

30 N.H. Maring, 'The individualism of Francis Wayland', in W.S. Hudson (ed.) *Baptist Concepts of the Church: a survey of the historical and theological issues which have produced changes in church order*, Chicago: Judson Press, 1959, p. 169.

31 E. Troeltsch, *The Social Teaching of the Christian Churches*, trans. O. Wyon, 2 vols, London: Allen & Unwin, 1931, vol. 1, pp. 328–43; vol. 2, pp. 706–11, 993–4. Troeltsch's definition of sect is problematic but his general typology is acceptable. For a more recent definition, see B.R. Wilson, 'An analysis of sect development', in B.R. Wilson (ed.) *Patterns of Sectarianism: organisation and ideology in social and religious movements*, London: Heinemann, 1967, pp. 22–45; B.R. Wilson, 'A typology of sects', in R. Robertson (ed.) *Sociology of Religion: selected readings*, Harmondsworth: Penguin, 1969, pp. 361–83.

32 A.C. Underwood, *A History of the English Baptists*, London: Baptist Union Publications Department, 1947, pp. 15–22.

33 I. Sellers, 'Edwardians, Anabaptists and the problem of Baptist origins', *Baptist Quarterly* 29, 1981, 97–112.

34 E.A. Payne, *The Fellowship of Believers: Baptist thought and practice yesterday and today*, London: Kingsgate Press, 1944, enlarged 1952.

35 M.A. Noll, *A History of Christianity in the United States and Canada*, Grand Rapids: Eerdmans, 1992, chs 11, 13; P. Johnson, *A History of the American People*, London: Weidenfeld & Nicolson, 1997, parts 5, 6.

36 I.M. Mullins, *Edgar Young Mullins: an intimate biography*, Nashville: Sunday School Board of the Southern Baptist Convention, 1929, p. 79.

37 E.Y. Mullins, *The Christian Religion in its Doctrinal Expression*, Philadelphia: Roger Williams Press, 1917, p. 3.

38 W.E. Ellis, *'A Man of Books and a Man of the People': E. Y. Mullins and the crisis of moderate Southern Baptist leadership*, Macon, GA: Mercer University Press, 1985, pp. 28–40.

39 I.M. Mullins, *Edgar Young Mullins*, pp. 102–18.

40 P. Schaff, *Modern Christianity: the German Reformation*, 2 vols, Edinburgh, 1888, vol. 1, pp. 4, 16, 24–5; T.M. Lindsay, *A History of the Reformation*, 2 vols, Edinburgh: T. & T. Clark, 1906, vol. 1, pp. 435–44.

41 A.V.G. Allen, *Christian Institutions*, Edinburgh, 1898.

42 E.Y. Mullins, *The Historical Significance of the Baptists*, Richmond: Virginia Baptist Historical Association, 1907, p. 9.

43 E.Y. Mullins, *The Axioms of Religion: a new interpretation of the Baptist faith*, Philadelphia: American Baptist Publication Society, 1908. See also edition by R.A. Mohler, T. George and D. George, Nashville: Broadman & Holman, 1997. The modern edition will be used here for all but the last few chapters; Mullins, *Axioms*, 1997, pp. 59, 121–2, 157–9.

44 H.L. McBeth, *The Baptist Heritage*, Nashville: Broadman Press, 1987, pp. 447–61.

45 Mullins made a number of pan-Protestant moves. He contributed to *The Fundamentals* but counted Shailer Mathews among his friends. His semi-orthodox doctrine can be seen in *The Baptist Faith and Message* (1925) but he was criticized by J.G. Machen for employing the liberal theological method of subjectivity for orthodox purposes. G.M. Marsden, *Fundamentalism and American Culture: the shaping of twentieth-century evangelicalism, 1870–1925*, Oxford: Oxford University Press, 1980, pp. 216–17.

46 Walter Rauschenbusch made a similar move. See Rauschenbusch, 'Why I am a Baptist' (1905–6), reprinted in *Christian Ethics Today* 1, 1995, 19–31; E.Y. Mullins,

'Why I am a Baptist', in *Twelve Modern Apostles and their Creeds*, ed. G.K. Chesterton et al. New York: Duffield, 1926, pp. 89–109.

47 Bloom, *American Religion*, pp. 46, 206.

48 Mullins, *Axioms*, 1997, chs 3, 5.

49 Since aesthetic impulses are respected by Mullins, such metaphors indicate his central position. 'God and the war', *Review and Expositor* 21, 1924, p. 448.

50 Mullins, *Axioms*, 1997, pp. 51–2, 63, 79, 111, 133–6, 139–40.

51 Ibid. pp. 76, 117, 119, 126, 135–6, 140.

52 Interestingly, the ecclesial section of the Independent Savoy Declaration and the Baptist Second London Confession reject the invisible interpretation found in the Westminster Confession, replacing it with detailed statements on the visible church.

53 Mullins, *Axioms*, 1997, pp. 42–3, 77–9, 118, 120, 123–5, 131, 174.

54 Cf. the nuanced understanding of mediation and priesthood in the work of Hanserd Knollys. *Christ Exalted*, London, 1646.

55 Mullins, *Axioms*, 1997, pp. 53–6, 68, 89, 94, 131, 150.

56 Ibid. pp. 50, 64, 66, 72, 99, 102–3, 123.

57 Mullins, *The Christian Religion*, pp. 57, 87–9, 93,193–5; W. James, *The Varieties of Religious Experience: a study in human nature*, London: Longmans, 1902, pp. 511–15; W. James, *Selected Writings*, ed. G.H. Bird, London: J.M. Dent, 1995, chs 11, 12.

58 Mullins, *The Christian Religion*, pp. 112–19, 344; Mullins, 'Book review', *Review and Expositor* 1, 1904, 249.

59 F. Humphreys, 'E.Y. Mullins', in T. George and D.S. Dockery (eds) *Baptist Theologians*, Nashville: Broadman Press, 1990, p. 346.

60 F.D.E. Schleiermacher, *The Christian Faith*, 2nd German edn trans. H.R. Mackintosh and J.S. Stewart, Edinburgh: T. & T. Clark, 1928, §§ 23–4. There is no ecclesiology in Mullins, *The Christian Religion*.

61 Mullins, *The Christian Religion*, pp. 61, 126, 196, 320.

62 Schleiermacher, *Christian Faith*, § 104; Mullins, *The Christian Religion*, pp. 303, 336–7.

63 F.D.E. Schleiermacher, *On Religion: speeches to its cultured despisers*, trans. R. Crouter, Cambridge: Cambridge University Press, 1988, § 16; Mullins, *The Christian Religion*, pp. 354–5, 362–6.

64 H.H. Hobbs and E.Y. Mullins, *The Axioms of Religion*, Nashville: Broadman Press, 1978, p. 120.

65 P.M. Harrison, *Authority and Power in the Free Church Tradition: a social case study of the American Baptist Convention*, Princeton, NJ: Princeton University Press, 1959, pp. 21–9; H. Cook, *What Baptists Stand For*, 3rd edn, London: Carey Kingsgate Press, 1958, pp. 9, 213, 220.

Chapter 16

The Charismatic Movement
The laicizing of Christianity?

David F. Wright

The third edition of *The Oxford Dictionary of the Christian Church* spares less than half a column for the 'Charismatic Renewal Movement', perhaps partly because it identifies it as 'A loosely-structured predominantly lay movement'. In the Roman Catholic Church, in particular, 'by *c.* 1980 it had become one of the main lay movements', and was represented as such at the 1987 Rome Synod of Bishops on the laity.[1] In *The Church is Charismatic* (1981), a World Council of Churches report on the movement and member churches' experience of it, the leading Catholic charismatic exponent Peter Hocken lists 'lay initiative' second in itemizing the distinctive praxis of the renewal.

> Besides the general participatory character of charismatic worship [evident even in 'the characteristic layout' of a 'square or circular arrangement'], charismatic gatherings provide various opportunities for personal initiative in prophecy, in spontaneous reading of scripture and in personal witnessing and sharing. There is a direct link between lay initiative in charismatic gatherings and lay initiative in evangelism outside the prayer meetings.[2]

A leader of charismatic renewal in the Episcopal Church in the USA, Raymond Davis, reported of his congregation in Fairfax, Virginia, that 'The Holy Spirit has raised up a lay ministry at Truro Church which has exceeded my fondest expectation!'[3]

These three comments all issue from circles or writers marked by strongly priestly or clerical leadership, over against which the lay dimension of charismatic renewal may have been easier to recognize. Such a reading may have been less obvious in traditions which have not favoured clerical–lay distinctions. Nevertheless, some of the core elements of charismatic experience might lead us to expect a radically laicizing movement in the making. Four constitutive features will be identified.

First, what has sometimes been called the neo-Pentecostal movement shares with Pentecostalism proper an absolutely central focus on the Pentecostal gift of the Holy Spirit, which Peter interpreted as the fulfilment of the prophecy of Joel 2.28–9. As one of the defining marks of the new covenant, Pentecost was the democratization of endowment with or by the Spirit of God, according to Acts 2.17–18. Not only men but women too; not merely priests, prophets, kings and judges, but youngsters and senior citizens also, and even slaves, male and female alike – 'all flesh' will receive the Spirit in the new order. Peter's emphasis falls more on universality than on social equality.[4] Pentecost is thus the charter for the parity of all God's people, in respect of reception of the Holy Spirit. As Lesslie Newbigin puts it, 'The Holy Spirit may be the last article of the Creed but in the New Testament it is the first fact of experience.'[5] If the sacramental focus of reception of the Spirit is baptism, then the domination of baby baptism must be partly, perhaps largely, responsible for the feeble sense of being a people of the Spirit evident in most mainline churches.

Second, charismatic doctrine insists on the bestowal of charismata, spiritual gifts, on the rank and file of the Christian community. To quote Hocken again: 'Many people, both participants in Charismatic Renewal and sympathetic observers, see the rediscovery of the spiritual gifts and their restoration to ordinary Christian life and ministry as the major contribution of Charismatic Renewal.'[6] We need not tarry over narrower questions – whether all the gifts discernible in the New Testament are equally available today, whether all the Spirit-baptized possess one or more charismata, and what is the relationship between tongues-speaking as initial evidence and as lasting gift. Without doubt, the renewal movement stands for the exercise of spiritual gifts of worship and ministry by lay Christians without formal appointment or authorization.

Expressed in other terms, charismatic religion is characterized, thirdly, by spiritual immediacy and directness, independent of priestly, ministerial or other human mediation. As Hocken notes in *The Glory and the Shame: reflections on the 20th-century outpouring of the Holy Spirit* (1994), charismatic anticipation here and now of what Christians will receive in fullness at the Parousia entails

> (1) an immediacy of relationship to the Triune God, that reveals in the human spirit the person of Jesus as Saviour and Lord, the presence and power of the Holy Spirit as well as the majesty and merciful love of the Father;
> (2) a corresponding immediacy upward to God in worship that makes possible spontaneous expression of praise, especially in the speech of tongues that expresses the human spirit without the mediation of the mind;
> (3) an immediacy of downward relationship of God to the Christian, that makes possible a reception of divine communication in the human spirit.[7]

This interpretation by a sympathetic insider undoubtedly pinpoints a fundamental element of charismatic spirituality.

There ensues, in the fourth place, an enhanced sense of the whole Christian community as the body animated as one by life in the Spirit. What is in view here is not the spawning of new expressions of communal living which the movement has fostered – from the Church of the Redeemer, Houston, Texas, to the Mother of God Community in Gaithersburg, Maryland – but what was highlighted in a booklet from the Methodist Church in Britain in 1973, which compared 'the Body Ministry of the Methodist Society' with that of charismatic Bible-study-and-prayer groups. In the latter 'the Spirit is making a reality' what Methodists had been trying to promote for decades. The report cites F.D. Bruner's dictum, 'Pentecostalism is Primitive Methodism's extended incarnation.'[8] Hocken again says it in a nutshell:

> More than in classical Pentecostalism and previous Protestant revivals, Charismatic Renewal is developing an awareness that the outpouring of God's Spirit is for the sake of the body of Christ and leads to a renewed sense of what it is for the church, both local and universal, to be Christ's body.[9]

An external observer acknowledges the same point:

> Members of the Charismatic Movement emphasize that they have come to a *new awareness of community* and to new community experiences. In this regard members often emphasize the connection between enjoyment of the community and *communal proclamation and glorification of God*.[10]

Dominant features like these four interrelated ones might be thought to feed naturally into a thoroughgoing laicization of Christianity in charismatic mode. Commentators sometimes cast this thrust of the movement as a threat to the special role of the ordained. The charismatic discovery of the abundance and diversity of gifts of the Spirit allegedly 'leads to dismantling the separation within the community into professionals who play the lead roles and laity who have only minor parts'.[11] J. Rodman Williams, one of the most sophisticated of charismatic theologians (the competition is not intense), in discussing the instrumental use of laying on of hands in baptism of the Spirit, states that

> The 'ministers' [of this action] may be clergy or laity; it makes no difference. In fact, it has been the humbling experience of some of us who are clergymen to have laymen place hands on us to receive this fullness of the Spirit. Obviously God is doing a mighty work today bound neither by office nor by rank.[12]

Among responses from member churches surveyed in the WCC report *The Church is Charismatic*, one finds the following, from the United Church of North India:

Should we not recognize that the celebration of the eucharist before it became the preserve of the ordained ministry was the legitimate and natural function of the layman and that structural hierarchical ordination bottled up the Holy Spirit with the laying-on-of-hands of ministers (order) with all the succeeding wrangles of 'apostolic succession' and the loss of charisma?[13]

And again, from the Church of the Czech Brethren:

Wherever the concept of the charismatically renewed congregation is thought of, the concept of the one-man leadership in the congregation is as well problematized . . . It is problematized there where the charismatic congregation prays for the fullness of the gifts of the Holy Spirit as well as for the preaching service and also for the teaching one. In this new concept the pastor becomes only one of the many gifted members of the congregation.[14]

Occasionally a writer who holds office in a firmly ordered church openly encourages charismatic empowerment of laypeople to defy order. Rex Davis, formerly subdean of Lincoln and author of *Locusts and Wild Honey* (1978), on the renewal and the ecumenical movement, has elsewhere expressed himself as follows:

[T]here is in charismatic circles a much greater willingness to share the eucharist with other denominations. This may be frowned upon, but it happens. A wildfire ecumenism around the eucharist is probably the most necessary thing for the churches today: people should feel free to neglect ecclesiastical inhibitions and discover that the ground will not swallow them up if they share openly and happily. Here church order is threatened. It is a good threat. Secondly, there is an invitation for greater participation by more people in different ways. This happens with other kinds of services, but it is itself a new kind of 'communion'. More importantly, a wider involvement of people who confess the authority of the Holy Spirit, and who, in a sense, assert their baptismal power, leads us rapidly towards a newer understanding of the priesthood of all believers.

Unfortunately, Davis follows his train of thought not towards that 'newer understanding' but towards the ordination of women (writing in 1984) and the challenge posed to Roman Catholic eucharistic order. He then asks, 'Is the Charismatic Renewal strong enough or courageous enough to pursue these lines of development to their ends? Probably not.'[15]

Though a cleric, Davis voices here the widespread impatience of laypeople at the slow progress ecumenical officialdom makes towards intercommunion. Insofar as charismatic community of experience pushes this impatience into uninhibited 'wildfire ecumenism', it embodies the populism that will not wait for the ecumenical professionals.

Davis writes of 'people who confess the authority of the Holy Spirit, and who, in a sense, assert their baptismal power'. In this context, 'empowerment' is a term that has shifted in meaning, from an earlier stress on the inner dynamic of the Spirit and his gifts (as in the song 'We are building a people of power'), to a more recent religious-rights concern for liberation, recognition and status, as in uses such as 'the empowerment of women in the church'. Has the Charismatic Movement's unquestioned insistence that all Christians are called to be Spirit-empowered led on to a quest for their empowerment in the later sense?

When this enquiry into the laicizing dimension of charismatic renewal leads us in this direction, it is essential – and no doubt long overdue – that important differences be recognized. The renewal is indeed a many-splendoured thing, which resists generalization on several counts. One of these is the sharp contrast between a charismatic presence in established denominations (i.e. the original Charismatic Movement of the early 1960s, distinguished from traditional Pentecostalism by remaining within the historic churches) and the independent or separatist charismatic sector, originally known as the house-church movement, later as Restorationism and now increasingly as the new churches.[16] Although this sector – itself diverse enough, with some groupings developing into quasi-denominations – remains in flux,[17] much of it represents the rejection of traditional church organizations and professes an acute antidenominationalism, sometimes in an explicit preference for 'kingdom' over 'church'.[18]

The 'new church' appellation is a not unhelpful one, insofar as charismatic separatism gathers up the outcomes of a veritable orgy of independent, often lay-led, church division and church starting. Martyn Percy, a forceful theological analyst in this territory, recalls fulfilling a training placement in a Lake District village with a population of 1,200, an Anglican congregation of 160, and no fewer than three new churches, each a split from its parent body (the first from the local Church of England) and together totalling less than 50 members.[19] If the Charismatic Movement (one shrinks in this context from calling it 'renewal') has nurtured the empowerment of lay Christians, it has displayed an almost anarchical face. Its do-it-yourself ecclesiology should be regarded as reaping the bitter harvest of the woefully weak doctrine of the church in much evangelicalism.

'Lay' in this connexion has often meant antiprofessional, even anti-intellectual. A consistent Restorationist finds in the gospels an original 12 who had no collegiate training, let alone degrees. Hostility to academic theology was already common among classic Pentecostals. It was ironic that Donald Gee, an eminence in British Pentecostalism in the middle decades of the twentieth century, at the age of 60 became principal of the reorganized Bible school of the Assemblies of God, even though he was self-educated –

and still faced criticism of Bible colleges in the Assemblies denomination.[20] 'Multiple tracks to ordination' in the charismatic world being interpreted means the absence of educational requirements for ordination.[21]

One of the problems encountered by anyone who studies the Charismatic Movement is the lack of systematic theology. (There is no article on the subject in the *Dictionary of Pentecostal and Charismatic Movements*.) To some degree this reflects a disparagement of doctrine. Indifference to doctrinal disagreements under the unitive primacy of Spirit-experience has allowed for an easy ecumenism. A universalized charismatic immediacy of access to the 'revelation' of God has in some quarters bred an impatience with book learning and fostered a populist, vulgar-evangelicalism. To this extent the movement has significantly contributed, chiefly in the new churches wing, to a radical laicizing of church life – a kind of plebeian throwback against the lifeless theological scholarship in which liberalism abounds.

Other paradoxes are worth recording. It has been among the house churches that some leaders like Bryn Jones and Terry Virgo have enjoyed a powerful personal hegemony. It is part of the paradox that such apostolic or quasi-episcopal figures have often themselves emerged from the ranks with no professional biblical and theological training or qualifications. By contrast, charismatic renewal within the traditional churches has commonly been clerically led. This has been particularly obvious in Anglican and Episcopalian churches – Dennis Bennett, Graham Pulkingham, Michael Harper, David Pytches, David Watson and others.[22] A Baptist writer has contrasted the differing charismatic experiences of English Baptists and Methodists. 'If a Baptist congregation wanted to go further down the Charismatic road, the minister was often the determining factor', and 'Part of the dynamic growth was due to the relationship between Baptist minister and congregation.' The looseness of the Methodist circuit system, on the other hand, ensured that 'A key ingredient in the acceptance and growth of renewal, the dynamic between shepherd and flock, was absent.'[23] The comment must bite more deeply, in casting light on Methodism's general debilitation.

By the same token, absence of able ministerial leadership must be a major cause of the failure of the movement to get far off the ground in the Church of Scotland – but not the only cause, for the Reformed-Presbyterian tradition has proved more resistant to charismatic inroads than any other historic confession.

Yet at the same time, the movement within the established denominations has rarely been characterized by submissive attachment to any special father-figure. As Hocken comments, charismatic renewal 'cannot be traced to any one prestigious figure, nor . . . can the whole movement be traced back to any one human source. Being part of this movement does not involve following any particular leader.' In this respect, a contrast is evident with major sectors of British evangelicalism, with their unhealthy subservience to the Lloyd-Joneses, Stills and Stotts of this world. The Charismatic Movement has generally seemed more communal or communitarian, more participatory, less driven by 'charismatic'(!) preachers and teachers. Sometimes the difference between the two has appeared somewhat like the difference between pre-Pentecost and post-Pentecost, despite the fact that charismatics have openly espoused the continuance of the prophetic gift in the church.

In the Restorationism of some new churches, 'a system of control' has been constructed known variously as 'discipling', 'heavy shepherding', sometimes simply 'submission', or even with colourless inoffensiveness as 'relatedness'.

> Discipling is a serious affair that covers every area of believers' lives: children submit to parents, wives to husbands, all to elders, who submit to apostles, who in turn (in collegiate fashion) submit to each other. Subjects for direction do not only include what are usually understood as spiritual matters; they include the financial, social and sexual matters of life.[24]

It is interesting that Andrew Walker should compare the strictness of this regimen (not to its advantage) with that of a monastic rule. It is surely helpful to view 'discipling' in this setting as tantamount to an attempt to live out quasi-monastic submission, communism and interdependence in secular dispersion, i.e. without the benefit of cloistered common life. It is also interesting to note the use made by one or two writers of the analogy with the earliest Christian monasticism: it was overwhelmingly lay, uninitiated and unauthorized by clergy, and in itself a critique of the urban, Hellenized church. In the realm of religious experience also it displayed obvious similarities with charismatic renewal. Once incorporated and regulated, by conciliar canons and bishops, this hermitic phase of the ascetic movement proved a mighty force in the growth and diffusion of catholic Christianity. The appeal of the analogy to Roman Catholic observers of charismatic stirrings is self-evident. It is too early to judge whether the analogy does not overestimate the importance of charismatic renewal in the Roman Catholic Church.

It may, however, be too facile a judgement to discern in the Charismatic Movement a thoroughgoing laicizing of Christianity. There seems to be little analysis of it as an essentially lay phenomenon. The *Dictionary of Pentecostal and Charismatic Movements* has no article on 'laity', nor on the general priesthood of believers. If all are Spirit-baptized and all exercise charismatic powers – if only in congregational prayer in tongues – then the self-understanding of a corporate royal priesthood may be redundant. The British Methodist booklet of 1973 claims the concept to be authentic Methodism now realized within its charismatic wing.

> A recent charismatic conference may be used to illustrate how the movement builds firmly upon this doctrine. During a worship session at the

conference many came forward for ministry. Some six or seven ordained clergy ministered by prayer and the laying on of hands whilst the rest of the people (some 800 or 900) prayed and sang devotionally. Whilst the ordained ministers were at work in the Lord, the whole body of believers was simultaneously at work . . . Mutual ministry was a reality![25]

An altogether more suggestive discussion of shared priesthood occurs in a Belgian Roman Catholic evaluation of the movement in 1979.

It is thus necessary to understand, in all its nuances, the relationship between the ministry of ordained priests and that priesthood which derives from baptism and is common to all the faithful . . .

If the priest is to exercise his proper and indispensable role, he must first of all have an attitude of receptivity and of brotherly union with the lay people. He should be, according to the inspired phrase of St Augustine, 'a Christian with the people, a priest for the people' . . . Otherwise, the priest could give the impression that he has a monopoly of wisdom and insight, that he is manipulating the group, that he is extinguishing the Spirit. As long as the priest judges the renewal from outside it, without entering into it spiritually, he will have difficulty in exercising any role of discernment. This is especially true since the renewal was born and continues to find its dynamic and life in a thoroughly lay setting.

. . . There must take place a veritable exchange of life between the priests and the lay people at the heart of the Catholic renewal if it is to avoid the danger of becoming a sort of para-church obeying laws of its own.[26]

Though the assumptions of this reflection will not obtain within charismatic evangelicalism, its wisdom would not be wholly lost on some reaches of evangelical clericalism.

On a broader canvas, it is undeniable that the Charismatic Movement has been one of the most prominent forces in fostering in wide swathes of Protestantism, especially evangelicalism, a broader participatory base in worship and ministry. Congregations admitting to no charismatic convictions sing charismatic songs. Fixation on spiritual gifts has rubbed off on mainliners in the form of heartier recognition of all- or multi-member ministry. This has long seemed to some observers the signal contribution that the movement might make to clericalist Presbyterianism of the Scottish variety. It is possible to have so much room for the word that little is left for the Spirit.

Resistance to the Charismatic Movement has often been fired by aversion from its damaging downside, which it is hard to exclude from consideration. Its doctrinal indifferentism, uncritical following of private revelations, subordination of scripture to experience, subversion of worship by mindless repetition, emotional excitement and entertainment – these and other features have portrayed to many evangelical minds a populist, dumbing-down of Christianity, a kind of tabloidization of evangelicalism. If this is the lay piety that charismaticism breeds, some want none of it. The trouble is that tabloidization is now almost universal in British culture, with the so-called quality broadsheet newspapers and BBC television channels swimming with the tide. The extraordinarily wide usefulness of the Alpha course – an introduction to the Christian faith produced by an Anglican charismatic stronghold, Holy Trinity, Brompton, in fashionable central London – suggests a sensitivity to a broad-based mood and temper in British society that evangelicals have not always displayed. The danger is that this charismatic version of evangelicalism becomes 'so largely an expression of cultural Modernism'.[27]

The epithet 'lay' can convey different nuances. Charismatic spirituality and worship easily seem exotic, extravagant, unearthly – the religion of the hot-house. As such they may be the very reverse of lay in character, if 'lay' has reference to the common life of Christians in human society. Religion may be popular, or populist, without being genuinely lay. Some critics reckon that charismatic Christianity shares the high-octane escapism manifest in contemporary culture in so many different ways. But much evangelicalism nurtures an in-house, church-centred piety that at times appears to aspire, unspokenly of course, for a quasi-monastic existence of separation from the world and of unceasing prayer.

When David Bebbington prophesies that the Charismatic Movement is poised to become the prevailing form of Protestantism in twenty-first-century Britain,[28] he is more likely to be proved a true prophet in England than in Scotland. Insofar as the movement represents a turn to the laity in the longer perspectives of evangelical history, it poses sharp questions not only about ordination (which is scarcely a securely grounded notion in the New Testament) but also about the role of professional expertise, the academic magisterium, in evangelical Protestantism. Evangelicalism that has come of age (so some dare claim) may have learnt too readily to hand over its vernacular Bible to a new caste of hermeneutical gurus.

The Charismatic Movement at its best may still help wider evangelicalism to rediscover the Spirit-filled and charismatic (Spirit-gift-graced) character of the whole church. This character is finely spelt out in a Catholic charismatic manifesto of 1974.

> The Holy Spirit dwells in the Church as a perpetual Pentecost . . . The Spirit dwelling in the Church and in the hearts of the faithful as in a temple is a gift to the whole Church. [1 Cor. 3:16] . . .
>
> Though the Spirit manifests himself in different ministries which serve different functions . . . the whole Church and all its members are

partakers of the Spirit. There are no special classes of Spirit-bearers, no separate groups of Spirit-filled believers. Fullness of life in the Spirit, participation in the abundant life in the Spirit, is a common possession of the whole Church, although not appropriated in equal measure by all . . .

The statement stresses the plurality but not equality of charisms. As manifestations of the Spirit – 'inseparable but not identical' – spiritual gifts are constitutive both of the nature of the church and of 'the nature of the Christian life in its communitarian and individual expression'. In this sense every Christian is a charismatic and therefore has a ministry to the church and the world.

A radical equality of charisms and ministries is not a principle of church life. One must also say that the charisms of the Spirit are without number. Finally, one of the bonds which binds laity and the hierarchy is the one Spirit manifesting himself in different service functions.

. . . Irenaeus said: 'Where the Church is, there is the Spirit, and where the Spirit of God is, there is the Church . . .' Charism is a principle of order in the Church in such a way that there is no distinction between the institutional and the charismatic Church.[29]

Lightly transposed out of a Catholic key, there sounds an authentically New Testament laicization, recalling the one undifferentiated *laos* of God living by the one Pentecostal Spirit.

Notes

1 F.L. Cross (ed.) *The Oxford Dictionary of the Christian Church*, 3rd edn, ed. E.A. Livingstone, Oxford: Oxford University Press, 1997, p. 321. The work remains disappointingly weak on evangelical Christianity in general.
2 P. Hocken, 'A survey of the worldwide Charismatic Movement', in A. Bittlinger (ed.) *The Church is Charismatic*, Geneva: World Council of Churches, 1981, pp. 117–47, at p. 124.
3 R.W. Davis, 'A story of integration', in M.P. Hamilton (ed.) *The Charismatic Movement*, Grand Rapids: Eerdmans, 1975, pp. 175–84, at p. 181.
4 The latter is stressed by M. Welker, *God the Spirit*, trans. J.F. Hoffmeyer, Minneapolis: Fortress Press, 1994, pp. 148–51.
5 L. Newbigin, *The Household of God: lectures on the nature of the church*, London: SCM, 1953, p. 89.
6 Bittlinger (ed.) *The Church is Charismatic*, p. 128.
7 P. Hocken, *The Glory and the Shame: reflections on the 20th-century outpouring of the Holy Spirit*, Guildford: Eagle, 1994, p. 61.
8 K. McDonnell (ed.) *Presence, Power, Praise: documents on the charismatic renewal*, 3 vols, Collegeville, MN: Liturgical Press, 1980, vol. 1, pp. 473, 482 (and cf. pp. 472–82 as a whole). This invaluable assemblage of churches' evaluations will henceforth be cited as McDonnell.
9 Bittlinger (ed.) *The Church is Charismatic*, p. 129.

10 Welker, *God the Spirit*, p. 12 (his italics).
11 Welker, *God the Spirit*, p. 12.
12 J.R. Williams, *The Era of the Spirit*, Plainfield, NJ: Logos International, 1971, p. 64.
13 Bittlinger (ed.) *The Church is Charismatic*, p. 49.
14 Ibid. pp. 49–50.
15 R. Davis, 'Living liturgically: the charismatic contribution', in D. Martin and P. Mullen (eds) *Strange Gifts? A guide to charismatic renewal*, Oxford: Blackwell, 1984, pp. 107–22, at pp. 110–11.
16 See especially A. Walker, *Restoring the Kingdom: the radical Christianity of the house church movement*, London: Hodder & Stoughton, 1985, with later editions.
17 See N. Wright, 'The nature and variety of Restorationism and the "house church" movement', in S. Hunt, M. Hamilton and T. Walter (eds) *Charismatic Christianity: sociological perspectives*, Basingstoke: Macmillan, 1997, pp. 60–76.
18 A. Walker, 'The theology of the "Restoration" house churches', in Martin and Mullen (eds) *Strange Gifts?*, pp. 208–16, at pp. 211, 214.
19 M. Percy, *Power and the Church: ecclesiology in an age of transition*, London: Cassell, 1998, pp. 189–90.
20 D.D. Bundy, in S.M. Burgess and G.B. McGee (eds) *Dictionary of Pentecostal and Charismatic Movements*, Grand Rapids: Regency Reference Library, 1988, pp. 330–2, at p. 331.
21 C.P. Wagner, in Burgess and McGee (eds) *Dictionary*, p. 193, including the reassurance that 'Academic training does not disqualify men and women from ordination.'
22 See Hocken, *Glory and Shame*, pp. 17–18.
23 D. McBain, 'Mainstream charismatics: some observations of Baptist renewal', in Hunt, Hamilton and Walter (eds) *Charismatic Christianity*, pp. 43–59, at p. 47.
24 Walker, in Martin and Mullen (eds) *Strange Gifts?*, pp. 212, 213.
25 McDonnell, vol. 1, p. 479.
26 McDonnell, vol. 2, pp. 498–9.
27 D.W. Bebbington, *Evangelicalism in Modern Britain: a history from the 1730s to the 1980s*, London: Unwin Hyman, 1989, p. 275.
28 Ibid. p. 247.
29 McDonnell, vol. 3, pp. 23–5.

Index

Africa 9, 169, 177, 190, 193; South Africa 194; West Africa 170, 178, 182
African Methodist Episcopal Church 8, 107–11
Aldwinckle, Stella 206, 209
Allen, Alexander 244, 245
Allen, Richard 107, 109
American churches: Baptist 97, 99, 101, 104, 142, 146; Congregationalist 96, 104, 142, 146, 149; Episcopalian 104, 142, 149, 253; Presbyterian 96, 97, 99, 104, 142, 149; see also African Methodist Episcopal Church; Methodism in America; Quakers; Southern Baptists
American Revolution 96, 105, 146
Ames, William 27, 31, 241
Anabaptism 29, 240
anticlerical tendency 9, 130
Archibald, Malcolm 210
aristocratic female patrons: church authorities 87; deference to male ministry 86; financial role 86; force of personality 89, 93; influence on women 93; private chaplains 86, 87, 88, 89, 92; proprietary chapels 8, 86, 87, 88, 92; public and private spheres 89, 91, 93; quasi-episcopal control 88, 91, 93; rejection of preaching role 89; religious fervour 89; theological students 86, 89, 92, 120; use of the home 8, 86, 88, 89, 90, 102
Arminianism 28, 101
Arminians 81
Asbury, Francis 101, 103, 104, 146
assurance of salvation: in Calvin's thought 36; in conversion narratives 40, 41; in Luther's thought 23;

normative for believers 19; post-Reformation emphasis on 30; puritan leaders on 28; reaction to political turmoil 39; second crisis 44; source of evangelical activism 67; see also conversion narratives; golden chain of salvation
Augustine 18, 43, 76, 80, 155
Austen, Jane: *Mansfield Park* 167, 168, 170
Austin, Margaret 69–70, 71, 73, 79, 81

Backus, Isaac 98, 99, 243
Baptist Missionary Society 144, 168, 175; *Periodical Accounts* 182
Baptists: American 97, 99, 101, 104, 142, 146; Baptist Union 198; Baptist World Alliance 236, 237; and Charismatic Movement 258; early confessions 241, 242; family networks 188, 189; General Baptists 236, 239, 240, 241, 243; open-Baptist Independents 40, 42; Particular Baptists 124, 175, 236, 240, 241; Philadelphia Baptist Association 243; polity of 197; separation from Wesleyans 120; see also American churches; Dissent; early Baptist thought; Independents; modern Baptist thought; Southern Baptists
Bateman, Winifred 193, 196
Baxter, Richard 27, 30, 31, 38, 43, 80
Bedford, itinerancy from 120
Bennett, Dennis 258
Benson, Joseph 127
Bevan, Frances 230
Beverley, Robert 217, 221, 223, 224
Beza, Theodore 31, 43

This book is due for return on or before the last date shown below.